LLYFRGELL COLEG MENAI LIBRARY
SAFLE FFRIDDOEDD SITE
BANGOR GWYNEDD LL57

C
BG
9

D0421221

Health and Safety
Management

STOC DYNNWYD YMAITH
LLYFRGELL COLEG MENAI
WITHDRAWN LIBRARY STOCK

LLYFRGELL COLEG MENAI LIBRARY

058790

We work with leading authors to develop the
strongest educational materials in business and
management, bringing cutting-edge thinking and best
learning practice to a global market.

Under a range of well-known imprints,
including Financial Times Prentice Hall, we craft high
quality print and electronic publications which help
readers to understand and apply their content, whether
studying or at work.

To find out more about the complete range of our
publishing, please visit us on the World Wide Web at:
www.pearsoned.co.uk

058790

STOC DYNNWYD YMAITH
LLYFRGELL COLEG MENAI

Health and Safety
Management

Principles and Best Practice

Colin W. Fuller
Luise H. Vassie

 Prentice Hall

FINANCIAL TIMES

An imprint of **Pearson Education**

Harlow, England • London • New York • Boston • San Francisco • Toronto • Sydney • Singapore • Hong Kong
Tokyo • Seoul • Taipei • New Delhi • Cape Town • Madrid • Mexico City • Amsterdam • Munich • Paris • Milan

Pearson Education Limited
Edinburgh Gate
Harlow
Essex CM20 2JE
England

and Associated Companies throughout the world

Visit us on the World Wide Web at:
www.pearsoned.co.uk

First published 2004

© Pearson Education Limited 2004

The rights of Colin W. Fuller and Luise H. Vassie to be identified as authors of this work
have been asserted by the authors in accordance with the Copyright, Designs and Patents
Act 1988.

All rights reserved. No part of this publication may be reproduced, stored in a retrieval
system, or transmitted in any form or by any means, electronic, mechanical,
photocopying, recording or otherwise, without either the prior written permission of
the publisher or a licence permitting restricted copying in the United Kingdom issued
by the Copyright Licensing Agency Ltd, 90 Tottenham Court Road, London W1T 4LP.

All trademarks used herein are the property of their respective owners. The use of any
trademark in this text does not vest in the author or publisher any trademark
ownership rights in such trademarks, nor does the use of such trademarks imply any
affiliation with or endorsement of this book by such owners.

ISBN 0 273 68482 5

British Library Cataloguing-in-Publication Data
A catalogue record for this book is available from the British Library

Library of Congress Cataloging-in-Publication Data
A catalog record for this book is available from the Library of Congress

10 9 8 7 6 5 4 3 2 1
08 07 06 05 04

Typeset in 9.5/12 pt Stone Serif by 30
Printed by Bell & Bain Ltd., Glasgow

The publisher's policy is to use paper manufactured from sustainable forests.

Contents

Preface

For many companies business success depends on taking opportunistic and speculative risks. These risks may be associated, for example, with the launch of a new product, process or service that, if successful, could bring prosperity, growth and profitability to the organisation. However, the launch may result, for example, in poor sales causing a loss in investment capital, product design failure resulting in customer claims for compensation, or plant failures resulting in environmental damage. In addition to these opportunistic risks, an organisation's routine activities involve operational risks in various forms. These risks could, for example, be associated with product or service quality, production output, emissions to the environment or employee health and safety.

Organisations have generally been more concerned with the consequences of financial risk, as a failure to control these can have an immediate impact on the viability of an organisation. In addition, financial risks have an effect on investors' perceptions of the short-, medium- and long-term trading prospects of a company, and this is reflected in a company's share value. The declaration of financial performance in a company's annual report assists in demonstrating that a company's directors have effectively managed the company's resources over the preceding 12 months. Effective management, however, requires the control of more than just financial risks; it requires systems of control for all the internal and external risks faced by an organisation. Failure to manage these risks can create serious consequences for an organisation and its stakeholders. The implementation of a risk management framework requires:

- identifying organisational hazards;
- assessing the risks associated with each hazard;
- evaluating the acceptability of the residual risks to the organisation; and
- implementing risk control measures.

Organisations that operate an open and honest management system following these principles are in a strong position to demonstrate 'corporate governance'.

This book sets health and safety management alongside the management of other internal and external risks faced by organisations. It advocates that the general risk management framework outlined above is applicable to the management of health and safety risks. In addition, the book adopts a holistic approach to the management of health and safety by proposing best practice techniques that are applicable on a global platform irrespective of the local legislation. The book is presented in two parts: in Part One the essential principles and concepts that underpin the management of health and safety in industrial, commercial and public sector organisations are introduced, and in Part Two the focus is on best practice techniques for health and safety management.

The aims of Part One are to discuss:

- the terminology of risk;
- the management options available for risk mitigation;
- the role of cultural theory, human needs and human error in risk management;
- the influence of risk perception and risk communication on the management of risk;
- the importance of economic and cost–benefit considerations in risk decision-making; and
- the context of health and safety risks.

The opening chapter discusses the terminology and definitions used in risk, the development of the concept of risk, the role of risk in modern society, the allocation of responsibilities for risk, and individual and societal risks. In addition, it explores the issue of quantification of risk and the concept of acceptability and tolerability of risk. In Chapter 2 health and safety risks are placed within the context of global risks, and the factors that influence risk management, including business continuity and disaster management, are discussed. Options available for mitigating risk within an organisational setting and the role of internal control are presented.

Individual and organisational personalities influence the ways in which people and organisations act and respond in risk situations and determine whether they display 'risk-taking' or 'risk-averse' behaviours: hence it is important to understand the factors that underpin personality and behaviour. Chapter 3 therefore outlines theories of personality, behaviour, human needs and social culture and discusses their roles in influencing an individual's and an organisation's motivation and propensity for taking risks and how these can lead to human error.

The way in which individuals and organisations perceive risks is an important issue for defining risk control strategies. Although people's perceptions can be changed, perception is a personal view that cannot be said to be right or wrong. Risk perception affects an individual's actions, conclusions and decisions on risk identification, risk estimation, risk evaluation and risk mitigation. Chapter 4 therefore outlines the complexities of human perception and its relationship with risk perception, and discusses the role of risk perception in risk management. Closely linked to risk perception is the issue of risk communication. Evidence has shown that the views of 'experts' and 'public' are different and often incompatible. Bridging the gap between opposing views of risk and persuading people and groups to change their perceptions of and attitudes towards a hazard or issue forms the focus of risk communication. Chapter 5 explains the role of individual attitudes in the process of communication, and addresses a number of specific issues associated with risk communication, such as risk comparisons, framing effects, trust and the social amplification of risk.

An essential principle of business risk management is grounded in economics. Companies incur costs not only from the consequences of accidents and ill-health but also from trying to prevent accidents and ill-health. It is important, therefore, to understand the economic balance between prevention and failure in health and safety management. Chapter 6 outlines the basic aspects of economics in order to explain how health and safety costs impact on the financial performance of an organisation. In addition, specific economic issues related to health and safety, such as budget constraints and the costs associated with performance standards, externalities and the selection of control measures, are discussed. Cost–benefit analysis techniques are used to support normative decisions on how to control risks. In order to perform these assessments, the appropriate information must be available and presented to decision-makers in a format that is readily understood. Chapter 7 discusses factors that affect cost and benefit analysis procedures and outlines their impact on decision-making. The issues associated with defining a valuation for life, injury and ill-health are also discussed within this context.

The final chapter in Part One considers the position of health and safety management within the overall context of business management. In addition, factors influencing and motivating organisations towards proactive health and safety management and the acceptance and demonstration of corporate responsibility for health and safety risks are discussed. Chapter 8 draws together the themes discussed in the preceding chapters and provides an introduction to the best practices that are discussed in Part Two.

The aims of Part Two are to discuss:

- the international, national and organisational approaches of health and safety management systems;
- the principles of risk assessment;
- the roles of physical, management and human factor controls in a risk mitigation strategy;
- the contributions of training and competence in risk control;
- the requirements of effective performance measurement;
- the techniques of auditing, benchmarking and continuous improvement; and
- the management of health and safety risks in the context of social responsibility and accountability.

Part Two commences by considering, in Chapter 9, the role of regulation in the management of health and safety and the evolution and structure of governmental and non-governmental regulation. In addition, some of the challenges posed by the harmonisation of health and safety regulation are discussed. This is followed, in Chapter 10, by a discussion of the principles and goals of organisational health and safety management systems. This chapter compares and contrasts six organisational management models that are applicable to health and safety.

In modern society, risk assessment provides the cornerstone of health and safety management. Chapter 11 introduces and discusses a wide range of general issues, a range of techniques for carrying out strategic and operational risk assessments, and the preparation of risk assessment reports. Factors affecting the preparation of a risk assessment in an environment of uncertainty are discussed, and the role of risk assessment in making decisions at government level is also outlined. Risk control is at the heart of effective risk management, and there are three generic options available: physical, procedural and people controls. Chapter 12 explores these options together with the hierarchy of controls principle, the relative merits and disadvantages of control strategies, and the implementation and maintenance of control measures. The role of operational standards, the principle of inherent safety in plant designs and safe systems of work are examined. The influence of risk control strategies on the development of a positive organisational safety culture is also discussed.

Chapter 13 addresses the roles of training and competence at all employee levels within an organisation, and their impact on health and safety performance. The principles of effective training using theories and practices of adult learning are discussed. In particular, training programme design, training needs analysis and training evaluation are examined.

A key aspect of health and safety management is the measurement of health and safety performance. Health and safety performance can be measured reactively in terms of the harms that occur, or proactively in terms of the inputs to a health and safety management system. Chapter 14 discusses the importance of performance measurement and the relative merits and difficulties associated with a range of reactive and proactive monitoring techniques. Organisations can maintain and improve their health and safety performance by learning through the use of audits and inspections. In order to continuously improve their health and safety management systems, organisations may seek to 'benchmark' their performance internally and externally. Chapter 15 discusses the roles and processes of health and safety audits and inspections, including the collection, assessment and interpretation of information, and examines the nature and role of benchmarking in health and safety management. In addition, this chapter discusses how the detailed objective analysis of data generated by the health and safety management system provides opportunities for continuous improvement in health and safety performance.

Having considered best practice techniques for the management of health and safety risks, Chapter 16 considers the social responsibility and accountability of individuals and organisations for the management of health and safety risks. It also considers their wider duty to improve health and safety performances at the organisational, national and international levels.

The book is intended for managers and directors with responsibilities for health and safety. Given that the text adopts a best practice approach, it meets or exceeds the requirements of legislative systems around the world, and therefore should have wide appeal within multinational organisations operating across countries and continents. The book will also be a key text for students studying undergraduate and postgraduate programmes in health and safety management and other management programmes that contain health and safety as a significant element, such as environmental, quality and general management programmes.

> But more than that we want you to leave here feeling that we all could make a very real difference to the world we live in if we could work together. In a world of –isms and –ologies, of expertise so refined that only experts understand it, we have brought together scientists, artists and technologists to create a distinctive culture, one that makes the possibilities of the future come to life in a way that we can all comprehend.

T. Smit *The Eden Project: The Guide*, 2001

About the authors

Dr Colin W. Fuller obtained a BSc in chemistry at Exeter University and a PhD in analytical chemistry at Strathclyde University. He then worked in the chemical and electricity sectors in areas such as research, operations, plant commissioning, quality, environment and health and safety management. Colin joined Loughborough University before moving with Dr Luise Vassie to the University of Leicester, where they established an MSc in Health and Safety Management by distance learning for managers working in industry and commerce. Colin acts as a consultant for a wide range of organisations, where he focuses on management training, auditing management systems and benchmarking organisational performance.

Research forms a major area of interest and was the catalyst for his move from industry to academia. His research interests include risk management, auditing, benchmarking, performance measurement and modelling health and safety management issues in industrial organisations and applying risk management principles within professional sports such as football, rugby and motor sport.

Colin is the author of over 50 peer-reviewed research publications and the author or editor of several books in the areas of analytical chemistry, environment, health and safety management and risk management in professional sport. Colin is a Fellow of the Royal Society of Chemistry and an Associate Member of FIFA's Medical Assessment and Research Centre.

Dr Luise H. Vassie obtained a BSc in physics and a PhD in laser physics at University College of Wales, Swansea. After completing her degrees, she investigated the feasibility of using laser-based techniques for monitoring the integrity of safety critical coatings/materials used in space vehicles in near earth orbit.

She joined Loughborough University initially to carry out research in the area of laser safety, which entailed the development of a knowledge-based system for auditing laser equipment. She also worked with several major companies to assist them in the development of laser safety systems. Later, she undertook research, postgraduate teaching and consultancy in health and safety management with a range of public and private sector organisations. Luise joined the University of Leicester to develop and present an MSc in Health and Safety Management with Dr Colin Fuller. Her research interests include employee participation, continuous improvement approaches and the role of global partnerships in health and safety management. She frequently works with industrial organisations on a wide range of health and safety issues, which are largely aimed at facilitating a philosophy of continuous improvement in health and safety management.

Luise is a Member of the Institute of Physics and a Member of the Institution of Occupational Safety and Health.

Acknowledgements

We are grateful to the following for permission to reproduce copyright material:

Table 2.1 and Table 2.2 from *Natural Catastrophes and Man-made Disasters in 2001: Storms and Earthquakes Lead to the Second-highest Losses in Insurance History*, from Swiss Re, Sigma no.1/2002; Figure 3.12 from *Reducing Error and Influencing Behaviour*, HSG48, 1999 with permission of the Health and Safety Executive ©Crown copyright 1999, reproduced with permission from the Controller of Her Majesty's Stationery Office; Table 4.2 from *Risk: Analysis, Perception and Management* by Pidgeon *et al.*, Royal Society, 1992; Table 8.2 from *Risk Management and Critical Protective Systems*, ed. by R. F. Cox, reproduced by permission of the Safety and Reliability Society, 1994; Table 11.3 from *The Philosophy of Risk* by J. C. Chicken and T. Posner, Thomas Telford, 1998; Table 11.7 from Development of a Hazard and Operability-based Method for Identifying Safety Management Vulnerabilities in High Risk Systems by R. Kennedy and B. Kirwin, from *Safety Science*, vol. 30, 1998, with permission from Elsevier Science; Figure 12.3 and Table 12.2 from *Functional Safety of Electrical/Electronic/Programmable Electronic Safety-related Systems*, IEC 61508, with thanks to the International Electrotechnical Commission (IEC) for permission to reproduce information from its International Standard IEC 61508-1; Figure 12.8, with thanks to the International Electrotechnical Commission (IEC) for permission to reproduce information from its International Standard IEC 61508-5. All extracts are copyright of IEC, Geneva, Switzerland. All rights reserved. Further information on the IEC is available from www.iec.ch. IEC has no responsibility for the placement and context in which the extracts and contents are reproduced by Pearson Education Ltd; nor is IEC in any way responsible for the other content or accuracy therein; Figure 15.3 from *Introducing Excellence* by the European Foundation for Quality Management, © EFQM, The EFQM Excellence model is a registered trademark.

We are grateful to Bob Dylan Music Co / Special Rider Music for permission to reprint lyrics from the following songs recorded by Bob Dylan:

Ballad of Donald White © 1962 by Warner Bros. Inc. Copyright renewed 1990 by Special Rider Music; *Gonna Change My Way of Thinking* © 1979 by Special Rider Music; *Everything is Broken* © 1989 by Special Rider Music; *Tryin' to Get to Heaven* © 1997 by Special Rider Music; *Outlaw Blues* © 1965 by Warner Bros. Inc.

Copyright renewed 1993 by Special Rider Music; *Union Sundown* © 1983 by Special Rider Music; *Blowin' in the Wind* © 1962 by Warner Bros. Inc. Copyright renewed 1990 by Special Rider Music; *Arthur McBride* © 1992 by Special Rider Music; *Shelter from the Storm* © 1974 by Ram's Horn Music; *Love Minus Zero / No Limit* © 1965 by Warner Bros. Inc. Copyright renewed 1993 by Special Rider Music; and *Who Killed Davey Moore?* © 1964 by Warner Bros. Inc. Copyright renewed 1992 by Special Rider Music. All rights reserved. International copyright secured. Reprint by permission.

In some instances we have been unable to trace the owners of copyright material, and we would appreciate any information that would enable us to do so.

Principles

The concept of risk

If I had some education
To give me a decent start,
I might have been a doctor or
A master in the arts.

– Bob Dylan, 'Ballad of Donald White' (1962)

Chapter contents

- Introduction
- Terminology and definitions in risk management
- Living with risk
- Risk in modern society
- Responsibilities for risk
- Quantification of risks
- Individuals and groups at risk
- Acceptable and tolerable levels of risk

Introduction

Every living organism is exposed to risk, either through genetic make-up or through the environment in which it exists. On the grand scale, Charles Darwin's (1859) book entitled *The Origin of Species* clearly demonstrated the risks and potential consequences of evolutionary life. Some species that evolve are appropriate to their environment and survive; most species that evolve, however, are doomed to extinction. Everyone voluntarily seeks risks, and everyone has risks thrust upon them. Every aspect of people's lives is influenced by risks, and from birth until death everyone takes risks or is subjected to risk on a daily basis. From conception onwards, babies are maintained in a relatively risk-free environment: first in their mother's womb, then subsequently in their cots, where just a mere call for assistance is more than enough to bring food and comfort at most times of the day and night. So why do babies constantly try to escape from this cocoon of safety and well-being by, for example, standing up, walking, climbing and exploring the unknown? The act of standing up, alone, increases one's level of risk because one can now fall down. Later in life, after many child-hood accidents and incidents, which result in cuts, bruises and broken bones, one finds that 'slips, trips and falls' still represent one of the major causes of accident and injury at work (Health and Safety Commission, 2003).

Throughout life, individuals constantly expose themselves, other people and the environment in which they live to many risks. Risks such as drinking alcohol and gambling can affect one's own health and financial status; poor driving habits can affect one's own and other people's safety on the roads; and using ozone-depleting chemicals can affect the environment. Individuals take risks because they perceive that the benefits, which may include long-term employment, financial reward or a pleasurable experience, outweigh the costs, which may include poor health, poor housing or a polluted environment.

A lifetime of exposure to risk therefore enables everyone intuitively to understand risk, to make decisions on risk, and to deal with risk. Based on this accumulated knowledge and experience, everyone feels entitled and able to contribute to debates on risk. However, in order to contribute effectively to these debates, one needs to be able to answer, for example, the questions: What is risk? Who is at risk? Why do people take risks? What, if any, is an acceptable level of risk? Who makes decisions on risk? and Who is responsible for the consequences of risk?

The aims of this chapter are to discuss the basic terminology and definitions used in risk, the development of the concept of risk within life, the role of risk in modern society, the allocation of responsibilities for risk, individual and societal risk, the quantification of risks, and the concepts of acceptability and tolerability of risk.

Terminology and definitions in risk management

The terminology used by stakeholders in risk management is often used in a loose and confusing way. There are differences in definitions and understanding of risk terminology across hazards, organisations, business sectors and countries. It is therefore important to establish and define the terminology that will be used throughout this book. These definitions, which offer a common platform from which the subjects of risk management and health and safety management can be discussed, have been compiled from three main sources:

■ Health and Safety Executive (UK) (1995): *Generic Terms and Concepts in the Assessment and Regulation of Industrial Risks (a discussion document)*;

■ Standards Australia and Standards New Zealand (1999): *AS/NZS 4360: 1999, Risk management*;

■ Royal Society (1992): *Risk: analysis, perception and management*.

Risk

Risk is the chance of a particular situation or event, which will have an impact upon an individual's, organisation's or society's objectives, occurring within a stated period of time. Risk, which is normally measured in terms of its consequences and the probability of these consequences occurring, is a measure of uncertainty, and it should therefore follow the normal laws of combining probabilities. Hence where a series of events must take place for an outcome to occur, the probability attached to each of the component events can be multiplied together in order to obtain the probability of the final consequence occurring. Risk may have either positive or negative outcomes: where negative outcomes result, the event will be referred to as an *adverse event*. In health and safety management, risk always refers to the chance of a negative outcome. Individual, social, work-based and environmental risks can be categorised as situational or event-based risks.

A *situational risk* exists where a hazard (or agent) may be continuously disposed to impact upon a system. The harmful properties of an agent are normally defined through a 'dose–effect' relationship and the susceptibility of the exposed system. This condition exists, for example, in the case of a chemical that has been identified through a dose–effect relationship to be carcinogenic to people or harmful to the environment.

An *event-based risk* exists where the probability of an event occurring arises from the failure, under certain circumstances, of protective systems, which may or may not have been implemented to control the risk. Protective systems may relate to physical controls, such as guards, to management controls, such as safe systems of work, or to human factors, such as the behaviour of an individual. An unplanned escape of chemicals from an industrial process, which represents an event-based risk, may for example have occurred through the failure of a plant safety mechanism, the application of an inadequate permit-to-work procedure, or the actions of an employee who has been incorrectly trained.

Probability is a quantified measure of the likelihood or frequency of a specific event or outcome occurring. Probability is the ratio of the number of specific events or outcomes occurring to the total number of possible events or outcomes. Probability is therefore expressed as a number between 0 and 1: the value 0 represents the situation where an event is impossible, and 1 represents the situation where an event is certain. Small values of probability are often expressed as a power to the base of 10: for example, a probability of 0.000 000 1 is expressed as 1×10^{-7}.

Frequency is a measure of the rate of occurrence of an event, expressed as the number of occurrences of an event in, for example, a given period of time, a given distance travelled, or a given number of events. Industrial accidents, which are often used as indicators of health and safety performance, are presented as accident frequencies. These may be reported, for example, as the number of fatalities, lost-time accidents or cases of ill health per 100 000 hours worked.

Likelihood is a qualitative measure of probability and frequency. Some people find it difficult to conceptualise the meaning of a probability of, for example, 1×10^{-7}, in the context of work-based activities. Therefore the qualitative measure of likelihood is used instead, in order to describe the number of times an event occurs. This parameter is often expressed in descriptive terms, such as 'frequent', 'probable', 'possible', 'unlikely', 'rare' or 'impossible', in order to convey the range of probabilities of an event occurring.

An *event* is an incident or situation that occurs in a particular place during a particular interval of time. An *adverse event* is an event that produces harm or damage. Events and adverse events can both occur in connection with speculative risks, but only adverse events can occur in the context of pure risks (see later). Adverse events may take place over short, medium or extended periods of time, and they may involve either a single action or several repeated actions. Adverse events may lead to either acute or chronic outcomes of harm. Hence an employee may, for example, suffer harm from noise as a result of a single exposure to a high intensity, of repeated exposures at low intensities, or of continuous exposure to a range of intensities over an extended period of time.

A *hazard* is a disposition, condition or situation that may be a source of potential harm, or which may potentially lead to damage. Disposition refers to properties that are intrinsic to a hazard and which will be harmful under certain circumstances. Sometimes the properties themselves, for example an irritant or carcinogen, may be referred to as the hazard rather than the chemical substance or article itself. Hazards can be classified in terms of their potential effects or severity – for example radiation, financial or environmental hazards.

Harm refers to injury, which requires repair, cure or which may be irreparable, to people or the environment. Events may give rise to effects that do not always lead to harm. The effect is the initial impact on the system, which may or may not then result in harm. For example, exposure to a dust may have an effect by causing a person to sneeze, but it does not result in harm to the person because, in this case, the body's immune system has protected the person from harm, by expelling the dust particles from the nose, trachea and lungs before any harm has been incurred.

Damage refers to an observable destruction of objects or to a negative financial consequence. Damage is normally used to refer to negative outcomes involving plant and equipment. For example, in a factory or an office, a fire or explosion may lead to direct damage to the plant, equipment and materials, but it may also lead to indirect financial losses through a failure to meet contractual obligations on delivery schedules or because alternative production arrangements, which may be required, prove expensive to install.

Detriment is a measure of the summation of all the harms to all the people and all the damage to all the properties that are affected by an adverse event. Detriment is a measure of the potential severity and probability of the consequences of an adverse event. The total detriment of a specified risk may therefore require the summation of the probabilities of a wide range of consequences of widely varying severity. Detriment can be expressed in a number of ways, for example as lost production or loss of life; however, it is normally expressed in financial terms, such as 'the expected loss in monetary value per year'. Detriment provides a simple numerical way of assessing the combined effects of an adverse event on people, the environment and property. This approach is therefore an essential precursor to the use of cost–benefit analysis techniques within a risk management system.

Loss is any negative consequence resulting from an adverse event. Loss is the sum of all the damage to property and all the harm to people, including any pain or suffering as well as any financial consequences. Loss is normally expressed in financial terms, and potential losses are often covered by insurance policies, as part of a risk mitigation strategy.

The interrelationships that exist between the terms discussed above for an event-based risk are illustrated in Figure 1.1.

Risk management

Risk management is the systematic application of management policies, procedures and practices to the tasks of identifying, analysing, evaluating, treating and monitoring risks. Risk management therefore implies that decisions have been made to accept certain known levels of risk, either with or without the implementation of risk control measures, but it invariably implies that a formal or informal cost–benefit analysis has been undertaken as part of the overall process.

Risk identification is the process of identifying situations and events that may give rise to potential losses for an organisation, and includes the identification of

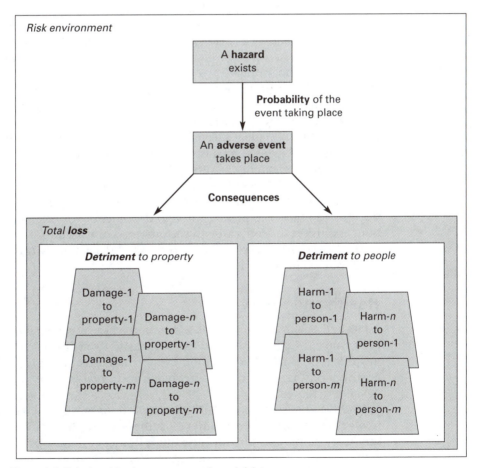

Figure 1.1 Relationships between event-based risk terms

hazards, the potential adverse events associated with these hazards, and the stakeholders, who may be affected by the adverse events.

Risk classification is the process of categorising risks into groups, which are identified either by their origins or by their potential impacts. Risks can be grouped either by their hazard type, such as chemical, electrical, industrial and natural sources, or by the consequences that they give rise to, such as financial, environmental and health and safety losses.

A *risk event* is the realisation of a potential loss into an actual loss. Risk, as outlined above, follows the mathematical principles of probability. Therefore, although the risk always exists, a loss may never actually be realised within the lifetime of an organisation, plant, process or piece of equipment. An actual loss occurs only following a risk event.

Risk assessment involves the processes of risk identification, risk estimation and risk evaluation. Risk assessment is an attempt to define the probability of certain outcomes resulting from specified adverse events. The process is based on arguments and judgements that have been derived from statistical data and/or comparisons with similar agents, events and situations that have occurred in the past either within the organisation or within other organisations.

Risk estimation is the identification of the outcomes of events and an estimation of the magnitude and probability of these outcomes. Risk estimation is used where it is considered that a degree of precision can be attributed to or claimed for the results obtained. There is a connotation that risk estimations are made by 'risk experts'. Risk estimations can be made on the basis of qualitative, semi-quantitative or quantitative predictions.

Risk evaluation is the process of determining the significance or acceptability of the estimated risks. Risk evaluation involves the application of the important issue of stakeholder risk perceptions, because these impact on the acceptability of the risks to the individual stakeholders. Risk evaluation also implies that a formal or informal cost–benefit analysis has been undertaken in order to reach conclusions on the acceptability, or otherwise, of the risks involved.

Risk mitigation is the process of defining and implementing measures to reduce or control exposures to risk. Risk mitigation or risk control measures incorporate the options of risk acceptance, through the processes of risk transfer or risk retention, and risk reduction, through the processes of risk control or risk avoidance.

The interrelationships between the risk management terms discussed above are illustrated in Figure 1.2.

Health and safety

A safe and healthy state refers to a situation where unacceptable risks, which can cause harm to people, do not exist. Clearly, from this definition, a safe and healthy state is an ideal situation rather than a reality. It is a state that many organisations aspire to reach but which most organisations would accept could never be achieved.

Health and safety management is the application of risk management principles to work-based activities in order to achieve the optimum level of health and safety for employees and all other stakeholders affected by the organisation's activities and risks. Effective health and safety management requires organisations to establish formal or informal policies, responsibilities and procedures in

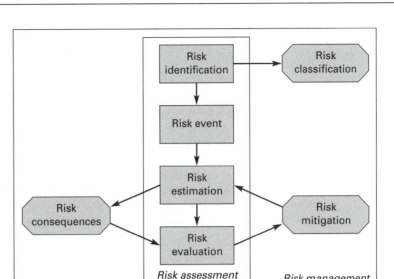

Figure 1.2 Relationships between risk management terms

order to achieve this aim. These arrangements must then be monitored, audited and reviewed in order to ensure that the organisation's procedures and standards are continuously improved or, at the very least, maintained.

Living with risk

There is a dilemma when dealing with people and risk. Some people appear to strive to reduce levels of risk, whereas other people look to increase their level of risk exposure. However, people invariably reduce or increase their exposure to risk selectively. Those people who aim to reduce their risk exposure are still normally prepared, for example, to use drugs and undergo surgery in medical treatments and eat dairy products, red meat and chocolates as part of their diet. People who strive to increase their voluntary exposure to risk often seek to reduce their exposure to work-based, environmental and financial risks.

Homo prudens strives constantly, if not always efficaciously, to avoid accidents.

But people do willingly take risks. Gamblers may not like losing, but they do like gambling. Zero-risk man is a figment of the imagination of the safety profession. *Homo prudens* is but one aspect of the human character. *Homo aleatorius* – dice man, gambling man, risk-taking man – also lurks within every one of us.

We respond to the promptings of *Homo aleatorius* because we have no choice; life is uncertain. And we respond because we want to; too much certainty is boring, unrewarding and belittling. The safety literature largely ignores *Homo aleatorius*, or, where it does acknowledge his existence, seeks to reform him. It assumes that everyone's risk thermostat is set to zero, or should be.

Adams (1995: 16–17)

The problem with 'risk' is that the more one knows about it, the more one realises how much more there is to know. The complexities of the subject and the different views of risk expressed by stakeholders ensure that debates and theories of risk are many and varied. Unfortunately, these discussions frequently become a battlefield between natural scientists and engineers, on the one side, and social scientists, on the other. Kasperson (1992) has summarised the problems created by the entrenched positions often taken by each side in the arguments and discussions about risk:

> Disciplinary and theoretical squabbles over the correctness of particular viewpoints have diverted energies from seeking out the meeting points of theory, from appreciating the particular contributions of alternative interpretations, and from fashioning more holistic analyses of hazard experience and its social meaning.
>
> The most striking disjuncture has been that between the 'technical' and the 'social or perceptual' analysis of hazards. The technical concept of risk focuses narrowly on the probability of events and the magnitude of the consequences that follow.
>
> Accordingly, social scientists have delighted in detailing the inadequacies of the technical concept: consequences can be satisfactorily identified only through analysis of human activity and values; 'damage' is socially dependent; social processes and setting influence the incidence of hazard events; human 'factors' are major contributors in hazard causation; management is rooted in social institutions and relationships. Yet, while discrediting the narrow technical conception of risk and the limitations of 'mandated' science, the social science critics have offered no coherent framework or approach for integrating the technical and social aspects of risk.
>
> Kasperson (1992:155)

The great majority of people are familiar with the concept of 'risk' in terms of gambling. A 'punter', who places a bet on the turn of a card, the throw of a dice or the result of a competition, has an anticipation of a win or some other benefit, but he or she also has the knowledge that there is the possibility of the loss of the stake money. However, not all risks have the prospect of a gain; some risks merely have the possibility of a loss associated with them. Hurricanes and floods bring only the prospect of damage; it is difficult to contemplate many people benefiting from these events other than the builders and manufacturers who are employed to repair the damage. Although insurance companies may benefit financially from covering these risks in terms of insurance premiums, they do not benefit from the consequences of the actual events.

When one refers to risk, one needs therefore to understand whether it is a 'speculative' risk or a 'pure' risk because, whereas speculative risks offer the possibilities of both a gain and a loss, pure risks provide only the prospect of a loss with no prospect of a gain. Examples of pure risk are provided by, for instance, environment, health, safety and quality issues, whereas speculative risks are illustrated by advertising, marketing, political, currency, stock market and gambling issues. When one gambles on the throw of the dice or the toss of a coin, one places a bet and takes a risk on the outcome. The bet is placed on the basis of predicting or guessing the outcomes of the risk event. The gamble or risk is based on the fact that, over hundreds of throws of the dice or tosses of a coin, the outcomes obtained will follow a clearly defined distribution, which can be predicted statistically: this is referred to as *aleatoric probability*. However, the outcome of any individual throw of the dice or toss of the coin has no dependence on the previous outcomes obtained. Individually, one has no control over the outcome of these purely probabilistically based events, unless of course one is prepared to cheat.

One must now question whether future organisational risks are related to the probabilities and consequences associated with past events, and whether future events are a continuation of events taking place in the present. Can one change or prevent risk events from taking place in an organisational setting or are they, like the toss of the coin, beyond one's control? Although organisational risk does relate to the uncertainty of the future, it also relates to situations and events over which we do have some level of control. This control is achieved through the process of risk management, which allows one to alter the odds and improve the chances of achieving the desired outcome.

Whether one believes that the outcome of future risk events can be influenced does, however, depend on one's view of life, and this will be discussed later within the context of cultural theory and risk perception.

Risk in modern society

Risk is not unique to modern society, as risk has always been a part of life. The difference is that, in modern society, the public have become more aware of some risks because they attract high levels of media attention. Those areas of risk that receive this media attention are not necessarily the areas with the highest levels of risk: for example, the number of accidents and deaths arising from leisure and home activities represents a major risk to most people, but does not receive significant media attention. This awareness of some risks rather than others has often been accentuated by the quantification of societal risk levels, in particular those related to health issues:

> For example, some experts now believe that between 40 and 50 per cent of all regular cigarette smokers will die prematurely as a result of their habit, which is a risk of 1 premature death for every 2 or 2.5 cases of lifetime exposure.
>
> Leiss and Chociolko (1994: 7)

Most people now live longer because, for example, the products that they use are generally safer, and the medical care products, procedures and treatments that have been developed in order to improve or maintain their health are more effective. However, these improvements are invariably accompanied by the introduction of new hazards, and exposures to these have raised concerns and sometimes alarm amongst the public. If exposure to risks makes individuals more concerned then they may become more risk averse, which will cause them to consequently avoid the use of these new technologies, procedures and treatments. If the probability and consequences of risk exposure to these new technologies are high then this may clearly be the correct course of action. However, where the risks from an activity, product or treatment are, in reality, very low, the individual may have exposed himself or herself to an unnecessarily higher level of risk, through risk-averse behaviour. If one assumes, for example, that a pharmaceutical company has developed an immunisation treatment for meningitis, this would have enormous health benefits for young people. If, unfortunately, there is an extremely remote chance that there may be undesirable side-effects from the use of this drug, then parents who are risk averse may reject the treatment and choose instead to expose their children to the risk of meningitis. In this case the very action of avoiding the extremely low risk from a meningitis immunisation programme would expose children, in general, to a much higher level of risk from the contraction of meningitis.

Although the rapid rate of technological development creates many opportunities and benefits, it also creates many hazards and risks. Developments must be thoroughly assessed in order to determine whether the overall level of risk exposure will be reduced or increased as a consequence of exposure to these new types of risk. A problem in modern society is that the main protagonists of new technologies are often biased in their views or are evasive in their comments about the costs and benefits of the risks associated with the technologies. This invariably leads to suspicions, amongst the public, about governments', scientists' and industrialists' motives, and about their reluctance to demonstrate corporate governance in commercial activities. These suspicions inevitably lead to a greater level of risk aversion amongst the public, simply because they do not trust the integrity of the people involved rather than through any real knowledge or belief that the technology itself is unsound or not beneficial.

An individual's susceptibility to risk can be defined by three components: the magnitude of the potential loss or consequence, the probability of the potential loss or consequence occurring, and the individual's level of exposure to the risk. Three issues affect the impact of these components: the measures in place to control the risk, the information provided about the risk, and the time that one has available to manage the risks (MacCrimmon and Wehrung, 1986). An individual can normally control only his or her exposure to a risk: for example not taking part in a particular activity, or reducing the level of consumption of a suspect foodstuff. An organisation can change the magnitude of the potential losses and the probability of an event taking place by improving the type and level of control measures in place, by increasing the level of information provided to stakeholders, by allocating adequate time in order to address the problems involved, and by providing adequate financial support to implement these measures.

The key issue involved in technological development in modern society is risk management through appropriate risk assessment and risk communication strategies. Governments, regulators and international bodies play a key role in managing the risks associated with modern developments of technology by first identifying the risks, then by assessing potential risk levels, and finally by defining acceptable levels of risk. One of the major problems associated with assessing and communicating new risk issues is connected with the way in which the public view the probabilities and consequences of risks. The public often view an event's probability of occurrence as being less important than the possible consequences:

Oftentimes in the public's view, the significance of an event's probability tends to decrease as conceivable consequences increase, until what is possible becomes more feared than what is probable.

Leiss and Chociolko (1994: 31)

The development of new technologies in modern society should be regarded as merely the process of trading new hazards for old hazards and new risks for old risks. Therefore either the benefits imparted by the new risks should be greater than the benefits obtained from the older risks, or the costs associated with the new risks should be lower than the costs associated with the older risks.

Responsibilities for risk

People who make decisions about introducing new risks, or who determine what is an acceptable or an unacceptable level of risk for individuals and/or society, are responsible for risk management. Most people realise that new technology brings new opportunities and benefits, but they also expect that those people who create and benefit from these technologies should also be responsible for the associated risks. The public expect governments and international bodies to take the lead in protecting people from these risks. People generally feel that they can control their exposure to risk as long as the exposure arises from their own voluntary actions. However, if exposure is involuntary and an unfavourable consequence occurs, their concerns will at some point turn to the issue of compensation, and to identifying the person who has the responsibility for agreeing and settling issues of compensation.

Whereas one may accept that there are clearly disproportionate benefits to be gained from exposing oneself to a risk, it is also important to be aware of who is responsible for the few undesirable outcomes when they do occur. A failure to allocate responsibility for losses arising from risks and to compensate those people suffering losses from risks will again lead to an increasing level of risk aversion in respect of new technologies.

In some situations the allocation of responsibility is clear and straightforward. For example, consider the situation where, as a result of driving his car too fast round a bend in the road on a beautiful summer's day, a driver swerves off the road and crashes into the front of a house. Setting aside the possibility, for example, that there was a type fault with the vehicle or that the vehicle had been inadequately serviced, the driver is quite clearly responsible either directly, or indirectly through his insurance company, for his actions and for compensation for any losses incurred by the householder. Compare this with the case where an eight-year-old child is blinded in one eye by a sharp component in a new toy. The child's parents bought the toy, which was designed for children of over 10 years of age, after seeing the product advertised on television. Does the responsibility for the injury rest with the child for playing with the toy, with the parents for buying an inappropriate toy, with the shopkeeper for not checking the age of the child who would be playing with the toy, with the television company for inadequately advertising the potential dangers of the toy to younger children, or with the manufacturers for not ensuring that their product is adequately marketed? The 'correct' allocation of responsibility can only be determined, in complex cases of this type, through lengthy and expensive legal liability cases.

Often the responsibility for compensation of losses that arise from risk activities falls disproportionately onto people who do not expose themselves to the risks. For example, should the cost for mountain rescue services fall on the population in general, or should it be borne solely by those people who expose themselves to the risk of climbing? An argument can be made that individuals take on this type of risk voluntarily, and they should know the level of risk associated with the activity. Therefore should a climber who takes on this risk expect to be rescued if he or she encounters difficulties? One could argue that this person knew the risks and therefore, if he or she has not provided their own emergency measures, should be left where they are with any resultant consequences. This situation is quite clearly different from the case of an individual who is exposed to involuntary risks when they may not be aware of or understand the risks associated with the activity. Therefore, for example, someone who is subjected to the fallout of toxic gases from an explosion at a chemical plant is entitled to expect hospital treatment for any injuries or ill-health sustained through no fault of their own. The responsibility for provision of treatment in this case should justifiably, therefore, be borne by the population at large and/or by the organisation that is responsible for the explosion at the factory.

Quantification of risks

Quantified values of risk are obtained from theoretical calculations and/or experiences of failure rates or non-conformances. Although risk is defined by the statistical parameters of probability, problems of understanding and interpreting values of risk are often not related to the values themselves but rather to the way in which different people interpret their significance. This arises because interpretation is also an issue of risk perception and risk communication rather than just risk quantification. Although most people accept that the potential outcomes of exposure to hazards can be quantified objectively, in terms for example of death, injury, ill-health and financial losses, risk is less easily quantified, as it is not possible to simply compartmentalise risks into 'objective' (statistical) and 'subjective' (perceived) risks (Slovic, 1992). This situation exists because all risk assessments involve human judgements, either directly or indirectly, and therefore these judgements will inevitably be based on subjective criteria (Royal Society, 1992).

Well-defined or quantified values of risk, which impart a degree of accuracy and precision, should assist one in developing risk control strategies. Risk, by definition, is a measure of uncertainty, and therefore, however reliable the statistical data, one cannot predict the exact outcome of risk situations. It must be remembered that quantified values of risk are normally based on historical data of events and/or consequences of risk events. These values relate to the general population who have been previously affected, rather than to the future risk of an individual within that population. It was reported (Hawkins and Fuller, 1999) that the average rate of injury to professional footballers was 27.7 injuries per 1000 player-hours of competition. Therefore, for a team of 11 players involved in 50 matches, one would predict that there would be a total of 23 injuries to this group of players over this period. However, one cannot predict from these data who will be injured or when the injuries will occur.

There is uncertainty with all quantified measurements of risk, but the uncertainties associated with statistical values of risk should be assessed against the alternatives of using stakeholders' guesses, beliefs and prejudices. If this approach were to be used in the process of risk management, it would be almost impossible to reach any conclusions on the acceptability of risks. There are, therefore, clear benefits to be gained from collecting and using statistical data. For example, although it may not be possible, with present scientific knowledge, to reduce the number and severity of floods, storms, hurricanes and earthquakes in specific areas of the world, statistical data will guide decisions on damage limitation measures, such as building and highway construction standards and locations for establishing centres of population. Similarly, the use of statistical data on product faults and deficiencies in process operations highlight areas where operational management can take appropriate risk control actions. Quantified data are also used successfully in epidemiological studies of health issues for defining risk levels associated with, for example, heart disease, lung cancer and mental illness. Often, this type of data is used to establish links between illness and disease among specific sections of the population, and exposures to occupational or environmental hazards.

Individuals and groups at risk

When completing a risk assessment, it is important to identify those stakeholders who may be affected by the risks. The definitions used to describe these stakeholders depend on the circumstances of the risks and the risk assessments being carried out. For general purposes of health and safety management, the population at risk consists of *statistical people*. Identifiable *groups of people*, for example those people living close to a nuclear power station or an airport, are subject to different levels of risk from these hazards than those experienced by a statistical person, who most probably will not be living in these areas. A *hypothetical person*, who is used to assess specific scenarios, is also different from a statistical person. Therefore, when carrying out a risk assessment, it is important to appreciate and identify which type of person is being included within the assessment. A further distinction should be made between risks to an individual, whether the individual is an identified, statistical or hypothetical person, in which case the risk is referred to as *individual risk*, and the risks to groups of people, in which case the risk is referred to as *societal risk*.

A statistical person has no special property, personality, living and working location or other distinguishing feature. By contrast, a hypothetical person or persons, who can also be treated for some purposes as a statistical person or persons as they are not identified individuals, is a person or group of people who have been defined solely to carry out a specific risk assessment. They may be people who live in a particular area and are subjected to specific risks, such as people who live near to natural rock formations and are exposed to radon gas, or people who live close to a motorway and are therefore exposed to high levels of vehicle exhaust fumes. A *critical group* is defined as a group of hypothetical people who are significantly more exposed to particular risks than a statistical person. An example of these would be young, newly qualified, male drivers of fast sports cars, as they are more likely to have an accident than more mature, experienced drivers.

Decisions on risk control measures are often influenced by the type of person or group of people affected by a risk. Accidents and injury to young children are regarded as being far less acceptable than accidents and injury to older people at work. This is particularly important where the identities of the people are known. In this case, the risk assessor knows exactly who will be affected rather than knowing that 'someone', who is unidentified, may be affected. Knowledge of the individuals affected invariably influences the type and level of risk control measures employed; this is particularly apparent in the deployment and financing of risk prevention and risk treatment measures.

Individual risk

Individual risk is the frequency with which a statistical, hypothetical or identified person may expect to sustain a specified level of harm as a result of an adverse event involving a specified hazard. Individual risk can be used to express the general level of risk to an individual in the general population (a statistical person) or to an individual in a specified section of the community (a hypothetical person). Individual risk does not normally refer to the risk sustained by an identifiable person, although it can be used in this context. If an individual is certain (or almost certain) to suffer injury as a result of an adverse event, then the individual risk level is the same as the risk associated with the adverse event itself taking place. This may be the case for the risk of an employee being fatally injured while working on a major hazard plant that may, under certain conditions, suffer a catastrophic explosion. On the other hand, where there is a risk of a major explosion taking place, but the probability of the employee being in the vicinity of the explosion when it occurs is only 1 in 100, the individual risk of a fatality to the operator is 100 times lower than the risk of the explosion itself taking place.

Occupational risk

Occupational risk is the frequency with which a hypothetical person may expect to sustain a specified level of harm as a result of an identified adverse event(s) involving a specified hazard while involved in work-based activities. Occupational risks are regularly reported by organisations as an indicator of their health and safety performance; regulatory bodies also use occupational accident frequencies in order to differentiate health and safety performances between organisations, between industrial sectors and between countries. Table 1.1 provides examples of fatal, major injury and over-three-day lost-time accident rates for a range of industrial sectors within the UK (Health and Safety Commission, 2003). These results illustrate the wide variations in injury severity and frequency of injury experienced by employees across industrial sectors. National responsible bodies use this type of data in order to target industrial sectors and promote injury prevention strategies.

Table 1.1 Occupational risks in the UK by industrial sectors (2002/03)

	Injuries per 100 000 employees		
Industrial sector	Fatalities	Major injuries	Over 3-day lost-time injuries
Agriculture	7	270	588
Chemicals manufacturing	0.9	169	656
Construction	5	375	792
Education	0	63	196
Financial services	0.3	32	124
Food products manufacturing	0.7	296	1908
Hotels and restaurants	0.1	56	192
Mining (coal)	0	685	5121
Transport (land)	4	234	1236

Refer to Health and Safety Commission (2003) for further data

Organisational risk

Organisational risk refers to the range of risks encountered by an organisation in carrying out its business activities. Organisational risks require the development of risk management programmes, either as a unified risk management programme across all types of hazard or as individual risk management programmes within each specialist area of risk. These risks include those associated, for example, with environment, quality, information technology, marketing, acquisitions, supply chain and health and safety. The management of all these risks is encompassed within the requirements of corporate governance (Turnbull, 1999). Corporate governance imposes a requirement on organisations to manage their businesses through a responsible risk management philosophy. Without taking risks, organisations are unlikely to survive in a competitive world but, equally, taking unacceptable risks will bring about the early demise of an organisation.

Organisational risks can also be expressed in terms that specifically indicate the risks associated with the organisation's activities. An example of this is used in air passenger transport, where fatal event rates are reported for world airlines (see Table 1.2; AirSafe.com, 2003). Fatal events, in this case, are defined as any event where at least one passenger is killed during a flight or where at least one passenger is injured during a flight and subsequently dies. A fatal event may be due to an accident or due to a deliberate act by another passenger(s) or crewmember(s).

Societal risk

Societal risk is defined as the risk of widespread or large-scale detriment from the realisation of a defined hazard. The implication is that the consequences of these risks would be on such a scale that they would provoke social and/or political comment such that the risks are effectively regulated through political processes and regulatory control mechanisms. Ball and Floyd (1998) suggested presenting these types of risk within three categories.

Collective risks are associated with accidents to vulnerable groups in particular, such as children and pregnant women. The risks are related to *diffuse* effects, which result from normal activities rather than from specific accidents or incidents.

Table 1.2 Fatal events and fatal event rates by airline, 1970–2002

Airline	Number of flights, $\times 10^6$	Number of events	Number of events per flight, $\times 10^{-6}$	Date of last event
Air Canada	4.8	3	0.63	1983
Air France	5.9	7	1.19	2000
British Airways	6.4	2	0.32	1985
Cathay Pacific	0.69	1	1.45	1972
China Airlines	0.90	10	11.1	2002
Cubana	0.33	8	24.0	1999 (2)
Delta Airlines	20.0	6	0.30	1997
Egypt Air	0.75	7	9.3	2002
Olympic Airways	1.8	3	1.67	1989
SAS	5.4	1	0.19	2001
Saudi Arabian Airlines	2.2	3	1.40	1996
South African Airways	1.6	1	0.63	1987

Source: AirSafe.com (2003)

Examples of these include the impact of dioxin emissions from incinerators and radioactive emissions from nuclear power stations, all of which are continuous processes rather than one-off events. The overall risk to society from collective risks is equal to the product of the individual risk and the number of people exposed.

Societal risks are described through the use of frequency–number distribution graphs, which define the frequency with which a certain level of fatalities occurs within the population. In this case, societal risks relate solely to harm to people and are referred to as *simple* risks. In more complex situations, where other harms in addition to those involving people may occur, criteria such as harm to the environment must also be included. These risks are referred to as *diverse* risks.

Societal concerns are those where the use of frequency–number graphs is considered to be inadequate at governmental level. At this strategic level of management it is important to take into consideration all aspects of risk, and the impacts that these may have on society. These impacts will therefore incorporate, for example, fatalities, injury, ill-health, environmental damage, economic costs and business interruption.

Acceptable and tolerable levels of risk

There are many social and technical problems associated with defining acceptable levels of risk. In attempting to define acceptable criteria for risk, Fischhoff *et al.* (1981) defined five generic issues that need to be addressed.

Uncertainty associated with the definition of the problem

In defining a risk problem, one may indicate, at the same time, how the problem could be solved. The problem definition may therefore signpost the decision-maker such that they consider a specific set of options rather than maintain an open mind on potential solutions. However, more often the problem is one of insufficient time being allocated to the problem definition rather than one of creating bias in solving the problem.

Difficulties associated with assessing the facts

Critical decisions on acceptable risk levels are often confused by the uncertainty associated with the risk values available. Uncertainty is well understood by natural scientists and engineers, who are used to reporting values with a level of uncertainty through the use of statistical parameters such as the mean and standard deviation. The issue of uncertainty is particularly important when dealing with very low-probability events that may have high-severity outcomes, for example in defining the acceptable risk levels in the design of a bridge or the approval of a drug.

Difficulties associated with assessing risk values

Where people are very familiar with a risk, they may already have a well-formed understanding and view of the problem. For new technologies this is much less likely to be the case. Quite often the public can be misled by being provided with only selective information or given extreme views on the subject. The worst-case scenario in debates on acceptable risk levels is where people have inadequate information, or in some cases no information at all, but still feel able and justified in influencing the debate.

Uncertainties about the impact of human factors

Those people who create new risks often also create the procedures for controlling them. They may therefore be so familiar with the 'risk problem' that they do not consider and question all the possible adverse events. There are two extreme views of the human factor element. The first of these is that people are very open, honest, rational and perceptive: they therefore make the best possible judgements on the risks associated with new hazards, in the interests of all stakeholders. The second view is that people are secretive, less than honest, irrational and limited in their perceptions: they therefore make judgements that meet their own agenda.

Difficulties associated with assessing the quality of the decision

A useful approach to determining the validity of a decision on acceptable levels of risk is to carry out a sensitivity analysis. In this process, a best estimate of an acceptable risk level is used to test the validity of the decision. Further iterative assessments are then carried out using refined estimates of the risk level until the best estimate is consistent with the known information.

Ideally one would like to live in a world where there was *negligible risk*, which could be considered as a state of existence where one would never need to consider the probability or consequences of adverse events. However, there is always risk in life because just being alive carries with it the risk of death. The fundamental risks that exist in the environment in which one lives and which are associated with the activities undertaken, as a part of day-to-day living, are referred to as *inherent risk*. *Pervasive risk* refers more to the environment in which one lives rather than to the specific activities undertaken by people. Within both social and occupational environments it is essential to agree on what may be considered to be an acceptable level of risk or, failing that, a tolerable level of risk. An *acceptable level of risk* can be considered to be one where one's own life, everyone else's life and the environment are not significantly affected, but where reasonable precautions are still required to achieve this condition. A *tolerable level of risk* is considered to be one that is knowingly accepted, on a regular basis, because the benefits accrued from tolerating the risk outweigh the costs. A tolerable level of risk is therefore not one that is negligible or one that can be ignored, but one that should be kept constantly under review. An *intolerable level of risk* is one that is above the tolerable level of risk.

The principle of 'as low as reasonably practicable' (ALARP)

Most people accept that there are three general levels of risk:

- risks that are so high that they are clearly intolerable to every member of society;
- risks that are so low that they can be regarded as negligible for every member of society; and
- risks that fall between these two levels, and which may require thought, discussion and mitigation action by different stakeholders before each group can decide whether the level of risk can be regarded as acceptable or tolerable.

Decisions about which risks fall into the first two categories do not occupy a major part of a risk manager's time; the main difficulties arise with making decisions about the risks falling within the third category. In these cases managers must decide whether the control procedures in place enable the residual risk levels to be regarded as being as low as one could reasonably expect. In determining whether a risk mitigation procedure is reasonably practicable, the implication is that a comparison has been made between the level of risk and the cost of eliminating or reducing the level of risk. If the cost of reducing the level of risk further is disproportionately high compared with the level of risk involved, then the current level of risk may be considered to be acceptable. Implementation of the *as low as reasonably practicable (ALARP)* principle implies that risk levels have been reduced as far as possible, taking into account the cost of the risk mitigation measures. The terms 'as low as reasonably achievable' (ALARA) and 'so far as is reasonably practicable' (SFAIRP) have similar meanings. The relationship between the ALARP principle and the terms 'intolerable', 'tolerable', 'acceptable' and 'negligible risk' is summarised in Figure 1.3.

The ALARP region, in terms of health and safety management, falls between the levels of negligible risk and intolerable risk. In this region one makes judgements, based on the levels of risk and the costs associated with controlling the risk, on whether to reduce the level of risk further or whether to accept the existing level of risk. As the consequences of risk in purely human terms are injury, ill-health and ultimately death, the balance of risk against costs of reduction requires that a value be placed on injury, ill-health and death (or life) in order to complete the cost–benefit analysis.

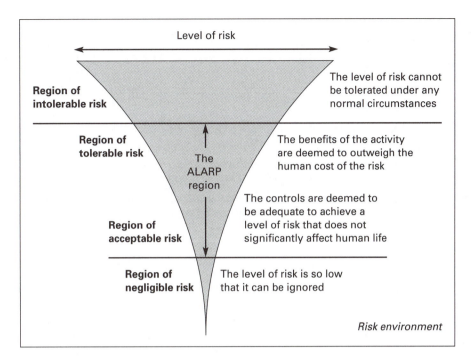

Figure 1.3 The principle of as low as reasonably practicable (ALARP) used in risk management

Summary

■ Models of risk management provide a framework within which the individual elements can be conceptualised and discussed.

■ Risk is an essential aspect of life, with everyone creating and accepting levels of risk throughout their lifetime. However, a balance is normally established between the levels of risk that are accepted by individuals, organisations and society and the cost of these risks to the stakeholders.

■ Speculative risks provide individuals and organisations with an opportunity to make gains as well as losses whereas pure risks only provide the opportunity for losses. Some risks follow defined probability distributions, while other risks can be controlled through effective risk management.

■ There is a balance between the levels of risk created and the benefits that are produced for society by new technologies. The responsibility for managing these risks, however, rests with the creators of the risks.

■ Risks to individuals and society generally fall within the four levels defined as negligible, acceptable, tolerable and intolerable. Risk is normally managed in organisations and society on the principle of reducing risk to a level which can be described by the phrase 'as low as reasonably practicable'.

Issues for review and discussion

- How would you define risk in the context of health and safety?

- Review the risks to which you are exposed within your personal, social and work-based environments.

- Review the risks to which you expose other people within your personal, social and work-based environments.

- Consider what level of control you have over your exposure to risk within your personal, social and work-based environments.

- Consider how you would define acceptable levels of risk for yourself in the context of voluntary and involuntary risks.

References

Adams, J. (1995) *Risk*. London: UCL Press.

AirSafe.com (2003) *Fatal Events and Fatal Event Rates by Airline*. http://airsafe.com

Ball, D.J. and Floyd, P.J. (1998) *Societal Risks*. Sudbury: Health and Safety Executive.

Darwin, C.R. (1859) *The Origin of Species*. London: John Murray.

Fischhoff, B., Lichtenstein, S., Slovic, P., Derby, S.L. and Keeney, R.L. (1981) *Acceptable Risk*. Cambridge: Cambridge University Press.

Hawkins, R.D. and Fuller, C.W. (1999) A prospective epidemiological study of injuries in four English professional football clubs. *British Journal of Sports Medicine*, **33**, 196–203.

Health and Safety Commission (2003) *Health and Safety Statistics, 2002/2003*. Sudbury: HSE Books.

Health and Safety Executive (1995) *Generic Terms and Concepts in the Assessment and Regulation of Industrial Risks (a discussion document)*. Sudbury: HSE Books.

Internal Control Working Party of the Institute of Chartered Accountants in England & Wales (1999) *Internal Control: Guidance for Directors on the Combined Code*. London: The Institute of Chartered Accountants in England & Wales.

Kasperson, R.E. (1992) The social amplification of risk: progress in developing an integrative framework. In: S. Krimsky and D. Golding (eds), *Social Theories of Risk*, 153–178. London: Praeger.

Leiss, W. and Chociolko, C. (1994) *Risk and Responsibility*. Quebec: McGill-Quenn's University Press.

MacCrimmon, K.R. and Wehrung, D.A. (1986) *Taking Risks: the Management of Uncertainty*. New York: The Free Press.

Royal Society (1992) *Risk: Analysis, Perception and Management*. London: Royal Society.

Slovic, P. (1992) Perceptions of risk: reflections on the psychometric paradigm. In: S. Krimsky and D. Golding (eds), *Social Theories of Risk*, 117–152. London: Praeger.

Standards Australia and Standards New Zealand (1999) AS/NZS 4360: 1999, *Risk Management*. Homebush: Standards Australia and Standards New Zealand.

Turnbull (1999) See: Internal Control Working Party of the Institute of Chartered Accountants in England & Wales (1999).

Risk management

Gonna change my way of thinking,
Make myself a different set of rules.
Gonna put my good foot forward,
And stop being influenced by fools.

– Bob Dylan, 'Gonna change my way of thinking' (1979)

Chapter contents

Introduction

Over the latter part of the twentieth century, societies in developed countries generally became healthier and safer places in which to live and work. However, in these countries people have become more concerned about risk issues, the results from risk assessments have become more contentious, the public have become more distrustful of scientists', industrialists' and politicians' statements on risk issues, and scientists, industrialists and politicians have become more frustrated about the public's understanding of risk.

Risk, which impacts on most aspects of business, social and personal life, arises from a variety of sources. For example, from:

- *naturally occurring events*, such as floods, earthquakes, volcanoes and drought;
- *work-based events*, such as the use of chemicals, machinery, electricity and scaffolding; and
- *personal activities*, such as sport, driving, drinking and smoking.

These risks can be conveniently categorised within groups defined by the source of the risk. For example:

- *environmental risks*, such as global warming, air pollution and river contamination;
- *financial risks*, such as currency exchange rates, share values and bank interest rates;
- *quality risks*, such as delivery schedules, production costs and product standards;
- *recreational risks*, such as mountaineering, swimming and gardening;
- *health risks*, such as blood pressure, hepatitis and malaria; and
- *occupational health and safety risks*, such as manual handling, noise and dust.

Categorising risks in this way defines the many subgroups of risk management and the specialist risk managers who are employed by industry and commerce in order to control them: for example, finance managers, environment managers, quality managers and health and safety managers. Although larger organisations may employ these and other specialist risk managers in order to provide corporate guidance and advice, it is an organisation's line managers who are responsible for the day-to-day management of risks. Operational managers, who are responsible for the risks arising from many hazards, must make decisions on the acceptability or unacceptability of risks in a range of circumstances. It is important, therefore, to understand what factors influence risk decisions, and how comparisons of different risks can be made. Unfortunately, there is no universally accepted scale for measuring and comparing risks across the range of hazards encountered. In broad terms, risk is defined as the probability that a certain event involving a specific hazard will result in a specified outcome, but because the outcomes from these events will almost certainly be different for each hazard, the risks must usually be defined by a specific set of criteria or parameters, such as:

- the probability of a production line losing output;
- the probability of a bridge collapsing;
- the probability of a sportsperson being injured; or
- the probability of an aeroplane crashing.

The decisions made on acceptable levels of risk will vary from person to person and from organisation to organisation, because they will depend on the risk philosophies and perceptions of the people, organisations and societies involved. The main aims of this chapter are to place organisational health and safety risks within the context of global risks, to discuss the factors that influence risk management, including business continuity and disaster management, to discuss the options available for mitigating risks, and to assess the role of internal control in the context of risk management.

World risks in context

Natural risks, such as meteor strikes, floods, droughts and pestilence, have existed throughout mankind's time on earth. However, there is a fundamental difference between these risks and modern risks. Mankind is now in an age of technology, where decisions may have the most profound effects on the future of mankind and other species on earth. Financial and human losses from occupational health and safety risks are normally considered to be small compared with those arising from worldwide natural catastrophes and man-made disasters. A *natural catastrophe* is considered to be an event caused by natural forces, such as flood, storm, earthquake, drought and cold, and a *man-made disaster* to be an event arising in conjunction with human activities, such as explosions/fires, transport, mining and construction (Swiss Re, 2002). Losses from natural catastrophes depend not only on the severity of the incident but also on the location where the catastrophe occurs, the density of population, and the nature of the building construction in the area. Events of this type usually result in a large number of individual insurance claims involving a number of insurance companies. Losses from man-made events usually occur in a small locality and involve only a very small number of insurance claims. The losses referred to in the published statistics for these events are made up of insured losses, and exclude liability claims: this form of reporting therefore tends to underestimate the total losses arising from man-made events, as these invariably lead to many liability claims.

The 20 most expensive events over the period 1970 to 2001, in terms of insurance losses, are presented in Table 2.1. Losses, which are quoted in US$m, have been corrected to 2001 values based on inflation rates in the United States over this period of time. These figures show that 19 of the top 20 insurance losses over this period occurred within Europe, Japan and the United States. In addition, 18 of the 20 largest insurance losses occurred from natural disasters, such as hurricanes, earthquakes and storms. Only two of the events included within this list arose from man-made events, namely explosions/fires on an offshore oilrig and a terrorist attack on a high-rise office complex.

Table 2.1 The 20 most expensive events in terms of insurance losses, 1970 to 2001

Insured loss (US$m)[a]	Number of victims	Year	Event	Country
20 200	38	1992	Hurricane Andrew	USA
19 000	>3000	2001	Terrorist attack, World Trade Center	USA
16 700	60	1994	Northridge earthquake	USA
7 300	51	1991	Typhoon Mireille	Japan
6 200	95	1990	Winter storm Daria	Europe
6 200	80	1999	Winter storm Lothar	Europe
5 990	61	1989	Hurricane Hugo	Puerto Rico
4 700	22	1987	Storms and floods	Europe
4 300	64	1990	Winter storm Vivian	Europe
4 300	26	1999	Typhoon Bart	Japan
3 800	600	1998	Hurricane Georges	USA
3 150	33	2001	Tropical storm Allison	USA
3 000	167	1988	Explosion on *Piper Alpha* oilrig	UK
2 900	6425	1995	Great Hanshin earthquake	Japan
2 600	45	1999	Winter storm Martin	Europe
2 500	70	1999	Hurricane Floyd	USA
2 400	59	1995	Hurricane Opal	USA
2 100	246	1993	Snowstorms and tornadoes	USA
2 000	4	1992	Hurricane Iniki	USA
1 900	–	2001	Hail, floods, tornadoes	USA

[a] *Indexed to 2001 values*
Source: Swiss Re, Sigma No. 1/2002

The 20 most expensive events over the period 1970 to 2001, in terms of death and missing persons, are presented in Table 2.2. The figures presented show that 18 of the worst 20 events were related to natural catastrophes, with only two related to man-made events: the nuclear accident at Chernobyl in the former USSR, and a burst dam in India. None of the 20 events occurred in Europe, Japan or the United States, and none of the events appeared in the top 20 greatest insurance losses.

These figures must be viewed in context, because the results refer to losses and fatalities from single, identifiable, catastrophic events. Therefore the statistics do not include insurance losses or fatalities arising from, for example, mesothelioma as a result of work with asbestos, and pneumoconiosis and silicosis as a result of work in coalmines. The total worldwide number of deaths from work-related health risks is very high, and significantly higher than the values presented in Table 2.2. However, because many work-related diseases do not become apparent in workers until at least 10 years after exposure, they do not create the same public impact as sudden major disasters, which normally gain worldwide publicity.

Table 2.2 The 20 most expensive events in terms of deaths, 1970 to 2001

Number of victims	Insured loss (US$m)[a]	Year	Event	Country
300 000	–	1970	Storm and flood	Bangladesh
250 000	–	1976	Earthquake	China
165 000	–	1986	Nuclear power plant incident	Former USSR
138 000	3	1991	Tropical cyclone Gorky	Bangladesh
60 000	–	1970	Earthquake	Peru
50 000	147	1990	Earthquake	Iran
25 000	–	1988	Earthquake	Former USSR
25 000	–	1978	Earthquake	Iran
23 000	–	1985	Volcanic eruption	Colombia
22 000	230	1976	Earthquake	Guatemala
19 000	1 000	1999	Earthquake	Turkey
15 000	100	2001	Earthquake	India/Pakistan
15 000	–	1978	Flooding	India
15 000	100	1999	Cyclone	India
15 000	501	1985	Earthquake	Mexico
15 000	–	1979	Dam burst	India
10 800	–	1971	Flooding	India
10 000	234	1999	Flooding, mudslides	Venezuela
10 000	–	1977	Cyclone	India
10 000	–	1985	Cyclone	Bangladesh

[a]*Indexed to 2001 values*
Source: Swiss Re, Sigma No. 1/2002

The International Labour Organization (ILO) have summarised the estimated levels of occupational fatalities, injuries and diseases worldwide. Their values (Table 2.3) clearly demonstrate the magnitude of the problem associated with accidents at work, because the *annual* number of worldwide occupational fatalities is greater than the worst worldwide disaster over the past 30 years. In addition, the figures demonstrate the differences in health and safety performance in the various areas of the world.

Table 2.3 Estimated number of worldwide work-related fatalities in 2002

World region	Fatalities
China	73 615
Established market economies	16 170
Former socialist economies in Europe	21 425
India	48 176
Latin America and Caribbean	29 594
Middle East	28 019
Other Asia and islands	83 048
Sub-Saharan Africa	54 705
World total	**354 752**

Source: ILO (2003)

The worldwide mortality level arising from occupational diseases is even greater than that arising from occupational accidents. Examples of the worldwide levels and causes of death from occupational diseases are illustrated in Table 2.4.

Table 2.4 Estimated number of deaths from work-related diseases in 2002

Cause of death	Work-related deaths
Communicable diseases	320 471
Malignant neoplasms	609 678
Respiratory system diseases	146 175
Circulatory system diseases	519 255
Neuro-psychiatric conditions	20 341
Digestive system diseases	22 566
Genitourinary system diseases	8 478
World total	**1 646 964**

Source: ILO (2003)

Risk management

Risk management covers the management of a wide range of high- and low-probability events, which may have high or low consequences. The management of high-consequence and low-probability events, such as earthquakes, storms and bomb explosions, is usually referred to as *disaster management* and the prevention and control of potential business disasters is normally referred to as *business continuity management*. The management of medium- to high-probability events coupled with low to medium consequences, such as environmental pollution and accidents and ill-health at work, is normally referred to as *operational risk management*. Successful business development strategies involve vision, creativity and a necessity to take risks; however, those people or businesses that willingly take or create risks with the aim of benefiting from them should be responsible for ensuring that adequate measures are in place to protect other people, their property and their money from the consequences that may arise from these risk-taking actions.

A simple definition of risk management is the prediction of risks and the identification and implementation of control measures to maintain these risks at an acceptable level. Risk management takes place at international, national, organisational and personal levels. At the international level the United Nations may, for example, be concerned about the risks from wars, floods and terrorist attacks because they may need to plan for the provision of military support or relief aid to the countries involved. At the national level a government may be concerned, for example, about the risks associated with the country's level of debt, because this may affect their ability to fund improvements in industrial efficiency or agricultural output. At the organisational level a company may, for example, be concerned about the security of its e-commerce systems because breaches of security may affect the confidence with which customers are prepared to provide the essential, financial information required for transactions over the Internet. Finally, at the personal level, an individual may be concerned, for example, about the risks of an accident because an injury may prevent that person from working and hence jeopardise their ability to maintain financial security. Therefore risk management covers a wide range of hazards, and these are often conveniently categorised under the general headings of environment, technical/economic and social/people hazards:

- *Environment hazards* include those issues that are outside the direct or immediate control of man, such as rain, snow, wind, drought and flood.
- *Technical/economic hazards* include those issues that arise from man-made or man-controlled systems, such as nuclear power generation, manufacturing industries, transport systems, building construction and finance.
- *Social/people hazards* include those issues that arise from social and human behaviour, such as war, crime, use of drugs and terrorism.

The Australian/New Zealand standard entitled *Risk Management* defines the risk management process as:

> The systematic application of management policies, procedures and practices to tasks of identifying, analysing, evaluating, treating and monitoring risk.
>
> Standards Australia/Standards New Zealand (1999: 5)

and the Royal Society defines risk management as:

> The process whereby decisions are made to accept a known or assessed risk and/or the implementation of actions to reduce the consequences or probability of occurrence.
>
> Royal Society (1992: 5)

Neither of these definitions states that risk management is about the elimination of risk; rather they refer to risk management as a process of managing risks within known and acceptable limits. However, levels of risk that may be regarded as acceptable will vary between hazards, countries and individuals. Although the development of consensus agreements on acceptable levels of risks, at the international, national, organisational and personal levels, is a complex and contentious issue, the importance of agreeing and setting risk levels at an optimum level cannot be overstated.

Defining acceptable levels of risk

Deliberations on risk levels usually depend on which hazards are involved, which stakeholders are affected, and whether exposure to the hazard is voluntary or involuntary. Even when acceptable levels of risk are based on statistical probability and are referred to as 'probability-based safety values', they can give rise to apparent anomalies and concerns to the public:

> It has not been true only since Chernobyl, but there it first became palpable to a broad public: safety and probable safety, seemingly so close, are worlds apart. The engineering sciences always have only probable safety at their command. Thus, even if two or three nuclear reactors blow up tomorrow, their statements remain true.
>
> Beck (1992: 107)

Therefore there often remains an unbridgeable gap between the technical and non-technical views of risk. For example, if the safety record of an individual airplane is, on average, 1 accident in every 10 000 000 flights, engineers may deem air travel to be a reliable form of transport with an acceptable level of risk. However, when all the flights of all the airplanes around the world are accumulated, each with an individual safety record of 1×10^{-7}, the probability is that several airplane crashes will occur each year – a situation borne out by observed events (see Table 1.2). Each crash, however, is clearly unacceptable to the public, in general, and to the people involved in the crashes, in particular.

Stakeholders who may be involved in discussions and decisions on acceptable levels of risk include politicians, employers, employees, trades unions, standards organisations, regulators, the media and pressure groups. Each of these groups is able to exert either a direct or an indirect influence on the levels of risk that are deemed to be acceptable. Some of the multidirectional interactions that can occur between stakeholders during debates on risk standards are summarised in Figure 2.1.

Decision analysis

In many sectors, risk managers were traditionally scientists or engineers, who estimated and evaluated the levels of risk associated with an activity or structure and then made a decision on whether these levels of risk were acceptable. Examples of this process are provided by civil engineers, who calculate the levels of risk associated with bridges and define the margins of error, and doctors, who assess the severity of a patient's illness, provide a prognosis, and then make decisions on how best to treat the patient. This approach worked well while there were the opportunities for these people to use trial and error and, hopefully, to learn from their mistakes. If an occasional bridge fell down or a patient died, it did not assume too great a significance in the minds of the public, as engineers and doctors were considered to be professional people who were well trained, well qualified and capable of making this type of decision. However, the important ethical issue related to this approach has been questioned in modern society:

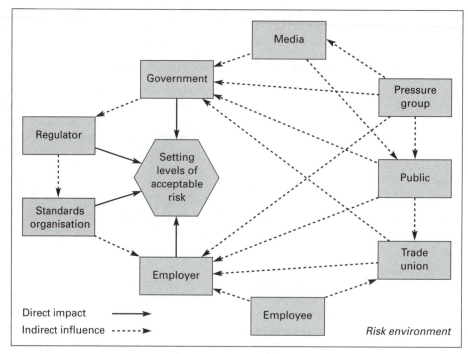

Figure 2.1 Stakeholders involved in influencing acceptable levels of risk

Test-tube babies must first be produced, genetically engineered artificial creatures released, in order that their properties and safety can be studied.

Engineers cannot let people's reactors blow up all around them in order to test their safety, unless they turn the world into a laboratory.

Beck (1992: 108)

The previous approach of 'let us have a go and see what happens' is now untenable in modern society, for several reasons. First, the emergence of totally new technologies has made the estimation of risks much more difficult; second, the use of trial and error is no longer deemed to be an acceptable method of learning as the potential consequences associated with some risks can be too high; and third, the experts are not necessarily in tune with the concerns of those people affected by the risks. The difficulty now experienced by politicians and regulators is that the range of risks to which modern society is exposed has increased to such an extent and to such a level of complexity that the public, who want to be involved in discussions on the acceptability of these risks, have no real prospect of understanding the problems involved or of reaching logical conclusions. Clearly, the only totally democratic route for agreeing acceptable levels of risk is for the public to vote on the level of acceptable risk in every case. However, this would be impossible to implement effectively, because the knowledge required by each individual, in order to analyse the problems, would be too great. The dilemma of this situation was summarised very simply by von Winterfeldt (1992):

The experts should not control society's technological choices, but the public and their political representatives are not sufficiently informed to assume complete control themselves.

von Winterfeldt (1992: 324)

This dilemma has led to discussions on developing qualitative and quantitative models of risk management in order to support the decision-making process (Beroggi and Aebi, 1996). Essentially, this process consists of defining the problem, gathering data and knowledge, and resolving the problem. Von Winterfeldt (1992) suggested using a five-step *decision analysis process* to address some of these problems when a range of stakeholders is involved: see Table 2.5.

Table 2.5 A multiple-stakeholder decision analysis process

Decision analysis step	Actions required
Formulate the problem	Translate the risk problem into a decision problem Identify the stakeholders Obtain broad stakeholder inputs and objectives
Develop objectives and attributes	Construct value trees for each stakeholder group Build a combined stakeholder value tree Develop attributes
Estimate the risks, costs, benefits and other impacts	Identify and select experts in the area of risk Train and assist in the decomposition of the problem Model the problem and collect data Elicit risk assessment values Aggregate information and comments across experts
Develop a utility model based on stakeholder evaluations	Elicit stakeholder value judgements on the options Test and build a multivariate utility model
Complete sensitivity analyses of the options available	Evaluate the alternatives Complete sensitivity analyses Define compromise options

Source: Adapted from von Winterfeldt (1992)

This approach is potentially very useful when broad agreement is required between stakeholders, because the problem is resolved through cooperative discussion. This was broadly the approach recommended by the UK Government (Office of Science and Technology, 1997) for dealing with issues where there may be significant scientific uncertainty, a range of scientific opinion, or potentially significant implications for sensitive areas of public policy. The approach advocated:

■ gathering scientific information from a number of sources, e.g. internal and external research programmes, advisory bodies, industry and academia;

■ involving non-scientific experts;

■ releasing available information to stakeholders for discussion;

■ incorporating risk communication among stakeholders; and

■ presenting the issues, uncertainties and policy options to the public for discussion and comment.

The following multi-stage management process has been proposed in order to improve the quality of scientific advice provided for government policy development in new areas of risk and, in particular, where the level and quality of evidence available is weak (OXERA, 2000):

- *Detect the issue.* The sooner an issue is identified the more time there is available to explore the issue and to define and analyse the options.

- *Establish the policy context and policy options.* Policy issues should be identified before seeking scientific advice, although it is possible that after scientific advice has been sought additional issues may be identified.

- *Define what the policy-maker needs to know.* The policy-maker must be sufficiently aware of the issues in order to determine what scientific information is required. It is important to separate the provision of the scientific advice from the definition of what scientific advice is required.

- *Choose the scientific advisory mechanism.* The advisory mechanism should be proportionate to the scale, complexity and importance of the policy issue.

- *Choose the advisers.* The choice of advisers should take into account the need to obtain an appropriate level of information and to balance the potential for bias and conflicts of interest among the advisers.

- *Agree and confirm the brief.* It is essential to define the role of the advisers in order to avoid scientific advisers providing judgements, which is the role of the policy-maker.

- *Prepare the scientific advice.* The advice should focus on providing perspectives on all the available relevant information and on providing estimates of the validity of this information. The information selected should not be biased by the views of the advisers.

- *Communicate the advice.* It is essential that scientific advice is provided to policy-makers in a comprehensible format.

- *Prepare advice on policy options.* The policy-maker must translate the scientific advice into policy options for the decision-maker.

- *Take the decision.* The decision-maker rather than the scientific adviser must be responsible for making the decision, and must consider the costs, risks and benefits associated with each option.

- *Audit and maintain the process.* The quality of scientific advice provided to policy-makers must be tested through quality assurance, peer review, audit and government scrutiny.

A risk management framework

Risk management is achieved through the processes of placing risks within the appropriate social, organisational or personal risk environment; identifying the hazards involved; identifying the risks associated with the hazards; assessing the risks; and controlling those risks using a range of mitigating options. This is an ongoing management cycle, which should be continuously monitored, audited and reviewed. The generalised management framework shown in Figure 2.2 illustrates this cycle.

Unfortunately, the management of risks is not quite as simple and straightforward as the process shown in Figure 2.2 might suggest, as there are many complicating factors within the cycle. Although it is generally accepted that the outcomes or consequences of exposure to hazards can be quantified in terms of death, injury, ill-health or financial loss, actual risk is less easily quantified, as it is not possible to simply compartmentalise risk into statistical or objective measures. All quantified risk assessments involve human judgements, either directly or indirectly, and these judgements are inevitably based on subjectivity, which in turn is based on people's perception of risk. Differences in risk perception will inevitably lead to differences, among individuals and groups, in the acceptability or unacceptability of risks. This situation is further complicated because stakeholders have developed an expectation that they will receive information and be involved in the decision-making process.

Risk management therefore requires organisations to establish a risk *policy* or strategy, which will be influenced by the *risk perceptions* of the stakeholders. The risk policy will require organisations to *plan* for how they will deal with the organisational risks through the process of *risk assessment*. Finally, the organisation must *implement* its risk control strategy and involve all stakeholders through the process of *risk communication*. The impact of these individual factors on the risk management process is illustrated within the framework shown in Figure 2.3.

A discussion of the issues related to risk perception, risk communication and risk assessment is presented in later chapters.

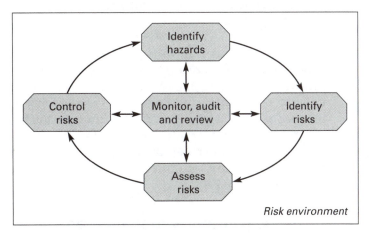

Figure 2.2 A framework for managing risk

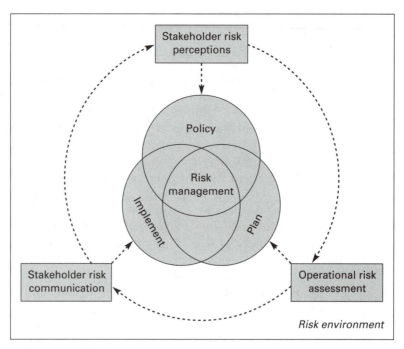

Figure 2.3 The roles of risk perception, risk assessment and risk communication within an organisation's risk management process

Business continuity and disaster management

However effective an organisation's risk management processes are in avoiding losses, unexpected situations can always occur. Dealing with these situations and their consequences is part of the broader picture of risk management, and is referred to as *business continuity management*. Business continuity management is not so much to do with the probability of an adverse event occurring or the associated consequences as with the impact that the event will have on the organisation's operations. The key aspects of business continuity management involve planning and implementing risk control strategies to avoid the possibility of an organisational emergency or crisis becoming a disaster. An *emergency* is regarded as an adverse event that *may* threaten the survival of an organisation if effective measures are not taken to control the situation. A *crisis* is the point at which management cannot decide on the most appropriate action to take in an emergency situation, and this may lead to a *disaster* through the loss of significant assets (Figure 2.4).

Business continuity management

Emergency management involves ensuring that an organisation has the ability to react to an adverse event, whereas crisis management involves ensuring that an organisation retains an effective and efficient decision-making capability. The aims of business continuity management are, therefore, to:

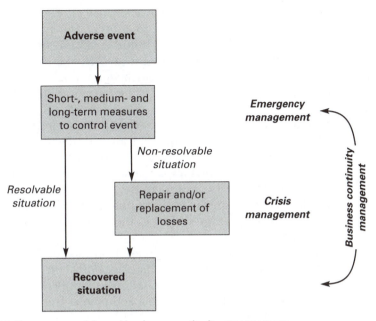

Figure 2.4 Emergency, crisis and business continuity management

■ maintain a business in its present state;

■ enable a business to continue operating; and

■ resume normal operations after a business interruption.

Most organisations' business continuity strategy involves the development and implementation of a continuity plan that can be used to manage emergencies and crises. This requires:

■ *Senior management commitment* to provide support and ownership of the principles of business continuity management.

■ *Procedures* to establish a management group who are responsible for managing the continuity programme. Key issues that this group should cover include:
   ■ establishing targets and timescales for deliverables;
   ■ preparing a budget;
   ■ defining regulatory, statutory and contractual obligations;
   ■ determining when specialist support is required and where this support can be obtained; and
   ■ organising a management team to take control in the event of a disaster.

■ *Identification of risks* that could lead to a corporate disaster. These would include, for example, risks that may have a major impact on:
   ■ corporate governance;
   ■ sales, cash flow, profits and market share;
   ■ corporate image and reputation;
   ■ contractual and legal obligations and liabilities; and
   ■ health, safety, environment and quality performance.

Sources of potential corporate disasters will clearly vary from one organisation to another and from one country to another, but they can be summarised within the internal:external – social:technical/economic framework shown in Figure 2.5.

If the risks can be defined by probability analysis, it may be possible to insure against the risks; however, if the risks are not definable, it may not be possible to achieve this. The principles of business continuity management are, not surprisingly, the same as those of risk management, and the apparent differences are more often in the terminology used than in the processes involved. The first stage is hazard identification, followed by an assessment of the impacts from these risks through a process referred to as *business impact analysis*, which is similar to the process of environmental impact analysis used in environmental management.

Business impact analysis identifies the primary and secondary impacts that a disaster may have on the business functions of an organisation. Primary impacts are those issues that are critical to the organisation's well-being, such as revenue generation, but they may also include the associated support functions required to ensure that primary activities are maintained. Secondary impacts are important but are not essential for achieving short-term organisational recovery. These will include many of the organisation's support functions. An important aspect of impact analysis is to determine and predict the dependence of one function's activities on the operational status of another function.

Business recovery strategies ensure that an organisation could recover from major disasters. Even though the probability of these events is rare, the consequences, if they are not managed effectively, can result in the collapse of the organisation. It is therefore essential to review and implement risk mitigation measures aimed at reducing the probability and/or severity of the potential business interruption scenarios. It is also important to develop a communication

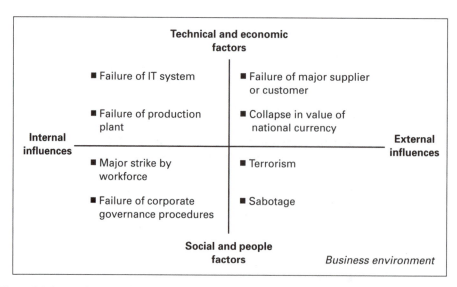

Figure 2.5 Internal: external – social: technical/economic framework of sources of corporate disasters

strategy in order to provide information to stakeholders, such as the media, shareholders, employees and regulators, during a crisis so that confidence in the organisation is maintained throughout the period.

Disaster management

Disaster recovery is the process that takes place during and after an organisational crisis in order to minimise business interruption and to return the organisation to a pre-disaster state as soon as possible. Disasters can occur without warning, at any time, often with profound and sometimes catastrophic effects on the business community. As Tansel (1995) pointed out, the best time to plan for a disaster is before the disaster occurs. There are typically three phases to a disaster:

- *The crisis period.* This period occurs during the early minutes and hours of a disaster, and normally establishes the type and scale of the problem.
- *The emergency response period.* This period may be very brief (hours) or last for an extended period (several days) of time; during this period critical decisions may have to be taken on how to deal with the short-, medium- and long-term problems affecting the organisation.
- *The disaster recovery and restoration period.* This period, which starts immediately after the event has occurred, may often last for several months; it finishes only when normal operations recommence.

Many companies have disaster recovery plans; however, few companies actually test them, which makes it unlikely that they will work effectively during a real disaster. There are several reasons why disaster recovery plans do not work in practice. These include the following:

- The interdependence of business functions is not appreciated.
- Business functions and managers are isolated within the plan.
- Early indications that the plan is not working are ignored or misinterpreted by those involved.
- The impact of the disaster on the organisation's IT systems is overlooked.
- The importance of training in public relations is overlooked.
- A crisis team is not established, trained and/or tested.

For any business in the private or public sector, an imperative is, therefore, the development of a contingency disaster plan, which has four objectives:

- to control the initial and any developing situation while continuing wherever possible to meet normal business requirements;
- to ensure as far as possible the health, safety and welfare of those affected by a disaster;
- to liaise with external agencies in controlling and recovering from the disaster; and
- to return the business to normality, as quickly as possible.

Risk mitigation

The complicating aspect of managing risk is that most risks are influenced by several interacting organisational factors, which can be categorised for simplicity as physical, management and human factors. Physical factors include, for example, equipment design, reliability and protection; management factors include, for example, work procedures, standards and inspections; and human factors include, for example, employee behaviour, competence and training. Each piece of equipment, operating procedure and employee issue can be addressed in turn, but the total residual risk in the overall system is greater than the sum of the residual risks from each of the components. This arises because there is a synergistic effect of one risk factor with another. Therefore a probabilistic risk assessment of individual failure modes for a piece of equipment, based solely on component reliability tests, would represent only part of the total risk because the interaction of, for example, equipment maintenance procedures and the operators on equipment performance must also be taken into account. The selection and implementation of appropriate options for dealing with risk is referred to as *risk treatment* or *risk mitigation*.

Most organisations have two fundamental mitigation options available for managing risks: they can either accept the risks, or they can reduce the risks. Risk acceptance options involve measures that reduce the financial impact of the risks on the organisation. Risk reduction options, on the other hand, involve the use of physical, management and human factor control measures in order to reduce the level of risk within the organisation. There are two sub-options available within each of the two main options. For risk acceptance these are risk transfer and risk retention, and for risk reduction these are risk control and risk avoidance. These options are summarised in Figure 2.6.

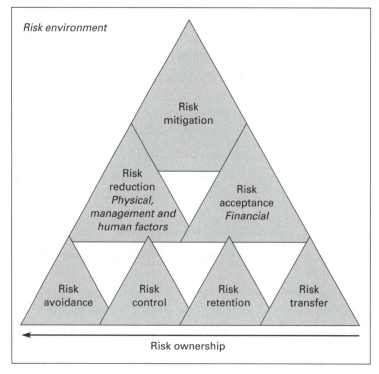

Figure 2.6 Options for risk mitigation

As the risk mitigation strategy shifts from risk acceptance to risk reduction, by moving from risk transfer through risk retention and risk control to risk avoidance, an organisation takes greater and greater ownership and responsibility for the control of the risks that it generates in carrying out its business.

Risk acceptance

Risk acceptance implies that an informed decision has been made to accept the consequences and likelihood of an occurrence of a specified risk. This option implies that the present levels of risk within the organisation are deemed to be at a level where it is not necessary to reduce them further. The consequences of adverse events are managed by making appropriate financial arrangements, which rely on the reactive compensation for failures in the organisation's operations.

Risk transfer

Risk transfer involves shifting the responsibility or burden for a specified risk to a third party. Insurance represents one of the principal options open to an organisation, when formulating a risk mitigation strategy. By taking out insurance, companies can offset some of the risks they face by transferring them to external agents. The purpose of insurance is to allow people to carry on their private or business lives with the reassurance that if they suffer a personal loss or damage to property or become liable to pay damages to third parties, their insurance company will provide an indemnity for them. Risk transfer, however, provides little incentive for an organisation to significantly reduce the level of organisational risk, as it offers the easy option of accepting current levels of risk by making financial arrangements to offset potential liabilities. Smallman (1996: 259), in fact, claimed that, because of the strength of insurance companies, 'the very term risk management is a euphemism for insurance management'.

All policies of insurance are fundamentally policies of *indemnity*. It is a matter of principle that the intention is to restore the policyholder to the position that they enjoyed immediately prior to the loss, which is substantially the same principle as for the award of damages in a civil law case. Normally, insurers will indemnify a policyholder through either the payment of cash or, at the insurer's option, reinstatement or replacement of the loss.

As discussed previously, risks can be categorised as *pure risks*, which may result in a loss but not in a gain, such as the risks of injury or fire, or as *speculative risks*, which may result in either a loss or a gain, such as buying a lottery ticket, investing in the stock market, or starting a new business venture. Only pure risks are *insurable risks*; if insurers covered speculative risks then the insured party would always be better off after the event than they were before the event. Insurable risks generally exhibit certain features. First, they must be pure risks; second, they must be capable of financial calculation; and third, the risk must be probabilistic, i.e. they may occur but they are not certain. Fourth, the event being insured must not be contrary to the public interest. Insurance premiums vary according to the perceived likelihood of loss, based on claim frequencies, and the potential loss involved, based on claim values.

Companies regard the insurance of some risks as essential for their business survival. First, it serves to protect them against sudden financial losses; and, second, it changes the unpredictability of risk from a loss of unknown severity occurring at an unknown time to an agreed cost at an agreed time. Risks that are typically covered by insurance include employer's liability, public liability, product liability, fire, and transport.

Risk retention

Risk retention involves intentionally or unintentionally retaining the responsibility or burden for a specified risk. Risk retention is itself made up of two subcategories:

- risk retention with knowledge, which is often referred to as the self-insurance approach; and
- risk retention without knowledge, which is caused by inadequate hazard identification and risk assessment.

Risk retention with knowledge

Risk retention with knowledge or self-insurance occurs where an organisation consciously accepts and retains a risk and deals with it by establishing an internal insurance fund. Usually such a decision will be taken only by large organisations, which may already have qualified insurance personnel capable of administering an insurance fund. Only those losses that are predictable through probabilistic calculations should be retained within an organisation. This approach can be used effectively by larger organisations – in particular where the company has a large portfolio of risks. It is important, however, for companies to avoid those situations where a single large risk could result in the company ending in bankruptcy. It is also important that a company does establish an insurance fund as part of the self-insurance approach, in order to cover potential liabilities, rather than just hoping that the liability situation will not arise or can be dealt with if and when it occurs.

The advantages of self-insurance are that insurance premiums should be lower, as there are no intermediaries expecting payments for costs, profits or commissions. The insured party also receives the benefit of investment income from the insurance fund that has been established, and keeps any profit accrued from it. An important aspect of self-insurance is that a company has an incentive to practise good risk management principles and thereby reduce the potential level of liabilities. There are, however, disadvantages to the self-insurance option. A self-insured company will normally establish its insurance fund based on a normal distribution of losses, which are calculated over an extended time period. Therefore, because risks are dependent on probability, the company loss may occur in 10 years' time or tomorrow – in which case insufficient funds may have been accrued in order to cope with a large loss or a large number of small losses occurring during the early years of the fund.

Risk retention without knowledge

Unidentified hazards and risks can arise from simple sources, such as inappropriate equipment and computer systems, ineffective permits to work and customer care procedures, and inadequate employee competence and training. It is essential, therefore, to keep organisational risks constantly under review, ensuring that any omissions identified are investigated and rectified.

The second way in which risks can be retained, without knowledge, within an organisation is through inadequate risk assessment. Although hazards may have been identified, the level of the residual risk associated with the hazards can be underestimated. This problem is often encountered where:

- employees without adequate experience of the hazards have carried out the risk assessment;
- risk assessors have received inadequate training; or
- risk assessment and risk evaluation standards have not been defined within the company.

Risk reduction

Risk reduction involves the application of appropriate techniques and principles in order to reduce either the consequences or the likelihood of an occurrence of a specified risk. These options provide a proactive approach by management in order to reduce the levels of organisational risk. The approach requires a constant review of hazards and risks in order to ensure that they are maintained at a level that is commensurate with the costs of reducing them further. This approach relates to the classic loss prevention approach advocated by Bird and Germain (1986), and is based on risk assessment.

Risk control

Risk control involves setting policies and standards, identifying hazards, identifying and evaluating the associated risks, and implementing changes to working procedures in order to eliminate or minimise specified risks through the use of physical, management and human factor controls. This approach provides the management system advocated by most risk managers, and also represents the *internal control* approach advocated within corporate governance principles (Turnbull, 1999).

The risk control approach places the management of risk firmly within the responsibility of an organisation's operational management. It also enables individual organisations to set their own standards, thereby enabling them to determine whether they wish to achieve minimum legal compliance or to provide a benchmark level of performance to which other organisations can aspire.

Risk avoidance

The ultimate, but normally unachievable, approach to risk mitigation is for an organisation to make an informed decision not to be associated with a specified risk. Every business activity, however, carries some level of risk, and the only way in which risk avoidance can be totally achieved, therefore, is for an organisation to cease trading. The normal risk avoidance approach adopted is to avoid certain types of risk by replacing one hazard with another hazard that hopefully has a lower level of risk attached to it.

Risk avoidance in some cases is often instigated by health and safety legislation, because the risks associated with certain hazards are considered to be so high that it is inappropriate to rely on employers to identify and control them. In the UK, for example, the importation and use of chrysotile (white asbestos) was banned through the Asbestos (Prohibitions) (Amendment) Regulations 1999. These regulations were implemented to support a wider risk avoidance approach taken within the European Union.

Risk management and corporate governance

The importance of a risk management approach within business management is clearly recognised within the guidance on corporate governance or internal control (Turnbull, 1999), and this link is specifically highlighted as one of its objectives:

> The guidance is based on the adoption by a company's board of a risk-based approach to establishing a sound system of internal control and reviewing its effectiveness.

> A company's system of internal control has a key role in the management of risks that are significant to the fulfilment of its business objectives.

> Turnbull (1999: 4)

Corporate governance recognises the principle of risk management, as defined within, for example, the Standards Australia/Standards New Zealand (1999) risk management standard: 'An internal control system encompasses the policies, processes, tasks, behaviours and other aspects of a company' (Turnbull, 1999: 7). The definition of risk proposed by the Royal Society (1992) is also supported within the guidance on internal control: 'The purpose of internal control is to help manage and control risk appropriately rather than eliminate it' (Turnbull, 1999: 5).

It is essential for a board of directors to avoid major shareholder losses arising from either unforeseen risks or poorly managed risks. In the case of a disaster, it is extremely important to ensure that a full and rapid recovery to normal operational status is achieved. Business continuity management and disaster management are therefore essential elements of the overall risk management programme, because the consequences of mismanagement of these risks are potentially devastating for an organisation.

Finally, corporate governance proposes that the effectiveness of a company's internal control system should be measured, and it emphasises the necessity of identifying hazards and risks, establishing a strategy for assessing and controlling risks, and monitoring company performance as part of the embedded management system (Turnbull, 1999). A clear link is therefore established between the guidance on internal control and the risk management framework shown in Figure 2.2. The guidance states:

It is the role of management to implement board policies on risk and control. In fulfilling its responsibilities, management should identify and evaluate the risks faced by the company for consideration by the board and design, operate and monitor a suitable system of internal control which implements the policies adopted by the board.

Turnbull (1999: 6)

Internal control can therefore be seen also to support the policy–planning–implementation cycle of the risk management process presented in Figure 2.3.

Summary

- Worldwide levels of risk associated with occupational health and safety issues can be defined in terms of financial and human losses. The human losses from work-related ill-health issues outweigh the losses from work-related safety issues.
- Establishing acceptable levels of risk is an important issue and one in which all stakeholders make an important contribution. In this context it is essential to develop a communication framework through which stakeholders can contribute to this decision-making process and reach consensus agreements.
- Risk perception, risk assessment and risk communication play important roles in developing policy within a risk management framework.
- Emergency management, crisis management and business continuity management represent critical elements within a risk management framework. Business continuity management helps to maintain a business in its present state, enables it to continue operating and resume normal operations after a business interruption.
- Mitigation of operational risks provides organisations with the opportunity to control risks at acceptable or tolerable levels.

Issues for review and discussion

- Consider how the consequences of national and international major accidents impact on your life.
- Assess the ways in which you can influence organisational and national levels of acceptable risk.
- Review the way in which risks are managed within your work environment.
- Consider how technical and social factors affect the level of risk in road transport.
- Review your strategy for managing personal risks.

References

Asbestos (Prohibitions) (Amendment) Regulations 1999. London: HMSO.

Beck, U. (1992) From industrial society to the risk society: questions of survival, social structure and ecological enlightenment. *Theory, Culture & Society*, **9**, 97–123.

Beroggi, G.E.G. and Aebi, M. (1996) Model formulation support in risk management. *Safety Science*, **24**, 121–142.

Bird, F.E. and Germain, G.L. (1986) *Practical Loss Control Leadership*. Loganville: Institute Press.

International Labour Organization (ILO) (2003) http:///laborsta.il/o.org

Office of Science and Technology (1997) *The Use of Scientific Advice in Policy Making*. London: Department of Trade and Industry.

Oxford Economic Research Associates Ltd (OXERA) (2000) *Policy, Risk and Science: Securing and Using Scientific Advice*. Contract Research Report 295/2000. Sudbury: HSE Books.

Royal Society (1992) *Risk: Analysis, Perception and Management*. London: The Royal Society.

Smallman, C. (1996) Challenging the orthodoxy in risk management. *Safety Science*, **22**, 245–262.

Standards Australia/Standards New Zealand (1999) *Risk Management*, AS/NZS 4360:1999. Homebush: Standards Australia Wellington: Standards New Zealand.

Swiss Re (2002) *Natural Catastrophes and Man-made Disasters in 2001: Storms and Earthquakes Lead to the Second-highest Losses in Insurance History*. Sigma No. 1/2002. Zurich: Swiss Reinsurance Company.

Tansel, B. (1995) Natural and manmade disasters: accepting and managing risks. *Safety Science*, **20**, 91–99.

Turnbull (1999) *Internal Control: Guidance for Directors on the Combined Code*. London: The Institute of Chartered Accountants in England & Wales.

von Winterfeldt, D. (1992) Expert knowledge and public values in risk management: the role of decision analysis. In: S. Krimsky and D. Golding (eds), *Social Theories of Risk*, 321–342. London: Praeger.

CHAPTER 3

Personality, behaviour and human error

Broken pipes, broken tools,
People bending broken rules.

– Bob Dylan, 'Everything is broken' (1989)

Chapter contents

Introduction

The propensity for people to accept high levels of some risks while rejecting much lower levels of other risks has already been referred to. In order to manage risk, it is important to discuss and understand why these differences occur, not only between individuals but also between organisations and countries. The propensity for taking risks is related to an individual's 'driving forces', which shape their personality, and to 'cultural influences', which exist within societies. Individuals have certain basic needs that must be satisfied in order to ensure their survival, such as the need for air to breathe, water to drink and food to eat, and these needs provide overriding driving forces for individuals to behave in certain ways. However, other needs also shape an individual's personality and behaviour, and these, in turn, impact on their propensity for taking risks. Similarly, there are fundamental needs that groups and organisations must satisfy in order to ensure survival, such as the need for groups to have cultural affiliation and for organisations to generate profits.

Individual and organisational personalities influence the ways in which people and organisations react to and respond to risk situations and determine whether they exhibit *risk-taking* or *risk-averse* behaviour. It is important to understand the underpinning factors affecting personality and behaviour, as these will influence the ways in which individuals and organisations react and how they will be motivated to achieve personal or corporate targets. The aims of this chapter are to outline theories of personality, behaviour, human needs and social cultures, and to discuss their roles in influencing an individual's motivation and propensity for taking risks. The underpinning theories of human error and models of human error are also discussed.

Personality and behaviour

Personality and behaviour are key determinants in risk management because the ways in which individuals respond to risk situations will influence organisational risk levels and determine which risk mitigation measures are most likely to be acceptable and/or effective. Although there are many theories of personality, they normally share the common assumption that personality belongs to the individual. Therefore studies of personality usually relate to individuals rather than to groups, although there are some views that accept the existence of *corporate personality*, when an organisation is treated as a single entity with its own personality. An individual's personality is generally considered to be stable and enduring. However, theories differ in how they characterise personality, with some theories using a defined set of traits or human dimensions that are common to everyone, and other theories using unique characteristics and qualities for each individual. Behavioural theories consider behaviour either to be consistent or to change from one situation to another. In the first case behaviour is determined and controlled mainly by personality, whereas in the latter case behaviour is determined and controlled by the situation rather than by the individual.

Personality

Personality can be defined as:

> those relatively stable and enduring aspects of individuals which distinguish them from other people, making them unique, but which at the same time allow people to be compared with each other.
>
> Gross (1996: 744)

This definition highlights two important points that should be considered in discussions on personality. The first point relates to whether an individual's personality consists of a mixture of permanent *traits* or characteristics, or whether it is composed of a unique set of traits. The second point relates to whether personality is simply a study of individuals or whether comparisons can be made of personalities between individuals. Psychologists who agree that personality is a mixture of permanent traits belong to what is referred to as the *psychometric group* or the *type and trait theorists*, as they use personality question-naires in order to identify common descriptors of personality. This approach is referred to as the *nomothetic* approach. The trait approach has resulted in the development of psychometric tests, which measure and compare individuals' personalities and which are frequently used in industry and commerce to select and recruit employees of a certain type. Psychologists who believe that everyone is an individual, on the other hand, follow the *idiographic* approach.

Personality traits

Kluckholm and Murray (1953) expounded the theory that 'every man is, in certain ways, like all other men, like some other men and like no other men'. Clearly, everyone has common features, such as physiological structure, whereas other features are common among groups, such as gender and social background. However, some traits make each person a unique individual who reacts to each risk situation in a particular way. Allport and Odbert (1936) identified several thousand traits that described individuals but, using statistical analysis techniques, they reduced this number of traits to just two general traits: *common traits* are applicable to all members of a group or cultural background, whereas *individual traits*, which are derived from an individual's life experiences, are split into three subgroups:

- *Cardinal traits* form the main influence on an individual's personality and relate to issues such as ambition, intolerance, anxiety and greed.
- *Central traits* form the basic components of an individual's personality and relate to the way in which they deal with life's events, such as integrity and love.
- *Secondary traits* are less important and relate to individual preferences, such as social and political affiliation.

Every trait, however, is not found in every individual, and even those traits that are common have different levels of importance and significance in different individuals. The differences in the relative importance of traits give rise to the differences between individuals in psychometric test results. When measuring an individual's personality, it must be recognised that it is only possible to compare one individual's personality with another personality, because personality is a relative measure.

Traits that form the foundation of an individual's personality are considered to be stable with time and situation. Therefore, if traits and/or personality define behaviour, an individual's behaviour will also be stable with time and situation. However, explaining an individual's behaviour simply as a function of situations and personality factors oversimplifies the issue. Other views of behaviour accommodate the contribution made by both factors by acknowledging the potential synergistic impact of situational and personality factors. Cattell (1965), for example, defined personality as a factor that determined behaviour in a defined situation and in a defined mood. This approach accepts that an individual's behaviour may change from day to day and situation to situation, and is in line with the viewpoint that behaviour is not driven solely by personality traits.

Clearly, a major problem in defining personality and consequently behaviour is the large number of underlying personality traits that can influence an individual's behaviour. Eysenck (1965) simplified the issue of personality by grouping traits into two dimensions placed on orthogonal axes that were labelled 'extrovert–introvert' and 'stable–unstable' (Table 3.1). The traits identified in Table 3.1, within each of the personality dimensions, should be considered as representing a continuous scale of values on which each individual rests according to how strong a particular trait is within their personality.

The extremes of the 'introvert–extrovert' dimension of personality would be described by the following characteristics:

■ *Introvert* tends to be a quiet, retiring person who takes life seriously. He or she places importance on ethical standards and tends to be pessimistic about outcomes.

■ *Extrovert* tends to be sociable and needs people to talk to, as he or she prefers other people's company to their own. He or she looks for excitement and is optimistic about outcomes.

The extremes of the 'stable–unstable' dimension of personality would be described by the following characteristics:

■ *Stable* tends to plan ahead and think before acting. He or she loathes acting on impulse, behaves in a controlled manner and is reliable.

■ *Unstable* tends to like taking chances, often acting on the spur of the moment. He or she likes changes, prefers to keep moving and doing things. He or she may lose their temper, be aggressive and be unreliable.

The unstable–extrovert describes a person who would be more likely to take risks, whereas the stable–introvert describes a person who would be more likely to be averse to taking risks.

Table 3.1 Dimensions of personality

Personality dimension	Personality traits
Stable–Extrovert	Responsive, easygoing, displays leadership, sociable, outgoing, carefree, talkative, lively
Unstable–Extrovert	Changeable, aggressive, impulsive, optimistic, excitable, restless, touchy, active
Stable–Introvert	Calm, careful, reliable, passive, peaceful, controlled, thoughtful, even-tempered
Unstable–Introvert	Rigid, quiet, sober, moody, anxious, reserved, unsociable, pessimistic

Source: Derived from Eysenck (1965)

Behaviour

Defining behaviour is very difficult because it requires understanding why people do things and also how and why they do things in a particular way. Theoretical approaches to behaviour include the following.

The *psychoanalytical or psychodynamic* approach relates behaviour to unconscious motives and wishes. Individuals are described as being in conflict between the opposing demands of the different parts of their personality, which were described by Freud as *id* (instincts), *ego* (the part of the id that has been influenced by one's perceptions and life experiences), and *superego* (developed morals and responses to authority). In this model, the ego component of behaviour provides the balance between fundamental desires (id) and the demands of authority to behave in a particular way (superego). An individual's unconscious traits, therefore, define his or her behaviour.

The *behaviourist or stimulus responsive* approach relates behaviour to the environmental and social conditions in which one lives, and refers to these as reinforcement conditions. People therefore respond to stimuli from the environment in which they live and work. The key behavioural learning process is provided by a *stimulus* followed by a *response*; this conditioning of an individual's behaviour is referred to as either *classical* (passive) or *operant* (active) conditioning.

The *humanistic, existentialistic or philosophic* approach relates behaviour to self-actualisation or self-realisation. Each person is regarded as an individual, who is unique and free to determine and to define what he or she wants to do. This approach accepts that past and present experiences are equally important influences on one's behaviour.

The *neurobiologic or biogenic* approach relates behaviour to processes taking place within the body's central nervous system, endocrine system and other biological systems. The body's nervous system brings to one's consciousness everything that one knows and remembers about the world, and controls many automatic bodily functions, such as the heartbeat and intestinal actions. The endocrine glands control the development of the body, maintain bodily equilibrium, and control activities such as growing, loving and being frightened. In this model, behaviour is regarded as a genetic, physiological and neurobiological process. The central nervous system, and the brain in particular, is the essential controlling element in defining an individual's behaviour.

The *cognitive* approach relates behaviour to an individual's mental processes. The brain, which acts like the central processing unit of a computer, records, analyses, stores and acts on the information and stimuli received. Outcomes and memories of previous events define one's perceptions of risk and provide important inputs into how one behaves in defined circumstances.

These models are important because they identify the driving forces that determine an individual's actions (Figure 3.1) and help to define approaches that might be utilised in order to change people's behaviour in the working environment. This is particularly important when choosing and implementing risk mitigation procedures that are based on human behaviour.

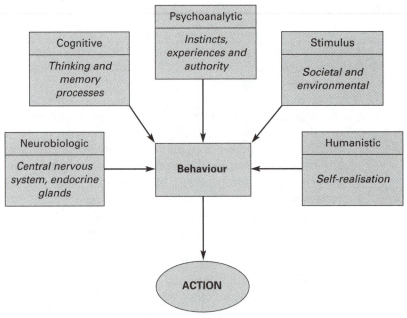

Figure 3.1 Models of human behaviour and their impact on individuals' actions

Motivation and models of human needs

Every manager has the challenge of managing employees' behaviours in order to achieve organisational targets. The transfer of knowledge, training and motivation provide ways in which employees' behaviours can be directed. Employee motivation is a difficult issue to analyse and describe as no two employees are the same and no two employees behave in the same way, because each has different reasons for being at work and different needs to satisfy. Two issues must be addressed in order to successfully motivate an employee:

- Employees must feel that they have gained personally from their actions. This is referred to as the *content theory of motivation* as it defines what employees want from an activity.

- Actions taken by employees must be directed, and this requires employees to know what, how and when to complete the actions. This is referred to as the *process theory of motivation.*

In order to motivate people to behave in a particular way, for example to be risk-averse in a work-based environment, it is essential to understand how people are likely to act in certain circumstances and at certain times. The motives that drive people to do something in a particular way relate to the needs and desires behind individuals' behaviours. These needs include the physiological need for food and drink, the need to be liked by people, and the need to achieve a position of power in industry or a position of trust within a community.

McClelland's model

McClelland (1961) identified two major needs in people:

- the need for achievement; and
- the need for affiliation.

If the need for achievement were strong, it would drive people to want to be successful whereas if the need for affiliation were strong, it would drive people to want to be with other people as part of a social or cultural group or to work as part of a team. McClelland (1961) argued that in those countries where people scored highly on measures of achievement motivation the countries were prosperous and showed high levels of economic growth, and where scores for achievement motivation were low the countries exhibited low levels of economic growth. The theory concluded that the drive to satisfy the need for achievement within a population brought about a prosperous and thriving economy in the country. However, it is always important in discussions of this type to consider which is the 'cause' and which is the 'effect', as it could equally be argued that a thriving economy generates a positive need for achievement.

Maslow's model

Maslow's (1954) model based on a hierarchy of human needs, which has been widely accepted and adopted as an explanation of human behaviour within work-based environments, argued that individuals were exposed to two types of motivational needs:

- Needs that ensured one's survival, such as personal health and safety, nutrition and reproduction, were referred to as *deficiency* needs.
- Needs that promoted the self-realisation of one's personal ambitions, such as a desire to acquire a range of skills, were referred to as *growth* needs.

Maslow proposed that people were subjected to a number of deficiency and growth needs that assume varying degrees of importance in different people. He classified these needs into a hierarchical group structure (Table 3.2), which assumed that a need lower down the structure would always be satisfied before a need higher up the structure. As each group of needs was satisfied the next group of needs assumed greater importance. At the top of the hierarchy was the need for self-realisation or the need to fulfil one's personal dreams and ambitions.

Table 3.2 Maslow's hierarchy of human needs

	Category	Examples
Growth	Self-realisation	Ambition
	Aesthetic	Beauty, symmetry
	Cognitive	Knowledge, understanding
	Esteem	Self-esteem, self-respect
	Belonging	Love, affection
	Health and safety	Protection from injury and ill-health
Deficiency	Physiological	Air, food, water

Source: Maslow (1954)

Maslow's theory has been used extensively because it indicates that people always have needs to fulfil, and if these needs can be identified there will always be a way of motivating people.

Rogers's model

Rogers's (1961) model identified two fundamental human needs that require satisfaction:

- positive regard, which referred to the need for individuals to be thought of positively by their peer group;
- self-actualisation, which was considered to be essential for an individual's personal development.

Herzberg's model

Herzberg's (1966) model identified two needs that were based on:

- hygiene factors, which referred to working conditions, such as safety, salary and work environment; and
- motivator factors, which referred to performance at work, such as job satisfaction, recognition and responsibility.

Herzberg's two-factor theory required an understanding of what contributed to job satisfaction and what contributed to job dissatisfaction, because these were not considered to be the same dimensions. According to Herzberg's theory, dissatisfaction resulted from the work not meeting the employee's needs – the *hygiene factors*. If employees were worried about safety or pay, they would not be able to concentrate on the work in hand. However, the provision of hygiene needs would not actually satisfy an employee as an individual's satisfaction level is dependent on motivators, such as the opportunity for individual achievement, peer group recognition and personal responsibility.

A comparison of models of motivation

Although there is a wide range of motivational theories, they do contain similarities (Figure 3.2). Each of the theories discussed proposed hierarchies of personal needs and social or cultural affiliation. Although McClelland's and Rogers's theories did not incorporate the basic physiological needs for breathing, eating and drinking, it could be argued that these did not need to be included because they were basic instincts. Similarly, McClelland and Rogers did not include health and safety needs, but this could be defended on the grounds that these were defined and compulsorily implemented within the requirements of health and safety legislation. The four models of motivation summarised in Figure 3.2 therefore proposed similar needs but categorised them under different factor headings.

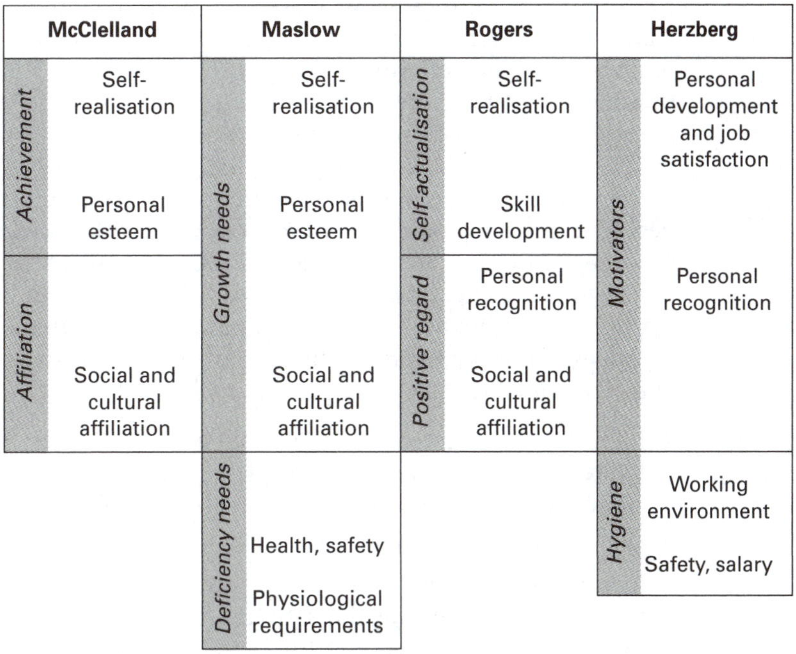

McClelland	Maslow	Rogers	Herzberg
Achievement — Self-realisation	*Growth needs* — Self-realisation	*Self-actualisation* — Self-realisation	*Motivators* — Personal development and job satisfaction
Achievement — Personal esteem	*Growth needs* — Personal esteem	*Self-actualisation* — Skill development	*Motivators* — Personal development and job satisfaction
Affiliation —	*Growth needs* —	*Positive regard* — Personal recognition	*Motivators* — Personal recognition
Affiliation — Social and cultural affiliation	*Growth needs* — Social and cultural affiliation	*Positive regard* — Social and cultural affiliation	*Motivators* — Personal recognition
	Deficiency needs —		*Hygiene* — Working environment
	Deficiency needs — Health, safety		*Hygiene* — Safety, salary
	Deficiency needs — Physiological requirements		*Hygiene* — Safety, salary

Figure 3.2 A comparison of motivational models

Behaviour modification

Theories of human motivation support the development of organisational motivation programmes by illustrating the role of non-economic factors in motivating people. Herzberg's theory highlighted the difference between intrinsic issues related to an individual's psychological rewards, such as recognition and achievement, and extrinsic issues related to an individual's material rewards, such as salary and job security. McClelland's theory raised the issue of inherited and learned needs, and introduced the role of cultural association. These theories, however, also identify the variations in factors and the potential differences in the requirements for motivational programmes across individual employees, industrial sectors and social and cultural groups. Motivation theories therefore emphasise that there is no single or simple answer to every situational problem and that, sometimes, it is better simply to recruit the right people, with the appropriate traits and personalities, for a job in the first place rather than try 'to fit square pegs into round holes'. This is particularly important when recruiting staff for high-risk activities, where risk-taking individuals could have potentially catastrophic effects.

An essential element of managing risks is the creation of a good working environment with good working procedures that are implemented effectively by competent and well-motivated employees. The principle behind establishing a well-motivated and efficient workforce is referred to as the *law of effect*. This claims that where there are several responses to the same situation, those responses that are accompanied or closely followed by employee satisfaction will become the preferred response, and employees will avoid those responses that are accompanied or closely followed by discomfort.

The stages in an employee behaviour modification programme should be, first, to reach a consensus view between individuals and the organisation on the desired or preferred outcomes from work-based risk situations and then to ensure that these outcomes are achieved in practice. In order that these programmes are successful, it is important to understand the interdependence of individual and organisational behaviours (Figure 3.3). Most behavioural modification programmes follow a standard approach involving eight steps (Vassie, 1998; Fleming and Lardner, 2000, 2002; Keil Centre, 2000):

1 Identify the target group of people and specify the behaviour(s) that one wishes to modify. At this stage it is important to ensure that the desired outcomes are realistic and achievable, within the timescales available.

2 Define the aims and objectives of the behavioural modification programme.

3 Identify performance indicators for the behaviours of the subjects involved in the programme, and/or the activities undertaken. Carry out a series of measurements of the subjects and/or activities over an appropriate period of time to establish benchmark performance levels.

4 Develop and define the behavioural modification programme.

5 Establish an implementation plan for the behavioural modification programme, with responsibilities, targets and timescales for each stage of the programme clearly identified.

6 Implement the behavioural modification programme.

7 Continue to monitor the performance of subjects and/or activities throughout the behavioural modification programme.

8 Review progress and then modify the behavioural modification programme if the results obtained indicate that the declared aims and objectives are not being achieved.

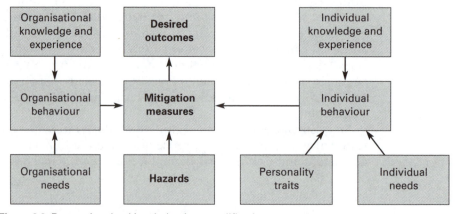

Figure 3.3 Factors involved in a behaviour modification programme

The role of cultural theories in risk management

Behavioural studies have often concentrated on issues of human needs and failed to accommodate the broader issues of human nature and social needs. One can consider the drives for food, drink, safety, love and esteem, but these do not address the issue of *why* people do things in a certain way. It is important, there-fore, to also consider the drives and needs of groups of people, together with the social and cultural issues associated with groups that affect the ways in which people do things. These issues have been addressed through the ideas encapsu-lated within *cultural theory*.

The way in which individuals and organisations understand, respond to and mitigate risks is an important element of the risk management process. However, although answers to these questions may provide an understanding of the per-sonal and organisational philosophies of risk strategies, they do not always help when managing risks that are difficult to understand, respond to or mitigate. Douglas and Wildavsky (1982) summarised this complex issue as follows:

> Can we know the risks we face, now or in the future? No, we cannot; but yes we must act as if we do. Some dangers are unknown; others are known, but not by us because no one person can know everything. Most people cannot be aware of most dangers at most times. Hence, no one can calculate precisely the total risk to be faced. How, then, do people decide which risks to take and which to ignore? On what basis are certain dangers guarded against and others relegated to secondary status?

> Douglas and Wildavsky (1982: 1)

Risk has been defined previously as the chance that a particular situation or event, which will have an impact upon objectives, will occur within a stated period of time. Whereas risk refers to the probability of an event occurring at some point in the future, future event-based risks will be affected by actions that are taken in the present. The actual process of risk assessment, which identifies that particular risk levels exist for individuals, groups or nations, raises people's awareness of the risks. Therefore, although future outcomes are invariably unknown, the very act of car-rying out a risk assessment may affect the way in which individuals and groups control and react to those risks, and this may affect the way in which the future unfolds. Those people who are aware of and understand the risk assessment results are more likely to implement additional personal preventive actions to reduce the likelihood of suffering harm than those people who are not aware of the risks. These actions would therefore change the levels of risk for these people. Hence, if risk assessment changes people's behaviour through an experiential learning process, risk assessment should be regarded as an ongoing process, which may be more appropriately referred to as risk reassessment.

Every action that each individual takes will directly or indirectly affect all future events. For example, the exact time at which one travels to work each day will impinge in a specific way on the activities of every person one contacts during that day. Although contact with other people may only result, for exam-ple, in them taking slightly different times to reach work, each contact will influence the sequence of subsequent events and actions of each of these people. As one has altered the actions of each of these people, they, in turn, will affect the actions of each and every person whom they come into contact with during that and subsequent days, and so on. Therefore, if each person were only to directly influence the actions of 10 other people each day, the total influence that one person could have on future events would grow exponentially to one million people after just six similar sequences and to one billion people after nine similar sequences. This concept has links with chaos theory, where there is an analogy of a butterfly flapping its wings and creating a cyclone on the other side of the world. Clearly, if random acts of meeting with people can potentially have such enormous impacts, specific actions taken each day at work could have an even bigger impact on fellow workers and those people that one comes into contact with as part of normal business activity.

In order to manage risk effectively in society, it is necessary to address three confounding factors:

- disagreement among stakeholders over the magnitude and importance of the risk problem;
- identification of those risk issues that can be universally regarded as representing the greatest importance to the greatest number of people; and
- the fact that risk events that are mitigated by society do not usually correspond with the events that present the greatest risks to most people.

The following examples illustrate these three issues:

- the disagreements expressed by stakeholders over the significance, validity and interpretation of the results available on global warming;
- the differences in social perspectives on the relative importance of health, political unrest and unemployment; and
- the arguments in the developed world over the level of support that should be provided for the prevention of flood, storm and earthquake damage in developing countries.

Concerns over risk and its mitigation are related to an understanding of the hazards and the personalities of the stakeholders involved. How one perceives, understands and influences the world's risk mitigation activities may have profound effects on one's own and other people's lives. An attempt to explain the ways in which people and organisations are likely to behave in different risk scenarios is therefore of fundamental importance in the process of successful risk management. At the national and international levels, governments are called upon to manage a wide variety of risks, which can be conveniently grouped and defined under four main headings (Douglas and Wildavsky, 1982):

- *relationships with other countries*, such as the fears created among a population by threats of invasion from hostile neighbours;
- *economic failure*, such as financial uncertainty created by inflationary or deflationary trading conditions;
- *social order*, such as national unrest brought about by a failure of law and order; and
- *environment*, such as health problems created by air pollution and contaminated drinking water.

These national issues occupy the time of politicians and provide them with their highest priorities, as control of these risks is more likely to ensure their political future and return to power. Individuals, on the other hand, may be more concerned about other issues, such as personal health problems, housing and long-term unemployment. As there are so many different views and opinions of which risks are the most important, it becomes very difficult – sometimes almost impossible – to obtain agreement or consensus among stakeholders on which issues to address and how to manage them. It helps, therefore, in understanding and ranking different risks if a framework can be developed in order to describe and explain the range of national, organisational and individual concerns over risk.

Douglas and Wildavsky (1982) proposed that risks should be viewed and categorised as a combination of the level of *knowledge* about the future risk and the level of *consensus* amongst stakeholders about the desired outcomes from the risks. They proposed a framework that can be represented on a two-dimensional grid system, which utilises values of 'risk knowledge' ranging from uncertain to certain, and values of 'consensus over outcome' ranging from contested to complete. This model identified four generic types of risk problem (Figure 3.4).

Type 1 problems are categorised by a well-defined knowledge about the level of future risk, for example through the quantification of the risk's consequences and probabilities, with a clear consensus about the desired outcomes. Risk mitigation programmes, which produce the best solution to the problem, would therefore be calculated from the data available. This type of problem usually relates to a technical problem that can be resolved through scientific or engineering calculations. An example would be the risks associated with the design and construction of a bridge.

Type 2 problems are categorised by a well-defined knowledge of what the future risks are but a lack of stakeholder agreement over what the desired outcomes are. The problem is usually one of resolving the disagreements between stakeholders over how to value the consequences of the risk. Solutions can be reached only through discussions of the potential consequences or through persuading some

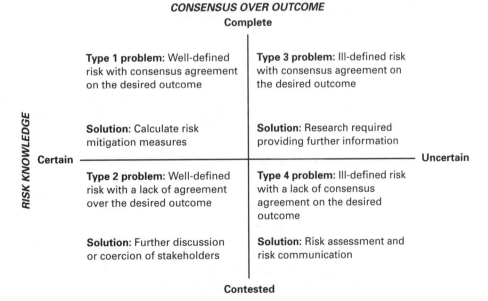

Figure 3.4 Categorising problems of risk

stakeholders to adopt a particular solution to the problem. An example would be a resolution of the level of acceptable risks associated with the use of nuclear power.

Type 3 problems are categorised by a consensus agreement about what needs to be achieved but a lack of knowledge about what the future levels of risk are. The solution to this type of problem is through the provision of suitable and sufficient information to stakeholders about the risk. This is invariably achieved through research. An example would be the risks associated with variant Creutzfeldt-Jakob disease.

Type 4 problems are categorised by insufficient knowledge about the future risks together with a lack of agreement on acceptable consequences. The approach for resolving problems of this type is through the use of risk assessment in order to obtain the best solution with the information available. This solution depends on achieving some level of social or organisational acceptance for the risks by controlling them within acceptable or tolerable risk levels. An example would be the risks associated with the development and use of genetically modified crops.

Douglas and Wildavsky (1982) argued that social principles, which guide behaviour, affect one's decisions on which risks cause the most concern. Frequently, accident statistics are presented only to support organisational and personal views of risk rather than to identify, quantify and control the risks within the workplace. Therefore the development of a cultural approach for explaining an individual's or group's views on risk provides a basis against which one can understand why people are more concerned about some problems and risks than others. Because different risks concern different groups of people in different ways, the adoption of a cultural approach to people and groups in society may help one to understand the issues involved. It may also allow one to determine which risk management policies are acceptable and which are not.

Cultural theories of risk

Cultural theories were developed originally for the anthropological study of animals and their behaviours. Cultural theories of risk are used to categorise and discuss people and groups at risk, but are rarely used in discussions related to technical matters, where scientific and engineering calculations and conclusions can resolve the risk issues. Cultural theory is regarded more as the theoretical ground for social scientists who are involved in discussing policy decisions, understanding the public's views on risk and debating differences in risk perceptions between pure scientists and social scientists. Cultural theories have been little used at the practical level within work-based environments, but they have many potential benefits if used in conjunction with the development of continuous improvement programmes and intervention strategies.

Cultural theories, which relate to social groups and the social relationships developed between groups within natural and work-based environments, regard the organisation or social group as the source of people's risk perceptions on issues. It is important, however, to consider which is the 'cause' and which is the 'effect', as it would not be unreasonable to argue that it is a particular risk perception that places one within a cultural group rather than vice versa.

The grid/group framework theory

Douglas (1970) developed a typology of social structure and view of nature that was based on an analysis of grid and group properties within social cultures.

The *group* dimension represents the level of incorporation of an individual within a social or organisational group.

- A weak group dimension represents a situation where interactions are open-ended, infrequent and restricted to certain specific activities. Individuals categorised as '*weak-group*' would tend to be 'loners', who are self-sufficient and competitive.

- A strong group dimension represents a situation where interactions are frequent and cover a very wide range of activities. Individuals categorised as '*strong-group*' would tend to be dependent on other people and would develop commonality of standards, needs and ambitions.

The *grid* dimension represents the type and nature of the social and organisational interactions that take place among the groups. The grid dimension is a measure of the constraints or classifications placed on individuals within different social and organisational groups. These classifications may be a function of organisational structure, social group, family or gender. The grid dimension acts independently of the group dimension.

- A weak grid dimension means that no one is precluded from taking on any role, whatever their current social or organisational standing, and therefore it represents a position of equality for all people.

- A strong grid dimension means that internal or external constraints are imposed on individuals with respect to the social or organisational roles that they can access.

Typical characteristics of weak and strong values within the group and grid dimensions (Rayner, 1992) are summarised in Table 3.3. The independent grid and group dimensions can be presented on two orthogonal axes. The 'group' axis may be viewed as moving from an individual (weak) to a collective (strong) way of living or working, and the 'grid' axis may be viewed as moving from a state of equality (weak) to a state of inequality (strong). Thompson *et al.* (1990) utilised this concept and identified a typology of human nature that contained four general descriptions of social or organisational ways of life (Table 3.4) described by their group and grid characteristics.

Table 3.3 Characteristics of group and grid dimensions

Dimension	Characteristic	Strength	
		Weak	*Strong*
Group	Interactions	Infrequent	Frequent
	Boundaries	Open	Closed
	Shared activities	Few	Many
Grid	Accountability	Horizontal	Vertical
	Specialisation	Low	High
	Role allocation	Achieved	Attributed

Source: Adapted from Rayner (1992)

Table 3.4 Typology of human nature

Typology	Strength of GRID dimension	Strength of GROUP dimension
Type 1: Individualist	Weak	Weak
Type 2: Fatalist	Strong	Weak
Type 3: Hierarchist	Strong	Strong
Type 4: Egalitarian	Weak	Strong

Type 1 (individualists) are independent and act in a way that is free from the control of other people. They will try to control the environment in which they work or live, strive to be recognised for their success, and try to influence others. Individualists are competitive, prepared to take high levels of risk, and will often seek to stretch the rules or take short cuts in order to achieve their goals. In situations where operational decisions are required, individualists may take decisions or corrective actions for procedures without reference to their colleagues or superiors. Individualists do not like to receive criticism of their actions by peers, supervisors or managers. They will tend to keep information to themselves rather than share it with fellow workers; this can lead to the loss of organisational learning. In terms of health and safety management, the view of individualists would be: *I am responsible for my own health and safety.*

Type 2 (fatalists) feel that they have little, if any, control over their life outcomes so they will make little attempt to change their lives through positive actions. They tend to accept changes to operational rules and procedures in order to get the job done. Fatalists do not tend to seek positions of control or influence: therefore they are more likely to be found carrying out routine activities. In terms of health and safety management, the view of fatalists would be: *there is little I can do to improve the level of health and safety.*

Type 3 (hierarchists) are aware of their place in an organisation or society, and will have a feeling of group identity and belonging: they will frequently work together and socialise together. Hierarchists are constrained in their activities by the social and organisational rules and procedures that relate to their jobs and positions, and they tend to resist change in their social and work environments. Hierarchists may be found in well-structured societies and organisations, such as the civil service or armed forces, where everyone knows and accepts their place. In terms of health and safety management, the view of hierarchists would be: *my health and safety is assured if I follow the rules and procedures.*

Type 4 (egalitarians) have strong social loyalties and allegiances, but do not like externally imposed rules and regulations. Egalitarians will support each other, especially in disputes with authority or in discussions with management over work procedures. Egalitarians operate in a work or social environment where everyone has a similar position and standing, and they prefer to operate through a system of democracy and leadership by personality, persuasion and example. Egalitarians often operate in single-skill groups and, if disputes arise, an individual from within the group will often appear in order to lead the group and resolve the problem. When the problem has been resolved the temporary leader will resume his or her normal role within the group. In terms of health and safety management, the view of egalitarians would be: *health and safety requires adapting procedures to fit the situation.*

Holling (1979) addressed the issue of how managers made decisions within a risk environment and found that, when managers had insufficient information but were still required to reach a decision, they often came to conclusions that were based on their beliefs about the environment within which they lived or worked. These beliefs could be grouped into what were referred to as 'nature benign', 'nature ephemeral' and 'nature perverse or tolerant'. Schwarz and Thompson (1990) added a fourth belief referred to as 'nature capricious'. These beliefs, which are referred to as the 'four myths of nature', are typically described by the ways in which a sphere (or nature) would behave in a range of landscapes (or social and work-based environments) (Figure 3.5).

Type 1 (nature benign) is predictable, plentiful, strong and recoverable from the actions of man. Managers who follow the benign style would be non-interventionist and assume that nature would manage itself, in the belief that man and nature would survive all the hazards and risks encountered.

Type 2 (nature capricious) is unpredictable, and wherever nature is pushed it will remain there and develop accordingly. It could be argued that this philosophy is similar to the principle behind Darwin's (1859) evolutionary theory and the phrase 'the survival of the fittest'. Managers who follow the capricious style believe that the outcomes of life and work-based events cannot be managed, and therefore they would take little action to reduce risks. They would not know whether the result of changes would be good or bad, but would believe that nature would always survive by developing in such a way that it would adapt to the new conditions.

Type 3 (nature perverse) is tolerant within limits but, if the risks became too great, harm would result from any adverse events that took place. In this situation risks to nature could be controlled through a goal-setting regulatory regime, whereby general guidelines were provided to managers in order to prevent

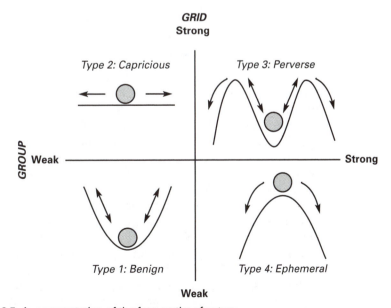

Figure 3.5 A representation of the four myths of nature

extremes of risk occurring that might result in irreparable harm to the environment or people. Managers who follow the perverse style would be reliant on an interventionist approach for the control of hazards and the reduction of risk.

Type 4 (nature ephemeral) is fragile and readily susceptible to harm: the smallest changes to prescribed operating systems would result in damage, which would be irreparable. High-risk environments must be treated carefully, and attention must be spent on details in order to prevent catastrophic consequences resulting from failures in physical, management or human factor control measures. Managers who follow the ephemeral style would take a precautionary route; they would not be prepared to take even the smallest risk with the environment or work-based processes for fear of the adverse outcomes.

The paradigms of human nature and the risk environment can be viewed together to illustrate how they complement each other:

- The *individualist* operates in a risk environment with a belief that nature can cope with whatever actions they take in order to achieve their aims and objectives.
- The *fatalist* operates in a risk environment with a belief that nature can be pushed in all directions but will survive the changes however great they may be.
- The *hierarchist* operates in a risk environment with a belief that nature can withstand most changes so long as the system is not changed by too large an amount.
- The *egalitarian* operates in a risk environment with a belief that nature must be treated carefully in order to prevent all accidents, incidents and catastrophes from occurring.

There is, however, an additional category of human nature, which is sometimes considered but usually omitted from the typology. This is the *hermit*, who withdraws totally from society, lives alone and does not impinge on the activities of anyone else. Although this is a viable way of life, it is not one that is encompassed within most spheres of social or work-based life.

Strengths and weaknesses of the cultural theory approach to risk management

Cultural theorists can be accused of ignoring the argument that human behaviour is based solely on self-interest. Economists and political scientists, by contrast, use the concept of self-interest to explain an individual's drive for financial and political power. By ignoring this concept, cultural theorists have effectively allowed individuals, industries and governments to claim that risk is a relative issue or a perception that is viewed differently by different groups. Risk perception and the complexities that this brings to risk management are discussed in the next chapter. There is also an argument of whether the knowledge and practice of risk mitigation in one context are relevant in other contexts. This can be illustrated simply by using the extreme example of trying to assess whether humans would be able to learn from animals if they could speak. The argument against the transfer of knowledge and experience between these completely different cultures is that, although humans might be able to hear what animals were saying, they would not actually understand what they were saying because communication would involve the use of animal philosophies, thoughts and concepts. There is a counter argument, however, that, even if one could not understand an alternative culture, the mere act of communicating and transferring knowledge between them would influence and inform the cultures of the two groups.

One can consider whether it is possible to link the theories of personality traits and human needs with cultural theory in order to determine the best ways of motivating different groups of people. For example, one could use the two motivational forces of 'personal achievement' and 'organisational affiliation' (Figure 3.2) as the two dimensions, with strong and weak characteristics, on the orthogonal framework (Figure 3.6). It becomes apparent that these two dimensions also identify four types of motivational needs, which are consistent with the four descriptions of human nature identified in Douglas's (1970) model of the grid–group theory of human nature. Comparing the descriptions provided earlier for individualists, fatalists, hierarchists and egalitarians, one would then expect:

- *individualists* to exhibit strong personal achievement and weak organisational affiliation dimensions – they would be pragmatic and would adopt whichever option provided them with the best opportunities;
- *fatalists* to exhibit weak personal achievement and weak organisational affiliation dimensions – they would be happy to work alone and watch the world go by;
- *hierarchists* to exhibit strong organisational affiliation and weak personal achievement dimensions – they would prefer well-organised communities but would prefer others to regulate and control the community;
- *egalitarians* to exhibit strong organisational affiliation and strong personal achievement dimensions – they would form pressure groups in order to change the world, and would strive to achieve targets that they considered to be socially and personally acceptable.

A similar comparison can be made between Eysenck's (1965) dimensions of personality (see Table 3.1) and the four types of human nature. Comparisons of this type can be helpful in defining the type and content of behaviour modification programmes, as these should be developed to suit different groups and different organisational settings.

Figure 3.6 Motivational needs as a function of human nature

It could be argued that cultural theories do nothing more than categorise individuals into four stereotypes. This is sometimes difficult for individuals to accept because of the high value that most people place on their own identity. What cultural theory does do, however, is emphasise that risk management is an issue of people management, and that the classification of people into *cultural stereotypes* highlights and reinforces the implication that political and social interests often drive the process of risk management. This is an important view, as risk mitigation measures, which are claimed to be neutral in their origins, are often implemented to achieve particular outcomes or fulfil self-interests.

Adams (1995) summarised both his objection to and his acceptance of the importance of cultural theory in risk management as follows:

> The insistence in cultural theory on the impossibility of more than 'five viable ways of life' I find unproven and unprovable, but I still find the theory useful. For me, limiting the number of risk-taking types to five is defensible, not just by theoretical speculation, but by virtue of five being a small and comprehensible number; theories of behaviour, to be useful and widely communicable, must be simple.
>
> Adams (1995: x)

Schwarz and Thompson (1990) summarised their views on the essential nature of accepting cultural pluralism as follows:

> The three active rationalities – the hierarchical, the individualistic and the egalitarian – structure the world in different and (in the right circumstances) complementary ways. And, lest it appear that, as usual, they have been missed out, we should stress that the fatalists too are essential (in their passive way), because each of the active rationalities seeks to advance its cause by mobilizing them. 'Just get the hierarchists and the egalitarians off their backs' say the individualists, 'and they'll soon lift themselves up by their bootstraps'.
>
> Schwarz and Thompson (1990: 12)

It is possible, however, that cultural theories limit the way in which countries, organisations and individuals view risks. A particular objection is from the viewpoint that people who may be classified in one way often behave in quite different ways from their expected stereotype in some situations. Additionally, even strongly constrained organisations, for example the armed forces, contain a range of stereotypical people within their cultural structure. Cultural theories should therefore be viewed more as a predictor of the most likely views and actions that may be taken by organisations and people. These predictors should be based on, for example, statistical averages, standard deviations and confidence limits. It is also important to understand the underlying principle that individuals may have components of each of the four (or five) types of human nature within their personality. Adams (1995: x) has again concisely and pointedly voiced this concern: 'I now see the stereotypes of cultural theory – egalitarians, individualists, hierarchists, fatalists and hermits – everywhere I look. But which am I?'

In the real world of risk management, it may be more helpful to incorporate these views, comments and concerns by developing a composite model of human nature, which can then be used to understand the complexities of man in social and work-based environments (Figure 3.7). In this way, individuals and

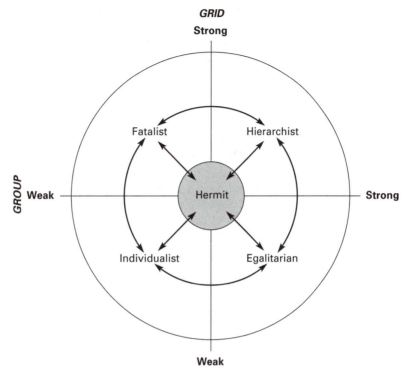

Figure 3.7 A composite model of human nature

groups could be identified with a dominant cultural type, whilst retaining elements of the other types. This would be more consistent with the view expressed by Kluckholm and Murray (1953) that 'every man is, in certain ways, like all other men, like some other men and like no other men'.

The importance of cultural theory in the context of risk is that it moves risk management from an issue that is discussed solely in terms of individual, local sources of risk to an issue that can be discussed in terms of wide-ranging international, social and political sources of risk. Schwarz and Thompson (1990) expressed the importance of incorporating all cultures into discussions of risk as follows:

> Our concern, therefore, should not be with which one is right (for that would be to insist that just one rationality had access to 'the truth') but rather with which is appropriate to the task at hand.
>
> We must learn to husband them and make the most of them. Divided we stand; united we fall.
>
> Schwarz and Thompson (1990: 13)

Finally, Bronowski (1973) discussed, at the beginning of his book *The Ascent of Man*, why theories of personality, behaviour and culture are so important for understanding the way in which man develops in social and organisational environments. His book helps to explain how man has changed and adapted over time to be able to deal with risk in order to survive:

His imagination, his reason, his emotional subtlety and toughness, make it possible for him not to accept the environment but to change it. And that series of inventions, by which man from age to age has remade his environment, is a different kind of evolution – not biological, but cultural evolution. I call that brilliant sequence of cultural peaks The Ascent of Man.

Bronowski (1973: 19–20)

Human error

All errors are deemed to be a direct consequence of human behaviour. Errors arise from either actions that are normally expected to produce the correct result but very occasionally fail or actions that may work but may also fail. Kirwan (1994) reasoned that even violations were a form of behaviour that might be acceptable on some occasions. Reason (1995) classified the causes of human error as:

- behavioural or 'what happened?';
- contextual or 'where did it happen?'; and
- conceptual or 'how did it happen?'.

The *behavioural level* provides superficial information about what caused an error. Errors are classified as observable issues associated with either the inputs, such as acts of omission or commission, or the outputs, such as the consequences of an error. Although this approach is widely used at the organisational and national levels, it has limited application because the same behavioural error may be caused by significantly different inputs and result in significantly different outputs from similar inputs.

The *contextual level* incorporates information about where an error occurred in terms of the workplace environment. This level of classification attempts to relate errors to the local conditions and circumstances that existed at the time of the error. Again this approach does not explain why similar workplace environments do not produce the same errors or why different workplace environments produce the same errors.

The *conceptual level* makes assumptions about the cognitive mechanisms involved in producing errors, and is based on making certain inferences about why an action took place rather than relying solely on the observable actions and the environment involved. This approach requires an understanding of the causes of human error.

Rasmussen (1996) commented:

Analyses of recent major accidents invariably have pointed to the role of human error; indeed it is often stated that 80–90 per cent of industrial accidents may be traced to this factor. Consequently considerable resources have been spent on human error research. Comprehensive programmes have been developed to define and quantify human errors, though without any significant success; reliable 'human error' databases still do not exist. The concept of human error is, in fact, very elusive.

Rasmussen (1996: 8)

Most operational procedures are made up of a number of individual actions, each of which can be completed either correctly or incorrectly. There is normally only one way in which each task can be completed entirely correctly but an infinite number of ways in which each task can be completed incorrectly. It could be predicted, therefore, from one's experience of life that many operations will be completed incorrectly. If it is assumed that a procedure is made up of five tasks that require human intervention (tasks A to E), with the probabilities of successful completion of each task equal to the values of P_A to P_E shown in Table 3.5, the overall probability of an error-free execution of the procedure is given by

$$\text{Probability of safe operation} \quad = \quad P_A \times P_B \times P_C \times P_D \times P_E$$
$$= \quad 0.978$$

Table 3.5 Probabilities of an error occurring in a procedure made up of five tasks involving human intervention

Task	Average number of errors observed per 1000 executions of task	Probability of correct operation
A	6	0.994 (P_A)
B	3	0.997 (P_B)
C	7	0.993 (P_C)
D	1	0.999 (P_D)
E	5	0.995 (P_E)
Probability of an error-free execution of the procedure:		0.978

In this case, statistically, two operations in every hundred will be completed incorrectly. Although the reliabilities associated with the individual tasks may appear to be high, the overall reliability of the procedure is considered to be low, particularly for activities that could lead to severe consequences. Although the overall reliability of a procedure may appear to be low from this type of calculation, the number of accidents actually observed is often much lower than predicted because employees take corrective actions before the consequences of an incorrect action become critical.

Constant and random human errors

It is important to differentiate between an error caused by a variation from an accepted or normal operational procedure and an error caused by a variation from a defined written operational procedure. For example, a production process may have a formal procedure that describes how a process should be carried out; however, because of design changes to the process, this procedure may no longer be appropriate and changes have, over time, been made to the way in which the process is controlled (the normal procedure). These changes, however, may not have been incorporated into the organisation's formal operational procedures (a human error in itself). Following an accident, it would be easy, in these circumstances, to identify an individual who has not followed the organisation's formal procedure: this could therefore be recorded as a violation of the organisation's rules and procedures.

Although human errors may or may not be common, health and safety managers should be interested in the predictability of these errors because predictable errors can be controlled. Human error prediction, however, depends on how well the circumstances that lead to the errors are understood. Human errors can present themselves as *constant errors* and *random errors*. Constant errors equate to the difference between the actual value and the observed value of a measurement (accuracy); random errors equate to the variation of the measurement about the mean (precision). Human error patterns can therefore be summarised by the statistical relationships shown in Figure 3.8.

This analogy illustrates why human error prediction is often based on probabilistic interpretations rather than precise causative reasons. If one considers, as an example, a task that requires an employee to set the operating temperature of a chemical reaction at a certain value, it is possible to explain the types of human behaviour that are described in Figure 3.8:

- *Region A* describes the actions of an employee who controls the reaction temperature at the wrong value in a highly predictable way.
- *Region B* describes the actions of an employee who controls the reaction temperature at the wrong value in a totally random way.
- *Region C* describes the actions of an employee who controls the reaction temperature in a totally random way but on average achieves the correct temperature.
- *Region D* describes the actions of an employee who controls the reaction temperature at the correct value with very little variation.

Human intention and error

In order to understand the impact of behaviour on accident causation, the concept of intention must be considered alongside human error. Reason (1995) stated:

> One psychologically useful way of distinguishing between the different kinds of intentional behaviour is on the basis of yes–no answers to three questions regarding a sequence of actions:
> Were the actions directed by some prior intention?
> Did the actions proceed as planned?
> Did they achieve their desired end?

Reason (1995: 5)

	Constant error	
	High	Low
Random error — Low	**Region A** Low accuracy + High precision	**Region D** High accuracy + High precision
Random error — High	**Region B** Low accuracy + Low precision	**Region C** High accuracy + Low precision

Figure 3.8 Classification of human behaviour in terms of random and constant errors

Prior intention implies not only that an action involved achieving a specific end result but also that there was an indication of how the end result might be achieved. However, although all intentional actions must involve intentions in the actions that are carried out, not all intentional actions must have prior intentions (Reason, 1995).

Intentional actions without prior intention relate to spontaneous activities or to actions that follow as a subsidiary action to an earlier action. For example, a *spontaneous activity* would be illustrated by the use of an emergency stop button on a piece of equipment by an employee when a work colleague is trapped in a moving part. There is clearly no prior intention to stop the equipment; the intention is involved solely in the action itself. A *subsidiary action* would be described by the action of a forklift truck driver when he or she raises the forks on the vehicle in order to remove a pallet of goods from a trailer. The driver's intention is to remove the goods from the vehicle; the intentional raising of the forks follows purely as a subsidiary action of the main intention.

Non-intentional actions and involuntary actions should not be categorised as human error, as human error should be applied only to actions that are intentional. If someone fell and grabbed at a nearby cable in order to prevent themselves from falling to the ground and consequently caused an electric short to occur that resulted in a fire, the person could not be accused of committing a human error for this act. Human error cannot be applied in the context of unintentional and involuntary actions because errors are related to the failure of actions to proceed as intended and the failure of intended actions to achieve a desired outcome.

Intended and unintended actions

It is necessary to examine whether intended actions proceeded as planned, and whether these planned actions achieved the desired outcomes.

Intended actions refer to an employee's actions that follow the intended path but fail to achieve the desired outcome. In these cases, the error arises through an inadequate plan of action, and this type of action is normally referred to as a *mistake*. Mistakes are brought about by a mismatch between the intention of the actions and the actual consequences arising from these actions. These errors result from failures of planning, and often result from management decision-making processes.

Unintended actions refer to actions that do not follow the intended route but which may or may not achieve the desired outcome. *Unintended actions achieving the desired outcome* are unlikely events but they are still possible. For example, an employee may intend to stop a machine but in the process of moving to the isolation switch he or she trips and as a result of reaching out to prevent a fall grabs at the isolation handle and pulls it into the 'off' position. The employee intended to stop the machine but did not intend to achieve this result by tripping over in the process. *Unintended actions not achieving the desired outcome* often occur with routine operations when another activity or person diverts an employee's attention; these actions are typified by actions carried out during moments of absentmindedness. These unintended actions are referred to as *lapses* and *slips* and are caused by a mismatch between the intended actions and the actions actually carried out.

Types of human error

Error types can be used to explain the presumed origin of errors within a context of the stages involved in conceiving and implementing an action sequence: Reason (1995) described these as the planning, storage and execution stages:

- *Planning* describes the processes involved in identifying the desired outcomes and defining how these will be achieved. Errors of this type are also referred to as *latent* errors.
- *Storage* describes the period and processes involved between the planning and execution stages of an action.
- *Execution* describes the processes involved in implementing the stored plan. Errors arising from this stage are also referred to as *active* errors.

The following definitions of human error (Reason, 1995) have gained general acceptance in the study of human error:

> Error will be taken as a generic term to encompass all those occasions in which a planned sequence of mental or physical activities fails to achieve its intended outcome, and when these failures cannot be attributed to the intervention of some chance agency. Slips and lapses are errors which result from some failure in the execution and/or storage of an action sequence, regardless of whether or not the plan which guided them was adequate to achieve its objective.
>
> Reason (1995: 9)

Slips and lapses tend to occur with activities that an operator is familiar with and which do not need constant conscious attention. These activities, which are also referred to as skill-based activities, are vulnerable when the operator's attention is distracted. Slips and lapses are often associated with acts of omission or commission. Slips are actions that can be described as implemented actions that were not planned, whereas lapses are forgotten actions. Mistakes are more complex to understand than slips and lapses but are generally regarded as actions that are incorrect but thought to be correct by the person carrying them out:

> Mistakes may be defined as deficiencies or failures in the judgemental and/or inferential processes involved in the selection of an objective or in the specification of the means to achieve it, irrespective of whether or not the actions directed by this decision-scheme run according to plan.
>
> Reason (1995: 9)

Reason (1995) divided the category of mistakes into two subcategories referred to as *failures of expertise* and *failures from a lack of expertise*:

- *Failures of expertise* refer to situations where an error occurs because a predefined plan is implemented inappropriately.
- *Failures from a lack of expertise* refer to situations where an error occurs because an individual has to develop an action plan based on their current inadequate level of knowledge.

Reason (1995) summarised his classification of error types in terms of the cognitive stages at which the errors occurred: see Table 3.6.

Table 3.6 Reason's classification of error types

Cognitive stage	Error type
	Mistake (lack of expertise)
Planning	Mistake (failure of expertise)
Storage	Lapse
Execution	Slip

Source: Reason (1995)

Rasmussen (1983) used a slightly different human error classification system, which was based on skill-, rule- and knowledge-based behaviours:

- *Skill-based behaviour* refers to those actions that are determined by an individual's stored patterns of behaviour such that the individual responds to signals automatically. Errors of this type are related to issues of force, space and/or time (Reason, 1995).

- *Rule-based behaviour* refers to those actions that take place under familiar circumstances using stored or accessible rules: this requires an individual to acknowledge that an action should be carried out in a predefined way and to select the appropriate rule for the circumstances. Errors of this type are related to incorrect assessments of situations that lead to the application of incorrect rules (Reason, 1995).

- *Knowledge-based behaviour* refers to those actions that are taken by an individual based on high-level problem solving, cognitive processes: this requires the individual to have an understanding of the underlying theories behind the process. Errors of this type are normally related to limitations in resources and/or incomplete or incorrect knowledge of the process (Reason, 1995).

Rasmussen's approach to the classification of error types is summarised in Table 3.7.

Table 3.7 Rasmussen's classification of error types

Performance level	Error type
Knowledge-based	Mistake
Rule-based	Lapse
Skill-based	Slip

Source: Rasmussen (1983)

Rasmussen's rule-based errors correspond to Reason's failure of expertise errors, and Rasmussen's knowledge-based errors correspond to Reason's failure through lack of expertise errors.

Human error recovery actions

Kirwan (1994) claimed that many human errors were recoverable before an accident or incident occurred, and he identified four scenarios or types of recovery action that achieved this:

- *Internal recovery* refers to situations where an individual has made an error but realises that this has happened and takes the necessary corrective actions, either immediately or at a later time.

- *External recovery* refers to situations where an individual has made an error but the working system creates a signal, such as an alarm, that prompts the same or another individual to take the necessary corrective actions either immediately or at a later time.

- *Independent human recovery* refers to situations where a second individual has monitored the actions of an individual and identifies that an error has occurred, and takes the necessary corrective actions either immediately or at a later time.

- *System recovery* refers to those situations where an individual has made an error but the system automatically corrects the mistake.

Violation errors

Violation errors, which refer to deliberate actions to break an operational rule or procedure, form a significant contributory factor in many accidents and incidents. However, most rule violations are not undertaken as deliberate or wilful actions to create an accident or incident: 'Most violations are motivated by a desire to carry out the job despite the prevailing constraints, goals and expectations' (Health and Safety Executive, 1999: 16).

Violations can be classified under the headings of routine, situational and exceptional violations (Health and Safety Executive, 1999).

Routine violations refer to situations where it has become custom and practice for employees to carry out work activities in ways that are different from those defined in the organisation's operating procedures and guidelines. These practices have developed through (Health and Safety Executive, 1999):

- a desire to take short cuts in order to save time and effort;
- the perception that the organisation's current procedures and/or guidelines are too restrictive;
- a belief that the organisation's current procedures and/or guidelines are no longer appropriate for the work to be carried out;
- a lack of management enforcement of the existing correct procedures and/or guidelines; or
- a belief by new employees that the current practices are the correct procedures.

Situational violations refer to situations where procedures and/or guidelines are disregarded owing to the current conditions under which the work activities must be carried out. These practices have developed because of (Health and Safety Executive, 1999):

- time pressures;
- inadequate staffing arrangements;
- inappropriate levels of competence of some employees;
- inadequate or inappropriate work equipment;
- poor environmental conditions;
- inability of the workforce to comply with the defined operating procedures under the specific circumstances in which the activity must be carried out; or
- a perception that the defined operating procedures are unsafe in the specific circumstances under which the activity must be carried out.

Exceptional violations are uncommon and occur when something unusual has happened in a process such as during an emergency. These situations arise where it is considered that (Health and Safety Executive, 1999):

- the only way to solve an urgent problem in the current circumstances is to break an accepted procedure or guideline; or
- the benefits from breaking an accepted procedure or guideline outweigh the costs.

Models of human error

A number of models of human error are used but most are derived from the work of Rasmussen (1983) and Reason (1995).

Domino theory

Heinrich (1969) developed the first model of human error based on the concept of cause and effect: this model is referred to as the *domino theory*. Heinrich postulated that a series of events were necessary for an accident to occur:

- People inherit or acquire faults as a result of their social environment, such as recklessness, stubbornness or lack of education.
- Hazards exist as a consequence of people's faults because the inherited or acquired faults create the ability to commit unsafe acts or to create unsafe conditions.
- Accidents occur as a result of personal hazards.
- Injuries can occur only as a result of an accident.

Heinrich's argument was that these factors acted like a row of dominoes: if one was knocked over, the other dominoes would be knocked over as well, resulting in an accident. However, if one domino was removed from the row of dominoes then, even if one domino was knocked over, the others would remain standing and an accident would not occur.

Intentional and unintentional behaviours

Reason (1995) described a model of human error based on the three questions related to intention, planning and outcomes of actions and the concepts of intentional and unintentional acts as inputs and slips, lapses and mistakes as potential outputs of these actions: see Figure 3.9.

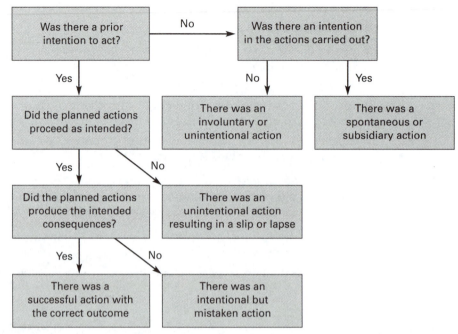

Figure 3.9 Human error and intentional behaviour
Source: Adapted from Reason (1995)

Active and latent errors

Reason (1995) presented a model of accident causation based on the concepts of latent and active errors: see Figure 3.10. He claimed that very few latent or active errors actually resulted in harm to people or the environment because normally most operational systems included sufficient layers of defence to prevent an accident. It was only when all the unsafe acts and conditions occurred concurrently or in the right sequence that an accident occurred.

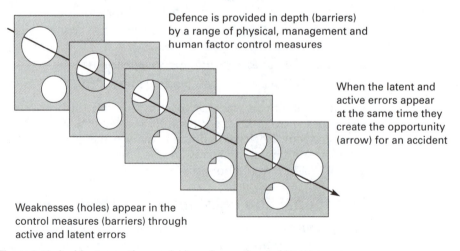

Figure 3.10 Accident causation model based on active and latent errors
Source: Adapted from Reason (1995)

Reason claimed:

> In a highly defended system, one of the most common accident scenarios involves the deliberate disabling of engineered safety features by operators in pursuit of what, at the time, seems a perfectly sensible goal but that fails to take account either of the side effects of these actions or of system characteristics. On other occasions, the defences are breached because the operators are unaware of concurrently created gaps in system security because they have an erroneous perception of the system state.
>
> Reason (1995: 209)

Personality types

The personality types of introversion and extroversion proposed by Eysenck have often been used to describe certain individuals' propensity to have accidents. Eysenck (1962) claimed that extroverts would be expected to exhibit higher accident rates than introverts because of their lower levels of care. Although there does appear to be some relationship between personality types and accident rates, the evidence is inconclusive (Lawton and Parker, 1998). It has been suggested that these associations may be related to an increased vulnerability to stress and to an increased willingness to take risks. Lawton and Parker (1998) suggested that the unstable extrovert is more likely to exhibit undesirable attitudes and cognitive biases that could lead to accidents whereas the unstable introvert may exhibit performance limitations when exposed to external pressures and therefore become easily distracted (Figure 3.11).

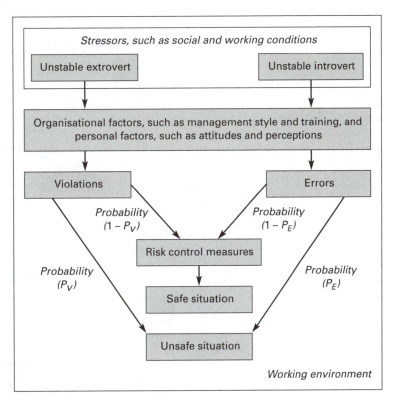

Figure 3.11 Accident and incident model based on personality, organisational and personal factors, and risk control measures

This model incorporated behavioural precursors to human errors, and illustrated the roles that chance and risk control measures play in the occurrence of an accident. The model also explained how management control could have a significant effect on human error and accident prevention.

Error types

The Health and Safety Executive (1999) presented a classification system for categorising the causes of human errors based on the work of Reason, Rasmussen and the discussion on violations presented above: see Figure 3.12.

Accident proneness

Farmer and Chambers (1926) used the term *accident proneness* in the context of a personal characteristic that created a propensity for an individual to have a significantly higher accident rate than other people working in a similar environment. The idea of accident proneness was, therefore, based on the concepts that:

■ different people exposed to the same hazards did not experience the same number of accidents; and

■ differences in accident rates among individuals resulted from differences in personalities.

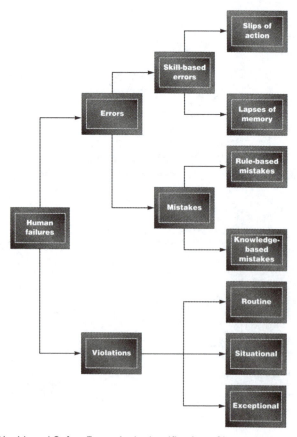

Figure 3.12 The Health and Safety Executive's classification of human errors
Source: Health and Safety Executive (1999) © Crown copyright 1999. Reproduced with permission from the Controller of Her Majesty's Stationery Office.

If differences in personality resulted in different accident rates, it should have been possible to identify those personality traits that caused the effect. Lawton and Parker (1998) reviewed issues such as employees' personality characteristics, cognitive capabilities and social factors, and Hale and Glendon (1987) reported that, in a limited number of studies, personality was related to accidents but the correlations were very weak. Major life events, such as marriage, death of a relative or close friend and the loss of employment, have been linked with traffic accidents (Selzer and Vinokur, 1974) and sports injuries (Junge, 2000), but these effects are short-lived and are not really associated with the phenomenon of workplace accident proneness. Glendon and McKenna (1995) summarised the arguments about personality traits and accident proneness as follows:

> It is almost certain that a combination of factors is responsible for the phenomenon that has been labelled as 'accident proneness' and that different clusters of factors attach to each individual. No personality trait for accident proneness has ever been isolated and it is unlikely to be worth looking for.
>
> Glendon and McKenna (1995: 161)

Accident proneness postulates that certain people may be more liable to have accidents than would be predicted by chance. In assessing the issue of accident proneness, it is important to understand and consider the statistical influence on the number of accidents and the number of people injured in a sample population (Uitenbroek, 1995). In statistical analyses, it must be assumed that every individual within the sample population has an equal chance of being involved in an accident and that the chance of suffering a further accident is not influenced by previous incidents. In this way the chance of an individual suffering an accident can be viewed purely as a random process. Over any given time period, the number of accidents in a population will therefore always be greater than or equal to the number of people having an accident, because some people will suffer accidents on more than one occasion. There are clearly invalid assumptions involved in this description because, for example, a person suffering a fatal accident could not return to the sample population and suffer a further accident. The published literature on accident proneness has focused on individuals, but the existence of *accident-prone operations* is a concept that is worthy of more consideration.

Summary

- The concept of common and individual traits can be used to explain an individual's personality. Personality is claimed to be a stable and enduring factor that influences an individual's behaviour.
- Behaviour, which determines an individual's actions in any situation, has been shown to be a function of the individual's unconscious motives, environment, desire for self-realisation, genetic make-up and cognitive processes.
- Individuals have a number of needs that can be grouped into the essential needs of life, such as food, air and safety, and other, higher needs, such as achieving personal esteem and satisfying ambitions. Addressing these needs can be used to motivate employees to achieve organisational targets.

- Theories of individual traits, personality, needs and motivation are used to explain why people do certain things, whereas cultural theories seek to explain why different groups of people behave in different ways. Social and organisational cultures are defined through the use of group and grid dimensions related to the level of incorporation of an individual into a group and the nature of the interactions between individuals and groups, respectively.

- Errors are deemed to be a consequence of human behaviour; however, the concept of intention must also be considered alongside human error when assessing the causes of accidents and incidents.

- Unintended actions that do not achieve the desired outcome are referred to as lapses and slips. Mistakes are brought about by a mismatch between the intention of the actions and the actual consequences arising from these actions.

Issues for review and discussion

- Consider which of Eysenck's traits are the dominant factors in your own personality.

- Assess where your personality fits on the 'stable–unstable' and 'introvert–extrovert' axes of personality.

- Consider which motivational factors have the greatest effect on your behaviour.

- Consider where you fit within the 'four myths of nature' model.

- Evaluate your views on rule violations in terms, for example, of road transport.

References

Adams, J. (1995) *Risk*. London: UCL Press.

Allport, G.W. and Odbert, H.S. (1936) Trait names: a psycho-lexical study. *Psychological Monographs: General and Applied,* Vol 47(1).

Bronowski, J. (1973) *The Ascent of Man*. London: British Broadcasting Corporation.

Cattell, R.B. (1965) *The Scientific Analysis of Personality*. Harmondsworth: Penguin.

Darwin, C. (1859) *The Origin of Species by Natural Selection*. London: John Murray.

Douglas, M. (1970) *Natural Symbols*. London: Barrie and Rockliff.

Douglas, M. and Wildavsky, A. (1982) *Risk and Culture: An Essay on the Selection of Technical and Environmental Dangers*. Berkeley: University of California Press.

Eysenck, H.J. (1962) The personality of drivers and pedestrians. *Medicine, Science and the Law*, **3**, 416–423.

Eysenck, H.J. (1965) *Fact and Fiction in Psychology*. Harmondsworth: Penguin.

Farmer, E. and Chambers, E.G. (1926) *A Psychological Study of Individual Differences in Accident Liability*. British Industrial Fatigue Research Board, Report No. 38. London: HMSO.

Fleming, M. and Lardner, R. (2000) *Behaviour Modification Programmes Establishing Best Practice*. OTR 2000/048. Sudbury: HSE Books.

Fleming, M. and Lardner, R. (2002) *Strategies to Promote Safe Behaviour as Part of a Health and Safety Management System*. CRR 430/2002. Sudbury: HSE Books.

Glendon, A.I. and McKenna, E.F. (1995) *Human Safety and Risk Management*. London: Chapman & Hall.

Gross, R. (1996) *Psychology: The Science of Mind and Behaviour*. London: Hodder & Stoughton.

Hale, A.R. and Glendon, A.I. (1987) *Individual Behaviour in the Control of Danger*. London: Elsevier.

Health and Safety Executive (1999) *Reducing Error and Influencing Behaviour*. HSG48. Sudbury: HSE Books.

Heinrich, H.W. (1969) *Industrial Accident Prevention*. New York: McGraw-Hill.

Herzberg, F. (1966) *Work and the Nature of Man*. Cleveland: World.

Holling, C.S. (1979) Myths of ecological stability. In: G. Smart and W. Stanbury (eds), *Studies in Crisis Management*. Montreal: Butterworth.

Junge, A. (2000) The influence of psychological factors on sports injuries. *American Journal of Sports Medicine*, **28**(5) S10–S15.

Keil Centre (2000) *Behaviour Modification to Improve Safety: Literature Review*. OTR 2000/003. Sudbury: HSE Books.

Kirwan, B. (1994) *A Guide to Practical Human Reliability Assessment*. London: Taylor & Francis.

Kluckholm, C. and Murray, H.A. (1953) Personality formation: The determinants. In: C. Kluckholm, H.A. Murray and D.M. Schneider (eds), *Personality in Nature, Society and Culture*. New York: Knopf.

Lawton, R. and Parker, D. (1998) *Individual Differences in Accident Liability: A Review*. CRR 175/1998. Sudbury: HSE Books.

Maslow, A. (1954) *Motivation and Personality*. New York: Harper & Row.

McClelland, D.C. (1961) *The Achieving Society*. Princeton: Van Nostrand.

Rasmussen, J. (1983) Skills, rules, knowledge: Signals, signs and symbols and other distinctions in human performance models. *IEEE Transactions: Systems, Man & Cybernetics*, **SMC-13**, 257–267.

Rasmussen, J. (1996) *Integrating Scientific Expertise into Regulatory Decision-making. Risk Management Issues – Doing Things Safely with Words, Rules and Laws*. San Domenico: European University Institute.

Rayner, S. (1992) Cultural theory and risk analysis. In: S. Krimsky and D. Golding (eds), *Social Theories of Risk*, 83–115. London: Praeger.

Reason, J. (1995) *Human Error*. Cambridge: Cambridge University Press.

Rogers, C.R. (1961) *On Becoming a Person*. Boston: Houghton Mifflin.

Schwarz, M. and Thompson, M. (1990) *Divided We Stand: Redefining Politics, Technology and Social Choice*. Hemel Hempstead: Harvester Wheatsheaf.

Selzer, M.L. and Vinokur, A. (1974) Life events, subjective stress and traffic accidents. *American Journal of Psychiatry*, **131**, 903–906.

Thompson, M., Ellis, R. and Wildavsky, A. (1990) *Cultural Theory*. Boulder, CO: Westview Press.

Uitenbroek, D.G. (1995) The mathematical relationship between the number of events in which people are injured and the number of people injured. *British Journal of Sports Medicine*, **29**, 126–128.

Vassie, L.H. (1998) A proactive team-based approach to continuous improvement in health and safety management. *Employee Relations*, **20**(6), 577–593.

LLYFRGELL COLEG MENAI LIBRARY

Risk perception

They tell me everything is gonna be all right
But I don't know what 'all right' even means.

– Bob Dylan, 'Tryin' to get to heaven' (1997)

Chapter contents

■ Introduction
■ Perception
■ Risk perception
■ Factors affecting risk perception
■ Cultural theory and risk perception
■ Risk homeostasis and risk compensation

Introduction

In the previous chapter, it was explained how the very act of carrying out a risk assessment could change the risks associated with an activity. Similarly, if one was just to think that a risk was high, one would consciously or unconsciously take actions to reduce that risk. Theories of behaviour predict that an individual will react to risks in a way that depends on their personal needs and personality traits. Cultural theory, similarly, predicts that different 'ways of life' produce different responses to risk. Adams (1995) summarised the complexities of assessing risk as follows:

> Risk is defined, by most of those who seek to measure it, as the product of the probability and utility of some future event. The future is uncertain and inescapably subjective; it does not exist except in the minds of people attempting to anticipate it. Our anticipations are formed by projecting past experience into the future. Our behaviour is guided by our anticipations. If we anticipate harm, we take avoiding action. Accident rates therefore cannot serve, even retrospectively, as measures of risk; if they are low, it does not necessarily indicate that the risk was low. It could be that a high risk was perceived and avoided.

Adams (1995: 30)

The only risks that one has no influence over are risks that are solely probabilistically based, such as the toss of a coin or the roll of a dice. This type of risk, however, is not usually encountered in a work environment, as work-based risks are affected by our and other people's actions, which are often linked to risk mitigation measures. The way in which individuals and organisations perceive risk is an important issue for several reasons: risk perception, for example, affects decisions and actions on risk identification, risk estimation, risk evaluation and risk mitigation. It can also affect the way in which individuals and organisations communicate the outcomes and conclusions obtained from risk assessments.

Richard Feynman (1985: 283), a Nobel prizewinner for physics, illustrated the problems associated with discussions and conclusions about perception when he described the difficulty of a group comprising a lawyer, a historian, a priest, a rabbi and a scientist in reaching a consensus view at an interdisciplinary conference: 'There's this meaningless inkblot, and the others ask you what you think you see, but when you tell them, they start arguing with you.'

Perception is a personal view; there are no right or wrong answers as to how risks should or should not influence one's views. An individual's perceptions can be changed, but their perceptions cannot be said to be wrong, however much one may disagree with them. It is important, therefore, to understand what issues affect an individual's perceptions, and their risk perceptions in particular. The aims of this chapter are to discuss the complexities of human perception, its relationship with risk perception and the role of risk perception, in determining individual and organisational actions.

Perception

Human perceptions are the conclusions and views that individuals reach about issues based on an accumulation of information and experiences from the world in which they live. The conclusions reached will be subject to individual influences, such as personality traits and needs, and to situational influences, such as social and work environments. An individual's understanding and interpretation of the sensory information received leads to conclusions and decisions about the actions he or she should take in particular situations.

Perception consists of two components: physical perception (or sensation), which occurs through the sensory system and provides the raw data; and cognitive perception, which occurs through psychological or mental processes and determines how one deals with the raw data. A useful description of perception is:

> Perception is not determined simply by stimulus patterns; rather it is a dynamic searching for the best interpretation of the available data. Perception involves going beyond the immediately given evidence of the senses.
>
> Gross (1996: 203)

One's physical perceptions of events and objects are normally very rapid, and this is an important factor that enables individuals to react quickly in times of danger. One's cognitive perceptions are formed over longer periods of time, and they may change as new information and experiences become available.

Physical perception

Physical perception is the process by which one receives information and experiences through the human sensory system, and is referred to as *sensation*. The sensory system operates through receptors, such as the eyes, ears, nose and skin, located throughout the body. The sensations that are recorded within the receptors generate electrical impulses, which are transmitted by sensory neurones to the *thalamus* in the brain. The thalamus sorts the information and then passes it to specialised sensory storage areas in the *cerebrum*, the largest part of the brain, where it is analysed and stored. Although sensory organs have a threshold value below which the human body will normally not respond, perception may sometimes still occur below these threshold values, in which case the responses are then referred to as *subliminal perception*. Damage to the sensory system is important not only because of the damage *per se* but also because it reduces the body's ability to identify and respond to future situations that may cause further harm.

Visual receptors or photoreceptor cells, which are located in the retina of the eye, contain chemicals that decolourise when exposed to light. This process changes the electrical potential within the photoreceptor cells and causes an electrical impulse to be sent to the brain. Visual perception may be impaired at birth but it may also deteriorate with age: these deficiencies may manifest themselves through, for example, poor response to light intensity, inability to focus on near or distant objects, or an inability to distinguish between certain colours (colour blindness). Damage to one eye can also affect an individual's binocular vision capabilities.

Auditory receptors detect sounds by the effect of air pressure waves on hair cells situated between two membranes in the inner ear, and this generates electrical impulses that are transmitted via the auditory nerve to the brain. Hearing loss may occur as a result of age (presbycusis, tinnitus) or as a result of exposure to high noise levels (threshold shift). Sound is also perceived through vibrations absorbed by the body.

Olfactory receptors identify smell, which was one of the first senses to evolve, and are capable of analysing highly complex information. Hair cells, which are covered with a fatty substance, in the *olfactory epithelium* area of the nose absorb molecules from the air onto their surface. This generates an electrical impulse that is passed directly to the *olfactory cortex* in the brain without passing through the thalamus.

Gustatory receptors identify taste and are closely linked with smell: the absence or deficiency of one of these receptors can significantly affect the capabilities of the other. Taste receptors are located in the *taste buds*, which are situated on the tongue and the palate of the mouth. These cells contain hair-like structures that respond when ingested material dissolves in the mouth's saliva. This response changes the chemical balance in the receptor cells, and this produces an electrical impulse that passes to the brain.

Tactile receptors record touch through three types of sensor that respond to pressure, temperature and pain. The response of pressure sensors, which are situated under the surface of the skin, depends on whether the sensors are situated in a sensitive or a non-sensitive part of the body. Temperature sensors consist of free nerve endings that respond to either hot or cold conditions. Pain, resulting for example from a cut, causes chemicals to be released within the skin; sensors consisting of free nerve endings detect these chemicals. All tactile sensors generate electrical impulses that are sent to the thalamus; however, pain impulses are also sent directly to the brain so that an injured person is able to respond more quickly to the pain and to take earlier corrective action.

Kinaesthetic receptors are situated throughout the body and provide information on muscle and joint movement (*proprioceptors*), body balance and body movement.

Cognitive perception

The sensory organs provide the raw data or stimulation to the brain, but this physical information must be translated into a psychological perception of the world. However, whether one's perceptions of life are derived solely from the physical sensations received through the sensory system or from one's knowledge, experiences and expectations of life is an important issue. Perception derived solely from physical sensations is referred to as direct or *bottom-up processing*, whereas perception derived from knowledge and learning is referred to as indirect or *top-down processing* (Gross, 1996). If one's interpretations of sensory data result mainly from education and experience of events, this is referred to as *empiricism*, whereas if they are dependent on genetically derived abilities, it is referred to as *nativism*. These two dimensions of perception, which are illustrated in Table 4.1, can give rise to four potential explanations of cognitive perception, although only three of these explanations are relevant in this context. These three explanations, which were described by Gregory, Gibson and the 'Gestalt group' of psychologists, are considered further.

Table 4.1 Typology of perception

Process of interpreting sensory data	Source of perception	
	Physical senses	Knowledge
Experience (empiricism)	Gibson's theory	Gregory's theory
Innate (nativism)	Gestalt theory	–

Gregory's theory

Gregory proposed that it was necessary to go beyond sensory evidence in order to arrive at conclusions about the surrounding environment (Gross, 1996). He referred to perception as an unconscious inference from the information received by the sensory system. Gregory's 'top-down – empiricist' theory is based on interpreting knowledge through experience.

He explained, for example, that although one often sees round shapes as ovals and square shapes as rectangles because of the effects of perspective, one knows (or thinks that one knows) what the shape should be. Therefore one mentally infers or registers the 'correct' shape: this is referred to as *shape and size constancy*. Similarly, one often perceives that objects and information are present (when in fact they are not) simply because one expects them to be present from previous experience. This effect or illusion, which is referred to as *perceptual hypothesis*, is based on one's attempts to reach logical conclusions about the sensory information received. Three examples of how visual information can be misinterpreted are shown in Figure 4.1:

- Illusion (a) appears to show that the line is not straight but is offset as it passes behind the parallel sides of the cylinder.
- Illusion (b) appears to show that there are two triangles present, when in reality there is only one, because certain parts of the three circles and the triangle are missing.
- Illusion (c) appears to show that the upper horizontal line is longer because of the visual perspective effect created by the sloping sides of the triangle.

These simple examples indicate how the human brain can be easily misled in the interpretation of visual information. Perceptual errors of this type can often lead to mistakes in the workplace.

Gibson's theory

Gibson's theory is concerned more with real-life perception than with laboratory-based examples of perception. In real life, one rarely receives sensory information relating to single objects because objects are always seen in a situational context, and one invariably receives multiple sensations at the same time. Gibson's 'bottom-up – empiricist theory' is based on sensory information interpreted through experience, and it encompasses the fact that one usually receives multiple images that form a 'rich picture'. For example, one learns to respond to a combination of sights, sounds and smells in the workplace, such as a process warning light, a fire alarm and a smell of escaping chemicals, to warn one that there is imminent danger.

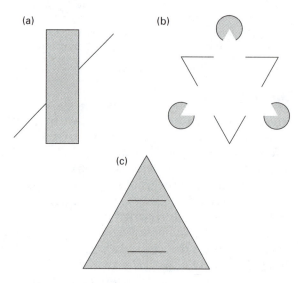

Figure 4.1 Examples of perceptual illusions

An important aspect of this theory is understanding the difference between 'seeing' and 'seeing as'. This relates to the fact that, although one sees something in one way, the image may be seen and interpreted in a different way because of previous experience. Gross (1996) summarised this point by quoting:

> What you see when you see a thing depends upon what the thing you see is. But what you see the thing as depends upon what you know about what you are seeing.
>
> Gross (1996: 215)

Perception described as 'seeing as' is almost always ambiguous, as the interpretation of what one sees is dependent on what one has seen in the past. The classic example of this is described as the Ames 'distorted room', which is constructed in such a way that it deliberately distorts an observer's perception of what they see. A simplified version of the 'distorted room' is shown in Figure 4.2.

Two drums (A and B) of the same size are shown in a closed room that is constructed in a distorted perspective. If someone viewed the two drums in the room through an observation window, he or she would reach one of two conclusions depending on their previous experience. If the observer did not know the types of drum in the room, their experience would tell them to accept that the room was normal and, therefore, drum A was much larger than drum B. However, if the observer knew the types of drum in the room and, therefore, knew that they were both the same size, they would conclude that the room was a distorted shape. The point of this example is that it illustrates a weakness in the Gibson theory of perception, because it is possible for one's experiences to lead to an incorrect perception of a real situation. This is an important point when considering the impact of human factors on accident causation.

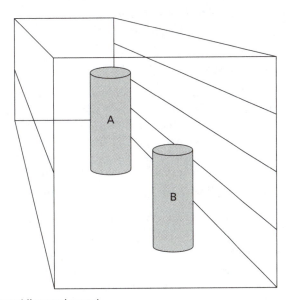

Figure 4.2 The Ames 'distorted room'

Gestalt theory

Gregory's theory of perception is dependent on the inferences that individuals make about their environment, whereas Gibson's theory is dependent on an individual's perceptions remaining constant. The Gestalt 'bottom-up – nativist' theory is based on one's *organisation* of the sensory data received, and it considers that the perception of the whole object is greater than the perception of the individual components. A simple example used to illustrate this point is the square. A square can be perceived as four lines, of equal length, joined together at right angles. However, a square conveys much more than this to an observer because it also has inherent properties of squareness. This effect is referred to as an *emergent property* and leads to the idea of *perceptual grouping*.

Gestalt theory argues that one does not perceive individual objects as a collection of individual sensations of sight, sound and smell, but as organised patterns or configurations. The principle of organisation is that one then perceives things as, for example, symmetrical, uniform and stable. This is achieved through a number of parameters:

- *proximity*, whereby elements that appear close together, in space or time, are perceived to belong together as a group even if they are not obviously similar;
- *closure*, whereby incomplete elements are finished in order to see complete elements that are then more easily perceived;
- *continuity and symmetry*, whereby elements are seen as a group rather than as the individual elements;
- *similarity*, whereby similar elements are perceived to belong together rather than as individual elements;
- *figure–ground*, whereby some elements are more prominent than others, so that the prominent element becomes the main focus of attention and the other elements become background information; and
- *part–whole relationship*, whereby the properties of individual elements are quite different from the properties of the whole product.

Perceptual set

In any environment, the brain receives an enormous amount of information from the sensory organs. These data are too much for the brain to cope with at any one time, and in many cases much of the information is not relevant to the activities being carried out at the same time. One therefore needs to limit the information that is acknowledged and processed by the brain at any moment in time to those aspects that are relevant. This process is referred to as *perceptual set*, which indicates a state of perceptual readiness to deal with situations that may arise (Gross, 1996).

The concept of perceptual set is applied in two ways: first, in the way that one has preconceived ideas or expectations that focus one's attention on particular aspects of the sensory information, i.e. as a *selector* of information; second, in the way that one knows how to react and deal with information, i.e. as an *interpreter* of information. Several parameters influence one's perceptual set, including parameters related to the individual and to the sensations received. Contributing parameters to perceptual set are illustrated in Figure 4.3.

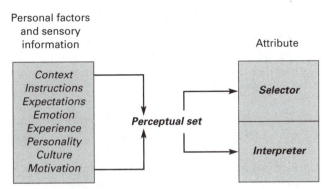

Figure 4.3 Relationship between personal factors and sensory information, perceptual set and attributes

It can now be appreciated how personality, behaviour and organisational and social culture, which were discussed in the previous chapter, can impact on and influence one's perceptions to a significant extent.

Risk perception

It is necessary to move from the general ideas and theories of human perception and how individuals gather and interpret sensory information to the specific subject of risk perception. In this context it is important to understand how sensory information relating to risk situations is interpreted. The most common theory of risk perception is referred to as *knowledge theory*, which implies that people perceive things or situations to be dangerous because they know (or think they know) that they are dangerous. If this were correct then people's actions and views would agree with their knowledge of the risks. Risk perception can also be discussed within *personality theory*, which identifies whether individuals have risk-averse or risk-taking behaviours; with *economic theory*, which is based on the premise that taking greater risks may produce greater rewards; with *political theory*, which holds that personal, organisational and political self-interests define risk perceptions; and with *cultural theory*, which proposes that what hazards individuals or groups fear, and how much they fear them, defines their perceptions of risk.

The study of perception and how the human mind engages risk has been a dominant theme in psychology within the context of *cognition*. Cognition is the mental process by which knowledge is acquired through perception, reasoning and intuition. Psychologists treat risk as a real and objective entity that is amenable to quantitative analysis. Psychologists have therefore tried to understand risks either by isolating and studying an aspect of the phenomenon in laboratory experiments, or by collecting and analysing data through social surveys. This type of research attempted to measure a 'perceived risk' against a 'calibrated or actual risk' within populations of individuals. Three common psychological theories of perception are the *cognitive* or *decision-making, psychometric* and *mental models* approaches.

Cognitive or decision-making approach

Kahneman and Tversky (1979) ascertained that the probability of people making rational choices was not related to logical decision-making. Lopes (1987) extended this idea and considered what motivated people into making certain choices and considered the context within which these decisions were made. This led to the identification of risk-averse and risk-seeking behaviours among different groups of people. The disadvantage of using laboratory-based risk perception studies of this type, however, is that they often have little relevance to real-life risk perceptions or the resultant levels of acceptable or tolerable risk that individuals are prepared to take. In addition, laboratory-based studies cannot take into account the wide range of hazards and risks encountered in real life, or the relative importance that individuals attach to these different hazards and risks.

Psychometric approach

Psychometric studies use a range of psychometric scales in order to produce quantified measures of the perceived risk associated with a variety of hazards within a population. Psychometric approaches to risk have attempted to consider qualitative characteristics of hazards and to measure the extent to which people perceive that particular risks would result in fatalities. Lichtenstein *et al.* (1978) studied how educated non-experts assessed the fatality rates associated with a number of known hazards, ranging from natural events to diseases. The experimental results, which were plotted against the known fatality rates for the hazards, showed that subjects had a tendency to overestimate the fatality rates for low-frequency risks, such as vaccinations and natural disasters, and to underestimate the fatality rates for high-frequency hazards, such as heart disease and cancer. It has subsequently been questioned whether this type of research demonstrated the public's confusion about risks from different hazards, because the views expressed depended heavily on whether the questions were framed in a positive or a negative way (Fischhoff, 1990). The benefit of psychometric studies, however, is that they have demonstrated the complexity of the factors that could influence risk perception amongst the public.

Mental models approach

Concerns about the need to consider the more qualitative dimensions of risk led some theorists to adopt the mental models approach, which explains how individuals explain events within their knowledge, experience, attitudes and beliefs. The approach was based on both decision-making and psychometric theories and aimed to improve the effectiveness of risk communication strategies for those people who needed to make informed choices about specific risks by considering and comparing lay and expert understandings of a particular hazard. Rich pictures or influence diagrams were constructed from both public and experts' views, and these were used to illustrate the differences in the perceived and known risks from hazards. The mental models approach has been criticised in a number of ways. For example, it has been argued that the interview techniques would not be sensitive enough to elicit the whole context within which subjects viewed a particular hazard, and no account was taken of the political and economic issues surrounding the examples used. This approach was significant, however, because it highlighted the contribution that social issues make to people's perceptions of risk.

Situation versus individual

An important debate about risk perception is whether the main determinant of risk perception, and thereafter risk behaviour, is the individual or the situation in which the individual operates. One argument proposed is that risk behaviour is defined by the situational context rather than by the individual's perceptions of the risk. Although it has generally been accepted that individual differences and situations interact to influence risk behaviour, Weyman and Kelly (1999) note:

> Unfortunately, this conclusion has not been carried over into the majority of studies of perception of risk, or risk-taking behaviour, most of which, although frequently acknowledging the influence of the other, effectively remain entrenched within one or other paradigm.
>
> Weyman and Kelly (1999: 53)

Research in this area has also been criticised because, although authors claimed to be measuring correlations between personality and risk-taking behaviour, they were in fact often measuring risk perception or attitudes to risk. The situation-versus-individual discussion is also related to the question of 'accident prone' individuals. There is some evidence that extroverts have more accidents than introverts, but this may also be related to the different risk perceptions of extroverts and the possibility that extroverts are more likely to report accidents than introverts. Studies that report that a small number of individuals have a disproportionate number of accidents are really only reporting a statistical phenomenon rather than providing an answer to the issue of accident proneness (Uitenbroek, 1995).

Factors affecting risk perception

Risk perception is not an absolute measure. Most measures and commentary on risk perception therefore relate to comparative views of risk – in other words, determining whether one risk is perceived to be greater or less than another risk. However, risk perception involves wider issues than just measured values of risk.

> Risk perception involves people's beliefs, attitudes, judgements and feelings as well as the wider social or cultural values and dispositions that people adopt, towards hazards and their benefits.
>
> Royal Society (1992: 89)

Measures of risk perception, however, are of paramount importance to the subject of risk communication, which involves communicating to stakeholders the relative significance of one risk compared with another. Fischhoff *et al.* (1978) and Lichtenstein *et al.* (1978) utilised a wide range of psychometric scaling procedures in order to obtain quantitative measures of risk perception. Their approaches included magnitude estimation, numerical rating scales, attitude questionnaires, word association and scenario generation techniques. The use of these techniques together is referred to as the *psychometric paradigm*, which assumes that people are capable of providing meaningful answers to, sometimes quite difficult, questions about risk. For example, how valid are questions such as 'How do you rate the risk of a fatality from an earthquake in Ecuador with the risk of a fatality from a motor accident on an autobahn in Germany?' An important assumption of the psychometric paradigm approach is that risk assessment is subjective because risk is not a tangible thing. One cannot see risk, because it exists only in the minds of those people who developed the concept in order to explain and deal with the hazards and problems existing in life. Qualitative and so-called quantitative risks both depend on a subjective assessment of risk. In addition, risk means different things to different people. Slovic (1992) outlined the complexities of the psychometric paradigm, but provided a usable definition of the term:

> In sum the psychometric paradigm encompasses a theoretical framework that assumes that risk is subjectively defined by individuals who may be influenced by a wide array of psychological, social, institutional and cultural factors. The paradigm assumes that, with appropriate design of survey instruments, many of these factors and their interrelationships can be quantified and modelled in order to illuminate the responses of individuals and their societies to the hazards that confront them.
>
> Slovic (1992: 20)

If the psychometric paradigm is used for risk perception research, there are three parameters that must be considered when defining the experimental design:

- the hazards or risk factors;
- the sample population that is providing information on the risks; and
- the dimensions of the risk used to assess the hazards.

Using people's judgements to measure risk generates significantly more problems than the much simpler option of using accident statistics to compare risks, because risk means different things to different people. For this reason, risk was often left undefined in order to encapsulate an individual's own understanding of risk (Slovic, 1992). One problem associated with using scales in psychometric assessments is that the scales are predefined by the researcher, and the subjects cannot therefore comment on the issues that are of specific importance to them. Nevertheless, certain qualitative parameters or dimensions of risk have been reported to have a negative effect on the public's perceptions of technological risks, such as 'kill size', 'fates worse than death' and 'involuntary risks' (Green and Brown, 1978a, 1978b; Otway and von Winterfeldt, 1982) (Table 4.2).

Table 4.2 Attributes having a negative influence on risk perception

Negative attributes of risk

Involuntary exposure to risk
Lack of personal control over outcomes
Uncertainty about probabilities or consequences of exposure
Lack of personal experience with the risk (fear of the unknown)
Difficulty in imagining risk exposure
Effects of exposure delayed in time
Genetic effects of exposure (threatens future generations)
Infrequent but catastrophic accidents ('kill size')
Benefits not highly visible
Benefits go to others (inequity)
Accidents caused by human failure rather than natural causes

Source: Pidgeon *et al.* (1992: Table 2;101)

Unknown and dread risks

Slovic presented many examples of the use of the psychometric paradigm for assessing risk perception (e.g. Slovic *et al.*, 1984; Slovic, 1987; Slovic *et al.*, 1987) and identified two strong factors referred to as 'dread/non-dread' and 'known/unknown' risks (Slovic, 1992). The key parameters or characteristics associated within these dimensions are presented in Table 4.3.

Table 4.3 Characteristics or parameters associated with the 'dread/non-dread' and 'known/unknown' risk perception factors

Risk factor	Characteristics associated with risk factor
Dread / non-dread	Feared / not feared
	Uncontrollable / controllable
	Global consequences / non-global consequences
	Fatal consequences / non-fatal consequences
	Risks not equitably distributed / risks equitably distributed
	Catastrophic consequences / non-catastrophic consequences
	High risk to future generations / low risk to future generations
	Not easily mitigated / easily reduced
	Risk level increasing / risk level decreasing
	Involuntary exposure to risk / voluntary exposure to risk
Known / unknown	Observable risk / non-observable risk
	Risk known to those exposed / risk unknown to those exposed
	Immediate consequences / delayed consequences
	Risk known to science / risk unknown to science

However, some of these aspects should not be translated simply into the working environment because, for example, as Adams and Thompson (2002) succinctly pointed out:

In the workplace, the distinction between voluntary and involuntary risk is frequently blurred, especially in intrinsically hazardous occupations such as fishing, scaffolding, deep-sea diving, or construction. The job can be seen to impose risks, but except in conditions of slavery or dire economic necessity, the job is voluntarily chosen.

Adams and Thompson (2002: 5)

The 'dread/non-dread' and 'known/unknown' factors were also presented on two orthogonal axes, which allowed four areas of risk perception to be identified. The positions that individual hazards occupied within this factor space were found to be dependent on laypeople's risk perceptions and attitudes towards the hazards (Figure 4.4).

The higher that a hazard scored on the dread and unknown risk dimensions, the more the individual desired that the risks associated with the hazard should be reduced through regulation, because respondents felt that these risks were too great to be left to individuals or organisations to self-regulate. However, hazards that were rated with high non-dread and known risk values were considered not to require political intervention, because respondents felt that these issues did not represent significant risks, and therefore the general public should be allowed to make up their own minds about the risks.

Experts' perceptions of the risks associated with the same hazards did not follow the factors identified for laypeople; instead experts appeared to view riskiness in the same way as the 'expected annual mortality values' for the hazards (Slovic *et al.*, 1979). The different foundations identified for the basis of risk perception between the public and the experts may explain the fundamental differences in their concerns about risk. They also go some way towards explaining why there are often difficulties for the two groups in reaching compromise decisions on risk issues.

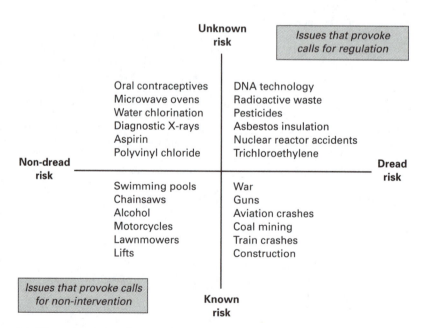

Figure 4.4 'Known' and 'dread' dimensions of risk perception and their relationships with the regulation of hazards

Affiliation bias

One's views on risk are quite likely to be influenced by factors such as familiarity and self-interest, and this can lead to either an understatement or an overstatement of the risks associated with a hazard. This issue is referred to as *affiliation bias*. In most developed countries there are official bodies that regulate risks and establish the appropriate standards associated with the hazards. Unfortunately, the public often do not believe the conclusions and proposals made by these 'independent' bodies, as they often perceive them to be working for the industries that they are meant to be regulating. This leads to conflict between the public, pressure groups, government and industrialists, with little chance of the various factions reaching agreement. Pidgeon *et al.* (2003) identified that, from a range of desirable attributes, the public rated 'acting in the public interest', 'accountability', effectiveness' and 'openness' as the most desirable attributes for risk regulators.

This situation is illustrated by the work of Slovic (1992) on the use and regulation of new chemicals. He addressed the issue of risk perception and the toxicological properties of chemicals through the following parameters:

- understanding the issue of toxicity;
- relationship between dose/exposure and risk;
- use of animal tests to determine human risk;
- attitudes towards the use of chemicals; and
- interpretation of toxicological evidence.

There were, unsurprisingly, differences of opinion between laypeople and toxicologists on the acceptability and the effects of small quantities of toxic chemicals. The public were generally averse to exposures to any level of a toxic substance, whereas toxicologists were more likely to take into account dose–effect relationships in their views. In addition, there were divergent opinions among the toxicologists about the validity of some test results on new chemicals. This, together with the ease with which stakeholders could obtain the appropriate 'expert support' for their own interpretations of the risks, may be a major cause of the public's distrust of experts' views on risk. An additional concern raised by this research was the affiliation bias expressed by toxicologists who were working directly with industry. This group tended to express a more 'benign' view of the risks associated with new chemicals than the views expressed by toxicologists working for government or academia. Of greatest concern was the propensity for toxicologists working with industry to be more confident of the validity of test results unless they showed a link with cancer, in which case they changed their views on the validity of the results obtained (Slovic, 1992).

Cognitive dissonance

Cognitive dissonance relates to how individuals change their attitudes to certain issues if two or more pieces of information or views are in apparent disagreement. Individuals usually deal with this in one of three ways: ignore one or more pieces of the evidence, change one or more of the views, or introduce an additional factor that explains the differences. Ball (1998) discussed this issue specifically in relation to sports activities in order to understand why individuals voluntarily take on high-risk sports activities, even though they are aware of the high risks involved. Cognitive dissonance goes some way towards explaining why, under certain circumstances, individuals in work-based environments will also undertake unsafe actions in order to complete a task, even when they know they are high risk, contravene accepted procedures, and do not accord with common sense.

Cultural theory and risk perception

Some researchers claim that there are differences in the way in which risk perceptions are developed between individuals and groups, and that risk perceptions correlate with social and cultural groups. Individual differences in risk perceptions are assumed to be dependent on variations in individuals' personality traits, which are considered to be stable with time. Group differences, however, are considered to be more dependent on current affiliations and the views held within social groups: social groups may have some long-standing beliefs and attitudes, but others may change with time.

Some results from psychometric assessments produced evidence of correlations between risk perception and culture, although the results were sometimes ambiguous. Independent factors that affect a particular issue are categorised as either proximal or distal variables. *Proximal* variables are closely related to the issue being assessed, whereas *distal* variables are less closely related to the issue. Unsurprisingly, correlations between the issues and proximal variables were usually stronger than the correlations with distal variables. Where cultural theory (a distal variable) was used to explain risk perception, the research results presented some theoretical difficulties. First, while one may intuitively expect a social group to influence risk perception, cultural groups – which are claimed to be stable in their views and attitudes – are also being correlated with risk perception, which is regarded as a changeable variable. Second, individuals may be members of several different social groups, such as family, work and leisure groups, and because each of these social groups may have different views on an issue, it is difficult to understand how an individual's risk perceptions may change as he or she moves from one of these social groups to another. Early work on the testing of correlations between cultural theory and risk perception (Wildavsky and Dake, 1990; Dake, 1991) compared respondents' perceptions on a series of social concerns, such as technology, environment, war, deviance and economic issues, with factors related to the respondents' knowledge, personality, political orientation and cultural biases. As a result of this research the authors observed:

> Cultural biases provide predictions of risk perceptions and risk-taking preferences that are more powerful than measures of knowledge and personality and at least as predictive as political orientation.
>
> Wildavsky and Dake (1990: 50)

This and other research (Brenot *et al.*, 1996; Peters and Slovic, 1996) identified what were claimed to be strong correlations between risk perception and culture.

However, the correlation coefficients of these reported 'strong correlations' ranged from 0.05 to 0.40. Sjoberg (1997), in particular, questioned the validity of many of these proposed relationships between risk perception and cultural theory. Sjoberg (1997) concluded from a reanalysis of published data, together with his own new results, that there were generally only very weak, but occasionally significant, correlations obtained between risk perception and measures related to cultural theory.

Risk homeostasis and risk compensation

Although theories of physical and cognitive perception, relationships between perception and risk perception and factors affecting an individual's risk perceptions have been discussed, none of the issues actually describes why people take risks. Adams (1995) comments:

> Human fallibility and the propensity to take risks are commonly asserted to be the root causes of accidents. How should responsibility for accidents be shared between these causes? The safety literature favours, overwhelmingly, human error as the cause of accidents. No one wants an accident, therefore, it is argued, if one occurs it must be a mistake, a miscalculation, a lapse of concentration or simple ignorance of the facts about a dangerous situation.
>
> Adams (1995: 16)

In the previous chapter, issues related to an individual's motivation and behaviour were discussed in the context of needs, personality and cultural theory. However, if an individual placed a high value on future life, he or she should be more likely to adopt safer behaviours now in order to gain from perceived future benefits (Bjorgvinsson and Wilde, 1996). A number of theories have been developed, particularly in the context of road traffic accidents, in order to explain why people take risks. Two models of risk-taking behaviour, which are referred to as risk homeostasis and risk compensation, are discussed here.

Risk homeostasis

Risk homeostasis is based on a *constant-risk hypothesis* (Wilde, 1982; Fuller, 1986), which postulates that individuals will always work towards a defined level of risk irrespective of the control measures put in place in order to reduce levels of risk. In broad terms, individuals define their own overall acceptable level or *target level* of risk. This target level of risk will be influenced by an individual's personality, needs and behaviour, and will be based on the individual's assessment of personal benefits and costs, of which money is only one of many utility factors. The central tenet of the risk homeostasis model is the ability of an individual to act as a risk comparator within what is essentially a cost–benefit analysis process. Individuals compare their target levels of risk with the risk levels associated with each of the options available to them to achieve the desired output. Their decisions are moderated by their perceptions of the risks involved (Figure 4.5). The application of the risk homeostasis theory outside the road transport environment, in which it was developed, is less well defined (Hoyes, 1994; Trimpop, 1996).

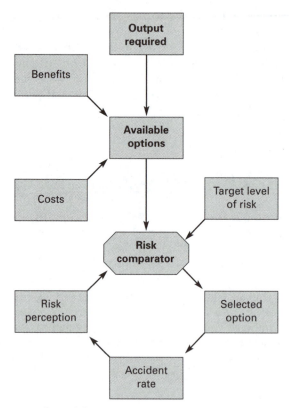

Figure 4.5 Risk homeostasis model

The risk homeostasis model should not be related to each risk environment in isolation, because individuals will decide on an acceptable (or tolerable) level of risk that is spread across a number of activities within a range of risk environments. Therefore a reduction in the level of risk exposure in one area may be compensated for by an increase in the level of risk in another area. For example, if an individual who desires a high level of risk works in an environment where risks are controlled to a very low level, he or she may decide to compensate for this through participation in high-risk sports activities. It is important not to underestimate the importance of personal estimates of costs and benefits in the decision-making process. A high target level of work-based risk may be tolerated if the alternative is for the operation to be closed down, with a loss of employment for the individual. Similarly, rewards for risk-averse behaviour may reduce an individual's target level of risk but, on the other hand, high rewards for achieving production targets may induce risk-taking behaviour.

Risk compensation

The risk compensation model, which was originally developed by Wilde (1976), was adapted by Adams (1985, 1988) and presented as the *risk thermostat* (Adams, 1995). Adams (1995) postulated that:

- everyone has a propensity to take risks within appropriate limits;
- the propensity to take risks varies from one individual to another, and the level of risk will depend on their personality, needs and motivational requirements;
- the propensity to take risks is influenced by the potential level of the rewards and the losses arising from risk-taking behaviours;
- individuals' perceptions of risk are influenced by their own and other people's experiences of accident losses;
- individuals' risk-taking decisions and behaviour represent a balancing act in which their perceptions of risk are balanced against their propensity to take risks; and
- benefits and losses arise from an individual taking risks, and the more risks an individual takes the greater the potential level of benefits and costs.

The interactions between these factors are summarised within the risk thermostat model (Adams, 1995) presented in Figure 4.6.

Adams (1995) emphasised, however, that the risk thermostat model was a conceptual model rather than a mathematical or operational model, and used it only in order to explain individuals' risk-taking behaviour. Adams (1995) likened the risk thermostat to a central heating system. The risk thermostat is set to the risk requirements of the individual, and – like the central heating thermostat – this level will vary from one individual to another and from one group to another. Where an individual's needs and personality give more weight to the benefits obtained from an action, the individual will be more prepared to take risks, whereas if they place more importance on minimising the costs arising from actions, they will be more risk-averse. In a similar way to the risk homeostasis theory, the risk thermostat should not be considered in one environment in isolation because it is made up of complex interactions involving a range of hazards, people, groups, organisations and countries. The magnitude or influence that risks from these different hazards and groups will have on an individual's risk thermostat will vary.

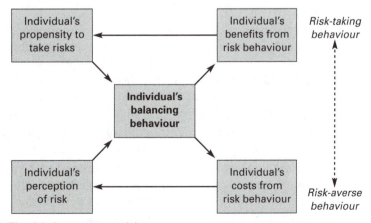

Figure 4.6 The risk thermostat model
Source: Adapted from Adams (1995)

Although the two models summarise how an individual's risk-taking behaviour is dependent on the costs and benefits accruing from risk-taking behaviour, the models are equally applicable for understanding and explaining corporate and governmental risk-taking behaviours. However, it should always be acknowledged that an organisation's risk-taking behaviour might not match that of its employees or the regulators. Understanding what issues influence a decision-making process enables more effective risk mitigation procedures to be developed at the organisational, national and international levels.

In understanding the role of risk perception in risk management, one should again consider the critical views expressed by Richard Feynman (1985: 283–4), who summarised his feelings towards a discussion on the ethics of equality as follows: 'Each of us talked about what we thought the "ethics of equality" was, from our own point of view, without paying any attention to the other guy's point of view.'

These sentiments also apply to discussions about risk perception, because each person's views of risk are equally valid as an individual's views of risk represent the reality of their own situation. Discussions about differences in risk perception should therefore relate only to the grounds on which these individual perceptions are based.

Summary

- This chapter has discussed the physical and cognitive components of perception. Physical perceptions, or sensations, are recorded by the body's sensory system and these signals are then interpreted within the brain in order to provide the psychological or cognitive perception.

- The human brain analyses and reacts to the sensory signals received using a combination of knowledge and experience. The concept of perceptual set explains how an individual is able to isolate and react to the most important signals received by the sensory system.

- Psychometric variables may be used in order to provide measures of an individual's risk perception. Individuals have a tendency to underestimate the levels of high-frequency risks and to overestimate the levels of low-frequency risks. Risk perceptions may be dependent on the levels of 'dread' and 'unknown' risk factors associated with hazards.

- Individuals' risk perceptions may be biased by self-interest factors, such as affiliation bias and cognitive dissonance, and there is some evidence to suggest that risk perceptions are also influenced by social affiliations and cultures.

- Risk-taking behaviours may be determined by a propensity for everyone to accept and take risks within acceptable levels. These risk-taking behaviours may be influenced by the individual's perceptions of the personal costs and benefits associated with the behaviours.

Issues for review and discussion

- Consider how physical perceptions affect an individual's behaviour.

- Assess where you would place the hazards of mountain climbing, driving, flu injections and genetically modified food on the perception dimensions of dread/non-dread and unknown/known risks.

- Consider which of the sensory organs makes the greatest contribution to health and safety at work.

- Review whether the risks associated with sport are affected by cognitive dissonance on the part of participants.

- Assess, within the context of the risk thermostat model, whether you exhibit risk-averse or risk-taking behaviour.

References

Adams, J. (1985) *Risk and Freedom: The Record of Road Safety Regulation.* London: Transport Publishing Projects.

Adams, J. (1988) Evaluating the effectiveness of road safety measures. *Traffic Engineering and Control*, **29** (June), 344–352.

Adams, J. (1995) *Risk.* London: UCL Press.

Adams, J. and Thompson, M. (2002) *Taking Account of Societal Concerns about Risk: Framing the Problem.* Sudbury: HSE Books.

Ball, J.D. (1998) Comparing the magnitudes of risks and benefits. *Sports Exercise and Injury*, **4**, 174–182.

Bjorgvinsson, T. and Wilde, G.J.S. (1996) Risky health and safety habits related to perceived value of the future. *Safety Science*, **22**, 27–33.

Brenot, J., Bonnefous, S. and Mays, C. (1996) Cultural theory and risk perception: validity and utility explored in the French context. *Radiation Protection Dosimetry*, **68**, 239–243.

Dake, K. (1991) Orienting dispositions in the perception of risk. *Journal of Cross-cultural Psychology*, **22**, 61–82.

Feynman, R.P. (1985) *'Surely You're Joking Mr Feynman!' Adventures of a Curious Character.* London: Norton.

Fischhoff, B. (1990) Psychology and public policy: a tool or toolmaker? *American Psychologist*, **45**, 647–653.

Fischhoff, B., Slovic, P., Lichtenstein, S., Read, S. and Combs, B. (1978) How safe is safe enough? A psychometric study of attitudes towards technological risks and benefits. *Policy Sciences*, **9**, 127–152.

Fuller, R.G.C. (1986) Reflections on risk homeostasis theory. In: B. Brehmer, H. Jungermann, P. Lourens and G. Sevon (eds), *New Directions in Research on Decision Making*, 263–273. New York: Elsevier Science.

Green, C.H. and Brown, R.A. (1978a) *Life Safety: What is it and How Much is it Worth?* CP52/78. Borehamwood: Building Research Establishment.

Green, C.H. and Brown, R.A. (1978b) Counting lives. *Journal of Occupational Accidents*, **2**, 55–70.

Gross, R. (1996) *Psychology: The Science of Mind and Behaviour*. London: Hodder & Stoughton.

Hoyes, T.W. (1994) Risk homeostasis theory: beyond transportational research. *Safety Science*, **17**, 77–89.

Kahneman, D. and Tversky, A. (1979) Prospect theory: an analysis of decision under risk. *Econometrica*, **47**(2), 263–291.

Lichtenstein, S., Slovic, P., Fischoff, B., Layman, M. and Combs, B. (1978) Judged frequency of lethal events. *Journal of Experimental Psychology: Human Learning and Memory*, **4**, 551–578.

Lopes, L.L. (1987) Between hope and fear: the psychology of risk. *Advances in Experimental Social Psychology*, **20**, 255–295.

Otway, H.J. and von Winterfeldt, D. (1982) Beyond acceptable risk: on the social acceptability of technologies. *Policy Sciences*, **14**, 247–256.

Peters, E. and Slovic, P. (1996) The role of affect and worldviews as orienting dispositions in the perception and acceptance of nuclear power. *Journal of Applied Social Psychology*, **26**, 1427–1453.

Pidgeon, N., Walls, J., Weyman, A. and Horlick-Jones, T. (2003) *Perceptions of Trust in the Health and Safety Executive as a Risk Regulator*. Sudbury: HSE Books.

Pidgeon *et al.* (1992) *Risk: analysis, perception and management*. London: The Royal Society.

Sjoberg, L. (1997) Explaining risk perception: an empirical evaluation of cultural theory. *Risk Decision and Policy*, **2**(2), 113–130.

Slovic, P. (1987) Perception of risk. *Science*, **236**, 280–285.

Slovic, P. (1992) Perceptions of risk: reflections on the psychometric paradigm. In: S. Krimsky and D. Golding (eds) *Social Theories of Risk*, 117–152. London: Praeger.

Slovic, P., Fischhoff, B. and Lichtenstein, S. (1979) Rating the risks. *Environment*, **21**(3), 14–20, 36–39.

Slovic, P., Lichtenstein, S. and Fischhoff, B. (1984) Modelling the societal impact of fatal accidents. *Management Science*, **30**, 464–474.

Slovic, P., McGregor, D. and Krauss, N.N. (1987) Perception of risk from automobile safety defects. *Accident Analysis and Prevention*, **19**, 359–373.

Trimpop, R.M. (1996) Risk homeostasis theory: problems of the past and promises for the future. *Safety Science*, **22**, 119–130.

Uitenbroek, D.G. (1995) The mathematical relationship between the number of events in which people are injured and the number of people injured. *British Journal of Sports Medicine*, **29**, 126–128.

Weyman, A.K. and Kelly, C.J. (1999) *Risk Perception and Risk Communication: A Review of Literature*. Contract Research Report (248/1999). Sudbury: HSE Books.

Wildavsky, A. and Dake, K. (1990) Theories of risk perception: who fears what and why? *Daedalus*, **119**(4), 41–60.

Wilde, G. (1976) The risk compensation theory of accident causation and its practical consequences for accident prevention. Paper presented at the annual meeting of the Osterreichische Gesellschaft für Unfallchirurgies, Salzburg.

Wilde, G.J.S. (1982) The theory of risk homeostasis: implications for safety and health. *Risk Analysis*, **2**, 209–225.

Risk communication

Don't ask me nothing about nothing,
I just might tell you the truth.

– Bob Dylan, 'Outlaw blues' (1965)

Chapter contents

- Introduction
- Communication
- The communication process
- The risk communication process
- Ranking and comparing risks
- Framing effects
- Social amplification of risk
- Trust and risk communication

Introduction

Risk communication assumed a significant role in the overall process of risk management as the need for governments and other organisations to inform stakeholders about issues of risk increased. The Royal Society (1992) commented:

> At first sight the task of communication might appear trivial given that most of us have little difficulty in conducting day-to-day interaction with colleagues, friends and associates. However, doing this effectively with diverse audiences, who possibly all hold different values and frames of reference with respect to the problem, where multiple feedback channels and competing messages (some out of our control) are available, and where interpretation is dependent upon subtle cultural factors, sets a more challenging task.
>
> The Royal Society (1992: 119)

Research has shown that the views expressed by 'risk experts' and 'the public' about risk issues were not only different but also often incompatible. Whereas scientists concentrated on 'quantified' estimates of risk, the public were more concerned about their 'innate feelings' or perceptions about risk issues. Bridging the gap between these opposing views of risk is the domain of risk communication. The aims of this chapter are to explain the role of individuals' attitudes in the process of communication and to address a number of specific issues associated with risk communication, such as risk comparisons, framing effects, trust and the social amplification of risk.

Communication

Communication is the general process of transferring information and ideas from one person or organisation to another person or organisation; *persuasive communication* has the specific aim of influencing individual or organisational *attitudes* about the subject being communicated. This process is of great importance in the context of risk management, where it is referred to as *risk communication*.

Attitudes

Although there are no simple, generally accepted definitions of attitude, most definitions have common elements. Allport (1935) considered attitude to be a mental and neural state of readiness that was organised through experience and which exerted a directive or dynamic influence over an individual's response to objects and situations with which it was related. Rokeach (1948) considered attitude to be a learned orientation or disposition towards an object or situation that provided a tendency to respond either favourably or unfavourably to an object or situation. Zimbardo and Leippe (1991) described attitude as an evaluative disposition towards some object. Rosenberg and Hovland (1960), who defined attitudes as a predisposition to respond to stimuli with certain responses, proposed a three-component model of attitudes in order to explain the ways in which individuals responded to stimuli (Figure 5.1).

Individuals and social groups operating within a situational context provide sources of stimuli that impact on an individual's attitudes in three ways, which generate three corresponding types of observable response:

- *Affective responses* are those that indicate how favourably or unfavourably an individual feels about the object or subject being discussed or communicated.
- *Cognitive responses* are those that indicate how objectively an individual views the object or subject being discussed or communicated.
- *Behavioural responses* are those that indicate how an individual intends to respond to the object or subject being discussed or communicated.

The terms 'attitude', 'belief' and 'value' are often used in the same context; however, psychologists generally regard them as having slightly different meanings, with the term 'attitude' often regarded as a mixture of beliefs and values. *Beliefs* describe one's knowledge about a subject, and it is the personal *values* that an individual puts on these beliefs that define his or her attitude towards an issue. Values

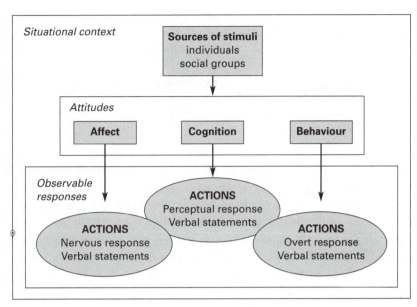

Figure 5.1 Three-component model of attitude illustrating an individual's responses to stimuli
Source: Adapted from Rosenberg and Hovland (1960)

serve two important functions: they provide standards against which to make judgements, and they motivate certain behaviours. Personal beliefs are moderated and attitudes developed about an issue through different types of values:

- *Theoretical values* relate to problem solving and the underlying theory.
- *Aesthetic values* relate to artistic aspects.
- *Political values* relate to national and international dimensions.
- *Economic values* relate to economic dimensions.
- *Social values* relate to social implications.
- *Moral values* relate to religious and moral concerns.

An individual's attitude towards an issue is built up from their personal views about a number of characteristics associated with the issue. Fishbein and Ajzen (1975) developed the *expectancy–value* model of attitudes, which described them as the sum of the expected values for each of the characteristics associated with an issue. Each characteristic is ascribed an 'expectancy' (probability) measure and a 'value' (positive or negative) measure for the outcome:

Measure ($^{I}C_{n}$) of characteristic n associated with issue I

$$= {}^{I}(\text{Expectancy})_{n} \times {}^{I}(\text{Value})_{n}$$

An individual's attitude (^{I}A) towards issue I $\quad = \Sigma\ (^{I}C_{n})$

The theory postulated that individuals would reach 'positive' or 'negative' attitudes towards an issue depending on whether the sum of all the characteristics of the issue was positive or negative. The depth of an individual's positive or negative feelings towards an issue was defined by the magnitude of the sum of the characteristic measures. However, individuals often only took into account one or two major characteristics of an issue when developing their attitudes rather than encompassing the full range of characteristics involved.

Changing people's attitudes and values

Katz (1960) outlined four functions or purposes associated with an individual's attitudes:

- *knowledge function*, whereby one gave meaning and direction to experiential learning – these provided a reference point for assessing future issues;
- *adjustive function*, whereby certain attitudes were displayed because they made one more socially acceptable – even though these attitudes were displayed, the individual might not necessarily believe in them;
- *value-expressive function*, whereby one achieved self-expression through cherished values, such as creating a feeling of personal integrity;
- *ego-defensive function*, whereby one avoided expressing one's ideas and weaknesses about an issue by displaying a different viewpoint.

These functions indicate how some attitudes could be deeply held and might therefore be difficult to change whereas other attitudes, which were less important to the individual, could be more easily influenced and changed. These functions also explain how communication and information can be used to change attitudes, and why different communication approaches would be required for different issues.

In all spheres of modern life, attempts are made to influence and persuade people to do something or to take a particular stance about an issue. All of these attempts are linked to changing people's attitudes about subjects or issues. Attitude change initiatives involve three stages:

- measuring the individual or group's attitudes towards the issue(s) before any attempt is made to change their views;
- implementing an attitude change programme that is related to the issue(s) on which an attitude change is required (this change programme may involve a range of persuasive communication processes, which can be either verbal or non-verbal in format); and
- re-measuring the individual or group's attitudes towards the issue(s) following the persuasive communication programme.

If the desired change in attitudes were achieved then the persuasive communication programme would be deemed to have been successful. However, in order to assess whether these programmes were successful, it would be necessary to have valid measures of individual and group attitudes.

Attitude measurement

Attitude is not a parameter that can be measured directly, because it is an abstract construct; therefore it is necessary to identify appropriate indirect indicators of attitude that can be measured. This is achieved by assuming that people's attitudes are defined by their beliefs and opinions about the subject under investigation. Attitude scales, which normally consist of verbal or written statements about the issues being assessed, assume that every respondent would ascribe the same meaning to the statements. Responses to attitude questionnaires are frequently analysed by exploratory or confirmatory factor analysis, in order to identify or confirm common themes. The Likert, semantic differential and Stapel scales provide three examples of indirect attitude measurements.

Likert scale

Likert scales provide measures of how closely individuals agree with different statements about a common theme, such as health and safety management. The Likert scale requires respondents to indicate whether they *strongly agree, agree, neither agree nor disagree, disagree* or *strongly disagree* with a series of statements. These Likert scales are sometimes also numbered in order to convey the concept of a graduated scale so that the data can then be treated as interval data, as this would allow a higher level of statistical analysis of the results. The Likert scale is one of the most commonly used scales in attitude measurements, because it provides statistically reliable data, and the attitude questionnaires are easy to construct. An example of the format used with the Likert scale is:

Statement	Strongly agree 1	Agree 2	Neither agree nor disagree 3	Disagree 4	Strongly disagree 5
All accidents in my organisation are reported to the manager.				X	
I am aware of my health and safety responsibilities.	X				
Health and safety training is provided for all new employees.			X		

Likert scales are sometimes criticised because respondents may not appreciate whether the view of 'neither agree nor disagree' is a view of neutrality, a 'don't know' response, or a genuine view somewhere between 'agree' and 'disagree'. A mid-point average score for all respondents can indicate not only a neutral or undecided viewpoint but also the presence of strongly polarised views, as views of 'strongly agree' at one extreme and 'strongly disagree' at the other extreme can provide an apparent position of neutrality when averaged.

Semantic differential scale

Semantic differential scales provide a series of measures about different aspects of a single issue. Each respondent marks on a series of semantic differentials (often seven-point scales) where their views fit with respect to the polarised views presented. It has been claimed that factor analysis, of all these bipolar response scales, provides just three general factors for any issue. These have been identified as:

- *activity factor*, such as fast/slow, active/inactive;
- *potency factor*, such as thick/thin, strong/weak;
- *evaluative factor*, such as clean/dirty, pleasant/unpleasant.

An example of the format used with semantic differential scales is:

Statement:	*How do you view the operational health and safety management in your organisation?*							
	1	2	3	4	5	6	7	
Well managed		X						Badly managed
Unimportant					X			Important
Beneficial			X					Non-beneficial

Semantic differential scales sometimes have a tendency to provide extreme views because respondents simply mark the scales at the extreme ends of the scales without considering intermediate levels of response. Although this type of response can also occur with Likert scales, it is more likely to occur in the case of semantic differentials because graded descriptors are not provided between the two extremes.

Stapel scale

Stapel scales again provide a series of measures about different aspects of a single issue. They provide a measure of attitude around central value judgements as respondents must indicate whether their views are positive or negative compared with the central null point.

An example of the format used with Stapel scales is:

Statement:			*How do you view the management of health and safety within your company?*			
+3	+2	+1	Issue	–1	–2	–3
		X	Effective			
			Proactive		X	
	X		Competent			

These scales are often used in order to provide a range of views about an issue, in the same way as the semantic differential scale. However, in this case the respondent is forced to choose a view on either side of the null point, which therefore precludes the choice of a neutral viewpoint.

Bias in attitude measurements

If the attitude survey instrument is not carefully designed, there is always the possibility that respondents' replies may be biased. This issue can be illustrated using Likert scales. The sequence of attitude statements in the survey instrument should be randomised, and statements should be framed in such a way that they present both positive and negative statements, which would anticipate a range of positive and negative views from the respondents. The following pairs of statements, which seek attitude measures of management performance in two areas of health and safety, illustrate the options available for framing the questions, together with the anticipated responses from employees working within a 'good' organisation:

A1: *My organisation ensures safe working conditions exist* (a positive statement anticipating a positive response); and

A2: *My organisation does not ensure safe working conditions exist* (a negative statement anticipating a negative response).

B1: *I sometimes take risks to get the job completed on time* (a positive statement anticipating a negative response); and

B2: *I do not take risks to get the job completed on time* (a negative statement anticipating a positive response).

The communication process

The effectiveness and efficiency of the communication process depends on the level of attention provided to the communicator by the receiver, the perceptual interpretation of the message by the receiver, the situational context in which the information is provided and the trust that the receiver has in the provider of the information. Key elements of this communication process are summarised in Figure 5.2.

Communicator

Key attributes of a communicator are status and credibility, appeal, trust and presentation.

Status and credibility are important because, in general, the more 'expert' a communicator is considered to be the more likely it is that people will be persuaded to change their attitudes about the issue. This can be illustrated by considering the credibility assigned to information provided by mass circulation newspapers compared with information presented in respected scientific journals. The status and credibility of a communicator is only important, however, when the recipient lacks personal information or experience about the issue.

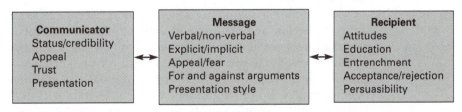

Figure 5.2 Key elements of the communication process

Appeal in a communicator is normally more persuasive than an unappealing communicator, and often an unappealing communicator can create the opposite effect to the desired one. This is especially true for political issues.

Trust is important because, if the perceived intentions or motives of a communicator are in doubt or questionable, then their message is less likely to be believed by the recipients. This will be especially true where the communicator is thought to have a vested interest in the message conveyed.

Presentation is closely linked to the factors of appeal and trust. If the communicator tries to impose his or her views in a way that is perceived to be threatening or aggressive, the recipient will be less inclined to listen to the communicator and may well become antagonistic towards them.

Message

Key attributes of the message are as follows.

Verbal or non-verbal relates to face-to-face communication normally being more effective than written information. With a face-to-face approach, the communicator can respond to any feedback received from the audience during the communication process and modify the message if necessary during the process in order to accommodate the objections or concerns of the recipient(s).

Explicit or implicit relates to whether the message should be presented as a clearly defined statement of facts about the issue or whether the recipient should be left with a requirement to draw out their own conclusions from the message. It is thought that if the recipients work out the final message for themselves, the message becomes more believable. This does, however, assume that the recipients have the ability to reach the desired conclusions about the issue; if they do not, then an explicit message would clearly be preferable from the communicator's point of view.

Appeal or fear is important because, although it is claimed to be possible to frighten people into listening and understanding a message, the audience may not necessarily respond to it. However, if people are told how to mitigate undesirable risks through acceptable, realistic and effective actions, it may be possible to change people's behaviours: this is referred to as *high availability*. There is also claimed to be an inverted 'bath-tub' response curve displayed by recipients to feared issues (Figure 5.3). If people's fears were low, they would not listen to the message, and therefore would take little or no action (Zone A); if the fears were intermediate, people would listen to the message and take appropriate actions (Zone B). However, if the fear levels were very high, people would feel that they could not influence matters, and therefore would ignore the message (Zone C) and take no action.

For-and-against arguments are generally more acceptable to educated audiences, as they appreciate and are influenced by two-sided arguments; less well-educated audiences are more likely to be persuaded by one-sided arguments.

Presentation style is particularly important for presentations involving for-and-against arguments, as it is important to present the arguments in the correct order. Generally, if both arguments were put forward within the same presentation, it would be preferable to put the opposing view first and to close the presentation by refuting this message. Barristers in most courts of law typically

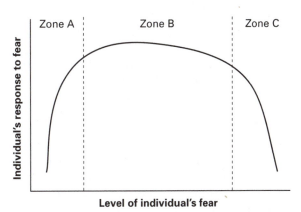

Figure 5.3 The inverted 'bath-tub' response to levels of fear

use this presentation style. In addition, recipients would be influenced by the confidence and sincerity with which the message was presented by the communicator.

Recipient

Key attributes of a recipient are as follows.

Attitudes are important, as it is the generation of a change in a recipient's attitude to a particular issue that is normally the main objective of the communication process.

Education of the recipient has been discussed above in the context of the one- and two-sided argument. In addition, education provides the recipient with the ability to understand more complex arguments and vice versa. The better informed people are about an issue the more difficult it is for a communicator to change their views. Educated people do not normally like to give the impression that they have been easily swayed in their views about an important issue, so they will therefore change their views only following strong arguments.

Entrenchment makes an individual more committed to a particular view about an issue, and therefore it is more difficult to change his or her views. If there are arguments against a particular stance on an issue, resistance will often be stronger than when there are no clear counter-arguments against the views being put forward. When an individual feels that a communicator is exerting unnecessary pressure during a presentation, he or she is more likely to react by taking the opposite view, because the pressure is perceived to be an infringement of one's rights to hold a different viewpoint. This is referred to as the communicator achieving a *negative attitude change*.

Acceptance and rejection describes the situation created where there is a large difference between the views of the recipient and the communicator about an issue: in these circumstances, it is less likely that the communicator will achieve a change in the recipient's attitudes. This is referred to as a situation where the desired attitude change is outside an individual's *latitude of acceptance*. Individuals often treat messages that are outside their latitude of acceptance with greater hostility than they deserve, whereas messages that are within their latitude of acceptance may be more acceptable.

Persuasibility defines the ease with which people can be persuaded to change their attitudes about an issue. People who have a low self-esteem, for example, may be more easily persuaded than those with a high self-esteem. This may be related to a lack of self-confidence in presenting a contradictory viewpoint to someone who appears to be in a position of authority or expertise.

Situation

Informal group situations are often more acceptable for discussions of controversial issues than formal meetings, as the ability to take part in a discussion is often considered to be preferable to a situation where individuals feel they are being lectured to about the issue. Also, in a formal situation, individuals may feel that they are being asked to put themselves in a position where they have to make a public statement about their attitudes on a particular subject or issue – a situation with which they may not feel comfortable.

Communication strategy

An effective communication strategy requires a plan within which targets, timescales and responsibilities have been identified. The plan should address four desired objectives:

- Define the key goals of the communication exercise by identifying what the main issues are and what messages must be communicated.
- Adopt an open and multidisciplinary approach to the communication process by involving, where possible, all stakeholders.
- Include information about the issue from all relevant sources, and avoid presenting an obviously one-sided or biased viewpoint.
- Prepare a balanced presentation for the messages being communicated, and avoid making claims that are clearly difficult to support.

An effective communication strategy should achieve an increased level of knowledge and understanding of the issues among the stakeholders, who should all feel that they have participated in the communication process and have been provided with an opportunity to present their views on the issue.

The risk communication process

Risk communication refers specifically to the process of communicating information about risks with the objective of changing or consolidating the recipients' views about an issue. A barrier to effective risk communication is a view held by many communicators with a vested interest that the risks associated with an issue are minimal and that the public and pressure groups exaggerate the levels of risk. Effective risk communication is more complex than simply a process of education as it depends on the actual and perceived characteristics of the communicators, the messages communicated, and the recipients. If the message were inappropriately presented or framed for the audience and/or the risks discussed, the risk communication process would be unlikely to be successful. A misconception held by many communicators is that any risk communication programme would improve public relations and decrease concerns about risk issues. Unfortunately, even the best risk communication programmes might not allay people's fears about an issue; however, a poor risk communication programme would almost certainly make a bad situation worse. For this reason much of the research carried out on risk communication has concentrated on the problems of communicating risk information and data effectively. The main problems encountered have been related to:

- presenting scientific risk data;
- the competence of risk communicators;
- the media reporting techniques and procedures for communicating risk issues; and
- the public's ability to evaluate and interpret risk data.

There are two classical approaches to risk communication: these are referred to as the one-way and the two-way communication approaches. Early strategies followed the one-way approach, which attempted to provide stakeholders with information about the hazard, the nature of the associated risks and the probability and the likely consequences of potential adverse events. The purpose of this process was to provide stakeholders with *reassurance* about the level of the potential problem; *persuasion* to take an appropriate view or to accept a course of action about a hazard; *awareness* of a potential problem; and *information* about the level of risk associated with a hazard. The one-way approach was often used where scientific or engineering-based communications of risks were involved, because the assumption was made that the public could not be involved in discussions because of their lack of knowledge and understanding of the issues. The main criticism of the one-way approach to risk communication is that it assumes that the communicator is altruistic and has no bias in the presentation of information.

Risk communication is now considered to be more a matter of presenting scientific information through an interactive exchange and an explanation of the risk factors with stakeholders. This two-way approach to risk communication was exemplified by the National Research Council of the National Academy of Sciences (1989), which defined risk communication as 'an interactive process of exchange of information and opinion amongst individuals, groups and institutions. The approach involved multiple messages about the nature of the risk.' They presented four reasons for effective risk communication:

- a desire by government and industry to inform the public;
- a desire by government and industry to counter public opposition;
- a desire by government to present a power-sharing process with the public; and
- a desire to improve the process of regulatory control.

Here risk communication was presented as an interactive process that involved an exchange of views, with an anticipation that a consensus view on the management of the risks could be reached among the stakeholders. An important aspect of this approach was the role that feedback and interaction played in the communication process. In the UK, the Inter-Departmental Liaison Group on Risk Assessment (1998) produced good practice guidance on risk communication for government departments, and highlighted four important aspects of the process:

- Integrate risk communication and risk regulation by engaging those stakeholders affected by risk issues.
- Listen to stakeholders' views and concerns.
- Tailor communications to the issue and the audience.
- Manage the communication process effectively.

Problems encountered with poor risk communication include the generation of unnecessary fears about hazards and their risks, a distrust of experts and government departments, and anger and resentment among those people most affected by the risks. Failure to comment on risk issues, particularly by industry and government, is often interpreted negatively by the public. In the absence of information, the public will often assume the worst-case scenario, as it would be assumed that, if the message were beneficial, the relevant parties would be quite prepared to present their viewpoints.

Concerns about risk among stakeholders often revolve around two aspects of the problem. The first is related to the *level of fear* generated by the hazard, and the second is related to the *emotive impact* raised by the level of risk. It is important to recognise that the emotive impact on stakeholders is not necessarily related to the actual level of harm that may arise from a hazard. Although both of these aspects must be addressed in a risk communication programme, it is important to identify which, if either, of the two components is the dominant issue in each case.

Level of fear

Levels of fear may arise through individuals' concerns for their own or the public's safety. For example, although one may have a genuine fear for anyone living next to a high-hazard chemical plant, the feelings of concern for oneself would be quite different. The communication programme therefore needs to address whom the risks would affect and how the risks would affect them. In these cases it might be helpful to compare the level of risk with other similar sources of risk in order to place the level of the problem into perspective.

Emotive impact

Emotive impact arises from perceptions of how risks might affect an individual rather than the actual level of injury. It is important not to trivialise stakeholders' emotive fears about risks, even when the communicator is confident that the risk levels are minimal, as this approach might harden the audience's views about the issue. The following provides a strategy for addressing the emotive impact of risks:

- Avoid making comparisons with other risks, as this could indicate that the communicator is not addressing the problem but is simply attempting to divert attention from the issue by identifying an issue with an even bigger risk.

- Discuss a full range of risk mitigation options, and explain how each of these would address the risks.
- Identify, where possible, the benefits associated with the risks and balance these against the known costs.

Risk communication strategies

The general principles of communication, which were discussed earlier, are equally valid for the issues of risk communication; however, there are three general approaches that should be considered when developing a risk communication strategy.

The *technical approach* uses the dissemination of technical information about a hazard and its associated risks as the main theme of the communication process, and technical experts such as scientists and engineers often prepare and present the information. The information should be presented in a factual way with little, if any, discussion with other stakeholders. The approach often fails because the communicators have not been trained in the necessary communication skills that are required to present information to the public and the media.

The *public relations approach* concentrates on getting the 'right message' across to stakeholders rather than a desire to present the scientific or technical justification for the message. There is little effort to educate or increase the stakeholders' understanding of the issues involved. Here the communicators might be highly trained in communication skills, but they would often lack the scientific background that would be required to answer technical questions about the hazards and risks.

The *multidisciplinary approach* aims to take the positive aspects of the technical and public relations approaches and to combine them with other relevant disciplines, such as toxicology, social science and economics, in order to present a holistic approach. The multidisciplinary approach provides a forum for public, industrial and governmental debate of risk issues, and presents a more rounded view of the risks than either of the individual approaches.

Ranking and comparing risks

A major problem associated with the risk communication process is the need to explain and communicate the probability and consequences of undesirable events in a way that would be acceptable to the recipients of the information. Early research in risk communication focused on trying to identify what the public perceived to be an acceptable level of risk in order to develop better ways of communicating the data outputs from risk assessments. However, attempts at communicating risk levels, for example as 1 in 10^6, often proved to be difficult or impossible because people experienced difficulty in understanding and interpreting statistical probabilities. Many people believe that risk is a discrete event, which either happens or does not happen. To the public, the information, for example, that the fatal accident rate in the manufacturing sector was 1 in 100 000 per year would appear to be so small that it could be ignored at any individual plant. However, because there might be one million people working in the manufacturing industry, the actual number of fatalities per year in this sector would, statistically, be 10. Therefore some researchers have used Likert-type scales to assess and communicate risk by using measures such as: *extremely unlikely, unlikely, possible, likely* and *probable* for the frequency of occurrence and *very slight, slight, minor, significant* and *major* for the consequences of adverse events. Objections to this approach relate to the difficulties of communicating the significance of low-probability, high-consequence risks. The subjective scales also make it difficult to interpret the results, because the phrases might have different meanings to different people.

Many people do not understand the concept of annualised risk, but there has also been concern because they do not understand the issue of *cumulative risk*. This issue can be illustrated by comparing two types of temperature control that may be used on a chemical plant to prevent overheating of a reactor vessel. On an annualised basis, one type of control is 99% reliable whereas a second type is only 95% reliable but cheaper. As there appears to be only a small difference in the performance, a decision might be taken to install the cheaper control system operating at 95% reliability. However, the cumulative performance difference between the two control systems would increase from 4% in the first year to over 30% by the tenth year.

It is generally accepted that risk comparisons are more meaningful to the public than the use of absolute values of risk, especially where the risks are very small. In addition, if fatality rates do not take exposure levels into account they may not indicate that some risks are related to certain risk factors, such as age. For example, fatality rates during pregnancy are higher for young women simply because women are generally under 40 years of age when they conceive. Fatality rates for lung cancer, on the other hand, are higher later in life because of the latency period involved with this type of disease. Various ways of presenting risks have been devised in order to overcome these and other problems. Wilson (1979) used the idea of listing activities that would increase one's chance of death in any one year by a factor of one in a million, for example:

- smoking 1.4 cigarettes;
- receiving one chest X-ray;
- living 150 years within 20 miles of a nuclear power station; and
- working one hour in a coal mine.

Cohen and Lee (1979) used the concept of loss of life expectancy from a lifetime of exposure to specified risks; for example:

- cigarette smoking: −2250 days;
- medical X-rays: −6 days;
- radiation from the nuclear industry: −0.02 days;
- coal mining: −1100 days.

Other approaches have compared risk levels with activities that the stakeholders may be more familiar with, for example stating that the risk of a fatality from working in a particular environment is more or less than the risk of a fatality from painting the outside of one's house. The incidence of risks can also be presented as the frequency of injury per thousand or million hours of exposure. For example, Hawkins and Fuller (1999) reported that the risk of injury in football was 4 per 1000 hours during training but 28 per 1000 hours during competition.

Differences in risk perception inevitably lead to differences in views of the acceptability or unacceptability of risks. Therefore risk perception is an important indicator of how an individual or a group might respond to a set of data that was presented to them. A problem with measuring risk perception is that people's ability to judge absolute levels of risk accurately is poor (Daamen *et al.*, 1986). Different people have different perspectives on risks: therefore one disadvantage claimed for using specific risk-rating scales is that they do not allow respondents to rate risks by the issues that are important to them (Slovic, 1992). One way of measuring the validity of an individual's judgement of risk, however, is to measure the way in which they perceive the level of risk of one activity compared with that of another activity and then to compare these views with statistical data for the same risks. Whereas the validity of some measures of risk comparison is subject to debate, the rank ordering of these risk judgements has been shown to be relatively consistent, and in line with the available statistical information (Daamen *et al.*, 1986). Fuller and Myerscough (2001) compared how race team members, officials and spectators together with safety managers compared the risks of motor racing with those of other sporting activities (Table 5.1). Although significant differences were observed between stakeholders for the relative risk perception scores across the five sports, their rank ordering of the scores was similar, and consistent with the published fatal accident rates for these sports.

Table 5.1 Average relative risk perception scores and fatal accident rates for sport activities compared with motor racing

Activity	FAR[a]	Average relative risk perception scores[b]				
		All	*Race teams*	*Race officials*	*Race spectators*	*Safety managers*
Climbing	237	+0.59	+0.60	+0.58	+0.45	+0.91
Motor racing	161	0	0	0	0	0
Horse riding	46	−0.16	+0.21	−0.19	−0.49	+0.09
Rugby	14	−0.39	−0.03	−0.23	−0.75	−0.41
Swimming	10	−0.74	−0.59	−0.77	−0.86	−0.68
Work	8	−	c	c	c	−0.77

[a] Fatal accident rate per 100 million days' participation.
[b] +1: higher risk; 0: equal risk; −1: lower risk (compared with motor racing).
[c] Information not requested.
Source: Fuller and Myerscough, 2001

Judgements and decisions about the acceptability of risks must include a consideration of the decision process as well as a consideration of the hazards and risks, because risk comparisons form only one part of the overall process. However, where risk comparisons are made, they should include a consideration of the following points:

- Comparisons should be made between similar types of risk.
- Data sources should be valid and credible.
- Strengths and weaknesses of the data and information should be provided.
- Data and information should be provided in order to present the audience with a full perspective of the problem.

Framing effects

Research within the area of risk communication and decision-making identified an important factor that is referred to as the *framing effect*. Framing effects, which relate to the context in which information is presented or 'framed', can lead to bias in the recipients' views of the risks. For example, Slovic (1993) commented on the anomaly created by the public's acceptance of the use of X-rays and chemicals in the medical domain, where they were perceived as high-benefit and low-risk hazards, compared with their non-acceptance in the industrial domain, where they were perceived as high-risk and low-benefit. Although, in theory, decision-making should not be affected by the way in which information is presented, this is not generally the case in practice.

The most common framing effect is that of the *domain effect*, which involves changing the description of a risk from a negative to a positive description by, for example, identifying the benefits associated with a risk rather than the losses. Where a choice must be made between two undesirable options, both options can be framed in terms of their relative gains rather than the losses, so that those people affected by the decision would be left with a positive feeling that they had made a real gain whichever decision was made. Similarly, decisions could be significantly influenced by whether the options available were phrased in terms of lives lost or lives saved. For example, if a new surgical procedure had been developed in order to cure a disease, the results could be framed in a number of ways, such as:

- 95% of operations were successful;
- 5% of operations were unsuccessful;
- 5 out of every 100 people undergoing the operation died; or
- 95 out of every 100 people undergoing the operation were cured.

Each of these statements communicates the same information, but the interpretation and conclusion reached by each individual about the surgical procedure would depend, for example, on whether the recipients were optimists or pessimists.

An important application of the framing effect is where communicators claim that the general public would receive substantial benefits from an activity, and that only a small group of people would be adversely affected. This could have the effect of minimising the perceived risk to the general public at the expense of the identified minority group, who would become isolated and exposed. The use of framing effects has wide implications, as it allows some individuals or groups to manipulate other people's decisions simply by choosing the format in which data are presented. This approach is routinely used in the advertising industry in order to present products and services in the best possible light. In a similar way, it has become common practice for politicians to use *spin-doctors* to frame communications so that they provide a positive image to what might otherwise be unpopular political communications.

Social amplification of risk

The hypothesis behind the *social amplification of risk* is that risk events interact with psychological, social, cultural, institutional and governmental processes, and this either increases or decreases perceptions of risk. The concept of risk amplification applies both to intensifying and to attenuating consequences of an event, but it relates mainly to the intensification of the risk perception process. In risk amplification, the impact of adverse events extends from the direct or primary costs of accidents and incidents, such as lost time, lost production and damaged equipment, to the indirect or secondary costs of the event, such as loss of sales and investor confidence. Secondary effects also include calls from the public for higher standards and legislation. A framework describing the risk amplification process, which is based on the proposals made by Kasperson *et al.* (1988), is presented in Figure 5.4.

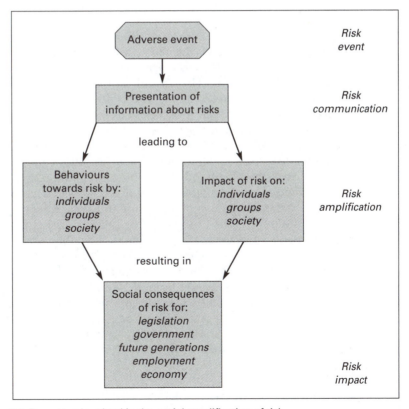

Figure 5.4 Processes involved in the social amplification of risk

The trigger (or adverse) event in the risk amplification process is normally an accident, a published report or a public statement about a risk situation. Depending on the issues and the risk perceptions of the stakeholders, some aspects of these adverse events would be selected, analysed and discussed further. The judgements reached by the stakeholders about these events would be communicated to other individuals and groups, who would in turn reach their own conclusions about the events. These conclusions might lead individuals and groups to change or consolidate their previously held views and behaviours. The groups and individuals therefore act as *amplification stations* for the risks by accentuating certain issues through their communications with other groups and by raising awareness of the social consequences. Where groups and individuals form part of larger social groupings, they are referred to as *social stations of amplification*. The communication flow and the behavioural responses to the information by these social stations of amplification can generate secondary effects that extend beyond the immediate boundaries of the people directly affected by the adverse events. These impacts may include:

- developing enduring risk perceptions related to technology and processes;
- impacting on local and national economies through, for example, tourism, property values and business confidence;
- creating political pressures through, for example, legislation and risk standards; or
- generating social disorder through, for example, protests, demonstrations and strikes.

The process of social amplification of risk has been compared to dropping a pebble in the centre of a still pond: the pebble initially disturbs just one part of the pond, but as the 'ripple effect' spreads it eventually causes the initial disturbance to affect every part of the pond. The amplification of risk, through communication processes, is clearly complex, and its effects depend on the social and organisational environments within which it occurs. Petts *et al.* (2001) also identified that different risks created different responses, and these responses were dependent on the risk profile. A high level of media coverage of risk issues and adverse events does not in itself lead to an amplification of the risks among the public, but it would certainly increase the likelihood of this process taking place. Following a study of adverse events, Kasperson (1992) presented a model outlining the causal relationships involved in the process of social amplification of risk (Figure 5.5).

At the same time, the physical consequences arising from the adverse event generate media coverage, which influences the public's risk perceptions and their responses. These public responses and the media attention to the adverse event initiate changes in the social dimensions of the risks through social, political or financial actions. In the longer term, the amplification of risk causes a change or consolidation of the public's risk perceptions, and this affects the way individuals and/or the public respond to future adverse events. Kasperson (1992) outlined a number of key observations about the causal relationships associated with the social amplification of risk:

- Society generally responds in a rational way to adverse events.
- The media coverage is proportional to the magnitude of the actual and/or perceived consequences of the adverse events.

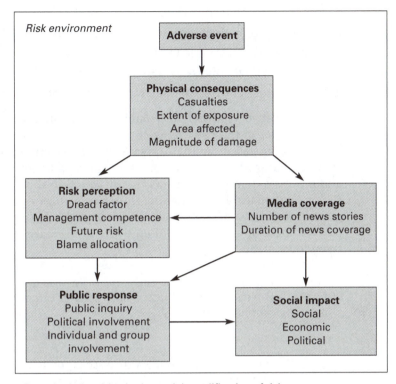

Figure 5.5 Causal relationships in the social amplification of risk

- The way in which the media and other groups present the effects of an adverse event influences society's perspectives of the hazards.

- The public's potential exposure to the consequences of an adverse event has a greater impact on risk perception than the actual consequences of the event. This effect is related to the differences in risk perceptions observed between the public and risk experts.

- Blame for adverse events has an influential effect on the public's interpretation of the consequences from an adverse event, particularly if the blame is attributable to industry or the government.

Trust and risk communication

Trust and distrust are important issues in risk management, and there is evidence that the trust and credibility of communicators are major factors in the process of risk communication (Slovic, 1993). Improved levels of trust, however, are not achieved simply by increasing the level or quality of the information supplied. An important aspect of trust is the stakeholders' perception of the communicator's independence: if the communicator is perceived to have an affiliation with the issue under discussion, then their credibility as a communicator is diminished. Renn and Levine (1991) suggested that there were five factors related to the issue of trust and credibility of the communicator:

- competence and technical expertise;
- objectivity so that messages are as free of bias as possible;
- fairness and an acknowledgement of alternative viewpoints;
- consistency in the messages and behaviours presented; and
- the recipient's faith in the source of the information or message presented.

Levels of trust and the preferred source of information are also dependent on the characteristics of the risks being communicated. Conservationists and pressure groups are trusted more than private companies and industry for information about environmental risks, whereas the public prefer information about products and processes from the producers and information about health risks from scientists. Confirmatory information from more than one source also generates greater trust in the data provided (Weyman and Kelly, 1999). Although it is difficult for communicators to build up trust among stakeholders, it is very easy for them to lose trust.

> One of the most fundamental qualities of trust has been known for ages. Trust is fragile. It is typically created rather slowly, but it can be destroyed in an instant – by a single mishap or mistake.
>
> (Slovic, 1993: 677)

The public have a natural bias towards distrust, which is referred to as the *asymmetry principle*. It is brought about for the following reasons:

- Adverse events are more visible than beneficial events, as they are more likely to attract media attention. Positive events are less easily defined, and they attract little media attention. For example, how would the safe operation of a train service be communicated to the public: an accident-free service for one year could be perceived as a single positive annual event or 365 positive daily events. One accident resulting in several fatalities, however, provides a very clear message that would be easily defined and very easily understood by the public.
- Negative events inevitably exert a greater influence on one's views than positive events. For example, one major plane crash might decrease one's willingness to fly, but 1000 successful flights would be unlikely to change one's willingness to fly.
- The public perceive bad news as more credible than good news. For example, people would believe studies that claimed that, because a chemical was hazardous to animals, it could also be considered to be a risk to humans, whereas the public would be unlikely to believe a study that claimed that because a chemical had no adverse effects on animals it could also be considered to have no adverse effects on humans.
- Whereas bad news reinforces the public's existing distrust of people, processes and products, good news alone does not allay existing fears about hazards. For example, a radiation leak at a nuclear reprocessing plant would add to existing concerns about nuclear safety, but claims for the safe operation of a nuclear power station would not allay concerns.

Certain groups of people within society are generally perceived to be more trustworthy than other groups: for example, politicians are among the least trusted whereas doctors are among the most trusted groups (Table 5.2). Slovic (1993: 676) illustrated how high levels of trust of certain groups can compensate for the fears associated with some hazards: 'Although X-rays and medicines pose significant risks, our relatively high degree of trust in the physicians who manage these devices makes them acceptable.'

Table 5.2 The public's level of trust in different groups of communicators

Level of trust	Members of the group
Most trusted	Physicians, academics, voluntary organisations
Average trust	Press, television, radio, pressure groups
Least trusted	Industrialists, politicians, consultants

One reason for a lack of trust is that, although the public accept that activities give rise to risks, they do not appreciate that if an accident occurs it could still be within the defined envelope of acceptable or tolerable levels of risks. This distrust arises because of the public's mistaken belief that a risk assessment equates to the removal of all risk rather than to the definition of a level of residual risk. In addition, it is often not understood that all the information required for a risk assessment may not be available or is incomplete at the time of the assessment. Therefore, if at some point in the future an accident occurs or additional information comes to light, a revised risk assessment could be interpreted as meaning that the original assessment was incorrect. It is important to demonstrate to employees and the public that important lessons can be learnt from accidents and near misses, but it is also important to ensure that they do not gain the impression that an accident necessarily relates to poor risk management. It is essential, therefore, to differentiate between accidents that were unforeseeable with the current levels of knowledge and those accidents that *were* caused by poor management. In the former case, open communication about the risk issues could prevent or minimise distrust among stakeholders. Arvai (2003) demonstrated that, when the public were made aware at the time of communicating risk decisions that participatory involvement of stakeholders had taken place during the decision-making process, they:

- were more supportive of the decisions reached;
- perceived the risks associated with the decision to be lower;
- perceived the benefits to be higher; and
- were more satisfied with the decision-making process.

In the UK, the Inter-Departmental Liaison Group on Risk Assessment (1998) identified four key issues that communicators should address in order to establish trust among stakeholders:

- Create *empathy* by engaging with the audience.
- Demonstrate *concern* for the people and their issues.
- Provide evidence of *commitment* to dealing with the issues.
- Explain the *benefits* that are associated with the risks.

Summary

- Communication is the process of transferring information and ideas between groups and individuals. Persuasive communication involves changing or consolidating an individual's or a group's attitudes about an issue.

- Attitude, which is an abstract construct that is defined by an individual's beliefs and values, is measured using indirect indicators that reflect the individual's views on a risk issue.

- The effectiveness of the communication process is determined by characteristics of the communicator, the message and the recipient. The level of fear about a hazard, the emotive impact of risks and framing effects can influence an individual's interpretation of risk information.

- Because the public have difficulty in interpreting quantified values of annualised and cumulative probabilities, risk-ranking techniques are often preferred for communicating and comparing levels of risk arising from different hazards.

- The impact of risk on society can be amplified through the process of risk communication among stakeholders, and this process is influenced by issues such as the recipient's level of trust or distrust of the communicator.

Issues for review and discussion

- Consider how you would evaluate employees' attitudes towards health and safety management.

- Review the reasons why you trust or distrust the risk information provided by politicians.

- Consider your strengths and weaknesses as a communicator.

- Consider how pressure groups and politicians use the domain effect to change people's attitudes towards hazards.

- Consider how you would attempt to change a work colleague's attitudes towards a high-risk activity.

References

Allport, G.W. (1935) Attitudes. In: C.M. Murchison (ed.) *Handbook of Social Psychology*. Worcester: Clark University Press.

Arvai, J.L. (2003) Using risk communication to disclose the outcome of a participatory decision-making process: effects on the perceived acceptability of risk-policy decisions. *Risk Analysis*, **23**, 281–289.

Cohen, B. and Lee, J. (1979) A catalog of risks. *Health Physics*, **36**, 707–722.

Daamen, D., Verplanken, B. and Midden, C. (1986) Accuracy and consistency of lay estimates of annual fatality rates. In: B. Brehmer, H. Jungermann, P. Lourens and G. Sevon (eds), *New Directions in Research on Decision Making*, 231–243. Elsevier: Amsterdam.

Fishbein, M. and Ajzen, I. (1975) *Belief, Attitude, Intention and Behaviour: An Introduction to Theory and Research*. Reading MA: Addison-Wesley.

Fuller, C.W. and Myerscough, F.E. (2001) Stakeholder perceptions of risk in motor sport. *Journal of Safety Research*, **32**, 345–358.

Hawkins, R.D. and Fuller, C.W. (1999) A prospective epidemiological study of injuries in four English professional football clubs. *British Journal of Sports Medicine*, **33**, 196–203.

Inter-Departmental Liaison Group on Risk Assessment (1998) *Risk Communication: A Guide to Regulatory Practice*. London: HMSO.

Kasperson, R.E. (1992) The social amplification of risk: progress in developing an integrative framework. In: S. Krimsky and D. Golding (eds), *Social Theories of Risk*, 153–178. London: Praeger.

Kasperson, R.E., Renn, O., Slovic, P., Brown, H.S., Emel, J., Goble, R., Kasperson, J.X. and Ratick, S. (1988) The social amplification of risk: a conceptual framework. *Risk Analysis*, **8**(2), 177–187.

Katz, D. (1960) The functional approach to the study of attitudes. *Public Opinion Quarterly*, **24**, 163–204.

National Academy of Sciences (1989) *Improving Risk Communication*. Washington, DC: National Academy Press.

Petts, J., Horlick-Jones, T. and Murdock, G. (2001) *Social Amplification of Risk: The Media and the Public*. CRR 329/2001. Sudbury: HSE Books.

Renn, O. and Levine, D. (1991) Credibility and trust in risk communication. In: R.E. Kasperson and P.J.M. Stallen (eds), *Communicating Risks to the Public*. Dordrecht: Kluwer.

Rokeach, M. (1948) Generalised mental rigidity as a factor in ethnocentrism. *Journal of Abnormal and Social Psychology*, **43**, 254–278.

Rosenberg, M.J. and Hovland, C.I. (1960) Cognitive, affective and behavioural components of attitudes. In: C.I. Hovland and M.J. Rosenberg (eds), *Attitude Organisation and Change*. New Haven: Yale University Press.

Royal Society (1992) *Risk: Analysis, Perception and Management*. London: The Royal Society.

Slovic, P. (1992) Perceptions of risk: reflections on the psychometric paradigm. In: S. Krimsky and D. Golding (eds), *Social Theories of Risk*, 117–152. Praeger: London.

Slovic, P. (1993) Perceived risk, trust and democracy. *Risk Analysis*, **13**, 675–683.

Weyman, A.K. and Kelly, C.J. (1999) *Risk Perception and Risk Communication: A Review of the Literature*. Sudbury: HSE Books.

Wilson, R. (1979) Analyzing the daily risks of life. *Technology Review*, **81**, 40–46.

Zimbardo, P.G. and Leippe, M.R. (1991) *The Psychology of Attitude Change and Social Influence*. London: McGraw-Hill.

CHAPTER 6

Economic issues

*When it costs too much to build it at home
You just build it cheaper some place else.*

– Bob Dylan, 'Union sundown' (1983)

Introduction

In order to indicate the financial impact that workplace accidents and ill-health have on organisations, many national health and safety bodies publish data showing the number of days lost through workplace accidents and ill-health. The European Agency for Safety and Health at Work (2002a), for example, stated:

Currently, every year nearly 5 million employees in the EU suffer from work-related accidents involving more than three days absence from work, and a further 5500 are killed. Besides the human suffering, these accidents have a strong economic impact on business, as 150 million workdays are lost and the insurance costs to be borne by industry add up to €20 billion.

These statistics alone, however, do not describe the full impact of accidents at work. This can be achieved only by considering the social and economic impact of accidents and ill-health on employees, employers and society (European Agency for Safety and Health at Work, 2002b).

Impacts on employees arise from:

■ *direct financial costs* such as lost earnings and personal expenses arising, for example, from hospital attendance, medication and transport; and

■ *human costs* such as the loss in quality of life caused by, for example, pain, stress and incapacity.

Impacts on employers arise from:

■ *operational costs* such as loss of output and repair or replacement of broken equipment;

■ *administrative costs* such as recruitment of replacement staff, increased insurance premiums and compensation costs; and

■ *goodwill costs* such as loss of public confidence in the ability of an organisation to manage health and safety issues.

Financial impacts on society arise from:

■ *taxes* that are used to provide medical services and social security payments for people injured at work; and

■ *prices of goods and services* that are increased in order to recover the additional operating costs caused by accidents and ill-health at work.

Although companies incur costs from accidents and ill-health, they also incur costs from trying to prevent them. It is important, therefore, to understand how a balance between prevention and failure is achieved in health and safety management. The aim of this chapter is to discuss fundamental aspects of economics in order to understand how health and safety costs impact on the financial performance of an organisation. In addition, specific economic issues related to issues such as budget constraints, performance standards, externalities and selection of control measures will be discussed.

Economic principles

Every society operates on the principle of trading goods and/or services. The process of business management defines what goods and services an organisation will produce, how these goods and services will be produced, and for whom the goods and services will be produced. Trading markets provide the forum within which suppliers of goods and services are brought together with potential customers. Economics is the study of these processes.

The following simple example illustrates the principles involved in the study of economics. One may need to buy a car in order to travel to work. Many people would like to buy an expensive, high-powered, exclusive sports car, but their limited financial resources mean that they will have to settle for a cheaper, mass-produced, low-powered car. The prices of the sports car and the mass-produced car have therefore defined the potential customers in the marketplace. From a car manufacturer's point of view, the design and development costs, employees' wages, production facilities, marketing, sales and profit will all contribute to the final price of the car. If people do not like the cars sufficiently at the prices quoted, nobody will buy the products and manufacturers will have to cut costs and profits in order to decrease the price of the cars until people do buy them. However, if the price at which people will buy the cars is below the production costs, the manufacturer will very soon become bankrupt.

Positive and normative economics

When discussing economic issues, it is important to differentiate between the two main branches of the subject.

Positive economics refers to the objective scientific descriptions, explanations and predictions of an economy and the desire to explain how society manages the supply and demand of goods and services. This approach involves the development of economic theories and models that enable movements in the economy to be predicted when changes are made. Positive economics relates to facts about the provision of goods and services and how these affect the economy rather than about how the economy should or should not be managed. Positive economics is therefore a pure science, which will enable one to predict how the economy will react, for example, to an increase or decrease in fuel tax or changes in exchange rates. It will not, however, relate to how the money raised from taxes should be used or distributed within society.

Normative economics refers to the policy decisions and views that individuals or groups have about a particular issue, and therefore relates to subjective judgements or preferences. There are no right or wrong answers about normative economic decisions, as they are determined solely by an individual's views.

Positive economics should be considered as providing unequivocal assessments of an economy. Normative economics deals with views and recommendations on how resources may be allocated to achieve economic targets. These are generally regarded as equivocal assessments based on personal, political or social viewpoints. These two aspects of economics can be illustrated by reference to the problems raised by work-based health and safety. When one refers to the fact that accidents and ill-health at work cost society large sums of money, one is using positive economics. However, when one refers to the issue of compensating people who are injured or suffer ill-health at work, one is referring to normative economics. It is important, therefore, when discussing the financial implications of any issue, to distinguish between the views expressed by an economist who is presenting information based on evidence and those of an economist who is merely presenting a personal perspective.

Market economies

The way in which decisions are made by societies about the allocation of national resources and the level of government intervention in these decisions define the type of market economy in place within a country.

Command economies exist in societies where governments make the decisions about the production and consumption of goods and services. In command economies, government planners define the production levels, designate who will produce what, set prices for the goods and services, and determine the wages of the workforce. However, as markets become more complex and new goods and services become available, it becomes increasingly difficult for government planners to keep up to date with developments and, sooner or later, the goods and services provided cease to satisfy consumer desires. This creates general unrest in the communities and creates widespread shortages of the desired goods and services and surpluses of those goods and services that are no longer required.

Free market economies exist in societies where governments do not interfere in the running of the economy. In a free market economy everyone is able to follow their own interests: individuals decide how they will work, how they will produce goods and services, and which goods and services they will buy. The theory of a free market economy is that those people who have good ideas will develop them for their own benefit, but society as a whole will also benefit as a consequence of this. Without a central government planning function, employees determine their conditions of employment through independent negotiation. Unfortunately, this does not always mean that employees and employers are negotiating from equal positions, and therefore employees may often be unhappy about their terms of employment and workplace conditions.

Mixed economies exist in societies where government and private enterprises work together. Governments may direct production and consumption through, for example, the use of taxation, rebates and the provision of health services, transport systems and the defence of the nation. Governments also implement some controls over how organisations may operate. Therefore there is a degree of freedom for individuals to follow their interests, but this is controlled within certain regulatory systems. In some mixed economies, governments may also act as producers of goods and services through, for example, the supply of utilities such as electricity, water and telecommunications and as consumers through, for example, the purchase of military and medical goods.

An organisation's success in a market economy depends on satisfying the needs of customers by producing the right goods and services at prices they are prepared to pay, and those of the workforce by offering competitive wages and acceptable conditions of employment.

Microeconomics and macroeconomics

Economic studies can be categorised by the analytical approach adopted for assessing economic issues.

Microeconomics considers the economic factors that are associated with particular commodities and issues. *General equilibrium theory* involves the study of every microeconomic analysis possible and the combination of the results in an attempt to define a complete economic picture. This, in reality, is an impossible objective. Microeconomics therefore generally relates to the detailed analysis of specific issues without considering the interactions that may or may not occur with other aspects of the economy. For example, one may carry out a detailed economic study of improving the standard of health and safety control measures in the rail industry without including an analysis of the impact that the cost of these improved standards may have on train timetables, the price of tickets and the cost of transporting goods around the country, or the impact that any of these issues may have on the country's economy. In some cases this is a valid analytical approach to take, but in other cases the consequential effects may be too great to be ignored.

Macroeconomics simplifies economic factors so that the interactions between issues can be modelled and interpreted more easily. For example, one would consider the transport sector as a whole rather than analysing just the rail industry. At the macroeconomic level economists are more interested in general trends within an economy than in the details associated with a particular issue.

Financing a market economy

Marketplaces trade money as well as goods and services: therefore money becomes a commodity. When companies wish to expand or replace obsolete plant and equipment, they may borrow money from banks and other financial institutions. The role of these financial organisations is therefore to bring companies and business investors together in order that they may both be in a position to make money out of a venture. An alternative route for investing money in a company is through the purchase of shares in the company. In this case the owners of the shares become the legal owners of the company, and they become interested in the way the company manages its business, as it will affect the return on their investment. This approach increases the risks of the investors, because shareholders lose all of their investment if the company becomes bankrupt. A shareholder, however, can lose only the money that they invested in the purchase of the shares, as they have no responsibility for any of the debts and/or liabilities associated with the company.

A board of directors, which makes the strategic decisions on how a company will operate, manages the activities of each company. The directors must present an annual summary of performance to the shareholders in order to demonstrate how the company has been managed. If a company cannot satisfactorily demonstrate that it is managing investors' money effectively and efficiently, the shareholders may lose confidence and decide to sell their shares. If a large enough number of shareholders repeat this process, the overall value of the company will eventually diminish as the demand for shares decreases. The requirement for companies to report on their internal control systems for managing organisational risks (Turnbull 1999) has further strengthened the position of shareholders in obtaining information about how companies are managed.

Supply and demand

Societies have to develop ways in which they can make decisions on what, how and for whom to produce goods and services. In most countries the balance between *supply*, which is determined by the producers, and *demand*, which is determined by the consumers, defines the price and quantity of goods and services in the marketplace, and this forms the basis of the *supply and demand equilibrium model* of economics.

Demand is defined as the quantity of goods and services that consumers may want to purchase at a specified price. Therefore there is no such thing as a specific demand for a product or service, because the demand will change depending on the price. Even if all goods and services were free to the consumer, there would be a limit on how much consumers could use: therefore there would be a demand figure even at this price. The *demand curve* defines the purchase characteristics of consumers at all conceivable prices, whereas the *quantity demanded* defines the purchase characteristics of consumers at a particular price.

Supply is defined as the quantity of goods and services that producers may want to sell at a specified price. In the same way that demand is not a specific value, supply also varies with the price attainable for the goods and services. The *supply curve* defines the production characteristics of suppliers at all conceivable prices, whereas the *quantity supplied* defines the production characteristics of suppliers at a particular price.

The interplay between supply and demand can be illustrated in terms of the market for quality chocolates. If demand for the chocolates exceeds the quantity available, then some potential customers will be disappointed because there will be a shortage. Clearly, at the prices charged the quantity of chocolates demanded exceeds the quantity supplied. However, if the chocolates were double the price, the quantity demanded would be lower and there might now even be a surplus to requirements. The quantity of chocolates demanded and supplied at all conceivable prices can be combined to produce supply and demand curves that will define the market for this particular type of chocolate (Figure 6.1). Although the supply and demand curves are shown, for illustrative purposes, as straight lines, they will in reality be curved.

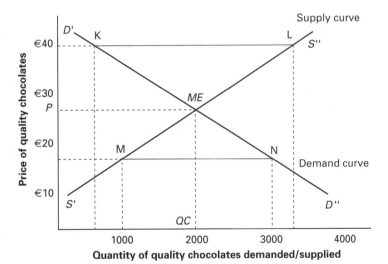

Figure 6.1 The supply and demand curves

Assuming all other things to be equal, the supply curve (*S'*–*S"*) shown in Figure 6.1 illustrates how the quantity of chocolates produced will increase as the price that can be charged increases. The demand curve (*D'*–*D"*), on the other hand, illustrates how the demand for chocolates will decrease as the price increases. The market equilibrium point (*ME*) is reached where the supply and demand curves cross: in this case at price *P* (€27 per box) and quantity of chocolates *QC* (2000 boxes). At €17 per box the demand for chocolates increases to 3000 boxes, but because of the costs involved the number of suppliers prepared to produce chocolates at this price decreases, resulting in the production of only 1000 boxes. The line M–N shows the deficit between the quantities supplied and demanded (2000 boxes). However, at €40 per box suppliers will be very pleased to produce large quantities of quality chocolates (3300), but consumers will feel that they are now overpriced and demand will fall (600 boxes), resulting in an excess of supply over demand equal to K–L (2700 boxes). These arguments are equally valid for the supply and demand of any commodity including, for example, train tickets, chemicals, cars, telephones and restaurant meals. In a free market economy producers and consumers define supply and demand, because producers are not required to produce and consumers are not required to consume goods and services if they feel that it is not beneficial to them.

At low prices only the most efficient companies will be able to make a profit, because their operating costs will still be below the market price. However, as prices increase, less efficient companies will be able to enter the market and make a profit – albeit not as big a profit as that of the efficient companies. As prices rise, companies will seek to increase output by working overtime and attempting to produce more goods from existing plant and equipment. There comes a point, however, when additional plant and equipment or improved technology will be required to produce more goods. Supply curves are therefore always presented for a given level of technology; as the technology improves, the supply curves will change because goods may now be produced more cheaply. A supply curve also represents the costs of production under specific operating conditions, and any changes to these conditions will change the costs of production and therefore the market price at which the company can profitably sell goods in the market. Similarly, government regulations may increase the costs of production through, for example, the imposition of higher health and safety or environmental standards. As costs increase, they move the supply curve upwards, and this causes the market equilibrium point to shift to the left.

All costs related to the production of goods and services, whether self-imposed, for example through employee wages, operational efficiency and quality of production, or externally imposed, for example through government intervention and insurance premiums, affect the long-term average cost (LAC) of production.

Long-term average cost of production

In a non-monopoly situation and in an unconstrained market, a company supplying goods and services at or below the market price should be able to sell as many goods and services as it wants to produce. However, whether a company can sustain the provision of goods and services in the long term depends on its profitability, which in turn depends on its long-term average cost of production. The average cost of production is defined as the total cost of production divided by the total output in goods and services. In the short term, companies may continue to trade by producing goods and services at costs that are greater than the price at which they can sell them: in this case, one should be more interested in the short-term average costs of production. However, to ensure the long-term viability of a company, the average cost of production must be less than the price at which the goods and services can be traded.

Inputs to production are any goods or services that are used to produce the output product. Inputs to the production function include, for example, labour costs, raw materials, plant, equipment, water and electricity. The *production function* defines the maximum output that can be produced from a defined level of inputs. The efficiency with which a company achieves a specified output will define its long-term average costs. For example, consider two companies that adopt different production strategies for the same product. The first company (A) uses a high level of labour with low levels of technology, whereas the second company (B) invests in new machinery and reduces its workforce level considerably. These two cost components must be considered when calculating the average costs of production. In addition, there will be other operating costs to consider that arise from, for example, quality, waste disposal, and costs of injuries and ill-health among employees. This situation is summarised in Table 6.1 for the costs associated with the production of 1000 units of output.

Table 6.1 Average costs of production

	Costs per 1000 units (£)			Average cost
	Machinery	Wages	Other	per unit (£)
Company A	10 000	25 000	2000	37.0
Company B	20 000	12 500	1000	33.5

In this example Company B produces the goods at a lower average cost per unit than Company A. However, if a new production manager arrives at Company B and he or she adopts lower health and safety standards than those previously accepted, the other costs will increase through higher levels of accidents and ill-health. If this increased the figure for 'other costs' to £5000, then the average cost per unit of production for Company B would increase to £37.5 and its average cost of production would become greater than that of Company A. These figures represent the average costs for the production of 1000 units of output, but the average cost figure may in fact change with the level of production: see Figure 6.2.

There are three main ways in which long-term average costs vary with the level of production:

- where long-term average costs decrease as the level of output increases – an *economy of scale* or an increasing *return to scale* (curve A–A);
- where long-term average costs increase as the level of output increases – a *diseconomy of scale* or a *decreasing return to scale* (curve B–B); and
- where long-term average costs remain stable as the level of output increases – a *constant return to scale* (curve C–C).

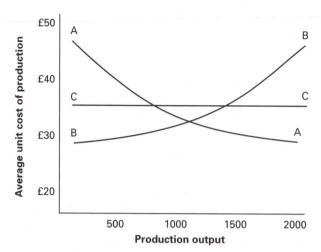

Figure 6.2 Economies and diseconomies of scale

Economies of scale arise because most companies have fixed costs associated with, for example, plant, equipment and the organisational management team. These costs, in broad terms, do not vary with production output and therefore, as production levels increase, these fixed costs are spread over a larger quantity of output. The contribution to the average unit cost therefore decreases as production levels increase. However, beyond a certain level it may be necessary to purchase more production facilities and to employ more staff: if this were the case, there might be a discontinuity in the average unit cost curve (A–A). In addition, some levels of technology become cost-effective only when production levels increase beyond a certain level. Diseconomies of scale arise because organisational management often becomes more difficult as a company becomes larger and more levels of management are required in order to control activities. Other reasons include the fact that as production levels increase the geographical location of the marketplace, for example, must grow, and therefore transport, marketing and sales costs increase. For these reasons a company's long-term average cost curve is more likely to follow the U-shape shown in Figure 6.3 than the shapes shown in Figure 6.2.

In the example shown in Figure 6.3, two companies are depicted with different long-term average costs of production (LAC_1 and LAC_2) for the same product. Both companies can sell their products in the market at a price of P_0. Company 1 can produce and sell goods at a profit, as long as its production levels fall between Q_1 and Q_2; outside these production levels the costs of production exceed the price that can be obtained in the market. Company 2, on the other hand, is in a situation where it cannot produce goods at a cost below the market price at any production levels. Company 2 may be able to sustain production at a loss in the short term, but it cannot continue to operate under these conditions for any significant length of time, as it would become bankrupt. Company 2 must therefore seek to identify and minimise its production costs in order to bring the long-term average costs below the market price.

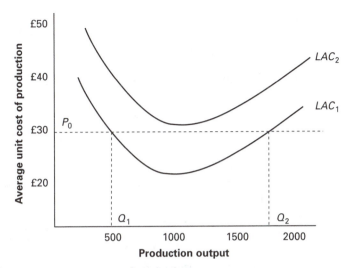

Figure 6.3 Long-term average costs of production

Budget constraint and choice

How individual consumers select the goods that they purchase depends on a number of factors, such as:

- the consumer's income;
- the prices at which goods and services are sold;
- the consumer's preferences for some goods and services over others; and
- the assumption that consumers will seek to maximise their satisfaction or *utility* through the choice of the goods and services purchased.

The first two of these issues define the consumer's *budget constraint*: that is, the amount of money available to spend and the consumption options available within these resources. As an example, assume that a student has $1000 available to spend on the purchase of textbooks in order to support their academic studies and for visits to football matches for leisure purposes. If each textbook costs $50 and each visit to a football match costs $25, Figure 6.4 illustrates the options available on how the student may spend the $1000.

The student can optimise his or her expenditure through the various combinations of textbooks and visits to football matches by ensuring that the combinations fall on the budget constraint line (A–B). Any combination that falls off this line will either overspend the budget (C) or underspend the budget (D). For example, the student could purchase 20 textbooks and forgo any visits to football matches, or visit 40 football matches and purchase no textbooks. The most likely decision by the student will be to choose a mixture of the two commodities, such as 10 textbooks and 20 visits to football matches, as this will satisfy the desire to achieve success in their academic studies but also the desire to enjoy some leisure activities.

The budget constraint line represents only the market options available within the resources available. It does not define an individual's preferences. In order to

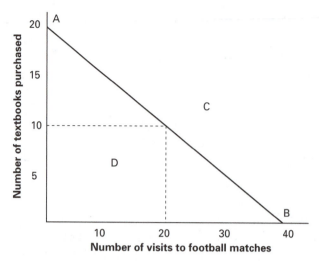

Figure 6.4 The budget constraint line

analyse this issue one must, for the time being, ignore the monetary cost of the commodities and consider only the intrinsic value of the goods and services to the consumer. In addition, one must make a number of assumptions:

- Consumers can rank different groups (bundles) of goods and services in the order of their preference or *utility value*. For example, if the student prefers 6 textbooks + 10 football matches (option X) to 8 textbooks + 8 football matches (option Y) and prefers option Y to 10 textbooks + 6 football matches (option Z), then the student must also prefer option X to option Z.

- Consumers prefer to have more goods and services rather than fewer. For example, the student will prefer 6 textbooks + 4 football matches to 6 textbooks + 3 football matches.

- Consumers have a *marginal rate of substitution* for one commodity compared with another commodity. Consumers will therefore demonstrate a diminishing marginal rate of substitution, because decreasing quantities of one type of product are given up to obtain equal increases in the quantity of the other product. This represents, for example, the number of textbooks that the student would give up to obtain 1 more visit to a football match, without changing the overall utility of the resulting bundle of books and football matches obtained. Hence, if the student has 10 textbooks and no visits to football matches, they may be prepared to give up 3 textbooks in order to obtain 1 visit to a football match, but be prepared to give up only 2 textbooks for a second visit to a football match.

Consumers' preferences are described by *indifference curves*, which identify those bundles of goods and services that provide the same utility or benefit to the consumer: see Figure 6.5. The shape of each curve incorporates the assumptions discussed above, and illustrates that a consumer will prefer to be on a higher indifference curve (B–B) than a lower curve (A–A) because all points on the higher curve (B–B) represent greater utility for the consumer – in this case, the total number of textbooks and visits to football matches. The actual shapes of the indifference curves will depend on the personal preferences of the consumers – for example how many textbooks they are prepared to give up for a visit to a football match.

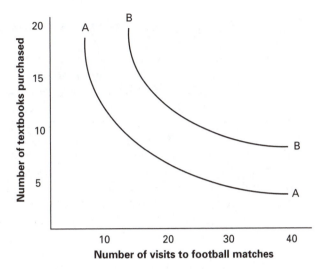

Figure 6.5 Indifference curves

It is now possible to combine the concept of budget constraint, shown in Figure 6.4, with the concept of indifference curves, shown in Figure 6.5, in order to define how consumers will spend their available budget: see Figure 6.6. Consumers can spend only up to their available budget: therefore any point on the budget constraint line (C–C) will satisfy this criterion. For example, option M falls on the budget constraint line with quantities of M_t textbooks and M_f football matches. Option N will also meet this criterion with quantities of N_t textbooks and N_f football matches. However, a third possibility is shown at option O, where the consumer obtains O_t textbooks and O_f visits to football matches. As this option provides greater utility, because it falls on a higher indifference curve (B–B) than the other two options, the consumer should make this choice.

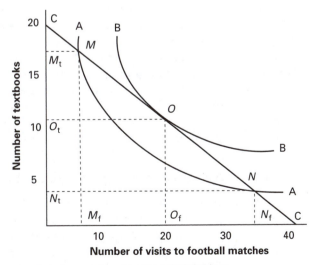

Figure 6.6 Consumers' choices on how to spend their budget

Risk management and economics

Individuals and organisations are exposed to risks from many activities. Generally speaking, individuals and organisations are prepared to take certain levels of risk in order to further their own interests, whether these are for personal or for business purposes. However, although one may be prepared to take risks, most people also prefer to have a system in place that compensates them, in case their risky activities result in significant losses. Insurance companies, which for a premium will underwrite most risks, normally fulfil this role. Insurance companies effectively spread the risks of an individual company over a large number of other companies so that the average outcome of all the risks from all the companies is in the insurance company's favour (Swiss Re, 2001). The risk capital generated from premiums must be sufficient to meet the potential liabilities of the policyholders.

An insurance company may insure a business property that is valued at $1 000 000 against earthquake damage for $10 000 per annum. Irrespective of whether the business property suffers earthquake damage, the company pays the premium of $10 000 to the insurance company, and the net value of the business has decreased to $990 000: this results from either still owning the property (valued at $1m) minus the $10 000 insurance premium or $1m insurance payout minus the premium of $10 000. A risk-taking organisation may decide not to insure the property against earthquake damage and gamble against the small risk of ending up with nothing in the event of an earthquake. A risk-averse organisation will insure the property in the knowledge that it will at least have $990 000, whatever happens. This appears to be a simple decision for both the insurance company and the business; however, if the insurance company's earthquake insurance business is all located in an earthquake region it has not actually spread its risk of suffering a loss. The insurance company has in fact taken on the same risk that the business had originally. In this case, if there is an earthquake in the region, all businesses will suffer a loss and the insurance company will have to pay out compensation to every business paying the insurance premium.

Another problem arises where an insurance company concentrates its business on risks associated with one hazard, such as asbestos products. In this case, the employees are not a random sample of the population, as it is known that asbestos workers are more likely to suffer from ill-health. Risk pooling, through insurance companies, is therefore an option only where the risks can genuinely be spread over a large number of independent people, groups and/or organisations. The reason why insurance companies may not insure against 'natural disasters' is simply because this type of risk event can have widespread consequences, and the risks cannot therefore be shared among large numbers of people.

Health and safety management and economics

Most managers will accept that accidents and ill-health disrupt normal operations and represent a potential addition to a company's operating costs. However, financial losses arise from many sources, including lost time, damaged plant and equipment, prosecution fines, and claims for damages from injured parties. Some losses are clear for all to see, such as a fire-damaged process plant, a derailed train or a collapsed scaffold. Other losses are less visible, such as

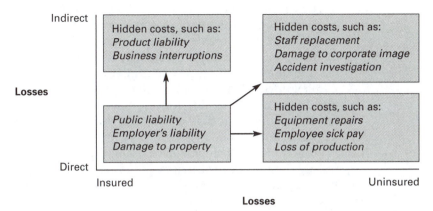

Figure 6.7 The hidden costs of accidents and ill-health

increased insurance premiums, business interruption and loss of goodwill. The idea of indirect costs of accidents comes from the work of Heinrich (1930), and has been manifested in the popular model of an iceberg, whereby direct costs are seen above the water line and the indirect costs are hidden below the water line. Organisational losses arising from workplace accidents and ill-health can be categorised within a framework of direct/indirect losses and insured/uninsured losses: see Figure 6.7.

The European Agency for Safety and Health at Work (1999) surveyed the member states within the European Union in order to estimate the national costs and proportions of gross national product (GNP) arising from accidents and ill-health at work. Their results are summarised in Table 6.2. The variations in the values reported were partly explained by the difficulty of measuring the exact economic losses associated with injuries and ill-health and the different reporting systems used in different countries. However, even though there was a wide range of values obtained (GNP: 0.4% to 4.0%), all the values were very high.

Table 6.2 Costs of work-related accidents and ill-health in the European Union

Country	Estimated costs (€bn)	Estimated proportion of GNP (%)
Austria	0.4	1.4
Belgium	4.3	2.3
Denmark	3.0	2.7
Finland	3.1	3.8
France	7.0	0.6
Germany	45.0	Not available
Greece	Not available	Not available
Ireland	0.2	0.4
Italy	28.0	3.2
Luxembourg	0.9	2.5
Netherlands	7.6	2.6
Portugal	0.3	0.4
Spain	Not available	3.0
Sweden	7.8	4.0
United Kingdom	36.4 to 58.1	1.1

Source: European Agency for Safety and Health at Work (1999)

The UK Health and Safety Executive (1993) also used a series of case studies to demonstrate the potential financial losses that can arise from accidents and ill-health. They presented the results as estimated annualised losses and related these figures to various financial parameters such as tender price, operating costs, profits, output and running costs, in order to demonstrate their impact. The losses were regarded as significant in each case. In four of the five case studies it was also possible to assess the differences between insured and uninsured costs. These results demonstrated that, on average, the uninsured losses were nearly 17 times higher than the insured losses.

Professional football provides a useful organisational setting for developing and testing theories of health and safety management because injury rates in this sector are at least three orders of magnitude higher than those in recognised high-risk occupations. Drawer and Fuller (2002) developed an economic framework for assessing the impact of players' injuries on team performance. The model utilised the economic interactions existing between the four parameters of quality, salaries, financial turnover and performance and assessed the impact that various levels of player injury would have on the playing and financial performance of a team. The authors suggested that the model, although developed for football, might have applications within other professional sports, and also within more conventional organisational settings such as manufacturing, provided that appropriate input and output parameters were used within the model.

Many organisations have adopted the total loss control approach to business management advocated by Bird and Germain (1990). In this approach, every event that incurs a loss is incorporated into the economic appraisal. Losses may arise, for example, from environmental (waste product), quality (out-of-specification production), energy (heat loss), productivity (plant downtime), and construction (variations to contract) issues as well as from health and safety issues. The Health and Safety Executive (1999) used a total loss approach to estimate the annual costs to employees, employers and society of workplace injuries and ill-health in the UK. They concluded that the total costs, at 1995/96 prices, were of the order of £6bn for employees, £5bn for employers and £12bn for society: this equated to around £900 per person employed every year. Related studies on the costs of work-based accidents have been undertaken in a number of other countries, such as Australia (Larsson and Betts, 1996), the Netherlands (van Beeck *et al.*, 1997), Norway (Kjellén *et al.*, 1997) and the USA (Farrow and Hayakawa, 2002).

The effect of externalities on health and safety management

The difficulties of gathering financial data on a national basis are understandable, but it is also often difficult to gather reliable data within individual organisations. Where companies have not correctly identified high-risk work activities, in particular those relating to potential ill-health, they will almost certainly have failed to allocate appropriate control measures. These companies' operating costs will therefore underestimate the full economic costs of accidents and ill-health, and society will have to provide the necessary support facilities for those employees incurring injuries and ill-health. These costs to society may arise from, for example, hospital treatment, industrial illness compensation and unemployment benefits. This issue is referred to as the effect of *externalities* on

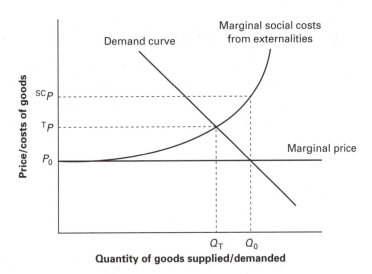

Figure 6.8 The effect of externalities on the supply and demand of goods and services

the cost of production. An externality occurs when one organisation's production or consumption decisions directly affect the production or consumption functions of other people or organisations by means other than the market price. This process is normally controlled by the removal of money from the economy through taxation. This is illustrated in Figure 6.8.

The marketplace sets the equilibrium marginal price for customers and suppliers at P_0 and the quantities supplied and demanded at Q_0. However, the true cost to society of producing at this level, when the social costs associated with accidents and ill-health are included, is ^{SC}P. If these additional costs were added to the price of the goods, the market should stabilise at a true price of ^{T}P and a supply/demand quantity of Q_T. There are a number of ways in which this anomaly can be addressed. In many countries, governments have taken an increasing role in regulating health and safety issues in order to ensure that companies achieve an acceptable level of health and safety management. This involvement includes a requirement that companies achieve certain standards of performance, the imposition of penalties for failing to achieve acceptable standards of performance, or the imposition of a health and safety taxation system. Similar approaches have been employed for environmental issues, where governments have imposed restrictions on gaseous emissions and disposals to landfill sites.

In the example shown in Figure 6.8, a government could recover the true costs of the externalities by imposing a tax on the goods or services that is equivalent to the value $[^{T}P - P_0]$. This would have the effect of maintaining the market price to the supplier at P_0 while increasing the price to the consumer to ^{T}P. This increase in price achieved through taxation would, as described above, reduce demand from Q_0 to Q_T. The tax revenue obtained from the supply of a quantity Q_T of goods or services that carry the tax element will produce $\{Q_T \times [^{T}P - P_0]\}$ revenue for the government. The government should then use this income in order to offset the total social costs of accidents and ill-health arising from the production and supply of these goods and services. The effect of externalities was estimated to be between £9.9bn and £14.1bn per year at 1995/96 prices in the UK (Health and Safety Executive, 1999).

Health and safety standards and economics

The costs of controlling health and safety risks within an organisation are made up from the costs associated with management, assurance and non-conformance:

■ *Management costs* include the costs of providing preventive control measures, such as guarding on machinery, fire sprinkler systems, safety interlocks, supervision, maintenance, personal protective equipment and training.

■ *Assurance costs* include the costs of monitoring performance, such as inspections, audits and reviews.

■ *Non-conformance costs* include the costs of all failures, such as injury, ill-health, damage to plant and equipment, prosecution, and damage to an organisation's reputation.

The impact of standards on the long-term average cost of production

In a survey of financial directors working in the public sector and the manufacturing and service industries (Chartered Institute of Management Accountants, 1994), the cost of compliance with health and safety regulations was identified most frequently (69%) as the business issue that had increased in cost by more than average. The main reason identified for the increase in the cost was stricter health and safety regulation. However, 89% of the respondents in the survey felt that tightening health and safety regulations was the correct thing to do.

The total cost of health and safety management will be directly related to an organisation's standards for health and safety. This occurs because the higher an organisation sets its standards, the greater will be the costs associated with management and assurance, and the lower will be the costs associated with non-conformance. The costs of management and assurance will rise exponentially as the level of standards increases within an organisation because of the law of diminishing returns, which describes the difficulties of trying to achieve the last small improvements in performance. The costs of failure will decrease exponentially as standards improve because as the accident rate is reduced there is less and less potential for further improvements. The total costs of health and safety risks ($^{HS}C_T$) in an organisation are, therefore, dependent on the costs of management (C_M), assurance (C_A) and failure (C_F), which are illustrated in Figure 6.9. These factors represent a direct operational cost to a company, and therefore they are reflected within the long-term average cost of production.

Effective, profitable companies will aim to operate in a way that minimises their risks and their costs in order to reduce the long-term average cost of production. Based purely on a risk management philosophy, a cost-effective company will therefore choose to establish health and safety standards that allow it to operate at the minimum cost point (*RM*), shown in Figure 6.9. At this point, the costs of prevention and assurance are balanced by the costs of failures. However, operating under these conditions means that organisations must accept that there will remain a significant level of injuries and ill-health associated with the company's operations.

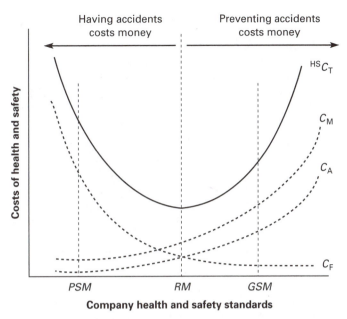

Figure 6.9 Costs of health and safety management as a function of standards

Companies that wish to operate with high moral and social principles may choose to reduce the incidence of injuries and ill-health among their employees and other stakeholders below the level defined by the risk management approach. In this case, they will choose to operate with higher health and safety standards at the position defined in Figure 6.9 as good health and safety management (*GSM*), where the costs associated with accidents and ill-health (C_F) are at a lower level than those at *RM*. However, these companies must accept that choosing to operate with these higher standards will lead to higher management and assurance costs (C_M and C_A) and an overall increase in the total costs, and this will increase the company's long-term average costs. This will ultimately impinge on the company's profits, and may also affect the company's long-term viability as a profitable organisation.

Poorly managed companies that choose to operate with low health and safety standards (*PSM*) will limit their costs for management and assurance (C_M and C_A) but will incur high total operating costs because the cost of failure (C_F) will be significantly higher. This approach may also jeopardise an organisation's long-term viability. In times of economic constraint, companies may decide to reduce expenditure on issues such as training and auditing because they do not appear to have an immediate impact on the organisation's production. These short-term savings, however, should be considered alongside the potential future losses, when the latent problems that build up during times of poor management are realised. Claims that accidents and ill-health cost a company more money than prevention are valid only up to a certain level of performance (RM); beyond this level, improving standards will cost a company more money than they save. There are, however, issues other than financial arguments that must be taken into account, such as the company's reputation for operating to high standards, as this will create a good public image, which may, for example, enable the company to attract and retain higher-quality employees.

The effect of a health and safety tax on performance

By imposing minimum health and safety standards on industry, a government is effectively increasing the operational costs of production for companies. The justification for taking this approach is that governments may have more information about the issues involved, and that they are more likely to be impartial in their judgements about the level and significance of the risks than the companies involved. Government imposition of minimum standards within a work environment reflects a judgement about risk perception, externalities and the human costs involved in injury and ill-health.

One problem for companies voluntarily choosing to operate with higher standards of health and safety than their competitors is that their operating costs may be higher. Therefore a uniform improvement in standards beyond the level defined by the risk management position RM in Figure 6.9 may be attainable only by government intervention. This can be achieved by ensuring that the full social costs of accidents and ill-health are added to the internal costs of accidents and ill-health. This approach increases the costs of failure to C_{F+SC} and creates a need to move to higher standards in order to achieve the new minimum cost position (RM_{SC}): see Figure 6.10. The increased costs arise because of the much higher spending required on management (C_M) and assurance (C_A) at this level of performance compared with the marginal gains obtained from the lower costs of failure (C_F).

The imposition of a direct health and safety tax on the products or services supplied by an industry sector would not achieve the same result because the tax would affect all consumers and all producers equally. The tax would increase costs but would not shift the minimum risk position to higher standards: there-

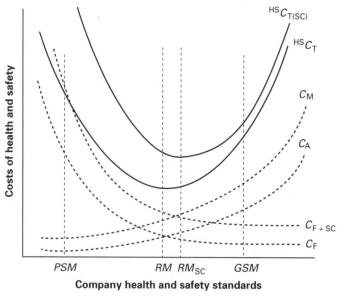

Figure 6.10 The effect on operational standards of imposing social costs for accidents and ill-health

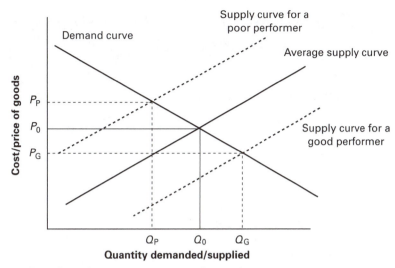

Figure 6.11 The effect of a tax on health and safety performance

fore there would be no net improvement in health and safety performance. However, if a government imposed a tax based on a company's accident and ill-health rates, it would have the effect of increasing the costs of poor performers selectively. This could be achieved, for example, through governments setting industry-wide accident rate targets with penalties imposed for poor performance (resulting in higher production costs) and rebates for good performers (resulting in lower production costs): see Figure 6.11. Demand for goods and services from poorly performing companies (Q_P) will decrease because their higher production costs will require a sale price of P_P in order to generate a profit, whereas there will be an increase in demand for well-performing companies (Q_G), which will be able to sell their products or services at P_G and still make a profit. Poorly performing companies will eventually cease to operate, because they will not be able to sell their higher-priced goods and services in the marketplace. This should result in a general improvement in health and safety performance as the poorly performing companies cease to trade.

If companies were charged the full social costs of accidents and ill-health associated with their work activities, it would force them to change their health and safety strategies in order to remain competitive. They would also need to become more proactive by investing in management and assurance rather than operating reactively by paying the costs associated with their failures. However, if penalty taxation were introduced, it would be important that additional resources were made available for independent inspections in order to ensure that industry-wide compliance with accident-reporting regulations was maintained. It is important that companies investing in prevention strategies complete effective cost–benefit analyses of the initiatives as, although the costs of the initiative may be similar for all companies, the resulting benefits may vary from company to company, because the returns will depend on where they currently fit on the costs versus standards graph shown in Figure 6.9.

Selecting health and safety control measures within a budget constraint

The allocation of resources to health and safety involves normative economic decisions. These decisions are based on organisational judgements about the relative importance of individual health and safety issues and also the relative importance of health and safety compared with other risks. As with many business parameters, health and safety control measures show a diminishing marginal rate of return on investment (the Pareto effect). For example, if a business considered only the use of physical controls within its safety strategy, the maximum safety benefit achievable from its total prevention budget (C_T) would be SB'_T; see Figure 6.12. This occurs because the provision of the second physical control measure provides less safety benefit than the first, the third measure less benefit than the second, and so on (Fuller, 2000). Therefore further increases in the number of physical safety control measures become less and less cost-effective, as they provide decreasing marginal improvements in safety benefit. If, however, the total budget available (C_T) was spread over a range of physical (C_1), management ($C_2 - C_1$) and human factor ($C_T - C_2$) control measures, the overall safety benefit could be raised from SB'_T to SB''_T: see Figure 6.12.

Safety-benefit curves and budget constraints

In the same way that indifference curves can be constructed to describe consumer utility, the utility derived from combinations of control measures can be described by a *safety-benefit curve* (Fuller, 2000). Figure 6.13 shows one example of a safety-benefit curve, SBC_1: this curve describes the locus of combinations of physical and management control measures that provide an equivalent level of safety benefit to an organisation. In the example shown, M_1 units of management controls together with P_1 units of physical controls provide the same level of safety benefit as M_2 units of management controls and P_2 units of physical controls. All safety-benefit

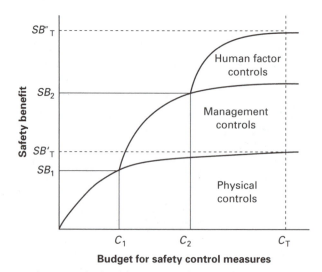

Figure 6.12 Increased returns obtained from a combination of control measures

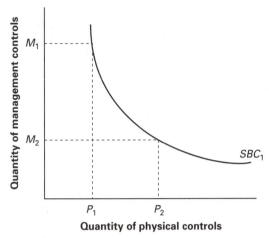

Figure 6.13 Safety benefit as a function of physical and management controls

curves will approach the two axes asymptotically because the effect of diminishing returns causes the marginal rate of safety benefit to be reduced with each increase in the quantity of control measures.

Companies also have to comply with their *budget constraints*, which limit the amount of money available for control measures, and this in turn affects the health and safety standards that can be achieved within the organisation. The maximum quantities of physical, management and human factor controls (Q_P, Q_M, and Q_{HF} respectively) that a company can provide within a budget constraint will depend on the unit prices of the physical, management and human factor controls (U_P, U_M and U_{HF} respectively). The budget available provides resources for the purchase of control measures that are defined by the value $[(Q_P \times U_P) + (Q_M \times U_M) + (Q_{HF} \times U_{HF})]$. Provided a company keeps within its budget constraint, it can provide any mix of control measures. However, the combinations of physical and management controls that fall on the budget constraint line AB, shown in Figure 6.14, represent control strategies that provide the maximum utilisation of the safety budget available.

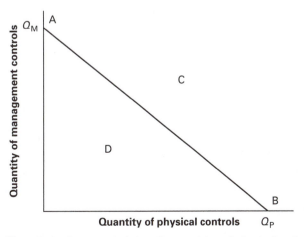

Figure 6.14 The effect of a budget constraint on the provision of physical and management control measures

As discussed previously for indifference curves (Figure 6.4), position A represents the maximum quantity of management controls that can be provided, and position B represents the maximum quantity of physical controls that can be provided within the budget. Point C, above the budget constraint line, represents an overexpenditure of the budget and point D, below the line, represents an underutilisation of the budget available. If safety-benefit curves are superimposed onto the budget constraint line, those combinations of control measures that provide defined levels of safety benefit and remain within the budget constraint can be identified: see Figure 6.15. The combinations of physical and management control measures $(M_1 + P_1)$, $(M_2 + P_2)$ and $(M_3 + P_3)$, identified by positions S_1, S_2 and S_3 respectively, all meet these criteria. However, because employees and employers desire (possibly for different reasons) the highest level of safety benefit available from their investment, any point falling on a higher safety-benefit curve is preferred to a point falling on a lower curve. Therefore the combination of physical and management controls $(M_1 + P_1)$ defined by position S_1, where the budget constraint line just forms a tangent to the safety-benefit curve SBC_2, represents the maximum safety benefit achievable within the budget constraint (A–B). This combination of control measures is preferred to either of the combinations of control measures defined at positions S_2 and S_3, which fall on the lower safety benefit curve SBC_1.

The same principles are valid if all three types of safety control measure, namely physical, management and human factors, are included in the analysis, but in this case a three-dimensional safety-benefit contour and a budget constraint plane are defined (Fuller, 2000).

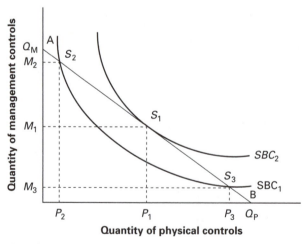

Figure 6.15 Selection of health and safety control measures within a budget constraint

Summary

- Positive economics describes objective, scientific descriptions of the supply and demand of goods and services, whereas normative economics describes policy decisions on how to manage an economy.

- Demand describes the quantity of goods and services that consumers wish to purchase, and supply describes the quantity of goods and services that suppliers wish to produce.

- An organisation's average cost of production is determined by dividing the total costs of producing the goods or services by the quantity produced. The costs of accidents and ill-health are one of the variable costs of production.

- The organisational costs of accidents and ill-health are made up of direct and indirect costs and insured and uninsured losses; some of the costs of organisational failures in health and safety management are borne by society through the provision of medical support and financial compensation for injured workers.

- Managing health and safety risks solely on risk management principles requires organisations to accept that accidents and ill-health will continue to occur; operating with higher health and safety standards based on moral and social principles will incur higher costs and increase the average cost of production for most organisations.

Issues for review and discussion

- Consider how you would define a costing strategy for the direct and indirect costs associated with accidents at work.

- Assess the differences required in a costing strategy that takes account of long-term health issues as well as short-term safety issues.

- Review the arguments for and against a company operating at the highest standards of health and safety management.

- Consider the validity of the statement 'Accidents cost money'.

- Review what information is required to provide a health and safety budget.

References

Bird, F.E. and Germain, G.L. (1990) *Practical Loss Control Leadership*. Loganville: International Loss Control Institute.

Chartered Institute of Management Accountants (1994) *The UK Economy and the Costs of Business*. London: Chartered Institute of Management Accountants.

Drawer, S. and Fuller, C.W. (2002) An economic framework for assessing the impact of injuries in professional football, *Safety Science*, **40**, 537–556.

European Agency for Safety and Health at Work (1999) *Economic Impact of Occupational Safety and Health in the Member States of the European Union*. Bilbao: European Agency for Safety and Health at Work.

European Agency for Safety and Health at Work (2002a) *New tools to improve occupational safety and health and to increase the competitiveness of your business.* Press release (10.09.2002). Bilbao: European Agency for Safety and Health at Work.

European Agency for Safety and Health at Work (2002b) *Inventory of Socioeconomic Costs of Work Accidents*, Factsheet 27. Bilbao: European Agency for Safety and Health at Work.

Farrow, S. and Hayakawa, H. (2002) Investing in safety: an analytical precautionary principle. *Journal of Safety Research* **33**, 165–174.

Fuller, C.W. (2000) Modelling continuous improvement and benchmarking processes through the use of benefit curves. *Benchmarking, An International Journal*, **7**(1), 35–51.

Health and Safety Executive (1993) *The Costs of Accidents at Work.* London: HMSO.

Health and Safety Executive (1999) *The Costs to Britain of Workplace Accidents and Work-related Ill-health in 1995/96.* Sudbury: HSE Books.

Heinrich, H.W. (1930) *Industrial Accidents and Safety. Monthly Labor Review.* Washington: US Department of Labor.

Kjellén, U., Boe, K. and Hagen, H.L. (1997) Economic effects of implementing internal control of health, safety and environment: a retrospective case study of an aluminium plant. *Safety Science*, **27**(2/3), 99–114.

Larsson, T.J. and Betts, N.J. (1996) The variation of occupational injury cost in Australia; estimates based on a small empirical study. *Safety Science*, **24**(2), 143–155.

Swiss Re (2001) *The Economics of Insurance.* Zurich: Swiss Re Publishing.

Turnbull (1999) *Internal Control: Guidance for Directors on the Combined Code.* London: Institute of Chartered Accountants in England & Wales.

van Beeck, E.F., van Roijen, L. and Mackenbach, J.P. (1997) Medical costs and economic production losses due to injuries in the Netherlands. *Journal of Trauma: Injury, Infection and Critical Care*, **42**(6), 1116–1123.

CHAPTER 7

Cost–benefit analysis

You know the cost of everything
And the value of nothing

– R. Ross, 'Bound to love' (1994)

Chapter contents

Introduction

Cost–benefit analysis and related techniques can be used to support normative decisions about risk control, but they cannot demonstrate whether one control measure is intrinsically better than another. The essential requirement of cost–benefit analysis is the provision of appropriate information on costs and benefits to decision-makers in a format that is readily understood and usable. Unfortunately, cost–benefit analysis is not a pure science; it requires the use of a number of debatable concepts, such as the value of a human life, the value of a healthy workplace, who pays the costs, and who receives the benefits. The aims of this chapter are to discuss factors related to cost–benefit analysis and to outline their impact on decision-making. Issues associated with valuing life, injury and ill-health are discussed within this context.

The role of cost–benefit analysis in legislation and standards

Individuals, organisations and society value the benefits of healthy and safe working environments in different ways. The driving factor for organisations is the long-term average costs for the production of goods and/or services, and this dictates that the allocation of resources to health and safety should be made on the basis that the marginal cost of control measures should be no more than the marginal cost of the injury or ill-health. Failure to adopt this approach results in an inefficient allocation of resources. The same argument applies to health and safety legislation and operational standards, because these should be implemented at a level where the marginal cost of the control measures is no more than the marginal cost of injury and ill-health.

Approach adopted in Europe

The European Agency for Safety and Health at Work (1999) concluded from an assessment of the perceived importance of cost–benefit analysis among the Member States that:

> At present there is a substantial interest in estimating the costs and benefits of occupational safety and health measures. Many Member States indicate that economic impact is a key issue at the moment. In others the interest in cost–benefit analysis is growing.
>
> European Agency for Safety and Health at Work (1999: 14)

The European Agency addressed the issue of whether cost–benefit analysis impacted on government decision-making about new health and safety measures, and concluded:

> In some Member States assessment of the economic impact is one of the standard pieces of information considered in political decision-making. However, the way economic assessments influence decision-making varies from one Member State to another. In general, where consensus with social partners is sought CBA usually influences the solutions adopted.
>
> In some Member States economic impact assessment is specifically meant to improve the effectiveness of legislation and to ensure that no unnecessary additional financial burden is created. Using an assessment method allows the socio-economic balance to be improved, as economic consequences are considered in a systematic way.
>
> European Agency for Safety and Health at Work (1999: 16)

The European Agency survey also assessed the way in which cost–benefit analysis assessments were carried out, and identified three approaches that were used within Europe:

- Estimates were made prior to health and safety measures being introduced (*ex ante* evaluation). In some Member States, *ex ante* impact assessments were often routine and sometimes mandatory.

- Estimates were made after health and safety measures had been implemented (*ex post* evaluation). In some countries the assessment of the effectiveness of measures concentrated on the health and safety benefits, and tended not to consider the economic costs of the measures introduced. One problem with *ex post* evaluations is that it may be some time before the benefits are apparent.

- Measurements were made of the economic efficiency of national occupational health and safety systems, although this type of evaluation was not used extensively.

The European Agency subsequently published a review of the socioeconomic costs of work accidents (European Agency for Safety and Health at Work, 2002a) and a simple guide on how economic appraisals of risk mitigation measures could be carried out within organisations (European Agency for Safety and Health at Work, 2002b). The guide recommended using a three-stage approach that identified the investment required, annual costs and cash flow.

Approach adopted in the United Kingdom

Cost–benefit analyses of regulatory proposals have been undertaken in the UK since 1982. The UK government published guidance (Cabinet Office, 1998, 2000) on the requirements for *regulatory impact assessments* of all new regulatory proposals.

> The assessment should include a clear statement of the objectives of the regulatory proposal and its likely effects. It should demonstrate that the proposal is the most effective means of meeting the stated objectives, set out the costs and benefits of the proposal, and identify who will be affected.
>
> Hallett (2000: 1)

The impact assessment involves a risk assessment in order to establish the scale of the issue being addressed and the potential benefits of the regulatory proposal. The proposal should be demonstrated to be the best available option from the range investigated, and this conclusion should be supported by cost–benefit analyses based on the lifetime of the proposal. The UK approach to changes in health and safety regulation advocates that employers, employees, trades unions, local authorities and other stakeholders should take part in the consultation process. Stakeholders are encouraged to comment on the information and analysis contained within the impact assessment and to formally respond to the proposals. Responsible government ministers are then required to state that 'the benefits justify the costs'. Cost–benefit analysis, however, is not the only issue that should be addressed when proposing new health and safety legislation. Fairness in the distribution of costs and benefits across society should also be considered, together with the political and social consequences of decisions associated with low-probability, high-consequence risks. Finally, where the baseline levels of risk are close to an intolerable level of risk, disproportionate costs compared with the potential benefits may be considered to be acceptable.

The UK government also published recommendations for setting health and safety standards (Health and Safety Executive, 1998), which called for:

- common frameworks to quantify costs and benefits;
- account to be taken of important ethical constraints; and
- greater consistency in the way in which costs of risk reduction and the public's values and preferences were evaluated.

Cost–benefit approaches in decision-making

Decisions related to the health and safety of people at work invariably involve choices between risk mitigation options. Although some decisions may be simple and obvious, such as providing high-visibility clothing for people working on public highways, other decisions may be less obvious, such as providing respiratory protective equipment for people working with grain. Within a limited health and safety budget, a health and safety manager may have to make decisions such as whether to allocate resources to reduce an already low probability of a fatality for a small number of the workforce or to reduce a higher probability of minor injuries for a large proportion of the workforce. In order to make these decisions, managers benefit from the use of evaluative models that can provide guidance on choosing the best value-for-money risk mitigation option available. Jones-Lee (1989) identified six approaches that decision-makers can use when making choices over risk mitigation options.

Subjective assessment

This approach avoids the need for accurate values of risk, and is used where the costs and/or benefits associated with one particular option are grossly different from the costs and/or benefits associated with other options. Although the management of health and safety risks raises concerns about the welfare of employees, it must still compete with other functions for the finite financial resources available. Generally, organisations tend to underresource control measures where the potential consequences are perceived to be minimal and to overresource control measures where the potential consequences are perceived to be very high. Therefore, to ensure that health and safety issues are correctly resourced, it is essential for important decisions not to be based on random, arbitrary or subjective decision-making processes. Examples of decisions leading to the provision of inadequate resources that resulted in major disasters include the incidents at Three Mile Island (USA, 1979), Bhopal (India, 1984), Chernobyl (Russia, 1986) and *Piper Alpha* (UK, 1988).

Informal judgement

Informal judgement is based on the assessor's perceptions of risk. This approach acknowledges the potential level of the consequences but avoids the problem of developing complex, formal economic assessment procedures. The main disadvantage of using informal judgements for making resource allocation decisions is that the methodology and conclusions reached are not auditable. A second problem is that the approach is subject to wide variations in the criteria that may be used by different people in the same situation and by the same people in different situations. Jones-Lee (1989) illustrated this point through the concept of *implicit value of safety or implicit value of life* (Table 7.1). The two projects illustrated have the same capital costs (£10m) associated with them. Safety project P1, which will reduce the number of fatalities per year by 3, will also produce a further £6m worth of environmental benefits. Safety project P2, on the other hand, will reduce the number of fatalities by 8 but will produce only £1m worth of environmental benefits.

Table 7.1 The implicit value of safety

	Capital costs of project (£k)	Number of fatalities avoided	Environmental benefits (£k)
Safety project P1	10 000	3	6000
Safety project P2	10 000	8	1000

A decision-maker who chooses P1 has implied that the value of life is less than or equal to £1m (calculated as [£6m – £1m]/[8 – 3]) simply because the additional £5m of environmental benefits obtained under P1 are considered to be worth more than the additional 5 lives saved under P2. Conversely, a decision-maker who chooses P2 rather than P1 has implied that the value of life is greater than or equal to £1m because the additional 5 lives saved under P2 are considered to be worth more than the additional £5m of environmental benefits obtained from P1. In fact, a decision-maker who makes a choice for or against any health and safety project places a value on human life or a related parameter. Therefore, although one may object on principle to the valuation of life, it is unavoidable when business decisions have to be made. This approach is effectively based on the principles of consumer choice and utility, and it enables one to define upper and lower boundaries for the implicit value of life. The approach appears to have a number of advantages, but empirical results indicate that informal judgements lead to inconsistencies in the allocation of implicit values of life, and this will therefore inevitably lead to an inefficient allocation of resources (Jones-Lee, 1989).

Health and safety standards

The use of standards appears to be an ideal way of managing organisational health and safety risks and of establishing consistent performance across sectors and countries. Unfortunately, this approach is subject to two critical weaknesses: the difficulty of defining acceptable and/or tolerable levels of risk, and the difficulty of identifying the criteria against which these standards can be judged. Additionally, an insistence on compliance with health and safety standards takes no account of the cost of compliance, and this can give rise to differences in the implicit values of life within different organisational and operational contexts.

Consider, for example, an organisation that produces the same goods at two production plants. Production plant A, which produces 400 000 units per year, has an accident rate of 2 fatalities per 100 000 units produced. Production plant B, which produces 200 000 units per year, has an accident rate of 6 fatalities per 100 000 units produced. The estimated annual costs of providing control measures that would reduce these accident rates to various values at the two production plants are shown in Table 7.2.

Table 7.2 Costs of reducing the fatal accident rates at two production plants

Fatality rate per 100 000 units produced	Production plant A		Production plant B	
	Number of fatalities per year	Annual cost of control measures (£k)	Number of fatalities per year	Annual cost of control measures (£k)
6.00			12	–
4.00			8	500
2.00	8	–	4	2000
1.50	6	200	3	3000
1.00	4	500	2	4500
0.50	2	1000	1	8000
0.25	1	1500	–	–
0	0	3000	0	14000

If the company sets a standard for health and safety performance across all production plants of 1.0 fatality per 100 000 units produced, the number of fatalities will be reduced from 8 to 4 at Plant A and from 12 to 2 at Plant B. The total improvement achieved by the company across both plants amounts to 14 lives. The total cost to the company of achieving this will be £5 000 000 (Plant A, £500 000; Plant B, £4 500 000). If one now considers the cost of avoiding one further fatality at Plant A, the value of life with a fatality rate of 1 has effectively been set at less than £250 000 (calculated as £[1 000 000 – 500 000] / 2), because the company is not prepared to spend a further £500 000 to reduce the number of fatalities by 2. In a similar way, if one considers the implicit cost of avoiding one further fatality at Plant B, the value of life has effectively been set at £3 500 000 (calculated as £[8 000 000 – 4 500 000] / 1). The imposition of a uniform standard of performance across all production plants has therefore created an inconsistency within the company over the valuation of human life.

An alternative option for the company is to spread the planned additional expenditure of £5 000 000 on control measures between Plant A and Plant B, such that the implicit value of life is the same at both locations. The company will now spend £1 500 000 at Plant A and £3 000 000 at Plant B. This will reduce the fatality rate to 0.25 and the number of fatalities at Plant A from 8 to 1, and the fatality rate at Plant B to 1.50 and the number of fatalities from 12 to 3. In this situation, the cost of avoiding one more fatality is £1 500 000 at both plants (calculated as Plant A: [£3.0m – £1.5m]; Plant B: [£4.5m – £3.0m]). The overall benefit obtained is a reduction in the total number of fatalities within the company from 20 to 4 (made up from Plant A, 7; Plant B, 9). Therefore the implementation of common operational standards and an inconsistent valuation of life would, in this example, cause two additional fatalities to employees with an additional expenditure of £500 000. The implementation of uniform operational standards in every case may not, therefore, create an efficient method of resource allocation.

Cost-effectiveness analysis

Cost-effectiveness analysis either maximises the health and safety benefits achieved within a given budget or minimises the cost of achieving a defined level of performance. Cost-effectiveness analysis normally compares a range of options that produces broadly similar benefits. The least-cost option that produces the desired outcomes is regarded as the most cost-effective choice. Cost-effectiveness analysis does not place a value on the benefit, so this approach is appropriate only where the health and safety budget has been fixed, and the assessment is used merely as a means of optimising performance within the budget. In this respect, cost-effectiveness analysis neither provides any information about the safety budget required nor differentiates between the effectiveness of a range of control options where the outputs are different.

Costing risk and valuing safety

It is often difficult to define the costs associated with risks or the value of benefits gained because these depend on circumstances and the perceptions of the people involved. For example, a production group in an organisation may include an allocation within their operational budget for fitting safety devices and providing equipment maintenance schedules so that production downtime is minimised in order to maximise output. These resource allocations based on production criteria, however, will also contribute to a safer work environment. However, the reverse can also occur, where expenditure in one favoured area can create an opportunity cost that reduces health and safety performance in another area (Hjalte *et al.*, 2003). There are a number of ways in which benefits may be valued within this approach.

Valuations based on organisational output use the concepts of 'gross output' or 'human capital', which define the cost of a fatality or accident as the discounted present value of an injured employee's future output. Account is also taken of other financial losses, such as damage to machinery, plant and product. The cost of preventing a fatality or accident is then regarded as an *averted loss*. From an employee's perspective this approach equates their value to an organisational output rather than to an intrinsic consideration of their value of life. To compensate for this, some output valuation methods also include a component for 'pain and suffering'.

Valuations based on an individual's welfare take into account the perceptions and preferences of the individuals affected by the risks. The difficulty associated with this approach is that it requires a measure of preference: this is achieved through the concept of an individual's *willingness to pay* for a particular health and safety control measure. The benefits of a project can then be assessed by summing each individual's 'willingness to pay' value and comparing this with the costs of the project.

Valuations based on life insurance consider the value of an averted fatality, injury or ill-health. This value is defined by the average value of every insurance policy that individuals have taken out in order to compensate themselves for potential losses. The weakness of this approach is that the amount insured will not necessarily relate to the amount that an individual will be willing to pay for his or her own health and safety. It is also quite conceivable that, although an individual may value their health and safety highly, they may through financial constraints have no insurance cover whatsoever. In contrast, an individual who may have little regard for their health and safety and is, therefore, prepared to undertake high-risk activities may have extensive life insurance cover.

Valuations based on litigation claims are not related to the value of a life lost or to an injury or ill-health sustained but to the legal liability attributable to an incident. This type of valuation will vary significantly from one country to another, owing to differences in national litigation cultures and systems. Compensation claims may be determined by, for example, lost income, pain and suffering and the number of dependants; therefore similar injuries may result in significant differences in compensation even within the same industrial sector and country.

Valuations based on an individual's value of time depend on lost life expectancy or impaired capabilities caused by an injury or ill-health. The weakness of this approach is that, although it is relatively easy to value working time through lost income, it is almost impossible to value lost leisure time or the loss of the ability to carry out certain tasks or activities. It is also very difficult to relate an individual's willingness to pay not to be incapacitated, as far as leisure activities are concerned, with the valuation that would be placed on these issues in a court of law.

Decision analysis

This approach involves identifying the major potential losses associated with each risk and defining them in terms of, for example, fatalities, injuries, ill-health, number of people involved, reduced production output or increased operational costs. These losses describe an organisation's risk utility function and represent the concerns that decision-makers should then consider. Decision analysis related to health and safety creates a conflict, as decision-makers must minimise the expected loss of life and also achieve an equitable distribution of the risk across the affected population. A weakness of this approach is that decision-makers must carry out complex assessments of the inputs and outputs of a range of risk control options, so that the effects of each of these options on the overall organisational risk utility function can be determined. It is possible that, in some circumstances, a risk control option may result in a negative change in the risk utility function. The decision analysis approach is often quite complex because there are no guidelines available as to which standards, if any, should be used when comparing, for example, an averted loss of life with an averted loss of production.

Value of life

For some people the mere act of attempting to place a value on someone's life is perceived as being morally and socially unacceptable. It is felt that money simply cannot be equated to the death, serious injury or ill-health of an individual. However, so far as decisions on the choice of health and safety control measures are concerned, it is essential to value life in order to equate the costs of prevention with a marginal reduction in the probability of a fatality, a serious injury or ill-health. The value of a statistical life is a common parameter used in cost–benefit analysis, but it raises emotive feelings among many people and for this reason, the concept is often framed in terms of 'the value of a life saved', 'the cost of a fatality averted' or 'the value of preventing a statistical fatality'.

Valuation of a life

The value of a life can be discussed in many ways (Viscusi, 1992). For example, it can be discussed in terms of the value of a specified individual as defined by the person concerned, in terms of a statistical person as defined by an independent assessor, or in terms of a statistical person as defined by their value to society.

The value of a person to society changes significantly with age (Figure 7.1). At the moment of birth, a child has little or no value to society, other than in terms of the love of the parents. The child then rapidly assumes a negative value to society because of the costs incurred in providing medical care, education and child support (Region A). As the child reaches maturity, around 18 years of age, he or she will begin to generate a net income to society through work activities and thereby contribute to the wealth of the nation (Region B). However, as he or she becomes older and reaches retirement age, the financial implications to society increase again through the costs associated with medical care and social support schemes (Region C).

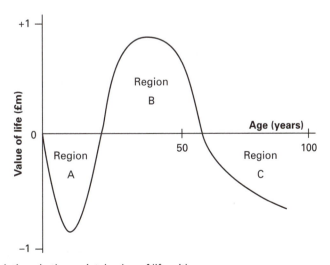

Figure 7.1 Variations in the societal value of life with age

Jones-Lee (1989) proposed a similar model for people aged between 16 and 70. The model, which was based on income generation, predicted an inverted U-shaped graph that started at a low value, peaked during early adulthood and middle age and decreased thereafter (Figure 7.2).

If values of life are calculated for everyone in a population, using either of the approaches described above, they will describe a log-normal distribution because not everyone has the same wealth-generating abilities: see Figure 7.3. It is then necessary to determine whether the value of life that should be used in cost–benefit analyses should be the mean, median or mode value of this distribution. Jones-Lee (1989) favoured the use of the median value because of the skewed distribution of the values obtained. If the mean value is used, the valuation is distorted to a disproportionately high value as a result of a relatively small number of very highly valued people.

Any decision to introduce control measures in order to reduce the probability of injury or ill-health implies that a value has been placed on life. The value assigned will reflect the preferences and concerns of the government, organisations, society and individuals. Where a valuation of life approach is used in cost–benefit analysis, the rejection of a specified control measure implies that the cost of the control measure is greater than the value of the life protected. The advantages (Hallett, 2000) of using a monetary value of life in cost–benefit analysis are that it helps to:

- make the decision-making process transparent;
- base the decisions on individual, societal, organisational and governmental preferences about risk; and
- achieve consistency in decision-making over time and across organisational settings.

One issue of concern to many people, however, is that cost–benefit analysis implies that a rescue attempt or a medical treatment of someone in danger should be abandoned if/when the costs exceed the value of life.

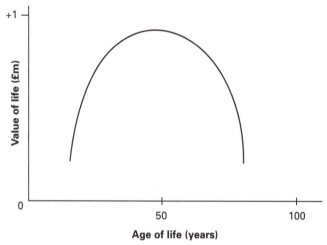

Figure 7.2 Variations in the value of life with age based on income generation
Source: Jones-Lee (1989)

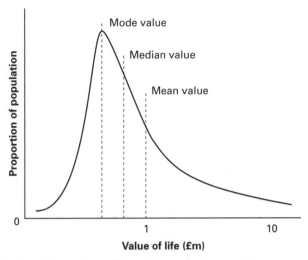

Figure 7.3 Distribution of the values of life within a sample population

Valuation of non-fatal injuries and ill-health

The numbers of non-fatal injuries and ill-health at work significantly exceed the number of fatalities (Health and Safety Commission, 2003), so it is important to establish valuations for injuries and ill-health of this type for use in cost–benefit analysis. In these cases, valuations tend to be based on income generation or the gross output capabilities of individuals. A complicating factor, however, is that the same injury may have different consequences for people working in different environments. The impact of risks on the health of workers can also be expressed in terms of measures such as 'years of potential life lost' (Bailer *et al.*, 2003) or 'years of life lost per year worked' (Park *et al.*, 2002); the latter method in particular provides a measure that is intuitively easier to understand and to communicate. One simple approach is to allocate *equivalent life or ratio values* for non-fatal injuries and diseases, which can then be used in cost–benefit calculations. Examples of possible values are shown in Table 7.3.

Table 7.3 Nominal equivalent life and ratio values used for injuries and ill-health in cost–benefit analyses

Injury/ill-health	Equivalent value of life	Ratio to fatality value
Fatality	1	1
Major injury (e.g. amputation)	0.1	10
Minor injury (e.g. sprain/strain)	0.005	200
Chronic illness (e.g. asbestosis)	0.5	2
Treatable illness (e.g. dermatitis)	0.01	100
First aid (e.g. cut finger)	0.0001	10 000

Willingness to pay and willingness to accept

Although the use of monetary values for loss of life, injury or ill-health may not be acceptable to many people, economists consider it to be a convenient method for assessing individual preferences for one option over other options. However, the monetary values that individuals place on a certain issue depend on how the issue is presented. This is referred to as the *willingness to pay* and *willingness to accept* question:

- willingness to pay (WTP) refers to how much someone is prepared to pay to prevent a loss occurring; whereas
- willingness to accept (WTA) refers to how much someone is prepared to accept in compensation for the loss of a benefit.

In theory, the WTP value should be the same as the WTA value. In practice, though, when individuals are asked to make preference choices, their WTA values are invariably higher than their WTP values. The key reason for this difference is an individual's preference to gain something rather than to lose something, as the negative impact of a loss is considered to be greater than the positive impact of an equivalent gain (Sugden *et al.*, 2000). This causes individuals to place a greater value on compensation (WTA). Kahneman and Tversky (1979) referred to this as *loss aversion*. Additionally, if individuals define a current benefit, such as their health and safety, as being beyond any value of compensation, it is not possible to carry out a cost–benefit analysis. The problems associated with these differences and the higher WTA values mean that governmental and organisational decisions based on cost–benefit analyses use WTP valuations.

WTP values for risk mitigation options are normally determined by two techniques: *revealed preference* and *contingent valuation* (Beattie *et al.*, 1998). The revealed preference approach obtains data from people based on real choices of trading money for risk. Contingent valuation obtains data from people on their WTP for hypothetical reductions in health and safety risks. However, there are a number of important issues surrounding the validity of the WTP approach in cost–benefit analysis. These include the following:

- WTP values often vary with the probability of death. If the probability of a fatality or a disease is very low, people tend to assume that the adverse event will occur to someone else rather than to themselves, and their WTP value reflects this view. However, if the probability of the adverse event is very high then an individual's WTP value increases. This is clearly an anomaly, because the value of a life should be independent of the probability of an event occurring. If a statistical life is valued at £1m, it implies that where there is a risk of death of 1 in 10^5 per year, the equivalent valuation per person is £10 (i.e. £1m/10^5).
- An individual's valuation of another person's life is likely to be less than the value they place on their own life. Therefore cost–benefit analyses should generally not consider a specified individual but always refer to a statistical person.
- Valuations of life and people's WTP for improved control measures to prevent further loss of life invariably increase after serious accidents or incidents even though the value of life and the probability of occurrence remain the same.
- Valuations of life often vary between organisations, industrial sectors, government departments and countries. These variations can be related to cultural and religious criteria, a company's ability to pay, the dread fear associated with some types of death, and the economic strength of different countries.

■ It is normally more difficult for individuals to allocate an equivalent life valuation to a major injury or disease than to a fatality. In reality, the costs to an individual or their family are often greater for a non-fatal injury than they are for a fatality.

Permissive and restrictive approaches to valuation

The best people to judge and define values of WTP and WTA are those people who may be directly affected by the risks and who will, therefore, incur the losses; they should, however, be people who are not anticipating or expecting a loss. Responses to questions about WTP and WTA values will clearly depend on personal views, but they may also depend on how the questions are framed; this is referred to as the *permissive* and *restrictive* effects. For example, if a construction worker on a building site were approached to determine his or her valuation of wearing a safety helmet on site, the responses would depend on the worker's personal views about head protection, but also on whether the options were presented in terms of his or her willingness to pay to wear head protection or willingness to accept compensation for not wearing head protection: see Table 7.4.

Table 7.4 Permissive and restrictive approaches to obtaining WTP and WTA valuations for wearing head protection

	Individual is against *wearing head protection*	*Individual is* for *wearing head protection*
Permissive approach	WTP for the right to continue not to wear head protection	WTP for the right to continue wearing head protection
Restrictive approach	WTA compensation for giving up the right not to wear head protection.	WTA compensation for giving up the right to wear head protection

The valuations that individuals identify in each of these four scenarios may be different. For example, if an individual is wealthy, he or she may be prepared to pay significantly more to retain his or her freedom of choice than someone who has limited financial resources. Similarly, someone who is wealthy is more likely to demand higher levels of compensation to give up something that they wish to do than someone with limited finances.

Valuing dread and future risks

Jones-Lee (1989) argued that, even if one accepts the WTP approach for the valuation of life, there are still a number of unresolved issues, such as:

■ Should the value of a life be the same for a fatality resulting from dread, involuntary and unknown risks as for a fatality resulting from non-dread, voluntary and known risks?

■ Should values of life for the present population be the same as those for future generations?

Valuations of life normally assume that the valuation is independent of the causation and time frame, and so all causes of injury and ill-health should be treated as equivalent events. However, people face a wide range of hazards and have different perceptions about the risks associated with dread/non-dread, voluntary/involuntary and known/unknown risk factors (Slovic, 1992). These different perceptions may lead to different valuations of life in different contexts (Beattie *et al.*, 2000). It has been suggested that where it is possible to obtain values of life for a statistical person for involuntary, dread risks the values may be several times higher than those obtained for non-dread, voluntary risks (Jones-Lee, 1989).

Values of life for future generations for risks such as radiation and genetically modified foods are more difficult to assess. Jones-Lee (1989) discussed two divergent opinions that can be taken:

- No account should be taken of the risks to people who are at present unborn.
- So far as possible, account should be taken of the interests of all present and future people who are or may be affected by risk decisions.

In addressing these two divergent views, he questioned:

- How is it possible to know or to take into account the views of an unborn child?
- If it is possible to take into account the views of an unborn individual, how should these views be weighted against the views of an individual living at the present time?

Jones-Lee (1989) concluded that the best compromise option was to take account of the interests of future generations and to assume that their views will be the same as those of people alive today.

Comparing costs and benefits

Risk assessments lead to the need to make judgements about risk control measures for work activities. These judgements therefore require assessors to consider how limited resources can be utilised most effectively. It is only valid to use cost–benefit analysis for risk assessment where the levels of risk fall within the ALARP region, because outside this region the risks are either trivial or intolerable. There is therefore a strong link between risk assessment and cost–benefit analysis, and this requires a number of issues to be considered (Health and Safety Executive, 1996), such as:

- How should risks and benefits be valued?
- How do risks and benefits vary with time?
- How should future costs and benefits be discounted?

In comparing costs and benefits within a risk assessment, one is effectively considering the input and output parameters of the activity.

Inputs are the resources required for risk mitigation, and *costs* are defined as the monetary value of these inputs.

Outputs are the products of the risk mitigation project, and the *outcomes* are the consequences expressed, for example, as reductions in the levels of injury and ill-health or other losses to the organisation. *Benefits* are defined as the sum of the monetary values of the outcomes to employees, employers and society in general: these benefits may be positive or negative in value. A negative benefit effectively becomes a cost in the cost–benefit equation.

Costs

Costs associated with workplace accidents and ill-health are borne by the injured person and their family, the employer and society in general.

Costs to employees and their families are made up from two components:

- *Financial costs* consist of loss of earnings, as a result of absence from work or loss of job, and personal costs associated with medical treatment.
- *Human costs* consist of a loss in the quality of life, such as the pain and suffering experienced by the employee and their family.

Costs to employers are made up from the loss of production output, payments to injured employees during their absence, first aid facilities and treatment, administrative costs, recruitment costs, damage to plant and equipment, compensation payments to injured employees, and legal costs associated with prosecutions and civil liability claims.

Costs to society are not simply the sum of the costs to employees and employers; they also include other costs, such as hospital treatment, fire, police and ambulance services, disability payments, social security payments, government departments, enforcement agencies, and costs of inquiries and prosecutions.

Opportunity costs

Accountants' views of costs and benefits are not the same as those of economists. Accountants provide a summary of an organisation's finances through the balance sheets presented in the annual financial statement. This provides information on, for example, the current valuations of plant and equipment, financial turnover, sales and profits. Accountants are interested in actual values that appear on the balance sheet and represent income or expenditure, but economists are more interested in costs and benefits as parameters that affect an organisation's decision-making processes about resource allocation. Economists often refer to a cost as an *opportunity cost*: 'Opportunity cost is the amount lost by not using the resource (labour or capital) in its best alternative use' (Begg *et al.*, 1991: 100).

In order to explain this further, consider a €30 000 investment in safety equipment for a process plant. It is anticipated that this investment will reduce accidents and provide a 'benefit' of €45 000 by way of reduced lost-time accidents, broken equipment, lost production, etc. The 'accounting profit' from this investment appears on the balance sheet as €15 000. However, because installation, commissioning, operation and maintenance of the safety equipment consume operators' time equivalent to 0.25 of a person over a year, at an annual salary of €50 000, there is an additional 'lost' resource of €12 500 that must be taken into account. This reduces the 'profit' to €2 500. In addition, one must take into account the potential benefits that could have been accrued from the €30 000 invested in the safety equipment. If this €30 000 had been invested with a return of 10% the lost income would be €3 000. When this figure is also taken into account, the original 'accounting profit' of €15 000 is further reduced, and the 'economic profit' actually becomes a €500 *loss*.

Benefits

In many situations the concepts of cost and benefit are easily understood. For example, if one buys a television, the cost is the price paid to the storekeeper and the benefit is the entertainment value accruing from watching the television pro-grammes. Similarly, if one buys food from a supermarket, the cost is the total price of the individual items purchased together with the energy required to cook the food, and the benefits are the satisfaction received from quelling hunger pains and the pleasure of eating the food. In each case one has gained tangible benefits that one did not have before incurring the costs.

When considering health and safety, an employee arrives at work in the morning in good health; during the day the organisation expends a large number of resources on health and safety management, and at the end of the day the employee goes home (hopefully) in the same state of good health. The costs associated with this activity are clear, but the benefits are less clear as the employee has gone home no better off than when he or she came to work in the morning. In this case the costs do not appear to have created a tangible benefit; they have instead *averted a potential loss*. This is an important concept in health and safety cost–benefit analyses. However, it could be considered that the organi-sation has received a tangible benefit in the form of the goodwill generated among its employees and society through the creation of a safe and healthy work environment.

Two further issues must be considered in relation to benefits and/or averted losses obtained from risk control initiatives. The first issue is that benefits accrue over a period of time, which is normally some time after the costs were incurred. It is therefore essential in cost–benefit analyses to take this factor into account by calculating the *discounted* or *net present values* of future benefits. The second issue is that it is often difficult, if not impossible, to define completely whether appar-ent benefits have actually resulted from the costs incurred. This issue can be assessed through the process of *sensitivity analysis*.

Discounting and net present values

Discounted values reflect the reality that a sum of money is normally worth more today than the same sum of money at some time in the future. This can be explained from the point that €1000 invested today will be worth €1100 in one year, or that €1000 worth of goods bought today will cost €1100 to purchase next year if the annual rate of inflation is 10%. Therefore costs incurred today must be compared with the benefits obtained at some time in the future but equated to today's values.

This situation can be described in general terms. If one invests €M at an interest rate of R, the value of the investment after the first year will be €$(M + MR)$ or €$M(1 + R)$. After the second year, the value of the investment will have increased further to €$([M + MR] + [M + MR]R)$ or €$M(1 + R)^2$. Through the process of compound interest, an initial investment of €M will grow to €$M(1 + R)^n$ after n years. An alternative way of viewing these figures is that, to achieve a benefit equal to €P in n years' time, one must have a benefit with a current net present value of €$P/(1 + R)^n$. Here the term $1/(1 + R)^n$ is termed the *discount factor* and the equivalent current value of €P is the *net present value*.

The effect of net present value on cost–benefit calculations is illustrated in Table 7.5; this example describes the costs and benefits associated with an investment of €10 000 in a safety initiative that produces benefits of €2000 each year for 10 years. The calculations assume an annual inflation rate of 10%. A simple calculation based on actual values indicates that the breakeven time for the project is 5 years, but the calculation of the cumulative net present value of the benefits shows that the true breakeven does not occur until the eighth year. In order to simplify the presentation in Table 7.5, no account has been taken of the opportunity costs associated with the original €10 000 investment or any additional future costs that may be required to maintain and operate the safety measures.

Table 7.5 The effect of net present values on the return on an investment

Year	Costs (€)	Net present value of costs (€)	Benefits, P (€)	Net present value of benefits, $P/(1+R)^n$ (€)	Cumulative net present value of benefits (€)
0	10 000	10 000	0	0	0
1	0	0	2 000	1 818	1 818
2	0	0	2 000	1 653	3 471
3	0	0	2 000	1 503	4 974
4	0	0	2 000	1 366	6 340
5	0	0	2 000	1 242	7 582
6	0	0	2 000	1 129	8 711
7	0	0	2 000	1 026	9 737
8	0	0	2 000	933	10 670
9	0	0	2 000	848	11 518
10	0	0	2 000	771	12 289
Total	**10 000**	**10 000**	**20 000**	**12 289**	**12 289**

n: year of project and $R = 0.1$

Cost-effectiveness and cost–benefit analyses

Cost-effectiveness analysis is used to maximise the return from a given budget, whereas cost–benefit analysis is used to assess whether the benefits of a project are greater than the costs (Johannesson, 1995).

Cost-effectiveness analysis

Cost-effectiveness analysis, which was discussed earlier, is used to compare the costs associated with a range of risk control measures that achieve similar benefits in order to identify the least cost option. No account is taken of the quality of the benefits achieved, because the analysis is based on the assumption that the defined safety benefits are achieved by all the options assessed. This approach is illustrated in Table 7.6 for two safety strategies costing different amounts and producing different quantities of the same outputs (accidents avoided).

Table 7.6 Cost-effectiveness analysis of two safety strategies

	Project costs (€)	Number of accidents avoided	Average cost per accident avoided (€)
Safety strategy S1	20 000	50	400
Safety strategy S2	18 000	30	600

The average cost per accident prevented through safety strategy S1 is €400 (€20 000/50) whereas the average cost per accident prevented through safety strategy S2 is €600 (€18 000/30). In order to use cost–effectiveness analysis to compare different strategies, they must share common outputs and be measured in similar terms. This is satisfied in the example presented, and therefore one concludes that safety strategy S1 is more cost-effective than safety strategy S2.

Cost–benefit analysis

Cost–benefit analysis takes the assessment a stage further by incorporating valuations of the costs and the benefits into the calculations. This necessitates monetary values being assigned to both the costs and the benefits so that a direct comparison can be made in order to obtain a cost–benefit ratio. The cost–benefit principle can be utilised and presented in several ways. For example:

- *Value of equivalent life*:

$$\text{Cost–benefit} = \frac{\text{Value of equivalent lives saved over the lifetime of project}}{\text{Cost of the control measures over their lifetime}}$$

- *Value of an averted loss*:

$$\text{Cost–benefit} = \frac{\text{Value of averted losses}}{\text{Cost of the control measures over their lifetime}}$$

- *Value of risk reduction*:

$$\text{Cost–benefit} = \frac{\text{Liability of original risk – liability of residual risk}}{\text{Cost of the control measures over their lifetime}}$$

Begg *et al.* (1991) state that decisions based on cost–benefit analysis should be reached in the following way:

> Compare the present value of the costs with the present value of the benefits. The action should be undertaken only if the present value of the benefits exceeds the present value of the costs.
>
> Begg *et al.* (1991: 201)

Therefore, in each of the examples presented above, if the cost–benefit ratio is greater than 1, the project can be accepted on the grounds that the benefits outweigh the costs, but if the ratio is less than 1 the project can be rejected on the grounds that the costs outweigh the benefits.

This cost–benefit approach is illustrated in Table 7.7, using the same safety strategies described for the cost-effectiveness example and presented in Table 7.6, with the added criterion that the benefit attributable to each accident avoided is €500.

Table 7.7 Cost–benefit analysis of two safety strategies

	Project costs (€)	Number of accidents avoided	Total benefit (€)	Net benefit (€)	Cost–benefit ratio
Safety strategy S1	20 000	50	25 000	+5000	1.25
Safety strategy S2	18 000	30	15 000	–3000	0.83

The cost–benefit analysis now shows that safety strategy S1 produces a net benefit of €5000 and a cost–benefit ratio of 1.25. Safety strategy S2, on the other hand, has a cost–benefit ratio of less than 1, and should therefore be rejected; the analysis also shows that the net benefit is a *loss* of €3000.

In the UK, around 200 employees out of a total workforce of around 20 million are killed at work each year (Health and Safety Commission, 2003). This represents a fatal accident rate for employees of 1 in 10^5 per year. If a new set of health and safety regulations could be introduced to reduce this accident rate to 0.8 in 10^5 per year, at an annual cost of £50 000 000, the government would need to calculate whether the new legislation would be cost-beneficial. For the purposes of this exercise the value of life is set at £2 000 000.

■ Liability of original risk was 20m (number of people in the national workforce) $\times$ 1 $\times$ 10^{-5} (probability of a fatality) $\times$ £2m (value of life) = 40×10^7.

■ Liability of residual risk is 20m (number of people in the national workforce) $\times$ 0.8 $\times$ 10^{-5} (probability of a fatality) $\times$ £2m (value of life) = 32×10^7.

The cost–benefit ratio for the new legislation is therefore

$$\text{Cost–benefit ratio} = \frac{(40 \times 10^7) - (32 \times 10^7)}{50 \times 10^{16}} \quad \text{(the cost of the control measure)}$$

$$= 1.6$$

Therefore, subject to the need to refine the calculation to take into account net present values and opportunity costs associated with the £50m investment and a sensitivity analysis to confirm that the net benefit value can be attributed to the intervention, it can be concluded that the new legislation would be cost-beneficial.

Sensitivity analysis

Cost–benefit analysis normally relies on the premise that there is a causal link between the benefits identified and the improvement measures implemented and, therefore, by implication the costs expended. If the benefits cannot be wholly linked to the costs then the validity of the calculations must be questioned. The example illustrated in Table 7.8 shows how the conclusions from a cost–benefit analysis can change depending on the level of the causal link between the costs of an intervention and the predicted benefits. The example presented describes a $20 000 investment in control measures, which results in a claimed $60 000 benefit through reduced numbers of accidents. The cost–benefit analysis is subjected to a sensitivity analysis, whereby the causal benefits that can be attributed to the safety intervention are attenuated to 75%, 50% and 25% of the total benefits obtained.

Table 7.8 Sensitivity analysis for a safety intervention

Cost of safety intervention ($)	Total safety benefits achieved ($)	% of benefits attributable to safety intervention	Benefit attributable to safety intervention ($)	Net benefit attributable to safety intervention ($)	Benefit/ cost ratio
20 000	60 000	100	60 000	40 000	3.00
20 000	60 000	75	45 000	25 000	2.25
20 000	60 000	50	30 000	10 000	1.50
20 000	60 000	25	15 000	−5 000	0.75

The net benefit varies from $40 000, with all benefits attributable to the safety intervention, to −$5000, where only 25% of the benefits can be attributed to the safety intervention.

Strengths and weaknesses of cost–benefit analysis

It should be remembered that cost–benefit analysis is a technique for evaluating future benefits against current and future costs. The lack of precision associated with cost–benefit analysis can give rise to significantly different outcomes in assessments of the same issues by different people. In addition, it is often easier to identify and evaluate the costs than the benefits. Costs of health and safety control measures are normally incurred by organisations, whereas a range of stakeholders who often bear none of the costs receive the benefits. Tudor (2000) described a ripple effect that can occur as benefits from health and safety improvement programmes spread across society. However, measuring these ripple benefits is even more difficult than measuring the direct benefits.

A significant argument against cost–benefit analysis is that, although it is an inaccurate technique, it creates an image of accuracy and precision. Many of the valuations used for the costs and benefits reflect the perceptions of the person carrying out the analysis rather than their real values. It is also often difficult to incorporate realistic calculations of the net present value of future costs and benefits into the analyses. Tudor (2000) defined three main philosophical problems with the cost–benefit process:

- inappropriate use of financial valuations of human health effects;
- inadequate justification for valuing human health effects on the basis of WTP research; and
- indeterminacy of the value of human life.

The main strength of cost–benefit analysis is that, although it has a number of weaknesses such as the value of life concept, it is better for evaluating projects than other techniques. In addition, because organisations have to justify their decisions, cost–benefit analysis provides an auditable assessment process. The technique also enables the additional costs incurred in implementing moral and social standards of health and safety to be evaluated. Frick (2000) summarised the strengths of the cost–benefit approach as:

- defining how to allocate limited resources efficiently; and
- revealing how the costs of work-related injuries and ill-health are offloaded onto society.

Although Frick (2000) claims that the cost–benefit approach underestimates the benefits and overestimates the costs of health and safety improvement programmes, the benefits of the technique are considerable:

> Cost–benefit analyses are thus important weapons in the intellectual arms race to win public opinion and make favourable political decisions. Their scientific basis and seemingly precise findings make them influential in defining social problems and solutions in the field of occupational safety and health. This impact is also growing in the European political occupational safety and health debate. Occupational safety and health activists – researchers, trade unionists, administrators and others – are generally still inexperienced and unskilled in this power game. However, if they combine the economic knowledge with their occupational safety and health competence before decisions are made, they can in the future turn cost–benefit analyses from obstructions to weapons to improve occupational safety and health.
>
> Frick (2000: 7)

Summary

- Some organisations and governments use cost–benefit analysis to support decisions on changes in health and safety legislation and standards.

- Cost–benefit methodologies can range from qualitative opinions to quantitative assessments, and can involve subjective assessments, informal judgements, standards, cost-effectiveness analysis, valuations of life and decision analysis.

- Quantitative cost–benefit analysis entails accepting that a valuation must be ascribed to human life; this can be determined in a number of ways, such as using an individual's organisational output, welfare, life insurance, litigation claims and value of time parameters.

- Valuations of life are most commonly based on the principle of an individual's willingness to pay to avoid a fatality, injury or ill-health. Valuations of non-fatal injuries and diseases are normally defined as fractions of an equivalent life or as the number of years of life lost per year exposed to a hazard. An individual's valuation of life is often increased when dread, involuntary and unknown risks are involved.

- Total costs and benefits to employees, employers and society must be included in a cost–benefit analysis, and the analysis must take into account opportunity costs associated with investments in risk control measures and discounted values where benefits are obtained at some future point in time.

Issues for review and discussion

- Evaluate why the 'willingness to pay' and 'willingness to accept' approaches to cost–benefit analysis will invariably produce different conclusions.

- Consider how the permissive and restrictive approaches to the valuation of life may be affected by the individual personalities of the people involved in making the choices.

- Review how cost–benefit analysis provides an input to decision-making in the choice of health and safety control measures.

- Assess whether it is acceptable to consider an 'averted loss' as a real benefit in cost–benefit analysis.

- Review the ways in which your value of life changes throughout your lifetime.

References

Bailer, A.J., Bena, J.F., Stayner, L.T., Halperin, W.E. and Park, R.M. (2003) External cause-specific summaries of occupational fatal injuries. Part II: An analysis of years of potential life lost. *American Journal of Industrial Medicine*, **43**, 251–261.

Beattie, J., Carthy, T., Chilton, S., Covey, J., Dolan, P., Hopkins, L., Jones-Lee, M., Loomes, G., Pidgeon, N., Robinson, A. and Spencer, A. (2000) *The Valuation of Benefits of Health and Safety Control: Final Report*. London: Health and Safety Executive.

Beattie, J., Chilton, S., Cookson, R., Hopkins, L., Jones-Lee, M., Loomes, G., Pidgeon, N., Robinson, A. and Spencer, A. (1998) *Valuing Health and Safety Controls: A Literature Review*. London: Health and Safety Executive.

Begg, D., Fischer, S. and Dornbusch, R. (1991) *Economics*. Maidenhead: McGraw-Hill.

Cabinet Office (1998) *The Better Regulation Guide*. London: Cabinet Office.

Cabinet Office (2000) *Good Policy Making: A Guide to Regulatory Impact Assessment*. London: Cabinet Office.

European Agency for Safety and Health at Work (1999) *Economic Impact of Occupational Safety and Health in the Member States of the European Union*. Bilbao: European Agency for Safety and Health at Work.

European Agency for Safety and Health at Work (2002a) *Inventory of Socioeconomic Costs of Work Accidents*. Bilbao: European Agency for Safety and Health at Work.

European Agency for Safety and Health at Work (2002b) *Economic Appraisal of Preventing Accidents at Company Level*. Factsheet 28. Bilbao: European Agency for Safety and Health at Work.

Frick, K. (2000) Uses and abuses. In: *The Role of CBA in Decision-making*, 38–40. Bilbao: European Agency for Safety and Health at Work.

Hallett, N. (2000) The UK experience. In: *The Role of CBA in Decision-making*, 12–13. Bilbao: European Agency for Safety and Health at Work.

Health and Safety Commission (2003) *Health and Safety Statistics 2002/03*. Sudbury: HSE Books.

Health and Safety Executive (1996) *Use of Risk Assessment within Government Departments*. Sudbury: HSE Books.

Health and Safety Executive (1998) *Risk Assessment and Risk Management: Improving Policy and Practice within Government Departments*. Sudbury: HSE Books.

Hjalte, K., Norinder, A., Persson, U. and Maraste, P. (2003) Health-health analysis: an alternative method for economic appraisal of health policy and safety regulation. Some empirical Swedish estimates. *Accident Analysis and Prevention*, **35**, 37–46.

Johannesson, M. (1995) The relationship between cost-effectiveness analysis and cost–benefit analysis. *Social Science & Medicine*, **41**(4), 483–489.

Jones-Lee, M.W. (1989) *The Economics of Safety and Physical Risk*. Oxford: Basil Blackwell.

Kahneman, D. and Tversky, A. (1979) Prospect theory: an analysis of decision under risk. *Econometrica*, **47**, 263–291.

Park, R.M., Bailer, A.J., Stayner, L.T., Halperin, W. and Gilbert, S.J. (2002) An alternative characterization of hazard in occupational epidemiology: years of life lost per years worked. *American Journal of Industrial Medicine*, **42**, 1–10.

Slovic, P. (1992) Perceptions of risk: reflections on the psychometric paradigm. In: S. Krimsky and D. Golding (eds), *Social Theories of Risk*, 117–152. London: Praeger.

Sugden, R., Bateman, I., Cubitt, R., Munro, A. and Starmer, C. (2000) Coping with loss aversion in stated preference studies. *Risk and Human Behaviour Newsletter*, **8**, 20–22.

Tudor, O. (2000) Strengths and weaknesses. In: *The Role of CBA in Decision-making*, 35–37. Bilbao: European Agency for Safety and Health at Work.

Viscusi, W.K. (1992) *Fatal Tradeoffs: Public and Private Responsibilities for Risk*. Oxford: Oxford University Press.

Managing health and safety risks

Yes and how many deaths will it take till he knows
That too many people have died?

– Bob Dylan, 'Blowin' in the wind' (1962)

Chapter contents

- Introduction
- The general role of health and safety standards
- Acceptable standards of health and safety
- Tolerability of risk as a health and safety standard
- Health and safety management in the context of risk and business management
- The holistic view of risk and business management
- The impact of changing work patterns on health and safety management
- Factors influencing the management of health and safety risks
- Factors motivating proactive health and safety management

Introduction

The quality of life for most people living in developed countries has improved significantly over the last 100 years. This improvement has been achieved largely through developments in technology and scientific discoveries. However, these changes have brought new risks associated with hazards such as nuclear power, transport systems, chemicals, stress and genetically modified organisms. There were two major social principles that influenced the management of occupational health and safety risks during this period of improvement (Dorman, 2000): the absolute right of individuals not to suffer injury and ill-health and the importance of equity in the way that costs and benefits were distributed among the population.

If the goal of firms is to maximize profits, the goal of the public health community is to minimize morbidity and mortality. The absolutist character of this mission, so alien to the economic mindset, draws on the tradition of medicine. Doctors, after all, do not ask whether the patient's health is worth the cost. If there is a remedy it must be taken. Health, from this perspective, is not a commodity to be traded off against other goods in the marketplace. Its value is thought to be incommensurable – a precondition for the enjoyment of any other value.

The second source of public activism in occupational safety and health draws on the workers' demand for justice and fairness on the job. Justice in this context means something very specific: no one should derive personal benefit by imposing hardships on others. Those who share in the profits of a firm, whether as owners or highly paid managers, should not do so at the expense of preventable risks to the workforce.

Dorman (2000: 1)

The public, therefore, justifiably expect that those people who benefit from developments in technology should bear the costs associated with them, and that governments should actively seek to protect the public and workers from high levels of risk. However, concerns over public health and justice for individuals, even during this period of rapid change, were never pursued in isolation from the costs associated with the attendant health and safety control measures. The difference in recent years is that cost–benefit analysis has assumed a more dominant role and social concerns a less prominent role in health and safety decision-making (European Agency for Safety and Health at Work, 2002a). Despite the change in direction, improvements in health and safety performance continued slowly, with no major step changes in the overall performances of organisations. For example, although the fatal accident rates for employees in the UK have decreased (Health and Safety Commission, 2003), the reductions are relatively small (Figure 8.1) compared with the developments and improvements in technology and management skills over the same period.

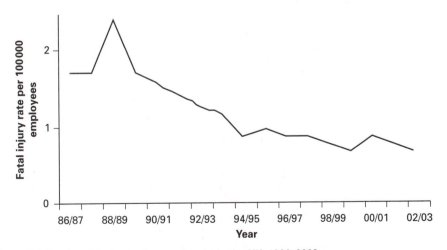

Figure 8.1 Fatal accident rates for employees in the UK, 1986–2003
Source: Derived from Health and Safety Commission (2003)

Similarly, the level of accidents and ill-health remains disappointingly high in Europe as a whole:

> Despite improvements in occupational safety over the last decade, around 5500 people lose their lives each year through work-related accidents in the European Union. More than 75 000 are so severely disabled that they can no longer work. Moreover, major surveys have found that people experience more physical problems at work than before, dispelling the often fashionable belief that new technology has eradicated difficulties such as manual lifting of heavy objects.
>
> Saari (2001: 3)

Standards provide a key input to health and safety management because they define the maximum acceptable level of risk that stakeholders should be exposed to. A wide range of international and national standards has been developed in order to cover many areas of health and safety management. These include a number of general management standards (Health and Safety Executive, 2000; Standards Australia, 2000; International Labour Organization, 2001), which are discussed in Chapter 10, and a range of specific standards for the control of physical hazards, such as electricity, machinery and fire, and health hazards, such as chemicals, radiation and noise.

The aims of this chapter are to discuss general issues related to health and safety standards and in particular to discuss the concept of standards based on the principle of a tolerable level of risk that employees and the general public would find acceptable under most circumstances. In addition the position of health and safety management within the overall context of business management, and factors influencing and motivating organisations to adopt proactive health and safety management systems, are discussed.

The general role of health and safety standards

The UK government, like many other governments, regulates a number of health and safety hazards, such as transport, nuclear power and fire, through legislation and standards. In the UK, the Inter-Departmental Liaison Group on Risk Assessment presented an argument for standards:

> In many areas of life people are free, and prefer to be free, to make their own decisions about their safety, but sometimes standards are needed. For consumers, standards may sometimes be the best way to provide them with the balance between cost and risk which reflects their preferences, because the information is otherwise very costly to obtain or too difficult to interpret. Third parties, for example living near a potentially dangerous industrial site, may have too little market power, or have too weak or too costly access to the law, to enable them to negotiate effectively with those who manage these health or safety risks. Producers can value standards which reduce uncertainty about exactly what balances of cost and safety will be acceptable in their labour and product markets. Some standards can be set and enforced satisfactorily by groups of producers or consumers, in response to market forces, but there is often also a role for government.
>
> ILGRA (1996: 4)

The nature of business entails producing a product or providing a service, in one form or another. These activities invariably require managing inputs to business premises and/or production facilities, producing goods and/or services through safe operational procedures, and managing the desired and undesired outputs from the premises and/or procedures. In order to achieve a satisfactory long-term financial performance, most businesses operate to defined standards. In defining these standards, organisations must take into account the fact that people who are associated with the inputs, the working environment and the outputs of the business will also affect the efficiency and effectiveness of these activities. Safety and health standards must therefore relate to physical, management *and* human factor issues. The Health and Safety Executive (1993) provided a framework for identifying when *and* how operational health and safety standards should be implemented: see Figure 8.2.

Standards are an essential prerequisite for the control of all functions in an organisation, and health and safety standards, in particular, enable managers to discuss the acceptability of control measures through the use of coherent and logical arguments.

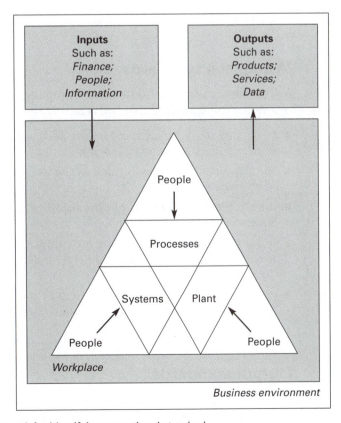

Figure 8.2 Framework for identifying operational standards

Input standards

Standards should be available for all premises, plant and equipment to ensure that health and safety issues are accounted for at their design, construction, operation, maintenance, modification and decommissioning stages. These issues are discussed later in Chapter 12 in the context of inherent safety and the safety lifecycle model. It is also essential to ensure that standards are incorporated into business input activities (Health and Safety Executive, 1993) through:

- *employees*, such as defining physical, intellectual and mental abilities through job specifications based on risk assessment;
- *design and selection of premises*, such as a consideration of the proposed and foreseeable uses, construction and contract specification;
- *design and selection of plant*, such as installation, operation, maintenance and decommissioning;
- *use of hazardous substances*, such as the incorporation of the principle of inherent safety and the selection of competent suppliers;
- *use of contractors*, such as selection procedures;
- *acquisitions and divestitures*, such as the identification of current and long-term health and safety risks associated with the organisation's activities; and
- *information*, such as maintaining an up-to-date system for relevant health and safety legislation, standards and codes of practice.

Workplace standards

The following issues illustrate some of the factors that should be included in an assessment of workplace standards (Health and Safety Executive, 1993):

- *health and safety management system*, such as policy, organisation, implementation, monitoring, audit and review;
- *use of hazardous substances*, such as the receipt, storage, use and transportation of chemicals;
- *use of contractors*, such as the provision of working documents and performance reviews;
- *emergency planning*, such as the identification of emergency scenarios, liaison with the emergency services and the implementation of emergency planning exercises; and
- *disaster and contingency planning*, such as the identification of disaster scenarios, preparation of contingency plans and the implementation of disaster planning exercises.

Output standards

Organisational outputs impact on society, and therefore it is even more important that these issues are carefully controlled through the implementation of acceptable and defined standards. The following issues illustrate some of the factors that should be included in output standards (Health and Safety Executive, 1993):

- *products*, such as packaging, transport, storage and use;

- *services*, such as the protection of recipients;

- *waste*, such as the safe off-site transport and disposal of liquid and solid materials and the control of atmospheric emissions;

- *information*, such as the provision of information about products and services to users;

- *public relations*, such as the supply of valid information to stakeholders about improvement and prohibition notices and corporate prosecutions, fines and convictions; and

- *health and safety performance data*, such as defining the criteria for and level of lost-time accidents and near-miss incidents.

Acceptable standards of health and safety

Some criteria for accepting certain levels of risk have been discussed in the context of risk management, risk assessment and risk perception: this discussion is continued here in the context of defining acceptable and tolerable standards of risk.

Factors influencing standards of health and safety

The important influences on standards of risk perception and risk communication have been discussed in Chapters 4 and 5; however, there are other factors that must also be taken into account when considering and defining health and safety standards (ILGRA, 1996).

Incident size: large incidents attract a disproportionate amount of attention from the public and the media, and this influences industrial and commercial organisations that are concerned about their public image. Governments are under pressure to set stricter industry standards where there is the potential for multiple fatality accidents to employees or, more importantly, to members of the public.

> It is widely held among regulators, but much less often among academics and other commentators, that people should as a general rule be less well protected from the risk of incidents that affect only one or a very few people at once than from the risks of incidents which affect many people – such as a major rail or air crash – although there is no consistent evidence that this reflects the preferences of those at risk.
>
> ILGRA (1996: 17)

One reason for imposing higher standards on risks that can create multiple fatalities is that the recovery costs for this type of incident are disproportionately higher than those from incidents involving single or just a few fatalities.

Pain and suffering: Arguments have been presented for imposing higher standards for hazards where there may be pain and/or suffering prior to death from hazards. This is of particular concern in terms of chronic health, such as respiratory disease, cancer and radiation sickness.

Familiarity: Although familiarity with some hazards, such as road transport, enables regulators to employ lower standards, there is no logical reason why this should affect tolerability of risk standards.

Observability and delay in impact: The invisibility of risks from some hazards, such as ionising and non-ionising radiation, can contribute to employees' and the public's concerns about standards. Similarly, delayed impacts from hazards such as cancer-inducing chemicals provide some people with greater cause for concern: this is related to the non-observability of the consequences at the time of the exposure. However, this issue is often related more to the lack of personal control over the risks, and because this requires a greater level of dependence on others to keep them informed about the risks. The public's lack of trust in providers of this information often engenders a desire for wider margins of error in the defined standards of risk. There is a contrary argument, however, that because delayed consequences are invariably more acceptable than immediate consequences, the standards for delayed consequences can be less strict.

Fairness or equity: It is widely felt that, when standards are set, the risk of a fatality should be spread equally across a large population rather than be concentrated within a small group. The reason for this is that the larger the population exposed to the risks or costs the more likely it is that the risk will be spread across those people who receive the benefits from the risk. An extreme example of fairness/unfairness occurs where the general public benefit from a risk but the costs are borne solely by one individual. Although the risk may be justified through cost–benefit analysis using the value of life concept, this individual is extremely unlikely to accept any valuation of life as compensation for his or her certain death.

Criteria used for defining standards

Although a completely rule-based approach to defining standards and health and safety regulations is unrealistic, it has been shown that criteria used for defining standards fall into three broad categories (Health and Safety Executive, 1999).

Equity-based criteria follow from the fundamental argument that each individual has a right to expect a certain level of protection from hazards. This premise leads to a universal standard of health and safety that should be acceptable in everyday life. This approach leads to the development of a maximum level of risk that an individual should be exposed to. If a risk assessment shows that the level of risk to an individual is greater than this maximum value then additional control measures should be introduced in order to reduce the level of risk. Values of risk above this standard are therefore defined as being unacceptable, under any conditions, whatever the benefits that may be accrued from them. The disadvantage of this approach is that it is often necessary to base decisions on worst-case scenarios, and these may not be related to normal experiences. In these cases the risks will be overestimated.

Utility-based criteria are obtained by making comparisons between the benefits obtained from incremental improvements in the level and quality of control measures and the cost of providing these additional control measures. This approach compares the costs of additional control measures with benefit parameters, such as lives saved and extended years of life, obtained from the control measures. The utility-based approach can be implemented in such a way that the cost–benefit analysis involved is strongly biased towards the benefits rather than the costs of additional protection. This is achieved, effectively, by inflating the values of lives saved and the added years of life that are obtained used in the calculations. This approach ignores the ethical issues and the arguments that some risks are not worth considering whatever the potential benefits.

Technology-based criteria are based on the premise that all employers should adopt industry best practices and the most up-to-date technology that is available to control the risks, whatever the work environment and whatever the circumstances. This approach would be unacceptable in some work sectors, and for some developing industries and countries, because it would preclude them from entering the marketplace with new products and services by placing an unacceptably high financial burden on their production processes.

Although there are a number of arguments for and against each of these criteria, the view adopted by most regulators is usually one of compromise between the three criteria. This enables regulators to set risk standards that take into account not just the costs and benefits but also the level of risk adopted by the general public in their personal lives.

Setting standards

A range of approaches have been developed for setting standards of health and safety.

Traditional approaches

An approach that is often adopted for health and safety standards is to declare that certain hazards, which are considered to be especially dangerous, should be made completely safe or as safe as possible. Historically, governments have used this approach, following major accidents, when they have been keen to ensure that 'it will never happen again' or 'it could never happen here' when an accident occurs in another country. Regulations and standards introduced in this way often cover management issues, such as training, inspections, audits, working procedures and plant design (ILGRA, 1996).

Other traditional approaches include the use of:

- *rules of thumb*, which entail not allowing risks to increase even where a clear case can be made that the balance of costs against benefits has shifted; and
- *margins of error*, which entail the practice of setting acceptable standards at a level that is an order of magnitude below the calculated value, on the grounds that the standard relates to a politically sensitive or socially undesirable hazard.

Tolerable, working and target standards

A number of approaches are used in this category, including:

- *maximum tolerable risks*, which set maximum levels for the number of fatalities per year based on ethical grounds;
- *working standards*, which are used to define good practice and are defined in terms of their value for money. This approach is used to gradually improve standards across different industries; and
- *target standards*, which are used by organisations and governments in order to set medium- and long-term health and safety objectives and to guide improvement programmes.

Standards based on cost–benefit analysis

In some cases standards are set after risks have been valued using cost–benefit analysis based on people's willingness to pay to reduce the levels of risk to a particular level. This approach is related to the principle of 'as low as reasonably practicable'.

Standards in safety-critical applications

In safety-critical applications, standards must reflect the probability that a specified safety device or system will perform its function correctly within a stated period of time. The higher the potential risk of injury and ill-health from a failure in a safety-critical protection system, the higher the level of confidence that is required from the safety standards. The normal approach to determining the standard of safety is through measurements of the probabilities of events taking place and the consequences associated with these events: see Table 8.1.

Table 8.1 Classification of risk

Probability	Consequences of incident				
	Insignificant	Minor	Moderate	Major	Catastrophic
Probable	2	3	3	4	4
Likely	1	2	3	3	4
Possible	1	2	2	3	3
Unlikely	1	1	2	2	3
Rare	1	1	1	1	2

Source: Johnston and Pugh (1994)

The resultant levels of risk (1–4) are used to define the standards required to ensure the achievement of a defined level of confidence that the risks will be controlled. The standards defined in this way are used to identify the necessary safety protection systems. Examples of the standards used in the verification processes in order to achieve the specified level of confidence in the performance of safety-critical protection systems are provided in Table 8.2 (Johnston and Pugh, 1994).

Absolute standards and relative standards

As discussed above, standards can be defined in terms of an absolute maximum level of risk or to a specific level of control measures. Alternatively, standards can be set in terms of a cost–benefit analysis. The choice between these two approaches invariably raises vigorous arguments between the protagonists of these divergent views. One group supports the view that safety should be managed through the use of considered views on the moral, legal and political implications, whereas the other group supports the view that safety can be effectively managed only through the use of standards based on risk calculations

Table 8.2 Verification standards recommended for safety-related protection systems

Verification procedure	Level of risk			
	1	**2**	**3**	**4**
Formal proof of operational system, including mathematical modelling where required.		✓	✓	✓✓
Probabilistic testing of failure rates through formal test procedures.		✓	✓	✓✓
Static analysis by inspection.	✓	✓✓	✓✓	✓✓
Dynamic testing through the implementation of test cases.	✓	✓✓	✓✓	✓✓
Application of metrics that are derived from computer codes in order to predict software outcomes.	✓	✓	✓	✓

✓   Recommended procedure
✓✓   Highly recommended procedure
Source: Johnston and Pugh (1994)

(ILGRA, 1996). In reality, governments compromise between these two viewpoints by regulating the control of risks either where market forces are too weak to influence standards or where certain individuals bear the costs but receive little direct benefit from the risk:

> In regulating risks to employees governments will generally wish to legislate to protect those who may have very little power against a seriously irresponsible employer. Nonetheless in a developed economy the main role of employee protection, as with consumer protection, should be to reflect people's willingness to pay for lower risks (and to accept more pay for higher risks) – not least because the costs of tighter standards are often reflected in incomes and other costs and benefits to employees and the local economy.
>
> Where the government is acting as an agent of the consumer, or of any other individuals who want a trade off, satisfactory to them, between higher risk and higher benefits, it is widely accepted, at least in the UK, that a cost–benefit approach to regulation is appropriate.
>
> ILGRA (1996: 11)

If individuals feel that the levels of risk to which they are exposed are too high, they can, at least in theory, change their employment and/or move to a different location to live. In practice, however, the majority of people cannot normally exercise this level of freedom for personal, social or economic reasons. Therefore, governments normally legislate or set standards in order to control risks at levels that are not unreasonably high. This presents a further alternative to the cost–benefit approach by setting standards for the upper limits of the tolerability of risk based on the principle of fairness.

Tolerability of risk as a health and safety standard

The tolerability of risk framework combines the equity-based and utility-based approaches for defining standards. This approach seeks to identify a just tolerable level of risk above which risk cannot be justified under any conditions and a lower level of risk that is broadly acceptable without implementing further risk control measures. The concept of tolerable risk standards has been discussed extensively, in the UK, in relation to the nuclear industry (Health and Safety Executive, 1988). It has been found that the higher levels of occupational risk of death in the UK are around 1 in 1000 per annum. These levels are found in the construction and other similar high-risk industrial sectors (Health and Safety Commission, 2003). It has been argued that, because employees normally accept this level of risk, it can be regarded as the dividing line between 'what is just tolerable and what is intolerable' (Health and Safety Executive, 1988). However, a member of the general public would not accept this level of risk from industrial and commercial activities that impinged on their daily lives. Therefore the Health and Safety Executive (1988) arbitrarily proposed that if the tolerable level of risk for employees is 1 in 1000 per annum, the maximum level that should be tolerated by a member of the public should be 1 in 10000 per annum. Regulators consider this level of risk to be reasonable because it is similar to the level of risk that a member of the public faces for a fatality in a road traffic accident, and this level of risk is generally accepted by the public. These two levels represent standards of risk that are just tolerable for employees and the public respectively.

It is important to differentiate between standards of risk that are just tolerable and standards of risk that are acceptable. For this reason, the Health and Safety Executive (1988) considered that a standard for an acceptable level of risk could be set at 1 in 1 000 000 per annum because this would be only a very small addition to the other general risks associated with normal life. For example, the current level of risk of a fatality at work in all UK industry is around 1 in 100 000 per annum (Health and Safety Commission, 2003). This level is 100 times lower than the level of risk considered to be the maximum level of tolerable risk to employees, and 10 times lower than the level of risk considered to be the maximum level of tolerable risk to the public, but 10 times higher than the level of risk considered to be acceptable.

The implications and application of standards based on the tolerability of risk

It is almost certain that there will always be conflicting views over what should be regarded as tolerable and acceptable levels of risk. Similarly, there will be disagreements over the individual responsibilities of government, employers and regulators in the definition of risk levels. If stakeholders worked together productively, it would not be unreasonable to expect that general agreement could be achieved for the management of health and safety risks in the working environment (Figure 8.3).

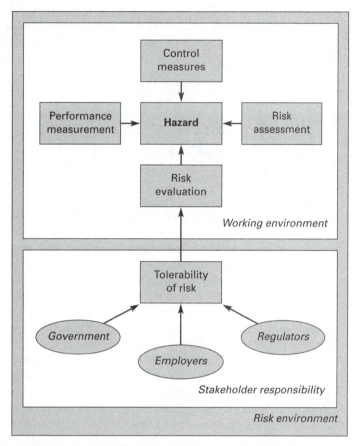

Figure 8.3 Stakeholder responsibilities for defining workplace standards

The responsibility for managing and regulating risks is often spread across several government departments and many organisations: therefore it is important that everyone involved in regulating health and safety risks is working to the same standards in order to avoid publishing conflicting viewpoints and requirements.

Probabilistic assessments of the risks associated with new plant and equipment begin at the specification and design stages and involve identifying *risk scenarios*. The probabilities and consequences arising from these situations are often reviewed through the use of hazard and operability studies and event tree analyses. This enables risk levels to be identified and assessed for compliance with the ALARP principle and the tolerability of risk criteria. This approach allows designers to produce plant and equipment in which there is an even distribution of the effectiveness of risk control measures across the whole plant and equipment rather than create some areas where the risks may be less than 1 in 1 000 000 and other areas where the risks may be as high as 1 in 1000.

If the tolerable risk levels for a major incident, at a high-risk plant, are 1 in 10 000 and there are 1000 high-risk plants each with a 20-year operational lifetime, there will statistically be two major incidents over their combined lifetimes. These incidents are referred to as *design-basis* incidents (Health and Safety Executive, 1988) in order to indicate that these incidents are anticipated

even when all the safety protection systems are working to their design performance levels. Higher failure rates or more serious incidents should occur only if
there is a difference between the design and actual performances of safety-related
control measures.

Health and safety management in the context of risk and business management

Business management is very closely linked to risk management. Business management involves translating the corporate strategy of an organisation into plans and
procedures that will deliver the specified short-, medium- and long-term business
aims and objectives. The overall strategy defines an organisation's business activities, such as whether the organisation will be involved in banking, energy,
telecommunications, food, transport, leisure, chemicals or oil. While undertaking
these business activities, there will be a need to make management decisions to
avoid or to minimise risks and to accept certain risks for commercial gain. Risk management is involved in all business activities and includes hazards associated with,
for example, the environment, quality, production, e-commerce, investment, currency markets and efficiency, as well as health and safety. It is important, therefore,
that health and safety managers do not become parochial over the issue of risk
management, and they should not lose sight of the wider, corporate risk picture.
Although health and safety management often assumes board-level importance
only at times of significant failures in health and safety control, it should be
assigned the same long-term importance as other business risks (Wright *et al.*, 2003).

In a study of the reasons behind major breakdowns in trading and investment
management, Broadley and Rhys (1997) identified what they referred to as the
'Ten Commandments of Risk Management':

1. *Understand your profits* – large profits you don't understand are more dangerous
   than large losses you do.
2. *Focus on distance* – operational risk increases with distance.
3. *Honour the Sabbath* – people who never take holidays are not necessarily
   paragons of corporate virtue.
4. *Prepare to pay* – there is no such thing as cheap risk management or segregation
   of duties.
5. *Invest with authority* – the Chief Executive Officer (CEO) is not the risk control
   function but a risk control function without the CEO's backing won't prosper.
6. *Reconcile with diligence* – reconciliation problems usually presage losses; a debit
   balance in a suspense account is usually not an asset.
7. *Track the cash* – accounting entries can be manipulated; cash disbursements
   cannot. Cash is the fundamental control.
8. *Respect business quality* – volume is no substitute for value.
9. *Ensure it adds up* – accounting losses reflect business realities.
10. *Watch your systems* – computer systems are an open door into the heart of your
    business, and their integrity and security are not as complete as you think.

Broadley and Rhys (1997: 76)

Although these commandments were directed specifically at financial risks, they have equal validity if translated into the requirements of occupational health and safety management.

The holistic view of risk and business management

The principles of risk management are the same for all hazards, but some risks, such as those associated with health, safety, environment and quality, are more naturally managed through common management systems than the risks associated with other hazards, such as finance, business development and foreign trade. Although the specific control procedures required for different hazards will vary, the consequences of adverse events associated with each of these hazards can be equally damaging to business performance, as shown in Table 8.3. It is therefore in the interests of any organisation to manage all risks effectively, and to do so as an integral part of the overall business management process.

Table 8.3 Consequences of adverse events on business performance

Risks to:	Examples of adverse business events		
	Minor (£1000)	Major (£100 000)	Severe (£10 000 000)
Physical assets: e.g. plant, equipment	Pump failure	Plant shutdown	Major factory fire
Human assets: e.g. employees, contractors	Minor injury	Major injury	Fatality
Product: e.g. quality, output	Inadequate packaging	Out-of-specification production run	Contaminated food product
Environment: e.g. air quality, food chain	Chemical spill to drain	Contaminating discharge to river	Radiation leak from nuclear installation
Customers: e.g. deliveries, goodwill	Delayed delivery	Delivery of sub-standard product	Loss of major customer

Cost–benefit analysis illustrates the importance of including health and safety within the context of the overall risk portfolio of an organisation, because costs incurred in reducing the risks associated with one business activity often produce benefits in other business areas. These benefits should clearly be taken into account through an overall assessment of the benefits provided by a project rather than from a parochial perspective of a single business function. As an example, one can consider the problem of leaking seals on solvent pumps at a chemical plant. The issue can be addressed by installing more effective pump seals, which significantly reduce the probability of leakage of flammable solvents. This solution requires fitting the new seal design on 400 pumps at an additional cost of £2500 per pump every five years. The total cost, therefore, amounts to £1m over five years or £200 000 per year. The improved seals will provide organisational benefits in terms of a reduced risk of fire damage to capital assets such as plant and equipment, reduced risk of injury and ill-health to operators through fire and inhalation of solvent vapours, reduced risk of environmental damage caused by solvent leaks escaping to drains, reduced risk of lost production as a result of plant downtime, and reduced risk of adverse publicity brought about by chemical leaks and fires. The organisation's estimation of the annual value of these benefits is shown in Table 8.4.

Table 8.4 Organisational benefits accruing from an improved pump seal design

Risks	Estimated annual benefits from new pump seal designs (£'000)
Health and safety	43
Environment	25
Capital assets	170
Production output	75
Public relations	38
Total	**351**

Clearly, a cost–benefit analysis based solely on the benefits from any one of these individual risks will not provide an argument to support the project because in each case the cost–benefit ratio is less than 1. However, if the sum of the annual benefits from all of the appropriate activities (£351 000) is compared with the annual additional cost of the new seals (£200 000), the cost–benefit ratio increases to nearly 1.8. This information provides suitable evidence in favour of implementing the project. Therefore, in this particular example, a marginal improvement in health and safety performance is obtained as a consequence of a business justification based primarily on the protection of the organisation's capital assets (£170 000) and production output (£75 000).

The impact of changing work patterns on health and safety management

Changes in the type and pattern of work in all countries have had a significant impact on health and safety management (Roy, 2003). Of major importance are the complexities associated with the changes and the speed with which the changes take place. Rapid changes create uncertainty within an organisation owing to lack of knowledge, experience and training (European Agency for Safety and Health at Work, 2002b), and organisations no longer have the luxury of working within a stable environment in which these changes can be absorbed slowly.

A major factor affecting businesses is the drive to achieve greater employee and production flexibility and customer focus (European Agency for Safety and Health at Work, 2002c). Wright (1996a) reviewed the main issues behind business re-engineering and concluded that, although the need to cut costs and improve productivity had not diminished over the previous 30 years, responses to the issues had changed. Initially, there was a great reliance on cutting costs through reduced staff levels and amalgamating departments. However, as competitive pressures increased and the options for cutting costs diminished, attention was turned towards communications, decision-making, cultural issues and workforce commitment as ways of improving competitiveness. Wright (1996a) identified that this required a shift from traditional command and control management structures to a management ethos of flexibility, customer satisfaction, accountability and empowerment. These changes have required organisations to concentrate more on core skills and activities and to increase the use of part-time workers, home workers, contractors, service support companies and overseas suppliers (Vassie, 2000). Concerns have been expressed (Health and Safety Commission, 1994) over how well health and safety legislation covers groups such as home workers, temporary workers and the self-employed, and changes in work patterns have led many organisations to reassess their risk portfolio. A more mobile workforce also means that organisations quickly lose the stability provided by long-serving employees who provide an essential source of corporate history. Many organisations continue to spend large amounts of time and effort developing new knowledge but little time and effort on retaining their existing knowledge built up from previous accidents and incidents.

The importance of global business has increased significantly for many organisations. This extension of trade boundaries is normally linked to international *collaboration* or *exploitation*. Reasons for increased collaboration are associated with issues of technical convergence between countries, the ending of closed economies, such as the former USSR, and new international trade initiatives between countries (Dorman, 2000). For many companies, operating in different areas of the world requires adapting to different social cultures and, until recently, operating to quite different performance standards. Nowadays, many multinational organisations aim and/or are expected to operate globally with high levels of health and safety performance irrespective of the country, culture or local standards of education and skills in which the work activities take place. One driving force for this change has been the move by major companies to proactive health and safety management styles, and this, coupled with the international convergence on corporate governance and risk control, has produced positive improvements in management attitudes in the developed economies towards health and safety in underdeveloped countries: 'In all our activities and operations, we will comply fully with legal requirements and meet or exceed [BP Amoco's] expectations wherever we operate in the world' (BP Amoco, 2001: 7).

These changes have revolutionised the performance of many international businesses operating worldwide and using labour, technology and management systems drawn from different companies, countries and cultures. Some companies, however, place production contracts for goods in developing countries simply because the opportunities of, for example, cheaper raw materials, lower labour costs, ready availability of development land, lower environmental standards and greater financial support provide attractive economic incentives. Although these contracts may bring developing countries financial benefits in the short term, they also often bring high costs in terms of health and safety in the medium and long term. Dorman (2000) reported, as an example, that fires in two toy factories in China and Thailand that were used by companies based in the developed world claimed 275 lives. Child labour is used throughout the developing world in order to compete and gain contracts from companies in the developed world; these children often work in conditions that would be abhorred by the public in those countries from where the contracts are placed.

These issues raise important moral and social questions when assessing the true organisational and social costs of occupational health and safety. If a company in the developed world can simply pass occupational health and safety risks over to underdeveloped countries, there is no external incentive for these companies to manage their risks. It is for this reason that the internationalisation of health and safety standards and legislation, such as that advocated by the International Labour Organisation and the European Union, and the adoption of international corporate health and safety policies by some major organisations are so important.

Factors influencing the management of health and safety risks

Ashby and Diacon (1996) identified compliance with legislation and avoidance of legal liability as the major motivational reasons among UK companies for managing health and safety risks. Wright (1998a) further identified that the responses to three questions determined whether health and safety and business management were driven by common goals within an organisation:

■ Was health and safety performance perceived as a critical commercial success factor?

■ Were the costs associated with occupational injury and ill-health perceived to be significant?

■ Were external pressures applied to the organisation in order to achieve specified health and safety performance targets?

If the answers to these questions were positive, it was usual for health and safety management to be considered as part of business management and to be implemented as a core management responsibility. However, some senior managers perceive health and safety to be a peripheral issue, and therefore do not manage these risks in the same way as mainstream business activities; often the only reason why they are even considered is because legislative, financial, social or corporate identity issues force them to be. Many major organisations prefer to concentrate solely on issues of quality, cost and cycle time:

> These priorities are considered prominent dimensions that significantly influence the success of any business. In contrast, an important influence on business success which has not received due attention is workplace safety. Furthermore, companies that emphasize workplace safety typically do so in order to reduce costs and conform to government regulations.
>
> Ansari and Modarress (1997: 389)

The reasons often quoted for why organisations manage health and safety issues at work are legal, financial and social factors; it can be argued, however, that all of these factors have a financial element. Non-compliance with legislation leads to financial implications from enforced improvements in performance or from prosecution. A desire to establish high social values of health and safety occurs because of the financial implications of providing compensation to employees who suffer occupational injuries and ill-health. Failures in health and safety management can also affect an organisation's corporate image through adverse media coverage, especially when multiple fatalities to employees and/or members of the public occur. This can have serious financial implications for companies through public demands for government intervention, reduced share value, and loss of confidence from customers.

Legal factors

Legislative compliance is a fundamental requirement for any organisation, and this is normally overseen by a national health and safety enforcement agency. However, financial restrictions mean that these agencies must make decisions on which organisations to inspect, how thoroughly to inspect, and when to inspect. Inevitably, larger organisations and higher-risk activities are inspected more frequently and with greater thoroughness than small and medium-sized companies and lower-risk activities. The apparent logic behind this approach is that larger companies are used as examples of what the enforcement authorities can do in cases of non-compliance. In some ways, however, this is often the wrong approach to take, because many larger companies have already progressed beyond legislative compliance as the main driving factor and take legislative compliance as a minimum level of performance rather than the desired level of performance. In these companies, failure to comply with a particular set of regulations is more likely to result from a genuine mistake than from a deliberate attempt to avoid implementation and/or compliance with legislation. Some smaller companies, however, take short cuts in health and safety in the belief that they are saving money and in the knowledge that they are unlikely to be inspected by the enforcement authority. Small and medium-sized companies often prefer prescriptive standards of performance and legislation to the goal-setting approach adopted in much of modern legislation because the prescriptive approach defines levels of acceptable performance, and this therefore removes the need for evaluative judgements on the part of the organisation's management.

Economic factors

The influence of economic factors on health and safety management is derived from the principle of loss control described by Bird and Germain (1990). In addition, competitive advantage is gained by an organisation through *constraining costs* or *adding value* (Deacon, 1997). Both of these approaches are beneficial, but they arise from different management strategies. Constraining costs requires the minimisation of operational costs, while at least maintaining current levels of performance. Although adding value may improve the desirability of a company's product or service it will not ensure business success, as the costs for the improved products or services may exceed the selling price. Managing health and safety risks effectively can constrain costs, enhance a company's public and commercial image, and ensure continued business with other companies that also demand high performance for the management of health and safety risks. Effective health and safety management may also add value to an organisation through contributions to quality schemes, productivity levels and employees' welfare. The profit line in an organisation's annual report does not differentiate between contributions from added value and cost constraint, but there is a limit to what can be achieved through cost constraint whereas, in theory, there is no limit to the gains that an organisation can make from added value. Ansari and Modarress (1997) highlighted the financial importance of managing health and safety for companies in the USA in the following way:

> Employer injury bills exceed $1250 per covered employee in 1993. This represents about 62 cents per worker per hour. If a company, for example, earns a 10 per cent net profit on sales, it must sell $12 500 of goods and services per employee per year simply to cover its injury costs.
>
> Ansari and Modarress (1997: 390)

Social factors

Enterprises normally take raw materials and turn them into saleable products or services through the process of adding value. Different companies, however, have different organisational approaches to the way they achieve this target. The idea of an organisational philosophy that addresses the social implications of work activities is becoming more common in some industries and countries. For example:

- DuPont's 'Safety Principles' include statements such as 'management is directly accountable for preventing injuries and occupational illnesses', 'safety is a condition of employment', and 'preventing injuries and occupational illnesses is good business' (DuPont, 1995).
- Johnson & Johnson's 'Credo' includes statements such as 'we are responsible to our employees, the men and women who work with us throughout the world', 'we must provide competent management and their actions must be just and ethical', and 'we are responsible to the communities in which we live and work and to the world community as well' (Johnson & Johnson, 2003).
- BP Amoco's 'Goals' state 'Our goals are simply stated – no accidents, no harm to people and no damage to the environment' (BP Amoco, 2001).

This type of management approach establishes a positive mindset among employees and encourages managers to take a social as well as a commercial approach to business management. Although many companies make these types of statement, it is only a few companies that have sufficient conviction to carry the ideals through and to implement the principles on a continuing, day-to-day basis. For many companies a proactive style of health and safety management is initiated and implemented only following a serious accident or incident. For individuals, their approach to health and safety is strongly influenced by first hand experience of accidents and ill-health. This is particularly true where an individual has been responsible for a situation in which a fellow worker or member of the public has suffered injury or ill-health.

Intrinsic and extrinsic factors

An alternative way of considering issues that affect the management of health and safety risks is to group them into *intrinsic factors*, which arise from an organisation's internal desire to achieve something, and *extrinsic factors*, which arise from an organisation's fear of external interference in its business activities (Table 8.5).

Table 8.5 Factors influencing health and safety management

Influencing factors	
A desire to:	*A fear of:*
Reduce operational costs	Bad publicity
Improve productivity	Prosecution
Improve employee morale	Enforced improvements
Maintain internal quality standards	Civil liability claims
Improve corporate image	Adverse stock market response

Source: Adapted from Wright (1998a)

The change in an organisation's health and safety management system from a reactive to a proactive style is often driven by a move from extrinsic to intrinsic influencing factors (Wright, 1996b): see Figure 8.4.

The forces arising from the external imposition of fines and/or improvement notices for failures to comply with health and safety legislation initially drive organisations through a reactive management style. Organisations then realise that the costs associated with this approach are excessive, and they progress towards a management style driven by economic factors and cost–benefit analyses. The final stage in the development of a mature and enduring health and safety management style is the move to a proactive approach that recognises that stakeholders' satisfaction with the organisation's management of health and safety is of greater importance.

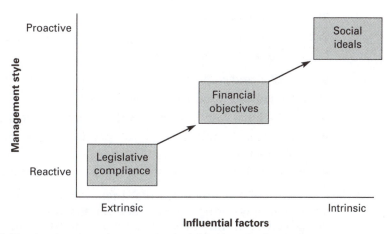

Figure 8.4 The development of an organisation's health and safety management style

Factors motivating proactive health and safety management

It is now generally accepted that the most effective way of managing organisational risks is through the use of a proactive management style, and this view is certainly valid in the specific case of health and safety risks. Unfortunately, acknowledged good practice and implemented practice do not always coincide. Wright (1998a, 1998b) suggested that there were two main factors that motivated organisations to initiate health and safety improvement programmes. These were the fear of loss of corporate credibility and the belief that it was correct to comply with health and safety legislation. There was a belief among organisations that:

> The adverse publicity, loss of confidence and regulatory attention subsequent to a serious incident will cause serious curtailment of operations, imposition of additional costs and loss of business/interruption of operations.
>
> Wright (1998a: iii–iv)

Other primary factors also motivate organisations to improve health and safety performance and a range of secondary factors have moderating effects. The primary factors create positive pressures on an organisation to initiate health and safety improvement programmes, and the secondary factors reduce the influence of the primary factors.

The primary reasons why organisations are motivated into initiating health and safety improvement programmes are linked to the issues of:

- maintaining corporate credibility;
- avoiding closure of or interruptions to operations;
- avoiding prosecutions and/or the issuing of improvement notices;
- complying with regulations;
- complying with stakeholder certification schemes;
- conforming with quality management systems;
- minimising the costs associated with injury and ill-health;
- increasing productivity; and
- improving employee morale.

The secondary factors that might mediate an organisation's intention to initiate health and safety improvement programmes are:

- individual and corporate levels of knowledge;
- individual and corporate risk perceptions;
- organisational costs associated with the improvement programme;
- management's and employees' previous experiences of accidents and incidents; and
- ease of implementation of the improvement programmes.

Wright (1998a) concluded that there was no single best practice regulatory strategy for motivating organisations to improve their health and safety performance. However, the most appropriate motivational approaches could be identified in a predictable way.

The *persuasion approach* requires the education and coercion of organisations to comply with current legislation through explanations of the reasons for and benefits of the legislation. This approach should be linked to discussions of ways in which compliance can be achieved in a cost-effective manner. Organisations that were most likely to be included within this approach came from high-risk industries in competitive markets.

The *compulsion approach* requires the imposition of well-defined standards of performance with little room for discussion of other options or variations from the prescribed targets. This approach should be accompanied by enforcement procedures and penalties for non-compliance. Organisations that were most likely to be included within this group came from small companies operating within a low-risk work environment.

Summary

- Health and safety standards provide a means of protecting vulnerable groups of employees, consumers and members of the public, but the responsibility for defining the standards rests with all stakeholders.
- The tolerability of risk framework identifies a just tolerable and an acceptable level of risk.
- Health and safety risks form one part of an organisation's business risks, and they should be treated with equal importance to other organisational risks. The public view of health and safety risks is that those people who benefit from the creation of risks should bear the costs of failure.
- Issues driving organisational health and safety management systems can be grouped under the headings of either legislative, financial and social factors or intrinsic and extrinsic factors.
- Health and safety management is considered to be a core management activity in some organisations only if failure is perceived to have a significant commercial impact.
- The major motivational factors for improving organisational health and safety performance are the fear of loss of corporate credibility and the belief that it is correct to comply with legislation. Proactive approaches to health and safety management provide a better long-term risk management strategy than reactive approaches.

Issues for review and discussion

- Consider why improvements in technology and management systems have not been matched by improvements in health and safety performance.
- Assess why many organisations do not treat health and safety risks on an equal basis with other organisational risks.
- Review the impact that health and safety risks may have on major business decisions.
- Consider whether expecting developing countries to adopt the same health and safety standards as developed countries is reasonable.
- Evaluate whether the business ethics of multinational organisations or legislation has the greater long-term impact on health and safety performance.

LLYFRGELL COLEG MENAI LIBRARY

References

Ansari, A. and Modarress, B. (1997) World-class strategies for safety: a Boeing approach. *International Journal of Operations & Production Management*, **17**(4), 389–398.

Ashby, S.G. and Diacon, S.R. (1996) Motives for occupational risk management in large UK companies. *Safety Science*, **22**, 229–243.

Bird, F.E. and Germain, G.L. (1990) *Practical Loss Control Leadership*. Loganville: International Loss Control Institute.

BP Amoco (2001) *Getting HSE Right: A Guide for BP Managers*. London: BP Amoco.

Broadley, P. and Rhys, M. (1997) Risk management: the 10 commandments. *Accountancy* (November), **120** 76.

Deacon, S. (1997) *Measuring Business Value in Health and Safety*. London: FT Pitman Publishing.

Dorman, P. (2000) Health, safety and global economics. In: *Health and Safety at Work: A Question of Costs and Benefits* 41–44. Bilbao: European Agency for Safety and Health at Work.

DuPont (1995) *Safety Training Observation Program*. Wilmington: E.I. DuPont de Nemours and Company.

European Agency for Safety and Health at Work (2002a) *Economic Appraisal of Preventing Accidents at Company Level*. Factsheet 28. Bilbao: European Agency for Safety and Health at Work.

European Agency for Safety and Health at Work (2002b) *New Trends in Accident Prevention due to the Changing World of Work*. Bilbao: European Agency for Safety and Health at Work.

European Agency for Safety and Health at Work (2002c) *New Forms of Contractual Relationships and the Implications for Occupational Safety and Health*. Bilbao: European Agency for Safety and Health at Work.

Health and Safety Commission (1994) *Health and Safety Commission Review of Legislation*. London: HSE Books.

Health and Safety Commission (2003) *Health and Safety Statistics 2002/2003*. Sudbury: HSE Books.

Health and Safety Executive (1988) *The Tolerability of Risks from Nuclear Power Stations*. London: HMSO.

Health and Safety Executive (1993) *Successful Health and Safety Management*. HS(G)65. Sudbury: HSE Books.

Health and Safety Executive (1999) *Reducing Risks, Protecting People*. C150. Sudbury: HSE Books.

Health and Safety Executive (2000) *Successful Health and Safety Management*. HSG65. Sudbury: HSE Books.

Inter-Departmental Liaison Group on Risk Assessment (1996) *The Setting of Safety Standards: A Report by an Interdepartmental Group and External Advisers*. London: HM Treasury.

International Labour Organization (2001) *Guidelines on Occupational Safety and Health Management Systems*. ILO-OSH 2001. Geneva: International Labour Organization.

Johnson & Johnson (2003) *Credo*. http://www.jnj.com

Johnston, I.H.A. and Pugh, S.D. (1994) System integrity classification: a practical application of integrity level concepts. In: R.F. Cox (ed.), *Risk Management and Critical Protective Systems* 7/1–7/15. Manchester: Sars Ltd.

Roy, M. (2003) Self-directed workteams and safety: a winning combination? *Safety Science*, **41**, 359–376.

Saari, J. (2001) Accident prevention today: one accident is too many. *Magazine of the European Agency for Safety and Health at Work*, **4** 3–5.

Standards Australia (2000) *Occupational Health and Safety Management Systems: Specifications with Guidance for Use*. AS 4801-2000. Strathfield: Standards Australia.

Vassie, L.H. (2000) Managing homeworking: health and safety responsibilities. *Employee Relations*, **22**(6), 540–554.

Wright, M.S. (1996a) *Business Re-engineering and Health and Safety Management: Literature Survey*. CRR 124. Sudbury: HSE Books.

Wright, M.S. (1996b) *Business Re-engineering and Health and Safety Management: Case Studies*. CRR 125. Sudbury: HSE Books.

Wright, M.S. (1998a) *Factors Motivating Proactive Health and Safety Management*. CRR 179. Sudbury: HSE Books.

Wright, M.S. (1998b) Why do we manage health and safety? *Occupational Safety & Health*, October, **28** 34–37.

Wright, M., Marsden, S. and Holmes, J. (2003) *Health and Safety Responsibilities of Company Directors and Management Board Members*. RR135. Sudbury: HSE Books.

PART TWO

Best Practice

Regulatory models for managing health and safety

The very use of the word regulation signals a toleration of the activity subject to control. Regulation is not an attempt to eradicate risk, crucially it is an attempt to manage it.

– Hutter (2001: 4)

Chapter contents

- Introduction
- The role of regulation in health and safety management
- National legislative systems
- Non-governmental regulation
- Challenges for health and safety regulation

Introduction

Legal frameworks, at national and international levels, currently set the boundaries within which business and society as a whole must operate. Initially, society's concerns and priorities were for the basic needs of life. However, with greater prosperity and improved standards of living came increased public demands for healthier and safer workplaces, cleaner environments, and safer commercial products. In addition, these demands were underpinned by the belief that national governments had an ever-increasing duty to protect people from involuntary harm. Governments therefore began to legislate in order to avoid the excesses of harm to society that had developed from increasing industrial activity. Initially regulation was through technical prescription, but it evolved to become goal-setting in nature. Governments, however, largely made their own judgements about which risks society would or would not tolerate. Industry, on the other hand, faced with the demands of a competitive global marketplace, required that health and safety and other regulations did not inhibit their global competitiveness or the development of new technologies.

This transition from a prescription to a goal-setting regime was accompanied by an increasing participation in regulation by non-governmental bodies.

The national challenge for health and safety regulation is extended by the current trend towards the internationalisation and harmonisation of regulations. Nowadays, regulation of health and safety is increasingly undertaken at an international level in the form of legally binding instruments on member states. This move towards internationalisation requires innovative forms of regulatory cooperation between countries, such as regulatory harmonisation, mutual recognition of standards, and removal of barriers to trade. Therefore effective regulation of workplace health and safety poses significant challenges to organisations in order to meet the aspirations of all stakeholders.

This chapter aims to provide an overview of the role of regulation in the management of health and safety risks, the evolution and structure of governmental regulations, and the role and development of non-governmental regulation. Finally, the challenges posed by the harmonisation of health and safety regulation is discussed.

The role of regulation in health and safety management

Regulation of health and safety risks and their management are inextricably linked. Regulation may be considered as the national means of managing health and safety risks, whereas corporate health and safety management is a form of organisational self-regulation. As with other regulatory practices, health and safety regulation takes many forms; however, statutory regulation in the form of national laws is the most common approach. Increasingly systems of self-regulation combine state and corporate systems, and this leads to a convergence of regulatory objectives and corporate strategy (Hutter and Power, 2000). Internal control is a particularly good example of the crossover between regulatory systems and corporate risk management.

A key challenge for legislators is the development and enactment of regulation that defines and protects not only the public's current interests but also their future interests, as society, technology and the economy evolve. Health and safety regulation is fundamentally different from other forms of regulation because it is generally concerned with the regulation of unintentional risk, unlike crimes such as fraud and burglary. The very nature of risk, which has been discussed in earlier chapters, presupposes that there will be a chance of an adverse outcome from a given activity. However, the activities that generate these risks may also provide benefits, such as products and services, employment opportunities and social networks, and therefore the risk of harm and the benefits are inextricably linked. It is impossible to prohibit harm absolutely, as risk cannot be reduced to zero. Therefore, given that the risk of harm is ever present, all that can be reasonably expected from regulation is that risk owners minimise the level of risk to others. Only when responsibility and accountability for adverse events can be proven can legal provisions be enacted. Although certain levels of risk are considered socially acceptable, the higher the potential for harm from an activity the more likely it is that the activity will be forbidden or regulated by law. However, the criteria and decision-making processes that define what is forbidden and what is not are not always based on scientific evidence (Seiler, 2002).

Some economists argue that the management of health and safety is a good economic business practice; furthermore, they argue that in the absence of regulatory control the adoption of a 'health and safety is good practice' approach should minimise business risk. However, Fuller (2000) identified that organisations operating on the basis of good practice risk management will seek to minimise operating costs, which inherently requires the acceptance of a level of injury and ill-health. Others argued that government regulation was a necessary part of the fabric of health and safety management because not all organisations will be motivated to follow the 'good business practice' argument (Wright, 1998). It has been claimed that risk levels can increase if the market regulates itself (Baram, 2002), and although civil litigation does indirectly promote safety, it is effective only where more proactive systems have failed (de Mol and van Gaalen, 2002). The contribution of health and safety legislation to health and safety performance is therefore difficult to assess; evidence suggests that it has been one important driver among a multitude of other factors (Hudson, 2002). Importantly, health and safety legislation provides a basic framework within which businesses must operate, and defines minimum standards that must be achieved.

Health and safety regulation in the industrialised countries, such as the United Kingdom, was founded in the industrial revolution of the nineteenth century. Early concerns focused on general issues of child labour and working hours, but issues relating to specific workplaces followed later. Prescriptive legislation evolved piecemeal over a period of time, and although some activities were regulated others remained unregulated (Hendy and Ford, 2001). In general, this resulted in an unstructured collection of laws that were complex, difficult to amend, and soon out of date. Following increases in the industrial accident rate, demand grew for statutory reform of the health and safety legislative system and, in particular, for worker involvement in the process. The UK government responded by establishing a committee of inquiry chaired by Lord Robens. The Robens (1972) Report, which signalled the beginning of a dramatic change in the way health and safety was regulated in the UK and other countries, recommended three areas for action:

- the introduction of a 'framework' Act to replace the existing legislation and to expand the application of health and safety laws;
- the creation of a single unified enforcement agency; and
- the adoption of a new philosophy that emphasised self-regulation and workforce involvement.

Employers were required to ensure that health and safety risks were managed *so far as reasonably practicable*, and in order to do so were provided with supporting codes of practice and guidance documents. The move towards goal-setting general duties was also witnessed elsewhere in Europe, North America and Australia (Gunningham and Johnstone, 2000).

The regulation of occupational health and safety has constituted a vital part of the work of the European Union since the 1950s, because it was perceived that this area of activity had important implications for Europe (Neal, 1998), as:

- common safety standards assisted economic integration;
- reductions in the human, social and economic costs of work-related accidents and ill-health brought about an increase in the quality of life;
- efficient work practices increased productivity and promoted better industrial relations; and
- regulation of certain major hazards should be harmonised at supranational level because of potential transboundary effects and the scale of resources involved.

The late 1980s and early 1990s witnessed a flood of European health and safety legislation that was pivotal in the development of health and safety in Member States. These developments in Europe represented a shift in regulatory policy 'from a relatively hierarchical one, characterised by deference to authority and technical expertise to a more egalitarian one defined by public mistrust of author-ity, technology and scientific expertise' (Vogel, 2001: p.11): this shift was driven by regulatory failures, the desire for European integration and public interest.

Although goal-setting regulatory systems do not require employers to intro-duce health and safety management systems, the goal-setting requirements do require evidence that employers have complied with their general duties (Gunningham and Johnstone, 2000). However, in the case of high-risk indus-tries, such as the nuclear, offshore and chemical sectors, UK regulations required operators of certain facilities to submit a safety case or report that demonstrated that they had managed specific risks.

In the UK and countries that adopt or follow the UK legislative system, such as Australia and Canada, the three regulatory approaches of technical prescrip-tion, goal-setting and safety case/report represent an evolutionary progression in proactive management. However, this evolution has not been universal; for example, in some countries technical prescription has been favoured over the goal-setting approach. These three approaches to regulation offer distinct differ-ences in risk control (Hopkins and Hale, 2002):

- *Technical prescription* provides rules for direct risk control.
- *Goal-setting regulation* specifies the outputs required but not the rules for achieving them.
- *Safety case/report regulation* specifies the requirements for the safety manage-ment system and/or requires that the safety management system adopted demonstrates how it controls the risks.

So far, the focus has been on the regulation of health and safety by government agencies/bodies in the form of legislation. However, the role played by non-governmental agencies in the regulation of health and safety has increased as national and international non-governmental organisations developed a variety of standards for various aspects of health and safety management. Organisations such as the United Nations (UN), the International Labour Organization (ILO) and the World Health Organization (WHO) all advocated that every person had the right to a work environment that enabled them to live a healthy and eco-nomically satisfying life. Occupational health and safety therefore forms a part of the wider world agenda on sustainable development. In developing countries, in particular, the well-being of a family unit is dependent on the health and safety of the working member of the group. Therefore, where the level of social protection of the workforce is low, families are at greater risk, and in these situations it is important for international organisations to define and implement health and safety strategies.

A key function of the ILO since its inception has been the establishment of international standards related to labour and social matters, including occupational health and safety. These standards, in the form of conventions and recommendations, influenced the ways in which health and safety risks were managed in ILO member states: for example, national legislation took into account the ILO requirements, trades unions used ILO standards to support arguments in bargaining for and promoting health and safety legislation, and governments consulted the ILO about the compatibility of proposed texts of national legislation with international labour standards.

WHO has been involved in health improvement programmes since 1950, and has worked closely with the ILO in this context through the Joint ILO/WHO Committee on Occupational Health. The constitution of WHO (2003) specifies that all people have a fundamental right to the highest achievable levels of health. Among a number of organisations, WHO also collaborates with the International Commission on Occupational Health (ICOH), the International Occupational Hygiene Association (IOHA) and the European Commission to protect and improve the working conditions of employees. The WHO General Programme of Work recognises the importance of monitoring and controlling the impact of work-related ill-health, and the European Union and the North American Free Trade Association (NAFTA) have also recognised the need to reduce the cases of ill-health at work. The Network of WHO Collaborating Centres in Occupational Health (World Health Organization, 2002) was created at a meeting in Helsinki in 1990, with the first meeting of the Network's member institutes held in Moscow in 1992. *The Declaration on Occupational Health for All* and its supporting document the *Global Strategy on Occupational Health for All* were both approved by the Second Meeting of the WHO Collaborating Centres in Occupational Health in Beijing in 1994 (World Health Organization, 2002). These documents provided guidance for the development of occupational health at international, national and local levels.

The national and international standards bodies have also played an increasing role in the regulation of health and safety. For example within Europe, where *New Approach Technical Directives* specify broad goal-setting essential requirements, product standards provide the technical detail in order to satisfy these essential requirements. Accordingly, the law does not need to be regularly adapted to accommodate technological progress, as an assessment of whether the essential requirements have been met is based on the state of technical knowledge defined within a standard. As industry participates in the standards development process, standards largely reflect the 'state of the art'. In this case, the regulatory efforts of government and non-governmental standards bodies complement and reinforce each other. The development and increasing application of health and safety management standards, such as BSI-OHSAS 18001 *Occupational Health and Safety Management Systems* (British Standards Institution, 1999), led to a number of non-governmental third parties offering certification of performance to these standards. Application of these standards, however, cannot guarantee successful management; they merely enable accredited auditors to attest to whether an organisation has met the requirements of the standard. Health and safety management systems standards are considered further in Chapter 10.

The final area of non-governmental regulation to be considered is that of corporate governance. In its simplest form, corporate governance can be described as an organisation's internal management arrangements that demonstrate to all stakeholders that the organisation's risks, such as health and safety, are adequately controlled. At the centre of these arrangements are an organisation's directors, who have a responsibility to ensure the long-term future of the organisation through profitable operations. The directors provide the company strategy for achieving this aim, and the operational management team implement the strategy on a day-to-day basis. Governance issues therefore address the control systems and performance measures related to how directors and senior managers achieve an organisation's strategic objectives. External laws, regulations, guidance, standards etc. support these internal control measures and provide a basis for achieving equality of competition between companies and countries by ensuring that they all meet minimum performance standards. The major external controls affecting a company usually relate to the national legal and standards framework in which the company operates. However, as an organisation's operations become more international in nature, they are more likely to be driven by worldwide industry best practices and international agreements and standards.

National legislative systems

The following sections consider legislative frameworks in developed and developing countries.

Developed countries

The general legal system operating in the United Kingdom is described as a *common law* system. In the early English legal system judgments were made on the basis of custom and practice, with the principles derived from judgments made in earlier cases creating binding precedents. The law relating to health and safety matters is a mixture of criminal law, which is set out in statutes, and common law, which is the substantive law and procedural rules created by prior judicial decisions. Legal judgments are based on both statute and common law, and the legal precedents established in the courts can apply to both civil actions and criminal prosecutions. Hendy and Ford (2001) and Barrett and Howells (2000) provided a detailed examination of the development of health and safety criminal and civil liabilities in the UK.

Criminal law is concerned with offences against individuals, society and the state, for which the offender may be prosecuted by the state, and if the accused is found guilty he or she is liable to be punished. Criminal cases are called *prosecutions* and are initiated by bodies representing the state. The prosecuting body aims to prove their assertion of guilt 'beyond reasonable doubt'. It is usual in a prosecution to require proof of a guilty mind (*mens rea*) on the part of the defendant – that is, the intention to perform the act. A crime or a criminal act is determined by judicial decisions, which then develop common law, or by legislation.

Civil law is concerned with disputes between individuals and/or organisations. Although the state provides the mechanism for civil actions to take place, the responsibility rests with individual parties to pursue and bring about a civil action. A claimant will bring an action against a defendant that, if successful, will result in civil remedies, which are defined by the judge, to compensate the claimant for their loss. The state takes no direct interest in these remedies. In terms of health and safety matters, victims of an accident most often bring civil actions. Such actions, if successful, result in the defendant paying the claimant damages in the form of financial compensation.

Statute law can relate to both civil and criminal proceedings and consists of Acts of Parliament and Rules, Regulations and Orders made within the parameters of an Act (Health and Safety Executive, 2002). Acts usually set out a framework of principles or objectives and use specific regulations or Orders to achieve these objectives. Acts of Parliament are referred to as *primary legislation*, with regulations made under Acts termed *subordinate* or *delegated legislation*. In the UK, the Health and Safety at Work etc. Act 1974 is the primary statutory instrument for the legislation of health and safety, whilst regulations set minimum standards for compliance with particular aspects of the Act. Codes of Practice may be issued to provide practical advice on how to comply with specific health and safety regulations. This mechanism effectively enables legislation to be kept up to date by revising the Code of Practice rather than the regulations. In the UK, failure to comply with an Approved Code of Practice (ACOP) does not in itself make a body liable in criminal or civil law. However, in criminal proceedings a failure to observe the terms of an ACOP constitutes proof of contravention of the relevant statutory duty unless there is proof that the defendant had complied with the legal duty in an equally acceptable way. The least formal rules in UK health and safety regulation are provided by Guidance Notes, which aim to assist employers in discharging their legal duties. Although they have no legal force, Guidance Notes may be used to establish what is considered to be reasonable practice within an industry. Guidance Notes are considered, therefore, to have 'quasi-legal' status.

Common law has evolved over hundreds of years as a result of judicial decisions. Common law, which is based on custom and practice, covers areas where statute law has not provided specific requirements. The accumulation of decisions in common law cases has resulted in a body of precedents, which are binding on future cases of a similar nature, unless they are subsequently overruled by a higher court or by statute. An employer must take reasonable care to protect employees from the risk of foreseeable injury, disease or death at work by providing and maintaining a safe place of work, safe plant and equipment, safe systems of work, and competent fellow employees. The employer's duty of care to employees derives from the existence of a contract of employment; however, a duty of care may also be owed to others who may be affected by an employer's activities. To avoid common law claims for compensation an employer must exercise what is considered reasonable under the particular circumstances. An employer can also be held liable for the actions of his employees if the actions take place in the course of employment: this is referred to as *vicarious liability*. Employees have a general duty of care towards themselves and other people, and therefore they can also be sued by someone who is injured as a result of a lack of reasonable care on their part.

Generally, in common law cases, the burden of proof rests with the claimant or plaintiff, who must demonstrate *'on the balance of probabilities'* that the defendant has been negligent. In order to achieve this, the claimant must show that the defendant owed him or her a duty of care, that there was a breach of this duty, that the breach led to the harm, and that the harm suffered was foreseeable. In the event that circumstances indicate that an accident could have occurred only through a lack of care – that is, negligence is inferred – the situation is known as *re ipsa loquitur* or 'let the facts speak for themselves'. In this case the defendant would have to demonstrate that they had not been negligent in the circumstances. Defences that can be offered against common law claims are: denial of negligence, there was no duty owed to the claimant, the accident was the sole fault of the claimant, the accident did not result from a lack of care, contributory negligence by the claimant, and the claimant knowingly accepted the risk associated with the activities (*volenti non fit injuria*). Damages are awarded based on a range of factors, such as the loss of a faculty, the permanent nature of an injury, and the effect on the ability of the claimant to earn a living. Awards for compensation may be reduced if there is an element of contributory negligence by the claimant, although the courts tend to minimise the significance of this.

The broad framework of the UK health and safety legislative system has influenced developments in health and safety legislation in many countries. Although these systems may be at different stages of evolution, some common and distinct features can be noted. Typically, they have:

■ a framework or enabling Act dealing with occupational health and safety;

■ subordinate regulations providing detail on specific aspects of health and safety;

■ codes of practice; and

■ national standards.

For example in *Australia*, which is a federation of six States and two Territories, each State or Territory has the responsibility for making laws (statutes) on workplace health and safety and for enforcing those laws within the area of its jurisdiction. Each has a principal occupational health and safety Act, which describes the broad duties of parties, such as employers, employees and manufacturers. The key principle within each Act is the 'duty of care' responsibility for employers to provide a safe place of work for employees. Specific regulations, which are also legally binding and enforceable, support the principal Act by providing more detailed requirements for specific hazards. The States and Territories advise employers on ways of complying with the requirements of the Acts and regulations by issuing Codes of Practice and Guidance Notes, which are supported by national health and safety standards developed by the National Occupational Health and Safety Commission.

National standards deal with specific workplace hazards such as plant equipment, noise, and hazardous environments. These standards make the regulation of occupational health and safety consistent throughout Australia. Other standards are established by the organisation Standards Australia, which is an independent body. Where it is appropriate, a State or Territory may decide to refer to an Australian Standard in its occupational health and safety regulations. When this happens employers must meet the requirements of the particular Australian Standard as well as other duties described within the legislation.

The National Occupational Health and Safety Commission declares National Codes of Practice to advise employers and workers of acceptable ways of meeting the national standards. Guidance Notes usually relate to declared national standards and/or Codes of Practice. They provide detailed practical guidance for use by unions, employers, management, health and safety committee representatives, safety officers, medical practitioners and others. In contrast to national standards and Codes of Practice, Guidance Notes may not be suitable for reference in State and Territory legislation. Enforcement of health and safety regulations is carried out by State and Territory inspectors, who have wide-ranging powers similar to those of Health and Safety Executive inspectors in the UK.

A similar legislative system operates in *Canada*, where each jurisdiction – province, territory and federal – has its own health and safety Act, which applies to most workplaces in that region. The government department responsible for occupational health and safety varies within each jurisdiction. Typically, it is a Ministry or Department of Labour; however, it may also be a workers' compensation board or commission. Basic elements, such as the rights and responsibilities of employers and employees, are similar in all jurisdictions across Canada; however, specific details of the legislation and how the legislation is enforced vary from one to another. In addition, provisions within health and safety regulations may be referred to as 'mandatory', 'discretionary' or 'directed by the Minister'.

Although broad similarities can be found between health and safety legislative systems, the playing field is far from level. Countries within the European Union provide good examples of the variations that can exist within one unified continent (European Agency for Safety and Health at Work, 2003; Commission of the European Communities, 2004). Four areas, which serve to highlight these variations, are legal systems, standards of proof, enforcement processes, and social security systems.

Legal systems

In the UK a distinction is drawn between criminal and civil law, in contrast to the systems in some other European countries. In the UK, the enforcement of health and safety is a criminal matter, which is separated from the administration of the compensation process for an injured party. The Netherlands, Spain and Italy adopt similar approaches to this, but in France and Germany regulation of health and safety is treated as a social insurance and criminal matter. In the UK, the pursuance of compensation by injured parties takes place independently of any criminal law and social insurance systems.

Standards of proof

The UK, Italy and the Netherlands impose broad principles of legal liability, and combine these with more detailed rules in specific areas, whereas in Germany more precise rules are to be found. Within the UK and the Netherlands duties are detailed in absolute and qualified terms, and the concept of 'reasonableness' is used. For example, in the UK some of the duties imposed by the Health and Safety at Work etc. Act 1974 and Regulations made under this Act are qualified by the term 'so far as is reasonably practicable'. A precedent for the definition of this phrase was set by the UK Court of Appeal in considering the case of *Edwards v National Coal Board* (1949). In this particular case the plaintiff was the widow of a coalminer who was killed underground by the collapse of a substantial part of a roadway. The Court of Appeal considered that the defendants failed to establish their defence under the relevant statutory provisions. Lord Justice Asquith described the standard of duty expected as follows:

> 'Reasonably practicable', as traditionally defined, is a narrower term than 'physically possible' and implies that a computation must be made in which the quantum of risk is placed on one scale and the sacrifice, whether in money, time, trouble, involved in the measures necessary to avert the risk is placed in the other; and that, if it be shown that there is a gross disproportion between them, the risk being insignificant in relation to the sacrifice, the person on whom the duty is laid discharges the burden of proving that compliance was not reasonably practicable.
>
> Hendy and Ford (1998: 25)

Thus a duty holder must weigh the severity of a risk against the cost of implementing measures to avoid or reduce the risk. Costs should be considered in terms of money, time and physical difficulty, and if the total costs are disproportionate in comparison with the risk, then it is unreasonable to expect the persons concerned to implement the measures. The size or financial situation of the organisation should be immaterial in these considerations.

In France, Germany and Spain there is no standard akin to the 'so far as is reasonably practicable' test used in the UK. France and Germany will implement what are apparently absolute duties in an appropriate situational context so that some qualification in duty is still applied. In Spain, however, there is a presumption of negligence when there is a breach of an absolute duty. There is also a considerable variation in the way in which legal liability is established across European countries. In general, an adversarial approach is adopted in the UK, which contrasts with the inquisitorial process adopted by other European states. For example, in the UK a failure to follow an Approved Code of Practice is read as a breach of statutory duty unless statutory compliance can be demonstrated by other means, whereas in the Netherlands and Italy the plaintiff has only to show that the injury was caused by work in order to place the onus on the employer to show reasonableness in their operations.

Enforcement processes

Member States vary in their choice of regulatory institution: in the UK a central agency (Health and Safety Executive, 2003) has primary responsibility, whereas in the Netherlands and Spain the regulatory function lies within a government ministry, and in Italy local health authorities carry out this role. The German system of enforcement is highly diffuse, with several parties involved including the police, state labour inspectorates and industrial insurance institutions. In France particular emphasis is placed on the role of the trade unions, which have the power to institute criminal proceedings, and the Labour Inspectorate. Many inspectorates have roles as promoters of health and safety, and therefore persuasion rather than penalty is the preferred route to compliance.

There is a wide difference across Member States in the principles adopted for taking enforcement actions and the approaches taken for seeking compliance. In the UK prosecutions are comparatively rare, with administrative sanctions and negotiations used far more frequently; prosecution is therefore not an automatic choice. In Italy criminal law is used less, owing to the inspection system, and in Germany it is also rare owing to the role of the social insurance system, which seeks compliance by negotiation. France makes more use of criminal sanctions, but this means that prosecutions are also limited. Although the duties of French employers are absolute, there appears to be considerable flexibility in interpretation, with inspectors again preferring to negotiate rather than to prosecute.

Social security systems

Social security systems also differ across European countries. In the UK, social security payments to injured parties do not affect an employer's overall liabilities, whereas in Spain social security law may impose additional compensatory liability on employers. Pursuance of a civil action independently of social security systems and criminal law provisions is a route available to the injured party in the UK and a number of other Member States. In Germany, however, the social security system does not permit civil actions between employers and employees, whereas in Spain civil and criminal liabilities are linked.

In countries where there are statutory requirements for employers to have accident insurance arrangements, employers are required to indemnify workers who are injured as a consequence of their work. In countries operating these systems, such as France, Spain and Italy, employers pay premiums to social security ministries or their agents. Insurance premiums are usually dependent on an organisation's accident performance and the level of risk inherent in the industrial sector within which the organisation operates. Employees can then bring a civil action against their employer only for pain and suffering and not for compensation, as this is dealt with via the social security system. Compensation in these systems is normally paid irrespective of fault.

Developing countries

In other parts of the world the development of occupational health and safety legislation lagged behind that in the industrialised countries. Nevertheless, significant changes have taken and are still taking place (Lowenson, 1998; Dwyer, 2000). For example, many multinational organisations, whose parent companies are located in Europe or the USA, operate in Southern Africa. Although there is some evidence to suggest that these organisations attempt to apply European and American policies, procedures and standards, in reality many African operations perform to lower standards. In addition, Southern African domestic operations involve smaller profit margins and less capital investment, and often operate under more hazardous conditions than the equivalent operations in Europe and the USA. More than half the Southern African population is employed in agriculture and in small-scale operations, with child labour a common feature. Legislation, which is being revised as a result of national and international pressures, reflects a shift towards a more holistic, participatory and broader vision of health and safety management rather than the narrow focus provided by 'workplace safety' and 'Factories Acts'. The new approach includes reducing risks by ensuring safe design, testing and choice of equipment, establishing safe work environments, and adapting the work to the workforce. These changes emphasise the internationalisation of health and safety management, as developing countries adopt approaches advocated by, for example, the ILO (2003).

In addition, the newer approach provides for tripartite occupational health and safety structures at national levels and bipartite structures at enterprise level. The national tripartite councils involve employers, unions and state representatives, and the bipartite structures, which have been created for the identification of hazards and implementation of standards, involve employers and employees. However, most laws still fail to provide workers with the right to refuse to undertake unsafe work; this situation is exacerbated by the relatively weak legal protection provided for workers against victimisation for reasonable health and safety actions. Hence, although the mechanism for bipartite structure exists in law, the shift towards employee control of risks is relatively limited. Given the major issues of unemployment and job security, it is unlikely that workers will take steps to stop dangerous work, thereby undermining their ability to avoid or reduce injury at work.

Despite the reforms taking place in developing countries, there are still many problems to be addressed, such as underdeveloped and poorly staffed systems of law enforcement, translating legal standards into practice, and developing clear and specific safety provisions for new processes and hazards. Nevertheless, the basic legal standards for occupational health and safety in developing countries are moving towards harmonisation, and corresponding more closely to the basic ILO standards set out in ILO Convention 155 (International Labour Organization, 1981a).

Non-governmental regulation

Non-governmental regulation plays an essential role in health and safety management of which national and international standards and corporate governance are particularly important.

International and national standards

The *International Labour Organization* (ILO) was set up in 1919, as part of the League of Nations, with the aims of improving workers' living standards and conditions of work throughout the world. The ILO, which is now an agency of the United Nations, is the only UN agency that operates as a tripartite organisation: the Governing Body, Committees and delegations to conferences are all composed of government, employers and trade union representatives. The key function of the ILO from its inception has been the establishment of international standards related to labour and social matters. These standards take the form of *Conventions* and *Recommendations*, of which approximately 70 deal with occupational health and safety matters. In addition, further guidance is provided through Codes of Practice, manuals and other instruments, such as resolutions, which are used to address particular problems. In contrast to the European Commission, which lays down mandatory legal requirements on health and safety matters for the Member States, the ILO operates on a voluntary compliance basis. However, the ILO, unlike the European Commission, is not required to pay close attention to the competitive implications of its regulatory activities. The relationship between the ILO and the European Union, in respect of occupational health and safety, has been a sensitive issue, as the European Union at times is perceived as reinventing the wheel when ILO instruments already exist and the Member States of the European Union are also members of the ILO.

Conventions are comparable to multilateral international treaties and are open to ratification by Member States. Once ratified by a Member State, conventions create specific binding obligations on that State. A State that has ratified a convention is expected to apply its provisions through national legislation or other appropriate means as indicated within the text of the convention. State governments are required to report on the application of ratified conventions, and the extent of compliance may be subjected to examination by the ILO. Any complaint about non-compliance, by the government of one State about another State or by an employers' or workers' organisation, may be investigated and acted upon by the ILO.

Recommendations are intended to offer guidance to Member States and often elaborate on the provisions made in a convention on the same subject. Member States are obliged to submit the texts of ILO recommendations to their legislative bodies, to report on any resulting action, and to report occasionally at the request of the ILO on the measures taken or envisaged to effect the provisions of the recommendations.

ILO occupational health and safety standards fall into four categories:

■ guiding policies for action, such as national policies;

■ defining protection in given industrial sectors, such as the construction industry;

■ defining protection against specific risks, such as ionising radiation; and

■ defining levels of protection, such as medical examinations for young workers.

The guiding policy on occupational health and safety is contained within the *Occupational Safety and Health Convention No. 155* (ILO, 1981a) and its accompanying *Occupational Health and Safety Recommendation No. 164* (ILO, 1981b). These documents prescribed the progressive application of comprehensive preventive measures and the adoption of a coherent national policy for occupational health and safety. They also prescribed establishing the responsibilities of employers for making work and work equipment safe and without risk to health, as well as the duties and rights of workers.

Through its SafeWork Programme, the ILO (2003) sought to extend the benefits of managing occupational safety and health achieved in the industrialised countries to the rest of the world. The primary objectives of this programme were to:

■ create worldwide awareness of the dimensions and consequences of work-related accidents, injuries and diseases;

■ promote the goal of basic protection for all workers in conformity with international labour standards; and

■ enhance the capacity of Member States and industry to design and implement effective preventative and protective policies and programmes.

A key development in support of the ILO SafeWork Programme was the introduction of the document *Guidelines on Occupational Safety and Health Management Systems* ILO-OSH 2001 (ILO, 2001), which is discussed in detail in Chapter 10.

International companies felt for many years that there was a need to agree on world standards in order to rationalise international trading processes, and this was the reason for establishing the *International Organization for Standardization* (ISO, 2003). International standardisation is already well established for many technologies, such as information processing and communications, textiles, energy production, shipbuilding, banking and financial services, but will continue to grow in importance for the foreseeable future. The main reasons for this are (ISO, 2003):

- worldwide progress in trade liberalisation;
- interpenetration of sectors;
- worldwide communication systems;
- global standards for emerging technologies; and
- developing countries.

The aim of international standards is to facilitate trade, exchange and technology transfer through (ISO, 2003):

- enhanced product quality at a reasonable price;
- improved health, safety and environmental protection, and reduction of waste;
- greater compatibility and interoperability of goods and services;
- simplification for improved usability;
- reduction in the variation of goods to reduce costs; and
- increased distribution efficiency and ease of maintenance.

Users have increased confidence in commodities that are produced in conformity with ISO standards, especially where there is an assurance of conformity available through certification by independent parties.

In order to facilitate the free movement of products in the *European Economic Area* (EEA) through the removal and prevention of trade barriers, a new approach to technical harmonisation was introduced in 1985. As a result product safety Directives set out broad essential requirements and standards were developed to provide the technical details needed to satisfy these requirements. Standards that are made in support of New Technical Approach Directives must be transposed into national standards of the Member States of the European Union, and pre-existing standards, which conflict with the harmonised standards, must be withdrawn. The application of harmonised European and other standards within the EEA remains voluntary, and manufacturers may apply other equivalent specifications in order to meet the essential requirements of the legislation. However, products manufactured in compliance with harmonised standards benefit from a presumption of conformity with the legislation, whereas products manufactured to other standards must demonstrate conformity. The development of the technical specifications required for the implementation of Directives is entrusted to the European standardisation organisations: namely Comité Européen de Normalisation (CEN, 2003), Comité Européen de Normalisation Electrotechnique

(CENELEC, 2003) and European Telecommunications Standards Institute (ETSI, 2003). The European standards organisations' aims are to promote voluntary technical harmonisation within Europe in conjunction with worldwide bodies and partners in Europe in order to diminish trade barriers and promote safety.

Corporate governance

Corporate governance issues became prominent in the early 1980s, in the United States of America, after company boards began introducing practices to avert hostile takeover bids. Many of these practices were seen to be for the benefit of company directors and against the best interests of shareholders. In the United Kingdom, in the late 1980s and early 1990s, greater public ownership and interest in companies came about through the government's privatisation of the nationalised utility companies. Also at this time in the UK there were a number of high-profile company failures, such as Polly Peck, Maxwell Communications and BCCI, where companies reported 'profits' in their last set of published accounts but then went into administration. In these cases directors were perceived to have presented the company finances in a favourable way by using a range of accounting techniques that acted against shareholders' best interests (Smith, 1992). These events brought about a distrust of large corporations and the motives of their directors, and this resulted in corporate activities coming under greater scrutiny from the public, the media and large institutional investment organisations. As a result, the 1990s witnessed a number of detailed examinations of corporate governance. Reports by Cadbury (1992) and Greenbury (1996) focused on the financial aspects of corporate governance. A further Committee on Corporate Governance was established in 1995 in the UK under the chairmanship of Sir Ronnie Hampel. The Hampel Committee produced their final report in 1998 and recognised that the definition of corporate governance used by the Cadbury Committee (1992) was restrictive as it excluded many activities involved in managing a company that were vital to its success. A key element introduced by the Hampel Committee into their *Principles of Corporate Governance* was the issue related to internal control.

> The board should maintain a sound system of internal control to safeguard shareholders' investment and the company's assets. This covers not only financial controls but operational and compliance controls, and risk management, since there are potential threats to shareholders' investment in each of these areas.
>
> Hampel (1998: 21)

This document clearly acknowledged for the first time the important impact that non-financial issues could have on the well-being of a company. Internal control now embraced a much wider range of risks including, for example, quality, environment and health and safety.

Following the work of the Hampel Committee, the London Stock Exchange, in 1998, published new Listing Rules together with Principles of Good Governance and a Code of Best Practice that was referred to as 'the Combined Code', which required companies incorporated in the UK to include in their annual reports statements of:

- how they had applied the principles of the Combined Code on corporate governance; and

- whether they had complied throughout the accounting period with the principles of the Combined Code.

The Institute of Chartered Accountants in England & Wales (ICAEW) agreed, with the London Stock Exchange, to produce guidance on implementing the requirements of the Combined Code in respect of internal control. This guidance was produced by the Internal Control Working Party of the ICAEW (1999), under the Chairmanship of Nigel Turnbull, in September 1999 and was entitled *Internal Control: Guidance for Directors on the Combined Code*.

Globalisation of corporate governance principles

Corporate governance codes or reports have been prepared on every continent of the world with the exception of Antarctica. Groups as diverse as investors, companies, regulators, directors, accountants and world trade organisations have all prepared corporate governance documents. Through a consultative process involving governments, the private sector, international organisations and other stakeholders, the Organisation for Economic Co-operation and Development (1999) developed the *Principles of Corporate Governance*.

The major systems of corporate governance are those based in Canada, Germany, Japan, UK and USA. The Canada, UK and USA models focus on the dispersion of controls or a goal-setting approach, whereas the German and Japanese models focus more on an ownership structure or a prescriptive approach. Many countries now advocate the use of corporate governance systems that reflect the broad responsibilities of all stakeholders. The positive impact that the principles of corporate governance have on business performance has been recognised and accepted as a component of an effective organisational management system on a worldwide basis. This acceptance, coupled with the globalisation of economies, led to an increasing convergence of corporate governance initiatives around the world, and as a consequence international issues are now considered alongside organisational and national issues, such as ethical investments and the transfer of environment, health and safety risks by the developed countries to the developing countries.

The Turnbull system of internal control

The Turnbull (1999) Working Party prepared guidance on how to implement the Combined Code provision D.2 and the associated provisions of D.2.1 and D.2.2. Principle D.2 of the Combined Code required a company board:

> to maintain a sound system of internal control to safeguard shareholders' investment and the company's assets.

Provision D.2.1 required directors to:

> at least annually conduct a review of the effectiveness of the group's system of internal control and should report to shareholders that they have done so; this review should include financial, operational and compliance controls and risk management.

Provision D.2.2 required companies:

> which do not have an internal audit function from time to time to review the need for one.

Risk is a fundamental part of business, and it is important that risk management and internal control are not viewed as ways of eliminating risk from business activities. Company value is often dependent on successful risk-taking ventures, and internal control should be viewed as one of the key means by which risk is managed at acceptable levels within an organisation. Directors are not required to review the effectiveness of the controls used to manage insignificant risks, but they are required to consider the residual risks associated with significant operational, compliance and financial controls. The objectives of internal control are to (i) reflect sound business practice; (ii) remain relevant over time; and (iii) enable each company to apply controls in a manner that takes account of its particular circumstances.

The guidance utilised a goal-setting management approach rather than a prescriptive approach, and required directors to use their judgement when reviewing how they had implemented the requirements of the Combined Code in terms of internal controls. The Report went on to say:

> The guidance is based on the adoption by a company's board of a risk-based approach to establishing a sound system of internal control and reviewing its effectiveness. This should be incorporated by the company within its normal management and governance processes. It should not be treated as a separate exercise undertaken to meet regulatory requirements.
>
> Turnbull (1999: 4)

These objectives provided the basis of corporate governance as they set out the requirement for a risk-based approach to management. This approach, however, required managers to understand and implement risk management within a much wider arena than the financial risks to which many were more accustomed. They were also required to understand the economic impact of risk management and the implementation of cost–benefit analysis arguments to justify and support management decisions on the control of organisational risks. This is a fundamental aspect of UK health and safety legislation, and is referred to as the 'so far as is reasonably practicable' or 'as low as is reasonably practicable' (ALARP) principle.

The guidance on internal control embraced the argument:

> A company's objectives, its internal organisation and the environment in which it operates are continually evolving and, as a result, the risks it faces are continually changing. A sound system of internal control therefore depends on a thorough and regular evaluation of the nature and extent of the risks to which the company is exposed. Since profits are, in part, the reward for successful risk-taking in business, the purpose of internal control is to help manage and control risk appropriately rather than to eliminate it.
>
> Turnbull (1999: 5)

Challenges for health and safety regulation

The achievement of common standards of health and safety management on a global basis is a valid aspiration, but there are many practical difficulties to be addressed before this can be achieved. For example, the vision of the European Union was to establish a 'level playing field' with common standards across all countries in order that a manufacturer in one Member State would be subject to the same regulatory regime as that of a manufacturer in another Member State. However, the measurement of equality of competition is complicated because it is difficult to define the costs of compliance through regulatory inputs such as preventive measures and outputs such as accident rates (Baldwin, 1992). Health and safety, which is intrinsically difficult to regulate effectively owing to the large range of hazards and the number and range of individuals and organisations, continues to pose a significant challenge. Issues related to differences in legal systems, legal standards of proof and the enforcement processes all impact on the issue of equality of regulation.

An alternative basis for the harmonisation of the regulation of health and safety management may be offered by a risk-based approach (Seiler, 2002). The use of risk-based decision-making as a basis for regulatory control is used in the USA for the control of carcinogenic and toxic substances. In a risk-based legislative framework the same acceptable level of risk is defined for all types of risk. On this basis, activities are legal if the risk associated with an activity is equal to or less than the defined acceptable level. This acceptable risk level may be achieved by whichever means the risk owner chooses. In contrast to the traditional legal approach to regulation, the risk-based approach is concerned with the residual risk resulting from an activity and not how the activity is carried out; it is therefore an output-oriented approach. The risk-based approach also accepts that there is always a certain residual risk but seeks to reduce this risk as far as possible rather than to specify that certain harms, such as a fatality, are illegal when it is impossible to prevent them absolutely. This approach offers rationality, but there are still many issues that must be addressed: for example, determination of acceptable and tolerable levels of risk, undesirable outcomes and the completeness of risk assessments (Seiler, 2002).

Kirwan *et al.* (2002) considered that the effective regulation of health and safety required:

- controllable technology;
- appropriate levels of resources;
- regulatory cooperation and willingness to comply; and
- an effective regulator

For technology to be controllable, the hazards associated with it must be well understood, the rate of change of technology must be manageable, and the profits generated from the technology must be adequate. Issues such as poor risk estimation, technology changing too fast (or too slow) and a lack of reinvestment of profits in health and safety impinge on the 'controllability' of technology. In addition, both the organisation and the regulator must have the required competence. Gunningham and Johnstone (2000) argued for a 'two-track' approach to regulation in which there was a more rigorous approach to enforcement and incentives that were used to provide greater encouragement for organisations to introduce health and safety management systems.

Summary

- Health and safety regulation is generally concerned with the regulation of unintentional risks. The activities that generate these risks may also provide benefits and therefore the risk of harm and the benefits are inextricably linked.

- Health and safety legislation is considered to be an important driver among many other influencing factors in shaping health and safety performance.

- The regulation of health and safety draws upon governmental and non-governmental regulation. Increasingly, non-government regulation in the form of international and national standards and corporate governance provide significant input to health and safety management.

- While there are a number of similarities between the legislative systems in the UK and other developed countries, variations exist in respect of legal systems, standards of proof enforcement processes and social security systems.

- There are several difficulties associated with the harmonisation of regulation. While a risk-based approach to regulation may be beneficial there are still difficulties associated with its implementation. Controllable technology, adequate resources, regulatory cooperation and an effective regulator are key inputs to effective regulation of health and safety.

Issues for review and discussion

- Consider the advantages and disadvantages of the internationalisation of health and safety regulation.

- Consider whether corporate governance adds to the existing legislative requirements for the management of health and safety risks.

- Examine the advantages and disadvantages of a risk-based approach to health and safety regulation.

- Review the relative contributions of government and non-government regulation to health and safety management.

- Examine how an organisation may evaluate the relevance of new health and safety regulation.

References

Baldwin, R. (1992) The limits of legislative harmonisation. In: R. Baldwin and T. Daintith (eds), *Harmonisation and Hazard: Regulating Workplace Health and Safety in the European Community*, 223–251. London: Graham and Trotman.

Baram, M. (2002) Biotechnology and social control. In: B. Kirwan, A. Hale and A. Hopkins (eds) *Changing Regulation: Controlling Risks in Society*, 217–230. Oxford: Elsevier Science.

Barrett, B. and Howells, R. (2000) *Occupational Health and Safety Law: Text and Materials*. London: Cavendish.

British Standards Institution (1999) *Occupational Health and Safety Management Systems: Specification* BSI-OHSAS 18001. London: British Standards Institution.

Cadbury, Sir A. (1992) *Report of the Committee on the Financial Aspects of Corporate Governance*. London: Gee Publishing.

Comité Européen de Normalisation (2003) http://www.cenorm.be

Comité Européen de Normalisation Electrotechnique (2003) http://www.cenelec.be

Commission of the European Communities (2004) *Communication from the Commission on the Practical Implementation of the Provisions of the Health and Safety at Work Directives 89/391, 89/654, 89/655, 89/656, 90/269 and 90/270*. COM(2004) 62.

De Mol, B. and van Gaalen, G. (2002) Medical device technology and patient protection: challenge for regulation and legislation. In: B. Kirwan, A. Hale and A. Hopkins (eds), *Changing Regulation: Controlling Risks in Society*, 195–215. Oxford: Elsevier Science.

Dwyer, T. (2000) A study on safety and health management at work: a multidimensional view from a developing country. In: K. Frick, P.L. Jensen, M. Quinlan and T. Wilthagen (eds), *Systematic Occupational Health and Safety Management: Perspectives on an International Development*, 149–174. Amsterdam: Pergamon.

Edwards v National Coal Board [1949], 1 AER 743.

European Agency for Safety and Health at Work (2003) http://agency.osha.eu.int

European Telecommunications Standards Institute (2003) http://www.etsi.org

Fuller, C.W. (2000) Modelling continuous improvement and benchmarking processes through the use of benefit curves. *Benchmarking: An International Journal*, 7(1), 35–51.

Greenbury, Sir R. (1996) *Report of the Study Group on Directors' Remuneration*. London: Gee Publishing.

Gunningham, N. and Johnstone, T.C. (2000) The legal construction of OHS management. In: K. Frick, P.L. Jensen, M. Quinlan and T. Wilthagen (eds), *Systematic Occupational Health and Safety Management: Perspectives on an International Development*, 125–146. Amsterdam: Pergamon.

Hampel, Sir R. (1998) *Report of the Committee on Corporate Governance*. London: Gee Publishing.

Health and Safety Executive (2002) *The Health and Safety System in Great Britain*. Sudbury: HSE Books.

Health and Safety Executive (2003) http://www.hse.gsi.gov.uk

Hendy, J. and Ford, M. (1998) *Redgrave, Fife and Machin: Health and Safety*. London: Butterworth.

Hendy, J. and Ford, M. (2001) *Munkman on Employer's Liability*. London: Butterworth.

Hopkins, A. and Hale, A. (2002) Issues in the regulation of safety: setting the scene. In: B. Kirwan, A. Hale and A. Hopkins (eds), *Changing Regulation: Controlling Risks in Society*, 1–12. Oxford: Elsevier Science.

Hudson, C. (2002) Judicial review. *The Safety and Health Practitioner*, 20(7), 28–30.

Hutter, B. (2001) *Regulation and Risk: Occupational Health and Safety on the Railways*. Oxford: Oxford University Press.

Hutter, B. and Power, M. (2000) *Risk Management and Business Regulation*. London: London School of Economics and Political Science.

Internal Control Working Party of the Institute of Chartered Accountants in England & Wales (1999) *Internal Control: Guidance for Directors on the Combined Code*. London: The Institute of Chartered Accountants in England & Wales.

International Labour Organization (1981a) *Occupational Safety and Health Convention, No. 155*. Geneva: International Labour Organization.

International Labour Organization (1981b) *Occupational Health and Safety Recommendation, No. 164*. Geneva: International Labour Organization.

International Labour Organization (2001) *Guidelines on Occupational Safety and Health Management Systems* ILO-OSH 2001. Geneva: International Labour Organization.

International Labour Organization (2003) http://www.ilo.org

International Organization for Standardization (2003) http://www.iso.ch

Kirwan, B., Hale, A. and Hopkins, A. (2002) Insights into safety regulation. In: B. Kirwan, A. Hale and A. Hopkins (eds) *Changing Regulation: Controlling Risks in Society*, 253–283. Oxford: Elsevier Science.

Lowenson, R. (1998) Occupational health and safety law in Southern Africa. *African Newsletter on Occupational Health and Safety*, **8**(3), 62–65.

Neal, A.C. (1998) Regulating health and safety at work: developing European Union policy for the millennium. *The International Journal of Comparative Labour Law and Industrial Relations*, **13**(3), 217–246.

Organisation for Economic Co-operation and Development (1999) *OECD Principles of Corporate Governance*. SG/CG(99)5. Paris: OECD.

Robens, Lord (1972) *Safety and Health at Work: Report of the Committee 1970-72 Cmnd 5034*. London: HMSO.

Seiler, H. (2002) Harmonised risk based regulation: a legal viewpoint. *Safety Science*, **40**, 31–49.

Smith, T. (1992) *Accounting for Growth: Stripping the Camouflage from Company Accounts*. London: Century Business.

Turnbull (1999) See Internal Control Working Party of the Institute of Chartered Accountants in England & Wales (1999).

Vogel, D. (2001) *The New Politics of Risk Regulation in Europe*. London: London School of Economics and Political Science.

World Health Organization (2002) *Global Strategy on Occupational Health for All: Principles of Occupational Health and Safety*. http://www.ccohs.ca/who

World Health Organization (2003) http://www.who.int

Wright, M. (1998) *Factors Motivating Proactive Health and Safety Management*. Sudbury: HSE Books.

Models for managing health and safety risks at the organisational level

There is so much talk about involvement of employees, quality of work life, communications and other poetic words. What is needed is involvement of management: get the management involved.

– Deming (1982a)

Chapter contents

- Introduction
- Principles of organisational management
- Organisational models for health and safety management
- Health and safety management system standards

Introduction

A balance must be maintained between the risks arising from an organisation's activities and the long-term efficiency and profitability of the organisation. Health and safety risks may significantly affect the achievement of business objectives: therefore management of these risks is vital in creating a sustainable, profitable and respected organisation. Although legislation in many countries requires that the health and safety of employees and others who may be affected by an organisation's undertaking be managed, organisations that adopt a proactive approach to health and safety are far more effective. The sound management principles of quality and business excellence are equally applicable to the management of health and safety. In fact, many commercially successful organisations excel at health and safety management simply because they apply the principles and practices that achieve business excellence.

Failure to manage health and safety within an organisation may lead to action by a regulatory body, but for many organisations the cost of prosecutions and fines is not significant. Furthermore, the internal costs of accidents, such as replacement labour, accident investigation, downtime and increased insurance premiums, are far greater than the external costs of fines and compensation. The publicity associated with a prosecution, however, will have a significantly more damaging effect and create a greater cost to the business through loss of reputation. Workplace accidents and ill-health also cause significant personal costs, pain and suffering among the injured workforce and their families.

The main aim of this chapter is to discuss the principles and goals of effective health and safety management using organisational management theories. Six key organisational models that are used for the management of health and safety are compared and contrasted.

Principles of organisational management

Development of management theories

Management experts have developed many theories and approaches to management, but the emergence of large-scale organisations in Europe and America in the late nineteenth and early twentieth centuries heralded the period in which many of the current management practices were developed (Bartol and Martin, 1998; Hannagan, 2002; Pettinger, 2002).

Taylor (1911) offered a scientific or problem-solving approach to management: this sought to question traditional work practices and find a 'best way' in which a task or activity could be completed. Appropriate employees were then selected, trained and required to perform their work activities in the precise manner prescribed. The approach sought to create prosperity for both the worker and the organisation. This approach, which was based on the concept of managing the work rather than simply treating work as a matter of custom and practice, led to higher productivity and profitability for organisations. Some of Taylor's innovations, such as the selection and training of employees and job analysis, are still advocated today. The 1920s and 1930s saw a number of further important developments, such as the principles of decentralisation, systematic approach to business objectives, business strategy, strategic planning and marketing (Drucker, 1999).

Fayol (1949) offered an administrative approach that defined five management functions: planning, organising, commanding, coordinating and controlling. Furthermore, he produced 14 principles of management, many of which were founded on personal experience and observation rather than on the analysis of research data. Weber (1947) added to this management approach and argued that business organisation should be highly structured with clear role definition, hierarchy of authority, a system of documented rules and procedures, competence and impartiality. Many of these factors are still to be found in the management practices used by large, complex modern organisations.

Mayo (1946), who was a proponent of the behavioural approach to management, considered that management approaches did not take sufficient account of employees, as they were more concerned with business objectives. Mayo (1946) therefore advocated that individual work groups should set the pace of production. This approach recognised employees' contributions, provided opportunities for development, allowed employees to air their grievances, enhanced job satisfaction and employee morale, and improved output.

Drucker, who has been a major contributor to modern management theories, considered that management was made up of three tasks of equal importance:

To think through and define the specific purpose and mission of the institution, whether business enterprise, hospital, or university.
To make work productive and the worker achieving.
To manage social impacts and social responsibilities.

Drucker (1999: 36)

The first task distinguished organisations from each other. For example, the specific purpose and mission of a business enterprise is normally economic performance, whereas a hospital's main purpose is the care of the sick. In achieving the second task, all organisations are alike because they all have people as their key resource, and therefore they must make this resource as effective and efficient as possible. In discharging the third task, which is to deliver goods and services, organisations impact on people and society as a whole, through, for example, their roles as employers and/or sources of waste. Drucker's approach to management embraced many aspects of the earlier models and produced a holistic view of organisational management by taking account of both economic and social perspectives.

Quality management systems emerged in the 1950s and 1960s through the pioneering work of Deming and Juran, who were associated with the postwar renaissance of Japanese industry, and Ishikawa, Crosby and Oakland (Bank, 2000). Deming considered that productivity could be improved by using statistical sampling to focus on process variability, and maintained that only management could eliminate common causes of variability that were systemic in the design/manufacturing process of a product. This philosophy led to a systematic approach to problem solving known as the Deming Wheel or the Plan–Do–Check–Act cycle (Figure 10.1), which was based on the work of Shewhart (1939) and which is found at the heart of many management systems. As a result of this work, there was an increasing recognition within organisations of the strategic importance of quality management (Juran, 1993).

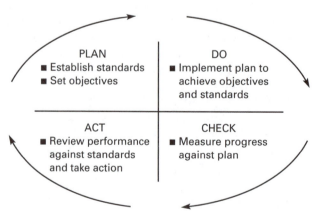

Figure 10.1 Plan–Do–Check–Act cycle
Source: Deming (1982b)

Total quality management (TQM) now penetrates a wide range of organisations, from industrial and commercial to the public sector and from large multinational organisations to small and medium-sized enterprises.

> People's expectations and demands for total quality are increasing all the time. Their impatience with systems that are poorly planned, services that fall ludicrously short of expectations and managers who fail to manage well is increasingly vocal.
>
> Bank (2000: ix)

The use of poor quality procedures and the disregard for quality procedures have always had major impacts on health and safety performance. For example, poor quality processes at the Bhopal pesticide plant in India resulted in a leak of methyl isocyanate gas in 1984 that cost the Union Carbide Corporation £420 million in compensation claims and caused over 200 000 immediate injuries, approximately 20 000 lasting injuries and 3400 fatalities (Bank, 2000). Incidents in the transport sector, such as the sinking of the *Herald of Free Enterprise* ferry in 1987 with the loss of 189 lives and the *Estonia* ferry in 1994 with the loss of 852 lives serve to further illustrate the consequences of a disregard for quality procedures (Bank, 2000).

The cornerstone of TQM is the notion that defect-free work is achievable by organisations for most of the time. This process is often referred to by phrases such as 'right first time', 'working smarter' or 'zero defects'. The TQM approach requires that management emphasis is placed on prevention, use of measurement tools, elimination of waste and error, and continuous improvement. Crosby (1980) considered that the purpose of quality management was to establish a management system that prevented defects from happening, as it is better to manage quality into products than to inspect defects out. Accidents and ill-health are clearly defects in a company's performance, and therefore a quality management system that is focused on the prevention of accidents, ill-health and incidents is beneficial. Current guidance on health and safety management (Health and Safety Executive, 2000) encourages the application of TQM to health and safety risks; however, it is reported that, in many organisations, emphasis on continuous improvement in health and safety lags behind that in other management areas (Osborne and Zairi, 1997).

Management theory in practice

Given that the key function of management is to maintain and develop an organisation, the role of management should be to act as both housekeeper and entrepreneur. The guidance document *Internal Control: Guidance for Directors on the Combined Code* (Turnbull, 1999) embraced the philosophy of business development and maintenance, and specified the requirements for a sound system of internal control. This guidance was based on risk management principles, and outlined the good business practices of developing policy, identifying responsibilities, establishing procedures, monitoring performance and reviewing the effectiveness of the overall internal control procedure. This management cycle is summarised in Figure 10.2.

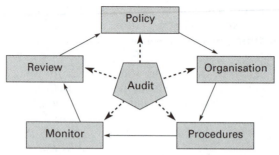

Figure 10.2 The management cycle

Policy

A policy defines the importance that management attaches to a particular issue. Policies that focus on an organisation's objectives should therefore be developed for all business activities. However, policies that are not relevant to an organisation are unlikely to receive commitment from employees.

> A policy is a general guideline for decision-making. It sets up the boundaries around decisions, including those that can be made and shutting out those that cannot. In this way it channels the thinking of organization members so that it is consistent with organizational objectives.
>
> Stoner and Wankel (1986: 91)

Policies clarify issues for all employees, engender consistent management behaviour, and make an organisation less dependent on the views of individuals. However, although it is common practice for senior management to delegate the task of implementing policies within an organisation, they should not delegate their responsibility for developing and reviewing it.

Organising

The effectiveness of an organisation depends on the management mechanisms through which the policies are put into action: these should coordinate the activities of employees in a way that creates administrative efficiency while developing their full potential. Organising human resources involves establishing employees' responsibilities and relationships, which in turn help to define the social environment or 'culture' within an organisation. This organisational culture impinges on and influences all aspects of work, and affects individual and group behaviours, job design and the planning and execution of procedures. A positive organisational culture is crucial for the implementation and continued development of effective policies, which themselves further contribute to the development of a positive culture. The process of organising also requires the development of standards and systems for monitoring the implementation of policies and objectives. Performance standards link individual responsibilities to outputs by identifying who is responsible for specific outcomes. In this respect the competence of individuals and the workforce as a whole must be considered in order to optimise performance.

Establishing procedures

A company policy and the identification of responsibilities alone cannot ensure the effective and efficient management of an organisation: all policy statements require procedures to make them work. These procedures provide the link between policy (what an organisation would like to achieve) and practice (what is actually happening). Policies will fail if they are fundamentally inappropriate or inadequate, if employers do not understand them, or – most often – if there are no valid procedures to support them. Well-designed procedures based on risk assessment offer a number of benefits, such as long-term stability, consistency in decision-making, and a knowledge that activities will be carried out within acceptable levels of risk.

Monitoring

In order to assess whether policies and procedures are effective and efficient, it is essential to monitor and measure operational performance against valid standards. The core requirement for monitoring performance is the availability of relevant information to make an assessment. Lucey (1987) advocated that this information should be timely, appropriate, accurate and of adequate detail, understandable and operational. Measurement provides the trigger for continuous improvement in performance, and this can lead to organisational growth and prosperity. Without performance measurement, improvements are difficult if not impossible to achieve.

Reviewing

A key part of good business practice is the regular assessment of the long-term effectiveness and efficiency of an organisation's management systems. Reviewing systems and performance therefore provides a feedback loop for senior management that enables the organisation to continually develop. Reviews should provide a balance between internal and external perspectives of company performance. Whereas internal local management undertake reviews as part of their routine operations and responsibilities, there is the danger with an internal review process that management will become complacent and accept that their current approaches are adequate. External review processes that are carried out by independent third parties, on the other hand, provide opportunities for identifying strengths and weaknesses and making comparisons with industry best practices.

Organisational models for health and safety management

Health and safety management came under considerable scrutiny by regulatory bodies, employers and the public following various disasters, such as the Chernobyl nuclear accident in 1986, the fire and explosion on the *Piper Alpha* oil rig in 1988, and the sinking of the *Estonia* ferry in 1994. In support of recommendations made in the document *Internal Control: Guidance for Directors on the Combined Code* (Turnbull, 1999), the UK Health and Safety Commission (2002) produced guidance for directors on their health and safety responsibilities (Wright *et al.*, 2003):

> The board needs to accept formally and publicly its collective role in providing health and safety leadership in its organisation.
>
> Each member of the board needs to accept their individual role in providing health and safety leadership for their organisation.
>
> The board needs to ensure that all board decisions reflect its health and safety intentions, as articulated in the health and safety policy statement.
>
> The board needs to recognise its role in engaging the active participation of their workers in improving health and safety.
>
> The board needs to ensure that it is kept informed of, and alert to, relevant health and safety risk management issues. The Health and Safety Commission recommends that boards appoint one of their number to be the 'health and safety director'.
>
> Health and Safety Commission (2002: 5–8)

Waring (1996) identified three general approaches to health and safety management systems: mechanical models, socio-technical models and human activity models. Analogies can be drawn between these models and the more mechanistic management approaches of Taylor (1911) and Fayol (1949) and the human relations approach of Mayo (1946), discussed earlier.

Mechanical models are often considered to be synonymous with highly technical industries, where engineered systems play a prominent role in achieving safety. Typically, these systems are highly prescriptive, use a large number of procedures, and make the assumption that employees perform in the manner defined by procedures. All formal human procedures are defined, analysed, prescribed, documented and audited, and there is little scope for flexibility. The strength of this approach lies in the systematic identification of activities, analysis of hazards, assessment of risks, and description of control measures. The mechanical model aligns itself with the prescriptive demands of quality standards, which enable third-party certification of procedures. Its weakness lies in the fact that it tends to focus on activities at the operational level, and tends not to be integrated into other management systems within the organisation. In addition, the approach makes the assumption that human control can be managed in the same way as engineering control, using the principles of reliability, predictability and repeatability. The model takes no account of informal 'soft' issues, such as organisational culture and power relationships.

Socio-technical models take account of the interactions between technology and people in order to develop work systems that are technically efficient but which also consider the social implications: this leads to a high level of employee job satisfaction. The socio-technical approach focuses on the efficiency of formal management systems but is supported by moves to manipulate and control the human contribution through staff selection, training and motivation. Each element of the management system therefore has both social and technical characteristics. Total quality management provides an example of this management approach. The strength of the socio-technical approach is that it recognises that people and technology interact and that this influences the management of health and safety. The weaknesses of the approach are similar to those presented for mechanical models, because the approach addresses mainly the formal functional aspects of safety management. People are considered important only because they can make the technical system function more efficiently, and because they are amenable to behaviour modification through stimulus–response methods, such as training and incentives.

Human activity models focus on people and consider the complexity of relationships and activities within organisations: the approach embodies a number of 'hard' and 'soft' management concepts. The model adopts a formal management system of control, monitoring, implementation and communication. However, as this approach alone cannot ensure effectiveness, the model also addresses informal aspects, such as culture, behaviour, motivation and risk perception. Individuals within an organisation are the creators of the culture, and to varying degrees their behaviour is in turn influenced by this culture. The strength of the human activity approach is that it avoids the oversimplification of human factors associated with the previous two approaches; however, the weakness of the approach lies in the complexities of understanding and managing human factors.

Hale *et al*. (1997) reviewed a range of models and concluded that there had been only limited attempts to produce rational and comprehensive models of safety management processes. Although the application of standards to health and safety management systems had demonstrated that several management functions could be considered within a quality assurance framework, coherent models that linked practice to principles had not been developed. Hale *et al*. (1997) modelled safety-related tasks using the *structured analysis and design technique* (SADT) to demonstrate that the appropriate inputs produced the desired outputs, for a given level of resources and control. This theoretical model was capable of describing the full range of activities within a safety management system, from technological processes to the development of strategy and policy.

Development of standards for health and safety management

Standards have been drawn up at both national and international levels for a range of management systems. Of particular note are the management standards available for quality, such as the ISO 9000 series, and the environment, such as the ISO 14001 series. Following the increasing level of application of these standards, attention turned to the development of an international generic standard for occupational health and safety management. In order to establish whether there was a need for such a standard, ISO arranged an international open workshop on 'Occupational Health and Safety Management Systems Standardisation' in 1996. This workshop attracted over 300 participants, representing the interests of governments, employers, labour groups and insurance bodies from 45 countries. There was a strong consensus at the workshop that the time was not yet right for an international standard, and this was accepted by the Technical Management Board within ISO in 1997. However, at the national level, a number of ISO members had already developed standards or were currently working in this area. For example, in the UK the British Standards Institution (1996) produced the standard *Guide to Occupational Health and Safety Management Systems BS8800*. In Australia, Standards Australia introduced the certifiable standard *Occupational Health and Safety Management Systems AS 4801-2000* (Standards Australia, 2000). The Spanish national standards body, Asociación Española de Normalización y Certificación (2003), offered their national standard to CEN for adoption as a European standard, and the Nederlands Normalisatie-instituut (2003) put forward the Dutch Standard NPR5001 to the Technical Management Board of ISO for adoption as a guidance document.

The Occupational Health and Safety Branch of the ILO commissioned the International Occupational Hygiene Association (IOHA), following discussion between both parties in 1997, to undertake a review of existing and proposed health and safety management systems in order to identify differences and similarities between the various systems. The IOHA were also invited to make recommendations on the harmonisation of the provisions within these documents and to prepare a draft outline ILO occupational health and safety management system standard. The review considered 24 standards from 15 countries including three international standards (Dalrymple *et al.*, 1998; Redinger and Levine, 1998). The key findings of the review were that the standards had strengths in areas such as risk assessment, hazard control and training, but weaknesses in areas such as management commitment, resource allocation and integration with other management processes. Concern was also expressed over variability in issues such as occupational health and employee participation. The report recommended that the ILO should produce a verifiable standard in consultation with ISO. The issue of occupational health and safety management systems therefore returned to the ISO agenda in early 2000, when members were asked to vote on a proposal from the British Standards Institution that a technical committee be established in order to transform the *Occupational Health and Safety Management Systems BS8800* into an ISO standard. This proposal was rejected, and the members' negative vote also led to ISO rejecting the ILO offer to collaborate on their project to develop an international standard for occupational health and safety management. ILO therefore progressed the findings of the IOHA report independently to produce guidelines on occupational health and safety management systems (ILO, 2001).

Existing management standards, such as those for quality and environment, sought to achieve success through a cycle of continuous improvement based on the work of Deming (1982b). However, standards cannot guarantee successful management, as they merely provide a system for third-party certification. Certification of health and safety management systems may be a determining factor in whether an organisation wins a contract, especially where the customer organisation specifies this as a condition of the contract. With these commercial pressures, some organisations have been obliged to follow the path of formal health and safety management systems in order to obtain certification.

Health and safety management system standards

Six management standards that are relevant to health and safety are briefly considered here in order to illustrate the range of systems available:

- AS/NZ 4360 *Risk Management* (Standards Australia/Standards New Zealand, 1999);
- AS 4801-2000 *Occupational Health and Safety Management Systems – Specification with Guidance for Use* (Standards Australia, 2000);
- BSI-OHSAS 18001 *Occupational Health and Safety Management Systems: Specification* (British Standards Institution, 1999);
- ISO 14001 *Environmental Management Systems – Specification with Guidance for Use* (International Organization for Standardization, 1996);
- ILO-OSH 2001 *Guidelines on Occupational Safety and Health Management Systems* (ILO, 2001); and
- HSG65 *Successful Health and Safety Management* (Health and Safety Executive, 2000).

AS/NZ 4360 *Risk Management* is a joint Australian and New Zealand standard providing generic guidance for establishing and implementing a risk management system: the standard advocates the identification, analysis, evaluation, treatment and ongoing monitoring of risks (Knight, 2002). First produced in 1995 and revised in 1999, the standard was well received in many industrial and commercial sectors. A key feature of this standard that made it widely accepted was that strategic and operational issues were considered and included within the risk management process: these included issues related to financial, quality, environment, competitive, political, social, client, cultural and legal aspects of the organisation's activities.

AS 4801-2000 *Occupational Health and Safety Management Systems: Specification for Use* is an Australian standard that provides guidance on the implementation, development and/or improvement of occupational health and safety management systems. This standard establishes an audit framework principally to enable independent external audits and assessments of the organisation's health and safety management system to be undertaken; however, it can also be used as a framework for internal audits. Although the standard shares common principles with ISO 9001 (quality) and ISO 14001 (environment) and encourages the integration of elements from these standards, it is more aligned to the risk management philosophies and methods described in AS/NZ 4360 Risk Management.

BSI-OHSAS 18001 *Occupational Health and Safety Management Systems: Specification* was developed by a consortium of certification organisations and standards bodies, such as British Standards Institution, National Standards Authority Ireland, Bureau Veritas Quality International, Det Norske Veritas and Lloyds Register. The standard was developed so that it was compatible with ISO 9001 and ISO 14001 in order to facilitate the integration of occupational health and safety risks within these management systems. Although the requirements for an occupational health and safety management system are included within the standard, it does not provide detailed specifications for the design of the management system. The aim of the standard is to provide criteria for the assessment and certification of an organisation's health and safety management system by third parties.

ISO 14001 *Environmental Management Systems – Specification with Guidance for Use* is fundamentally an international generic environment management system. It also provides guidance on the implementation of the standard within the overall management system of an organisation. However, an examination of the definitions contained within the standard reveals that the approach presented includes health and safety issues, because environment is defined as 'surroundings in which an organization operates, including air, water, land, natural resources, flora, fauna, humans and their interrelation' (International Organization for Standardization, 1996: 1), and an environmental effect as 'any change to the environment, whether adverse or beneficial, wholly or partially resulting from an organization's activities, products or services' (International Organization for Standardization, 1996: 2).

ILO-OSH 2001 *Guidelines on Occupational Safety and Health Management Systems* provides guidance at national and organisational levels. At the national level, guidance is provided for establishing a framework supported by national regulations. At the organisational level, guidance is provided on the integration of the occupational health and safety management system within the organisation's overall management arrangements. The guidance is intended to motivate stakeholders to continually improve their health and safety performance.

HSG65 *Successful Health and Safety Management* was first developed by the UK Health and Safety Executive's Accident Prevention and Advisory Unit in 1991 as a practical guide for directors, managers and health and safety representatives rather than as a management standard. The fundamental message in the guide is that organisations should manage health and safety risks with the same degree of expertise and to the same standards as other core business activities. The guide, however, does not provide the same level of prescription for the health and safety management system as that provided in the standards described above. Instead, the guide discusses issues in a more general manner and indicates what represents good health and safety management practice within a general management framework.

With the exception of HSG65 and ILO-OSH 2001, all the models are based on the normal approaches adopted within typical national and international standards. Those management models presented as standards are, therefore, goal-setting and define what must be achieved; for example 'the organisation shall establish and maintain an occupational health and safety management system' (Standards Australia, 2000). However, these standards do not specify how an organisation can achieve the requirements. Three of the standards-based models, namely BSI-OHSAS 18001, AS 4801-2000 and ISO 14001, allow for third-party certification of compliance. A further standard, BS8800 *Guide to Occupational Health and Safety Management Systems* (British Standards Institution, 1996), offers guidance on the principles of good health and safety management, and suggests two management approaches that are based on the HSG65 and ISO 14001 models. Although ILO-OSH 2001 is a guidance document, it is presented in the format of goals that 'should' be achieved, and therefore it is more prescriptive than HSG65.

All of the health and safety models presented have a management philosophy and cycle that are very similar to those presented in the general management model illustrated in Figure 10.2. Models based on ISO 14001 consider the planning stage, for example establishing legal requirements, setting health and safety objectives and establishing health and safety programmes, to come between defining the policy and establishing organisational arrangements, such as structure, responsibility, competence, consultation and communication. The models based on HSG65 and ILO-OSH 2001, on the other hand, place the planning stage between defining the organisational arrangements and establishing operational procedures (implementation). All of the models therefore illustrate that good practice principles for health and safety management are the same as those for general management. Table 10.1 summarises and compares the structures of the health and safety management models discussed above.

Table 10.1 Key elements of individual health and safety management models

AS/NZ 4360	AS 4801-2000	OHSAS 18001	ISO 14001	ILO-OSH 2001	HSG65
Policy	Occupational health and safety policy	Occupational health and safety policy	Occupational health and safety policy	Policy	Occupational health and safety policy
Planning and resources	Planning	Planning	Planning	Organising	Organising
Implementation	Implementation	Implementation and operation	Implementation and operation	Planning and implementation	Planning and implementation
Monitoring	Measurement and evaluation	Checking and corrective action	Checking and corrective action	Evaluation	Measuring performance
Management review	Management review	Management review	Management review	Action for improvement	Audit and review

These models contain six main elements: policy, organising, planning and implementing, monitoring, auditing, and reviewing. These elements are discussed below in the context of health and safety management.

Policy

The models are all broadly similar in their description of the role and function of the health and safety policy. Furthermore, they all state that it is the responsibility of senior management to define the policy and to ensure that it is understood, implemented and maintained at all levels of the organisation. With the exception of HSG65, the standards all describe how the policy should be relevant to both the nature and the scale of the organisation's risks. Key issues that are covered within policy include the following:

- Comply with national legal requirements as a minimum.
- Continually improve performance.
- Ensure that the policy is understood, implemented and maintained at all levels of the organisation.

- Ensure that all employees are made aware of their individual obligations.

- Provide employees with the necessary skills and knowledge to discharge their obligations.

- Review the policy periodically in order to ensure that it remains relevant and appropriate to the organisation.

With the exception of HSG65, all the models indicate that the policy should be made publicly available. HSG65, however, discusses management's responsibility to provide adequate resources to set and publish health and safety objectives, to involve and consult employees in order to gain commitment to the policy, and to implement the policy.

Organising

In order to translate health and safety policies into action, organisations should define employees' responsibilities and relationships so they will promote a positive health and safety culture and secure the implementation and continued development of the policy. Gaining control is essential in all management functions and requires the commitment of all employees to achieve the organisation's health and safety objectives. Central to this theme is the premise that ultimate responsibility for implementing the health and safety policy rests with the highest level of management (Wright *et al.*, 2003).

Key issues in organising health and safety management are as follows:

- Define responsibilities and accountabilities of management and ensure that people have the necessary resources to carry out their responsibilities.

- Make arrangements for the provision of health and safety specialist advice and services.

- Set performance standards that link responsibilities to defined targets or outputs.

- Allocate appropriate resources in order to achieve health and safety targets.

- Make effective arrangements for employee involvement and consultation in health and safety issues.

- Make arrangements for the effective internal and external communication of health and safety information.

Planning and implementing

Planning is essential to the implementation of health and safety policies, and this issue is addressed by all of the management models. Adequate risk control can be achieved only through the coordinated actions of everyone within an organisation. All the models advocate a requirement to establish and maintain procedures for the ongoing identification of hazards, assessment of risks, and implementation of appropriate control measures. Models based on ISO 14001 outline that this process of risk control should include routine and non-routine activities and the activities of employees and non-employees. The hazard identification and risk assessment methodology should be defined, appropriate to the activities and risks involved, up to date and documented. HSG65 is less prescriptive than the other systems about the way in which the planning element should be developed, as it recognises that arrangements will depend upon the complexity of the organisation and current health and safety standards. ILO-OSH 2001 makes specific mention of requirements to assess the impact of internal and external changes on occupational health and safety and the incorporation of health and safety issues in procurement and contracting functions.

Other important issues included within the planning and implementing element are as follows:

- Provide input to the identification of control options.
- Provide targets for monitoring performance.
- Identify legislative requirements.
- Establish and achieve health and safety objectives at functional level.
- Aim for continuous improvement.
- Plan regular reviews.

Risk assessment is discussed in Chapter 11 and risk control in Chapter 12.

Monitoring

Monitoring the implementation of health and safety management policies and procedures is an essential aspect of improving health and safety performance as it allows an organisation to determine whether prescribed standards are achieved and are in line with organisational objectives. All the models advocate establishing and maintaining procedures to monitor and measure health and safety performance on a regular basis through:

- Use of appropriate qualitative and quantitative measures.
- Proactive measures of performance that monitor compliance with the health and safety management system and legislation.
- Reactive measures of performance that monitor deficiencies in health and safety management performance.
- Recording performance data that facilitate corrective and preventative management actions.
- Investigation and documentation of the causes of accidents, incidents and non-conformances and the initiation and completion of corrective and preventative actions.

Performance measurement is discussed in Chapter 14.

Auditing

HSG65 emphasises the role of line management in auditing health and safety issues and the contribution that this makes to reinforcing management's commitment to health and safety as a business objective. It further highlights the benefits of providing feedback on health and safety performance before an accident, incident or ill-health occurs, as this motivates employees towards continuous improvement. All the standards advocate auditing the health and safety management system, and wherever possible independent personnel should carry out the audit. Models based on ISO 14001 further specify that procedures should be in place to record the results of health and safety audits. Clearly, this ensures that documentary evidence is available to demonstrate conformance with the standards so that certification may be obtained from a third party. Auditing is discussed in Chapter 15.

Reviewing

Reviewing is the final stage of all the health and safety management models. This process provides an organisation with information in order to maintain and continuously improve its ability to manage health and safety risks. In carrying out a review, senior management should take account of audit data when considering whether changes to elements of the health and safety management system are required. Changes in circumstances, such as management delayering and new legislation, should also be considered at the review stage. HSG65 advocates reviewing performance at various management levels within an organisation and on varying timescales to provide the basis for a continuous improvement philosophy. HSG65 also notes that organisations may extend the review process by benchmarking health and safety management performance against other organisations. Benchmarking is discussed in Chapter 15.

Summary

- Many of the key developments in management practices, which were developed in the late nineteenth and early twentieth century, provide the basis of management practice in modern organisations.
- The basic elements of a good management system are: developing policy, organising, developing procedures, monitoring performance and reviewing the effectiveness of the management system.
- Health and safety management systems have evolved in the wake of a number of multiple fatality events and developments in legislation. Approaches to health and safety management systems are categorised as mechanical, socio-technical and human activity.
- The health and safety management system standards are essentially based on the same principles of management as those applied to general management. Management systems based on ISO 14001, OHSAS 18001 and AS 4801-2000 are more prescriptive than those based on HSG65 and, to an extent, ILO-OSH 2001, which give a greater consideration to the role of people in the management of health and safety risks.

Issues for review and discussion

- Compare the similarities and differences in the management of health and safety risks with the management of other organisational risks.
- Examine the feasibility of managing health and safety risks using Deming's Plan–Do–Check–Act quality cycle.
- Consider the advantages and disadvantages of certifiable compared with non-certifiable health and safety management standards.
- Assess the key aspects of an organisation's health and safety policy.
- Review the organisational benefits of implementing a recognised formal health and safety management system.

References

Asociación Española de Normalización y Certificación (2003) http://www.aenor.es

Bank, J. (2000) *The Essence of Total Quality Management*. Harlow: Prentice Hall.

Bartol, K.M. and Martin, D.C. (1998) *Management*. Boston: Irwin McGraw-Hill.

British Standards Institution (1996) *Guide to Occupational Health and Safety Management Systems*. BS8800. London: British Standards Institution.

British Standards Institution (1999) *Occupational Health and Safety Management Systems: Specification*. BSI-OHSAS 18001. London: British Standards Institution.

Crosby, P.B. (1980) *Quality is Free*. Mentor: New York.

Dalrymple, H., Redinger, C., Dyjack, D., Levine, S. and Mansdorf, Z. (1998) *Occupational Health and Safety Management Systems: Review and Analysis of International, National, and Regional Systems and Proposals for a New International Document*. Geneva: ILO.

Deming, W.E. (1982a) *Quality, Productivity and Competitive Position*. Cambridge, MA: MIT Press.

Deming, W.E. (1982b) *Out of the Crisis*. USA: Cambridge University Press.

Drucker, P.F. (1999) *Management: Tasks, Responsibilities, Practices*. Oxford: Butterworth-Heinemann.

Fayol, H. (1949) *General and Industrial Management*. London: Pitman.

Hale, A.R., Heming, B.H.J., Carthey, J. and Kirwan, B. (1997) Modelling of safety management systems. *Safety Science*, **26**(1/2), 121–140.

Hannagan, T. (2002) *Management: Concepts and Practices*. Harlow: Prentice Hall.

Health and Safety Commission (2002) *Directors' Responsibilities for Health and Safety*. INDG343. Sudbury: HSE Books.

Health and Safety Executive (2000) *Successful Health and Safety Management*. HSG65. Sudbury: HSE Books.

Internal Control Working Party of the Institute of Chartered Accountants in England & Wales (1999) *Internal Control: Guidance for Directors on the Combined Code*. London: Internal Control Working Party of the Institute of Chartered Accountants in England & Wales.

International Labour Organization (2001) *Guidelines on Occupational Safety and Health Management Systems*. ILO-OSH 2001. Geneva: International Labour Office.

International Organization for Standardization (1996) ISO 14001 *Environmental Management Systems – Specification With Guidance for Use*. Geneva: International Organization for Standardization.

Juran, J. (1993) Made in the USA: a renaissance in quality. *Harvard Business Review*, July–August, **71**, 42–50.

Knight, K.W. (2002) Developing a risk management standard. *Safety Science*, **40**, 69–74.

Lucey, T. (1987) *Management Information Systems*. Eastleigh: DP Publications.

Mayo, E. (1946) *The Social Problems of an Industrial Civilisation*. London: Routledge & Kegan Paul.

Nederlands Normalisatie-instituut (2003) http://www.nen.nl

Osborne, J. and Zairi, M. (1997) *Total Quality Management and the Management of Health and Safety*. CRR153. Sudbury: HSE Books.

Pettinger, R. (2002) *Introduction to Management*. Basingstoke: Palgrave.

Redinger, C.F. and Levine, S.P. (1998) Development and evaluation of the Michigan Occupational Health and Safety Management System Assessment Instrument: a universal OHSMS performance measurement tool. *American Industrial Hygiene Journal*, **59**, 572–581.

Shewhart, W.A. (1939) *Statistical Method from the Viewpoint of Quality Control*. New York: Dover Publications.

Standards Australia (2000) *Occupational Health and Safety Management Systems – Specification with Guidance for Use*. AS 4801-2000. Strathfield: Standards Australia.

Standards Australia/Standards New Zealand (1999) *Risk Management*. AS/NZ 4360: 1999. Strathfield: Standards Australia.

Stoner, J.A.F. and Wankel, C. (1986) *Management*. Englewood Cliffs: Prentice Hall.

Taylor, F.W. (1911) *The Principles of Scientific Management*. New York: Harper Bros.

Turnbull, N. (1999) See: Internal Control Working Party of the Institute of Chartered Accountants in England & Wales (1999).

Waring, A. (1996) *Safety Management Systems*. London: Chapman & Hall.

Weber, M. (1947) *Theory of Social and Economic Organization*. New York: Oxford University Press.

Wright, M., Marsden, S. and Holmes, J. (2003) *Health and Safety Responsibilities of Company Directors and Management Board Members*. RR135/2003. Sudbury: HSE Books.

Risk assessment

All hazards and dangers we barter on chance.

– Bob Dylan, 'Arthur McBride' (1992)

Chapter contents

Introduction

In modern society, risk assessment provides the cornerstone of health and safety management. Not only are risk assessments a legal requirement in many countries, but they are also based on sound business practice and common sense. Risk assessment in essence is a straightforward process, but although some of the techniques are simple, many of them are overly complex for basic or routine health and safety risks encountered in most workplaces. An effective assessment provides businesses with a record that health and safety risks have been identified and evaluated, and a confirmation that appropriate control measures have been implemented in order to manage the risks within acceptable or tolerable limits. Calverd (2000) presented an interesting and important viewpoint about the assessment and management of risks by considering the apparent anomalies that often occur in everyday life.

We were not offered beef on the bone (acute hazard nil, risk of long-term effects from chronic consumption known to be less than one in two million) by our trained and certificated chef. He was under no obligation to tell us which of his products contained peanuts (1 in 200 people are allergic, and press reports suggest about one life-threatening allergic reaction per week in the UK). The students were taught how to obtain and record a patient's consent to an examination that would at worst subject them to a 1 in 20 000 risk of developing a fatal tumour in the next 20 years. (The natural risk is about 1 in 5.) I drove home. As a sober middle-aged professional, I subject other road users to a 1 in 10 000 risk of fatal injury each year, but I don't need their signed consent before driving.

It seems to me that the degree of regulation of a hazard is mostly determined by the precision with which it can be measured and controlled, and the smallness of the group responsible for dispensing it. Public perception – and thence the law – has very little to do with the actual probability or impact of a hazard.

Calverd (2000: 60)

The aims of this chapter are to introduce and discuss a wide range of general issues associated with the risk assessment process and the preparation of risk assessment reports. Factors affecting the preparation of risk assessments in an environment of uncertainty are discussed, and the role of risk assessment in making decisions at government level is also outlined. A range of qualitative and quantitative techniques for carrying out strategic and operational risk assessments is discussed.

The purpose of risk assessment

Employers within the European Union are required under health and safety legislation to ensure the health and safety of their workforce and anyone else whom it may reasonably be possible to foresee may be affected by the employer's activities. In the UK these requirements are incorporated within a range of health and safety regulations but, although there are differences between the specific requirements of each set of regulations because of the nature and properties of the hazards covered, the general requirements for the risk assessment are the same. The purpose of a risk assessment is to enable an employer to identify the risks associated with their work activities, to evaluate the levels of these risks, to identify adequate risk control measures for the protection of stakeholders, and to provide appropriate information and training to employees (Gadd *et al.*, 2003).

If the evaluation reveals that the residual levels of risk are unacceptably high then the provision of control measures should be reviewed and, if necessary, upgraded in order to reduce the level of residual risk to an acceptable level. The European Commission, in their guidance document on risk assessment, stated:

Whilst the purpose of risk assessment includes the prevention of occupational risks, and this should always be the goal, it will not always be achievable in practice. Where elimination of risk cannot be realized, then the risks should be reduced and the residual risk controlled. At a later stage, as part of a review programme, such residual risks will be reassessed and the possibility of elimination or further reduction of the risk, perhaps in the light of new knowledge, can be reconsidered.

European Commission (1996: 11)

Risk assessment has therefore become a focal point of the European Union's policy on occupational health and safety management, as it has in many other countries. For example, it is also a fundamental part of the Australian Standard *Occupational Health and Safety Management Systems* (Standards Australia, 2000), which states that all risks shall be assessed and have risk control priorities assigned to them based on the level of the risk identified.

The risk assessment process

A risk assessment is a formalised management procedure that is undertaken in order to identify the measures that are required to comply with national legislation and standards relating to the control of specific hazards present within a business. Organisations would normally be expected to maintain records of any significant findings from these risk assessments in a written or electronic format. These findings should be readily accessible for inspection by stakeholders such as employees, safety representatives and government inspectors. *Significant findings*, in the context of health and safety risk assessments, would normally include the identified hazards, the stakeholders who may be affected by the hazards, the risks, and the measures put in place in order to control the risks. Work-based risk assessments should consider only significant risks associated with work activities, and should not attempt to assess insignificant risks or risks that are part of normal everyday life.

The responsibility for completing risk assessments rests solely with the employer; although, where an employer feels that they do not have the necessary skills and expertise to complete the risk assessment, they may employ an expert(s) to assist them. This assistance does not, however, remove the responsibility and/or the accountability of employers for completing risk assessments. Risk assessments for most activities should be valid for a reasonable period of time and should normally require reviewing only on an annual or biennial basis. However, if an employer suspects that the levels of risk have changed, new evidence becomes available about the risks, or an accident or significant incident occurs, then the employer should review the validity of the assessment.

The risk assessment process is simple in theory, but it often assumes complexity in practice when the elements of the process are not clearly understood. This complexity is not necessarily related to mathematical or theoretical aspects of the process but more to the conceptual issues associated with risk assessment. Risk management is a matter of dealing with future adverse events for which the probability of occurrence and the consequences are unknown. If the probability and the consequences of an adverse event were known, there would be no element of risk as the outcome would be defined. For example, if a gambler knew that the next throw of the dice would result in the number 2, he or she could place a bet with absolute certainty of winning; there would be no risk of losing. Similarly, if one knew that the next train to leave the railway station would crash and result in 25 fatalities, there would be an absolute certainty of loss of life. Understanding risk, therefore, means appreciating that one is dealing with the possibility that something may or may not occur in the future; risk does not deal with what is happening in the present. Risk is a conceptual issue that involves understanding the nature, context, probability and consequences of risk.

Nature of risk

Risk can be assessed as:

- an individual's perception of risk;
- a group's perception of risk;
- a calculated risk; or
- a true risk.

Individual risk perception is the risk that an individual associates with an event or situation, and is influenced by issues such as voluntary/involuntary and dread/non-dread risks and affiliation bias (see Chapter 4).

Group risk perceptions arise from cultural, social and political perspectives and ideals about a hazard (see Chapter 3).

Calculated risk is related to the qualitative or quantitative values ascribed to a risk by the risk assessor. For example, a parent makes a qualitative risk assessment when telling a young child that he or she may be killed if they run across a busy road. A road safety expert, on the other hand, will rely on quantified data provided by age-related, time-based accident statistics for the particular road type in order to make a quantitative risk assessment.

True risk is the value that all risk assessments strive to achieve; however, because of the illusory nature of risk it is an impossible value to validate, as one would require an infinite database of information related to every event and consequence that had ever taken place and then try to relate this information to what might or might not occur in the future.

Context of risk

Risk must always be placed in a particular context. If one were interested in the risk of fatalities to air passengers it would clearly be ridiculous to consider the issue of fatalities to mountaineers. The context of risk is therefore related, for example, to the stakeholders, the location, the equipment, the process, the weather, the time of day, the organisation, and the sector in which the risk occurs. In addition to the physical context, one must also consider the cultural, social and political context of the risk, as these aspects also affect the decision-making process of risk assessment. The context of the risk therefore provides the envelope or the environment within which a risk assessment is carried out: without a context limitation the risks may be considered to impact on the whole world. It is of course quite possible that, in some examples, the context of the risk is the whole world: for example, risk assessments associated with global warming, population expansion and provision of world aid would need to be carried out at this level. However, the wider the context of the risk, the less precise the risk estimation will be, because the validity of the data used in the assessment becomes more and more uncertain.

Probability of risk

The issue of probability will be dealt with in more detail later in this chapter, but some general issues will be discussed here. Elms (1992: 31) suggested that the development of an understanding of probability involved the interplay of philosophers, mathematicians and practitioners in the following way: '... the first to get the ideas right, the second to ensure a rigorous framework and the last to relate it all to reality and practical usefulness'. Elms outlined a range of possible meanings and definitions for probability using the three categories of structural, frequentist and subjective.

Structural

Structural probability is determined by the way in which the issue is described or established. For instance, a pack of cards has 52 cards and within this pack there are 4 cards designated as an 'Ace'. In a randomly sorted pack of cards the probability that an Ace will be dealt as the first card is therefore 4 in 52. Similarly, if 1000 unique lottery tickets are sold, the probability of any individual ticket winning is 1 in 1000. There is no need for anyone to make any measurements or assumptions about these probabilities, as they are absolute values, which are determined solely by the structure of the risk environment. This approach, however, provides only the theoretical answer; it does not take into account any perturbations from the ideal, such as the possibility that the cards may be marked, or that the dealer may be a cheat, or certain cards may have been lost from the pack.

Frequentist

There is an argument that the true probability can only be determined by experiment as this will determine the real situation rather than the hypothetical value. In this case a large number of experimental data points are collected and a frequency of occurrence is calculated. For instance, the number of fatal accidents occurring in defined workplaces can be recorded (say 51) together with the total number of employee days worked (say 255 000). The probability of a fatality occurring is therefore calculated as 51 in 255 000. This incidence can be normalised, for comparative purposes, to 100 000 employee-days worked, in which case the probability of a fatality would be defined as 20 per 100 000 employee-days. The disadvantage of this simple mathematical approach is that it does not produce an underlying theory of accident causation, which might be helpful for predicting what future accident statistics will be and which, in turn, would provide information on how the level of accidents might be reduced.

Subjective

A major problem associated with both of the above approaches is that information may simply not be available for the risk assessor to define the probabilities. For instance, a production manager may wish to define the reliability of a new production facility in order to ensure that the correct maintenance arrangements are implemented. In this case the manager will need to estimate the probability of a facility breakdown based on his or her experience together with the experience of any other people who can provide useful information about the new facility. In making this estimate the manager will be making a subjective assessment, because it will depend on how he or she interprets the available information. The great majority of risk assessments made in industry and commerce are based to some extent on this subjective approach. This is a perfectly valid approach provided that there is no attempt by the assessor to imply that there is a higher level of confidence for the outcome of the risk assessment than is deserved.

Consequences of risk

Defining the consequences of risk is more straightforward than defining probability, but it still has its own problems. These problems are related to the diversity of harms that may be encountered in the workplace and to the continuum nature of the severity of the harms that may arise. For instance, a fire at an oil storage facility may cause structural damage through heat stress on supporting steelwork, environmental damage through atmospheric emissions, production damage through loss of equipment, and health and safety damage through injury and loss of life. The range of severity values that may occur within each type of harm compounds the problem of defining consequences further. In the example above, harm to people may vary from minor smoke inhalation to fatalities, and harm to the environment may vary from minor smoke emissions to major oil spillages. Where a range of harms must be considered, assigning monetary values and integrating the effects across all the levels of severity may help to define the overall consequences. In some instances it may be necessary to consider harm within only one context, such as environmental or health and safety issues. It may also be necessary to consider the difference between acute harm, which occurs now and manifests its consequences immediately, and chronic harm, which occurs at some point in the future.

Risk specification in health and safety management

An important issue in health and safety risk management is related to whether the risk assessment is being used to assess individual risks or societal risks.

Individual risk

Individual risks relate to the probability of a statistical, hypothetical or identified individual suffering a specified, general or undefined harm under specified or non-specified conditions. Individual risks are normally expressed as events or numbers of people affected per specified time period, such as fatalities per 100 000 hours or 10^8 hours, in which case it is referred to as the *fatal accident rate* (FAR), or as periods of time lost as a result of a specified event(s), such as the number of days of life lost as a result of smoking 10 cigarettes per day.

There is a major issue in assessing risk that is related to the variability in the susceptibility of individuals to various types of harm. This manifests itself when considering the impact of chemicals on the health of individuals. For example, if a sample of 100 people from the general population was exposed to the same concentration of a chemical for the same length of time the effects that the chemical would have on these people would vary significantly. A small proportion of the people would be hardly affected at all, whereas a small proportion would be seriously affected and in an extreme case might die. These variations occur because some people are very susceptible to certain substances whereas other people are immune to their effects. Therefore it is often very difficult to define either a maximum concentration or a maximum time to which all people should be exposed. One suggestion is that the worst-case scenario should be considered by adopting the stance that the most vulnerable person should be assessed, in order to ensure that no one will be affected. However, the problems with this approach are how to identify the most vulnerable person exposed and how to deal with a situation where there is no value at which no one would be affected. As an example, should a person who has a severe mental or physical disability be used as the benchmark for all issues related to work-based activities, or would a more reasonable approach be to assume that this person would not be exposed to the hazards anyway – in which case they need not be considered when setting the limits for individual risk? Therefore, because of these difficulties, regulators normally use the concept of an average response to a hazard, and they accept that some people will be more affected and other people will be less affected.

Societal risk

Often an organisation is more concerned about the risks that it may present to the wider population than to individuals: in this case it is concerned with societal risk. In dealing with societal risks, organisations are effectively taking into account the possibility of a disaster occurring. It is important to account separately for single disastrous events, which may give rise to the same number of fatalities as a multitude of unrelated events involving single fatalities, because major events of this type affect identifiable groups within a country, and their consequences may have major impacts on these communities. In addition, disasters can have international consequences, and these often have more far-reaching effects than a number of single fatality events. Individual risk relates simply to the probability of an event causing harm to an individual; for societal risk the problem is more complex. In this case it is not only the probability of the adverse event occurring but also the potential number of fatalities that must be considered. Therefore it is necessary to consider the probabilities for a series of incidents taking place, each of which produces a different number of fatalities. The approach most often adopted for describing societal risk is referred to as the societal or *frequency–number (FN) curve*. The mathematical basis of this approach is discussed in more detail later in the chapter.

Completing a risk assessment

Elms (1992) provided a useful framework for describing and understanding the stages of the risk assessment process:

- Establish the purpose of the risk assessment.
- Understand the problem.
- Define the scale of the risk assessment.

- Develop risk models.
- Obtain relevant risk data.
- Carry out the risk assessment.
- Communicate the risk assessment results to stakeholders.

As Elms (1992) pointed out, these stages are not necessarily sequential but are often a mixture of simultaneous, sequential and iterative stages.

Establishing the purpose of the risk assessment

The first stage of the risk assessment must clearly establish the aims and identify what the risk assessment results are required for, as these will determine the direction and depth of the overall assessment. The assessment may, for example, be required for statutory, operational, cost–benefit, political or public inquiry purposes. Each of these purposes, or combinations of purposes, provides equally valid reasons for completing a risk assessment, but the ideal format and presentation of the final risk assessment may vary. The important aspect at this stage is to identify whether there are any conflicting requirements so that they can be accommodated in a way that does not invalidate the final results.

Understanding the problems associated with the risk assessment

In daily life, everyone deals with risks: 'Everyone is a true risk expert in the original sense of the word; we have all been trained by practice and experience in the management of risk' (Adams, 1995: 1). In the work environment, however, assessors must familiarise themselves with the key issues, processes and hazards associated with the specific risk assessment, and this requires the risk assessor or risk team to be demonstrably competent to carry out the assessment process.

> A person shall be regarded as competent where he has sufficient training and experience or knowledge and other qualities to enable him properly to assist in undertaking the measures.
>
> Health and Safety Commission (1999: 17)

Knowledge: the essential areas of knowledge that a competent assessor would require include, for example, the:

- general legislation relating to risk assessment;
- specific legislation relating to the hazards and processes involved;
- physical, management and human factor control procedures;
- workplace monitoring and health surveillance procedures; and
- the process of risk assessment.

Experience: the essential areas of experience that a competent risk assessor would require include, for example, the:

- work processes and hazards being assessed;
- operating procedures;

- potential departures from routine operations;
- potential emergency situations;
- ability to coordinate diverse technical and management information; and
- ability to produce reasoned conclusions from technical information.

In some situations it will be important to establish the hidden risks as well as the visible risks. For example, many risks associated with operating a power station and flying an aircraft are self-evident, although different. However, there are also some important issues that may not be immediately apparent, or at first sight appear to be important, such as the fact that a power station exists at a single location and operates within a single set of legal requirements, operating procedures and, broadly speaking, employees. An aircraft, on the other hand, may be required to operate at airports in many countries with quite diverse legal systems, cultures, operating procedures, languages and employees. These differences will inevitably create additional risks for an airline operator that a power station operator would not have to consider.

An essential aspect of risk assessment is identifying and understanding the hazards encountered and the potential departures from routine operations that may occur. This may require the assessors to familiarise themselves with a range of hazard assessment techniques, such as *hazard and operability* (HAZOP) studies and *failure modes and effects analysis* (FMEA). In complex situations, it is a fundamental requirement to understand how different hazards and their associated risks impact on each other, as quite often they create synergistic effects. For example, although working with certain chemicals may have an adverse effect on employees' health, workers who also smoke or are pregnant may be significantly more at risk.

Defining the scale of the risk assessment

Risk assessments can be very expensive to complete in terms of manpower and financial resources: therefore this stage of the process should identify the scale of the assessment required and ensure that the remainder of the assessment is consistent with the scale defined. It is essential to ensure that the level of the completed risk assessment is commensurate with the risks involved, as additional and unnecessary work at a later date will be uneconomic. This situation can be avoided in more complex studies by using broad-brush assessments, such as rapid risk ranking, in the first instance in order to identify those key areas that require a greater depth of investigation. It is important, however, that this initial study is not so superficial that important issues are overlooked.

Developing models for the risk assessment

Risk assessments are only as good as the hazard identification, risk estimation and evaluation processes and the competence of the assessors. The adequacy of a risk assessment is greatly enhanced through the use of risk models, which guide the risk assessor carefully through the process. Common models used include *event tree analysis* (ETA), FMEA and HAZOP studies. Each potential hazard that exists and each potential adverse event that may take place should be identified and included within the model. Probability values may then be assigned to adverse events together with realistic potential outcomes. By including each of these events in the model it will prove easier to incorporate cost–benefit and/or cost-effectiveness analysis steps in order to assess existing or improved control options.

In estimating the level of risk associated with work activities, the interacting aspects of plant and equipment design, management and operational procedures and operator competence and behaviour should be considered. It is also important to consider the external control requirements, such as legislation, standards and codes of practice, as well as the internal control requirements that are imposed by the company's health and safety philosophy: see Figure 11.1.

Obtaining data for the risk assessment

Data are rarely available in the exact format required for a risk assessment, because the data available often relate to different workforces, workplaces and equipment. It is always necessary, therefore, to consider the validity of the data being used for the assessment in order to be aware of their impact on any sensitivity analyses carried out on potential control measures. In particular, it is important to identify whether the probability data available are structural, frequentist or subjective in nature because data employed in risk assessments are often obtained from sources with a range of validities. For example, in order to complete a comprehensive risk assessment, it may be necessary to incorporate equipment reliability data from a supplier, management systems reliability data from company audits, and human reliability data from accident statistics. These different data sources must be brought together in order to complete the holistic assessment required for an operational activity.

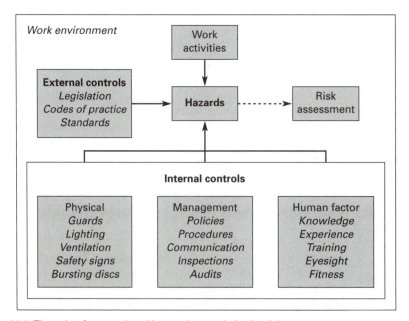

Figure 11.1 The role of external and internal controls in the risk assessment process

The risk assessment should reflect both the probability that an adverse event will occur and the potential severity of the harm or consequences that may arise. Data sources that may be used for defining harm and probability may include:

- *Harm*
  - chemical toxicity data, which describe the potential for harm;
  - workplace monitoring and survey data, which describe the potential magnitude of the harm;
  - occupational accident statistics, which describe the history of harm; and
  - manpower levels, which identify the potential population at risk of harm.

- *Probability*
  - accident and incident frequency statistics, which determine the likelihood of harm occurring;
  - operational procedures, which define the length of time the hazard may exist and give rise to the risk; and
  - work patterns, which define the length of time people may be exposed to the hazard.

Where specific data are not available, it may be necessary to rely on best estimates obtained from other closely or, in some cases, remotely related situations and activities. In these cases it is even more important to assess the validity of the data and its appropriateness and applicability to the risks being assessed. It is also often better to use qualitative risk data in an assessment and accept the limitations that this brings to the assessment rather than try to claim unrealistic accuracy and/or precision for poor-quality quantitative data.

Carrying out the risk assessment

The overall risk assessment process is summarised in Figure 11.2.

A simple qualitative or semi-quantitative risk assessment may require only a single round of assessment in order to provide an acceptable and valid conclusion. However, as the complexity and quantitative nature of the risk assessment increases, it will become more important to include iterations within the process. This is necessary because the assessment may progress from a broad outline or overview of the risks to the inclusion of more detailed and thorough models related to individual hazards and risks.

When carrying out a risk assessment, there are a number of ways in which the work activities may be grouped or structured. The two most common approaches are to address the risks by either operations or hazards. The preferred approach will very much be influenced by the existing management and operational procedures within a company. In the absence of other factors, it is usually more appropriate, logical and cost-effective to group work activities by operations. This approach will invariably bring health and safety management into line with the way in which most other company functions, such as finance, environment and production management, are treated. In this way line managers will clearly understand their responsibilities and appreciate how the risks can be managed within the financial constraints of individual management units. Where several

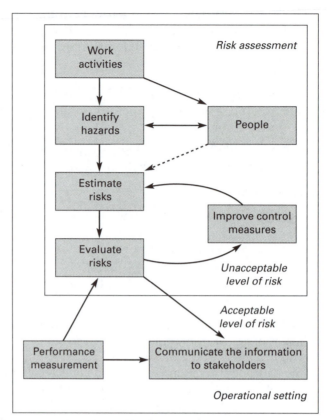

Figure 11.2 The risk assessment process

interacting management functions or operational processes are incorporated within a single risk assessment, it is important to ensure that the results provided by each function and/or process are equally valid when considered alongside the results from other functions. This may require quite detailed and complex engineering, scientific and management assessments to be undertaken, and there may also be a necessity to undertake sensitivity analyses in order to test the validity of the range of values obtained within the risk model. Finally, it may be beneficial to identify and record the limitations and boundaries of the risk assessment model employed, as it is always better to declare openly where there may be limitations in the conclusions from a risk assessment rather than try to cover them up. It is not unusual for weaknesses in a risk assessment to occur because the technical information required for the risk assessment is not available rather than because there is an inherent weakness in the process itself.

When carrying out a risk assessment, it is essential that the assessor observes all aspects of the operational processes and is familiar with and understands the activities involved. Frequently what an assessor thinks will happen or expects to happen and what actually happens are not the same. Therefore operations should be discussed with operators and supervisors, as these are invariably the people most familiar with the way in which activities are really carried out, and they will be aware of potential variations to the written procedures.

In order to ensure consistency across an organisation's operations and between risk assessors, an essential and important element of the risk assessment process is to establish organisational standards. This requires the definition of standards for both harm and probability, for use during the risk estimation stage. Standards for the risk evaluation stage will typically define a number of action levels, such as:

- *Action level 1*: The risk levels are so low that they may be considered to be trivial under all known operating conditions.
- *Action level 2*: The risk levels are low enough for them to be considered to be acceptable under the present conditions, but operations should be kept under review in order to ensure that this condition is maintained or improved.
- *Action level 3*: The risk levels are high although tolerable at present; operating conditions should be reviewed in order to identify means of improving control measures, which should be implemented within a specified time period.
- *Action level 4*: The risk levels are so high that they are considered intolerable, and therefore operations should be stopped until improved control measures have been identified and implemented.

Communicating the results of the risk assessment

In many ways a risk assessment is valueless unless its results are communicated effectively to all stakeholders. However, although communication is an important aspect of the whole process, it is often the most difficult to undertake satisfactorily in practice. The main problem associated with this part of the process is that one is identifying and then declaring to stakeholders that there are risks associated with the organisation's activities. Some stakeholders may misconstrue this as an indication that the organisation is not adequately managing the risks to employees and/or the public. This issue is particularly important where potential fatalities are concerned and/or where involuntary and dread risks are involved. An approach taken by many organisations involved in large projects that may potentially have a significant impact on the public is to involve stakeholders during all stages of the development of the project through a series of open consultative meetings and discussions.

Risk assessment in an environment of uncertainty

Uncertainty exists in all decision-making processes; if there was no uncertainty involved, management would be a very simple activity. However, it is important to differentiate between uncertainty and ignorance, as these are quite different issues in risk assessment. Ignorance of the existence of hazards and/or ignorance of potential adverse events associated with hazards are potential weaknesses of any risk assessment because the risks associated with these will not be accounted for in the overall assessment process. Uncertainty, on the other hand, means that although one knows about the hazards and/or the adverse events, the extent to which they may affect the overall risk level is unclear. The Health and Safety Executive (2001) have identified three sources of uncertainty in respect of risk assessment.

Knowledge uncertainty arises when knowledge is represented by data with poorly defined statistics. This problem can normally be overcome by using more sophisticated statistical tests, including confidence limits and sensitivity analysis. These approaches help to define the relative importance of individual components within the risk assessment and enable further actions to be prioritised in order to ensure that resources are directed to the most important issues.

Modelling uncertainty concerns the validity of the model employed in the risk assessment. For example, a risk model employed to assess the strength of a bridge under particular weather conditions may be unreliable under certain levels of stress. Therefore the predicted failure conditions will have a level of confidence that is strongly dependent on the constraints imposed by the model employed. Failings in this area can be minimised by using an independent expert peer-review process when complex models and calculations are required.

Limited predictability or unpredictability arises where there is a high level of sensitivity attached to the values employed in the risk assessment models. For example, if a slight variation in the starting value of a calculation results in significantly different outcomes under adverse conditions, then, although the model predictions will start from the same state, the outcomes may be unpredictable and/or unreliable.

When ascribing probability values to the likelihood of an adverse event occurring, it is easy to make the mistake of assuming that the probability is an absolute value. In reality, the same person can undertake the same operation in the same place on several different occasions and the chance of an accident occurring will be different each time. The reasons behind this include issues such as small changes in the physical environment of the risk and in the human behaviour of the people involved; these variations will change the envelope of conditions within which the events take place. Each individual has their own probability function for each activity, and this will describe the probability of the outcomes for that event for that person: see Figure 11.3.

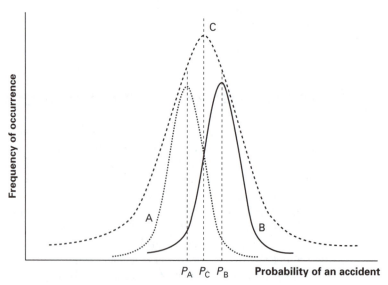

Figure 11.3 The impact of individuals on organisational risk probability

Figure 11.3 describes the risk probability functions for two operators (A and B) carrying out the same activity, at the same location. Operator A carries out the task with, on average, a lower probability (P_A) of having an accident than operator B (P_B). The risk probability function C describes the summed probability function for the work activity at this location for the two operators (A and B), and (P_C) represents the average probability applicable to the organisation for this particular activity using these two particular operators. The summed probability function (P_C) therefore represents the probability that should be included in the organisational risk assessment, as this represents the best estimate of the overall probability of an accident for the organisation. However, if the risks to particular individuals are of interest, it is more correct to use individual probability functions, as these will reflect the specific nature of the individual. As, for example, the number of people involved in an activity increases and the number of locations where the activity takes place increases, the variability or uncertainty associated with the probability value will also increase.

McQuaid (1995: S39) stated: 'Risk assessment provides a rational approach to making decisions or drawing inferences in the face of uncertainty.' Although not everyone may be quite as positive as this about the benefits of risk assessment, it remains true that currently risk assessment provides the only realistic approach to making difficult decisions in an uncertain world. Cooke (1997) has discussed and illustrated the statistical issues associated with uncertainty modelling. The Health and Safety Executive (2001), on the other hand, summarised a simpler and more practical approach to handling the uncertainty associated with data describing the probability and consequences of an event: see Figure 11.4. The vertical axis represents the uncertainty associated with the probability that the harmful consequences of an adverse event will be realised, and the horizontal axis shows the uncertainty associated with the actual consequences of the event. Hence in the lower left region of the diagram, where the levels of uncertainty associated with the probability and the consequences are very low, the risk

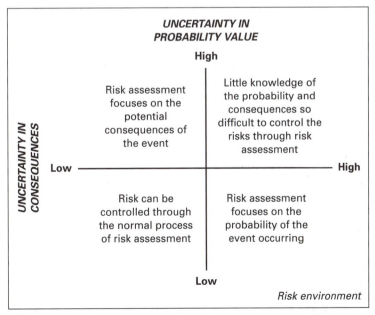

Figure 11.4 Dealing with uncertainty in risk assessments

assessment can be validated. However, as one moves along either axis into areas of greater uncertainty, it will be necessary to make assumptions that cannot be validated. Therefore in those areas where there is a very high level of uncertainty attached to the probability values (upper left region) the assessment will focus more on the potential consequences, and where there is a very high level of uncertainty associated with the consequences (lower right region) the assessment will focus more on the probability of the event taking place. Where there are relatively high levels of uncertainty attached to both the probability value and the consequences (central region), one has to rely on historic data and experiences with generic hazards to obtain meaningful results from a risk assessment. Finally, where there are very high levels of uncertainty attached to both the probability and the consequences (upper right region), risk assessment offers little of value.

It is important to understand that although increasing levels of information about risks may lead to a decrease in the level of uncertainty, it does not change the mean probability value associated with an adverse event. This is related to the normal statistical issues of mean and standard deviation, which are associated with any probability function: see Figure 11.5. In this example there are two distributions (M and N) that describe the probability of the same event occurring: both distributions have the same mean probability value (P) but they have different levels of uncertainty or standard deviation values. Distribution M clearly has a smaller standard deviation (σ_M) and therefore a lower level of uncertainty attached to the probability value P than that associated with the distribution N (σ_N).

This issue can be illustrated by reference to the information obtained from organisational plant audits or inspections. Although audits may provide statistical information on the reliability of various pieces of operational equipment, collecting the information does not change the probability of a failure actually occurring. In this case, changes in probability can be achieved only through a change in the maintenance schedules or operational procedures employed in the process. What the audit information does provide, however, is greater confidence in the validity of the conclusions reached regarding the probability of a failure.

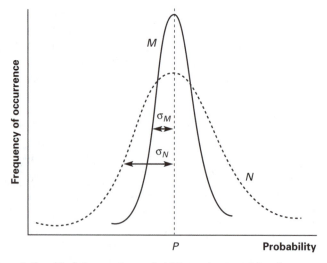

Figure 11.5 The relationship between the probability and uncertainty of an event occurring

The use of risk assessment in decision-making at government level

McQuaid (1995) discussed the issues surrounding the use of risk assessment in government, and highlighted the fact that the introduction of regulations in response to outside pressures can result in overregulation in some areas and underregulation in other areas of health and safety. This problem may be minimised, however, through the appropriate use of risk assessment.

> The resolution of the conflicting pressures on Government involves political judgements, but the process of risk assessment is nowadays an essential component of the exercise. Indeed, the Government wants the practice of risk assessment to epitomize the process of policy-making in the field of Government regulation.
>
> McQuaid (1995: S39)

The Health and Safety Executive (2001) outlined a six-stage process for reaching national decisions on health and safety in the United Kingdom:

Stage 1: Deciding whether the issue is primarily one for the Health and Safety Executive or Health and Safety Commission.

Stage 2: Defining and characterising the issue.

Stage 3: Examining the options available for addressing the issue, and their merits.

Stage 4: Adopting a particular course of action for addressing the issue efficiently and in good time, informed by the findings of the second and third points above and in the expectation that as far as possible it will be supported by stakeholders.

Stage 5: Implementing the decisions.

Stage 6: Evaluating the effectiveness of actions taken and revisiting the decisions and their implementation if necessary.

> Health and Safety Executive (2001: 21)

Governments have to address a wider range of health and safety issues than individual organisations, and therefore governmental risk assessments are far more wide-ranging than those typically completed at the organisational level. Governments often use risk assessment in order to extrapolate current data on risks to new and possibly untested areas of risk: therefore governments must balance the scientifically based judgements of risk with the public perceptions of risk before a final conclusion can be reached. Although the public's risk perceptions may not indicate a significant level of concern about a hazard, the government's decisions must also take into account the overall burden of risk on certain sectors of society when formulating legislation.

Governments invariably adopt a precautionary principle in risk decisions when the level of uncertainty about the risks is high. The precautionary approach requires that any assumptions that are made about the risks should be tested through techniques such as sensitivity analysis. Where hazards may give rise to irreversible and potentially severe consequences, such as cancer, and where there is a high level of uncertainty attached to the probability of an adverse event occurring, greater importance should be given to the potential consequences than the probability that the adverse events will occur. Where there is greater uncertainty about the consequences then worst-case scenarios should be considered (Health and Safety Executive, 2001).

Recording the results of a risk assessment

An essential element of risk assessment is recording the results in a format that is compatible with the requirements of the stakeholders. The European Commission (1996) outlined the main issues that should be incorporated within a risk assessment, and indicated that the record of the assessment should show:

- that a programme of risk assessments at work has been implemented and effectively carried out;
- how the programme was carried out;
- special or unusual risks (e.g. infectious risks at work);
- groups of workers facing particular risks (e.g. local authority workers who enter drains or sewers, electrical maintenance workers, crane drivers, etc);
- other risks of concern;
- as appropriate, the decisions made in the assessment of risk, including the information on which those decisions were based where published standards or guidance are not available;
- published standards or guidance otherwise applied (e.g. machine guarding standards);
- recommendations for measures to further reduce risk or otherwise improve protection;
- arrangements for review of assessments.

European Commission (1996: 28–29)

Risk assessments are frequently produced because they are a legislative requirement, but they also offer a very useful management tool as they provide an effective means of drawing together operational information and summarising the justification for the implementation of control measures. A risk assessment can be used to identify the baseline levels of risk associated with operational activities before control measures have been put in place and then to show how various levels of control may impact on the residual level of risk. This information can be particularly useful when cost-saving measures are being reviewed by senior management, as it identifies the impact that, for example, a reduction in plant maintenance or manning levels may have on the level of risk. Risk assessments also provide a way of defining the competence levels required of employees working in particular operations.

The preferred format of a risk assessment will depend on a number of factors, such as whether health and safety management is incorporated within a quality management system, whether the assessment is a formal document required for a high-hazard facility, or whether it is a routine assessment for a low- or medium-hazard activity. Whatever reporting format is used, the documentation should be presented in a manner that is:

- applicable to the type of operations being assessed;
- an effective means of identifying and recording risk control measures;
- cost-effective, in terms of preparation time, effort and financial commitment;
- a positive aid for managers, supervisors and operators in controlling risks; and
- an auditable route for reviewing the conclusions obtained from the risk assessment.

It is helpful if organisational risk assessments follow a common format and form part of a structured quality management system. For most organisations, whatever their size, it is also helpful to prepare a formal documented management system for completing and recording risk assessments so that they can be referenced, filed and accessed easily. A simple example of a framework in which an organisation's activities can be accommodated and referenced is illustrated in Figure 11.6.

The work involved in the preparation and presentation of individual health and safety risk assessments can be significantly reduced if the process is supported by a high-quality, well-documented company health and safety manual. This manual, which should contain relevant, general information on each type of hazard encountered within the organisation, can be cross-referenced in individual risk assessments so that the level of repetition in the documentation is reduced to the minimum. For each hazard covered in a company's health and safety manual information should be provided, where appropriate, on:

- legislation and codes of practice;
- standards and guidance documents;
- physical and management control procedures;

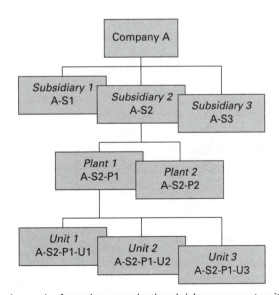

Figure 11.6 Structuring and referencing organisational risk assessments within a quality management system

- maintenance and inspection schedules;
- safety signs;
- personal protective equipment; and
- competence levels for operators, supervisors and managers.

A generic approach to risk assessment is acceptable for many risks, particularly for low-level risks, provided that the assessment is relevant for the hazards at each location covered by the assessment. However, a compromise approach that falls between the individual and the generic approaches is often preferred. In this case a generic assessment provides the major part of the assessment, but an option is provided that allows additional information to be included in order to cover minor variations. Whichever approach is adopted, however, the risk assessor should sign the document and the location manager should then sign to accept the results of the risk assessment. Two formats for reporting risk assessments will be considered in more detail in order to illustrate the key issues that should be addressed when recording risk assessment findings. Although the discussion presented focuses on the requirements for a production facility, the comments are also valid for other organisational settings. The first format provides a general assessment approach that can be utilised in the majority of cases; the second format is applicable more for the assessment of high-hazard operations.

All assessments should be reviewed on a regular basis; however, this review may only entail confirming that the results of the original assessment are still valid and that there have been no accidents or incidents that give reason to suspect that the original assessment is no longer valid. When significant changes are made to an operation, such as manning levels, equipment and operational procedures, it is important to review and possibly reassess the whole operation. An assessment should also be reviewed if, for example, any of the following situations arise:

- legislative requirements change;
- periodic inspections of control measures show that a deterioration in their performance has occurred;
- monitoring programmes show that the control measures are no longer providing adequate protection to employees;
- employees report adverse health effects;
- new scientific information becomes available about the risks associated with the hazards;
- improved control measures become available;
- operational procedures change; or
- significant changes are made in the workplace environment.

General format

The risk assessment document should contain four main sections, which cover the issues of general information, specific information, assessment results, and management approval of the document.

Section 1: General information

This section should define, with the use of drawings, plant and equipment identification codes, the location and processes covered by the assessment. Those people responsible for each part of the process, equipment or facility should be identified in terms of their job titles: these may include, for example, the plant manager, maintenance manager, shift supervisor and quality assurance manager. The manning regimes, such as shift or day work, adopted for operating the facility and equipment should be presented, together with the number, experience and training requirements for the employees.

Sufficient information should be provided about the process so that its purpose, operations and hazards can be reasonably and readily identified. This information provides the boundaries or envelope for the applicability of the risk assessment. The introduction of new equipment and changes to the operational procedures or maintenance schedules may impact on these boundaries. Similarly, changes in, for example, the number of operators or their competence may also significantly change the validity of a risk assessment.

Section 2: Specific information

This section should contain information about the hazards associated with the work activities described in Section 1 of the report and those people whom it may reasonably be foreseen may be affected by the hazards. Reference should be made to the appropriate company safety manual in order to provide relevant information about each hazard together with generic risk mitigation measures. The specific operational procedures should be referenced, and non-generic risk control procedures should be described together with the reasons for the variation. Potential departures from normal operating envelopes should be identified, together with the control measures that have been put in place in order to control them. Reports on the commissioning and operation of the facility should be referenced and, in particular, any operational limitations that were imposed at commissioning should be described.

The people affected by the operations will include the operators, but others, such as fitters, electricians, scaffolders, site cleaners, contractors, delivery drivers and visitors, may also be affected at various times. Any restrictions placed on the access to the facility or equipment, by any of these groups of people at any time, should be highlighted and the appropriate personnel control signs indicated. Historic data and reports pertaining to accidents, incidents and near misses at the facility should be referenced together with company or public reports or information derived from incidents at other related facilities.

Section 3: Assessment results

Specialist risk assessment reports related to specific parts of the facility that may, for example, have been prepared by equipment suppliers should be referenced in this section. The assessment methodology employed, together with the organisation's standards for risk estimation and evaluation, should be referenced or described in detail if a non-generic approach has been adopted. Recommendations for improvements in control measures, with responsibilities and timescales for implementation, should be identified. The results of cost–benefit and cost-effectiveness analyses that may have been used to support recommendations should be presented, together with the conclusions and reasons for the recommendations. A clear statement should be presented that summarises the conclusions reached from the risk assessment, together with the acceptability, or otherwise, of the residual levels of risk associated with the activities.

Section 4: Management approval

The final section of the assessment should contain the organisation's acceptance of the results of the assessment. This should include the assessment date, the proposed review date for the assessment, the assessor's signature, and the operation manager's signature of acceptance of the validity of the risk assessment.

Safety case and safety report formats

In the United Kingdom the Health and Safety Executive requires certain specified high-hazard operations to produce formal safety cases, such as for offshore oil rig operations (Health and Safety Executive, 1998a), and safety reports, such as for high-hazard chemical operations (Health and Safety Executive, 1999). In the offshore industry the impact of the safety case approach has been particularly important:

> The impact of the safety case regime has been far wider than was initially envisaged, either by the industry, or by the HSE. There have been substantial improvements in the overall management of offshore risks, which has been reflected in the fall in the numbers of accidents and incidents over the last few years.
>
> Health and Safety Executive (1998a: i)

In principle, the differences between the requirements of a general risk assessment and the more specific requirements of a safety case or safety report are only in the level of information and detail required.

> The principal requirements to be demonstrated in a safety case are that:
>
> (a) the management system is adequate to ensure compliance with statutory health and safety requirements;
>
> (b) adequate arrangements have been made for audit, and for audit reporting; and
>
> (c) all hazards with the potential to cause a major accident have been identified, their risks evaluated, and measures taken to reduce the risks to people affected by those hazards to as low as is reasonably practicable (ALARP).
>
> Health and Safety Executive (1998a: 1–2)

The following guidance (Health and Safety Executive, 1998a, 1999) summarises the general requirements for information that should be included in safety cases and safety reports.

Factual information

The supporting material should, where appropriate, include:

- a general description of the operations in order to provide an overview and understanding of the purpose of the facility and its activities;
- a location plan of the facility and a summary of the local environment;
- the general structure and design of the facility;
- the design of the operational equipment and the development of the operational procedures;
- staffing levels;
- descriptions of all primary functions of the facility;
- a summary of all hazardous materials at the facility; and
- the safety features incorporated into the management system for the facility.

Management of health and safety

A safety case should demonstrate that the management systems in place are adequate to control the risks and to ensure compliance with legislation. The management system should therefore address the issues of:

- policy;
- organisation;
- planning and standards;
- performance measurement; and
- audit and review.

Control of major hazards

A safety case should demonstrate that all significant hazards have been identified, their associated risks have been evaluated, and appropriate control measures have been put in place in order to reduce the risks to an acceptable level. The following issues should, therefore, be addressed:

- foreseeable hazards should be identified through a structured process, which should be appropriate to the level of risks involved;
- all adverse events that could lead to a major accident should be identified;
- all significant risks arising from the hazards should be evaluated, and risk control decisions should be based on sound engineering arguments and principles;
- human factor effects should be incorporated;
- safety-critical tasks should be identified and their impact assessed;
- where quantified risk assessment is incorporated into the process, uncertainty issues should be taken into account;
- the reasoning behind the choice of control measures should be fully documented;
- the principle of inherently safe design should be incorporated into the design of the installation; and

- control and mitigation measures for major accidents should be included within the management system.

Incorporating safety and reliability

In order to demonstrate that adequate safety and reliability have been incorporated into a high-hazard facility, the following issues should be addressed in a safety case or report:

- the facility should be designed to an appropriate standard, with the operating envelope for the facility clearly outlined;
- design issues related to redundancy and diversity, susceptibility to adverse events, facility layout, reliability, availability and survivability of emergency services, containment, structural integrity, impact of operational excursions outside design conditions, safety-related control systems, human factors, and identification of locations containing flammable materials should all be considered;
- the facility should be constructed to an adequate level of safety and reliability, and procedures should be implemented in order to demonstrate that changes to the original design are controlled;
- the facility should be operated to an adequate level of safety and reliability, and the procedures should cover abnormal conditions that are outside the normal envelope of operational conditions. The procedures should include, for example, start-up, shut-down, maintenance, temporary override and emergency conditions;
- the facility should be maintained to an adequate level of safety and reliability in order to prevent major accidents and to limit the consequences of this type of event; and
- the facility should be modified and decommissioned to an adequate level of safety and reliability; in particular, the management procedures should ensure that modifications to the facility are properly designed, installed, commissioned and tested.

Emergency response measures

A major element of safety cases and safety reports relates to a demonstration that suitable procedures are in place for the management of emergencies and major incidents through the availability of site emergency plans. The report should therefore cover issues related to:

- on-site mitigation measures, such as emergency shut-down procedures;
- emergency response measures, such as the roles and responsibilities of key personnel, isolation procedures, communication routes, evacuation points, and places of refuge for employees;
- on-site and off-site emergency response facilities, such as firefighting and medical services; and
- training personnel and testing emergency response systems.

Probability, reliability and maintainability

Two related and important issues in risk assessment are the frequency or probability that an event will occur and the reliability with which, for example, a facility or piece of equipment operates or an operator undertakes a task in a specified manner. A third issue that must also be considered in this context is equipment maintainability.

Probability and frequency

The likelihood that certain events may take place may be defined by a frequency value, which expresses the number of occurrences over a stated period of time, such as events per day or per year, or as a probability, which expresses the percentage likelihood of an event occurring on a scale from 0 (impossible) to 1 (certain). There are three general ways of describing the probability distribution of an uncertain function: probability density function, cumulative probability function, and complementary cumulative probability function.

Probability density function

The most common format for showing the distribution of a function is the probability density function (PDF), such as a Gaussian, Poisson or log-normal distribution. A typical probability distribution is shown in Figure 11.7(a). The *mode* value of a distribution of this type is the value most likely to occur, and is shown by the peak of the distribution function. The *median* value of a distribution occurs where the percentage probability that a value will be greater or less than the specified value is 50:50. The *mean* or *average* value corresponds to the point that equals the sum of all the values divided by the number of values. A symmetric, normal or Gaussian distribution has equal values for the mode, median and mean, whereas other types of probability density function have different values for each of these parameters: see, for example, Figure 7.3.

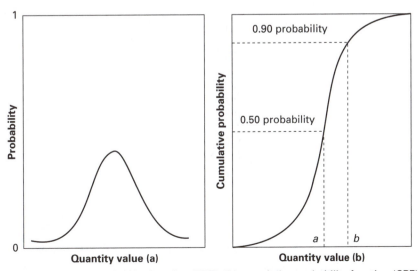

Figure 11.7 (a) Probability density function (PDF); (b) cumulative probability function (CPF)

Cumulative probability function

Figure 11.7(b) describes the cumulative probability function (CPF). This curve is derived from the PDF and vice versa; the CPF is the integral of the PDF and the PDF is the differential of the CPF. The height of the CPF, at any point on the x-axis, is equivalent to the probability that the actual value of the function will be less than or equal to the specified value on the x-axis. By using percentile values, confidence limits can be incorporated into the quantity value. For example, the 50% value (equivalent to a probability value of 0.5) represents the quantity value a, at which there is a 50% probability that the actual value will be less than or equal to this value, and the 90% value (equivalent to a probability value of 0.9) represents the quantity value b, at which there is a 90% probability that the actual quantity value will be less than or equal to this quantity value: see Figure 11.7(b). CPF curves are often plotted on logarithmic scales because the probability and quantity values range over several orders of magnitude.

Complementary cumulative probability function and FN-curves

Figure 11.8 describes the complementary cumulative probability function (CCPF), which is the complement of the CPF curve; in this case the height of the curve on the y-axis provides the probability that a value will be greater than the specified value on the x-axis.

The CCPF curve is the origin of the frequency–number (FN) curve that is often used to describe societal risk. FN-curves are normally plotted on logarithmic scales because the probability and quantity values may range over several orders of magnitude: the y-axis scale is typically presented as a frequency, such as the 'number of accidents per year with N or more fatalities' and the x-axis as the 'number of fatalities in an incident'. FN-curves are used to describe societal risk because they provide the cumulative frequency at which a specified or greater number of people may die in an event per year. The frequency value at $N=1$

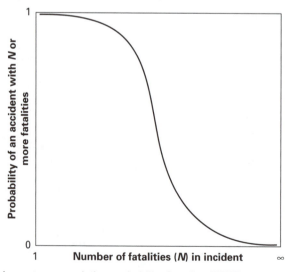

Figure 11.8 Complementary cumulative probability function (CCPF)

therefore represents in this case the frequency of occurrence of all fatal accidents. In practice FN-curves are developed for major facilities that have the potential to impact on society in general: these curves are then compared with a standard or acceptable FN-curve. If the curve for a new facility falls below the standard FN-curve then the level of risk is considered to be acceptable, and the further below the standard FN-curve that the line falls the safer the new facility is considered to be. A problem that may occur with this approach is that the shape of the FN-curve is different from the shape of the standard FN-curve such that part of the facility curve falls above and part below the standard curve. In this case it is not clear whether the overall risk of the new installation is greater or less than the acceptable standard (Evans, 2003).

Reliability

Reliability is the probability that a piece of equipment, for example, is able to perform its defined function under stated conditions for a stated period of time or for a stated demand (Institution of Chemical Engineers, 1985). If a high level of reliability of engineered safety features is required, particularly in safety-critical areas of an operation, design engineers should build high levels of equipment redundancy and diversity into the process.

- *Redundancy* refers to the ability to perform the same defined operational function by a number of independent but identical means (Institution of Chemical Engineers, 1985).
- *Diversity* refers to the ability to perform the same defined operational function by a number of independent and different means (Institution of Chemical Engineers, 1985).

Andrews and Moss (1993) have presented a detailed description of the principles and theory of network reliability, but the operation of simple series, parallel and mixed networks provides an understanding of the underlying principles of network reliability.

Series network

In processes using series networks, any component failure cannot be accepted because there is no redundancy built into the system (Figure 11.9). In this case the overall system will fail if any of the three individual components (A, B or C) fails.

If the reliabilities of the three components (A, B and C) in Figure 11.9 are R_A, R_B and R_C, respectively, the overall system reliability (R_S) of this three-component series network is given by:

$$R_S = R_A \times R_B \times R_C$$

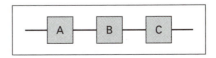

Figure 11.9 Reliability: three-component series network

Parallel network

In order to ensure that a system will continue to operate provided that at least one of its individual components operates, the components must be placed in parallel (Figure 11.10). In this case the system will fail only if all three components (A, B and C) fail, because a double level of redundancy/diversity is built into the design of the system, and there will always be a path through the system as long as any one of these components continues to operate.

If the reliabilities of each of the three components (A, B and C) shown in Figure 11.10 are R_A, R_B and R_C, respectively, the overall system reliability (R_S) is given by

$$R_S = 1 - [(1 - R_A) \times (1 - R_B) \times (1 - R_C)]$$

Clearly the reliability of the overall system increases as the level of redundancy is increased, but the return on investment decreases as the level of redundancy increases.

Mixed series and parallel network

If a system is made up from a mixture of series and parallel components (see for example Figure 11.11), the overall system reliability calculations can be simplified by assessing the reliability of each of the system's components in stages.

The first stage of the simplification involves combining the series components into an equivalent single operational component; in this case A and B can be combined and C and D can be combined:

$$^{AB}R_S = R_A \times R_B$$

and

$$^{CD}R_S = R_C \times R_D$$

These combined components can then be treated as two components in parallel, which gives the overall system reliability value as

$$^{ABCD}R_S = 1 - [(1 - {}^{AB}R_S) \times (1 - {}^{CD}R_S)]$$

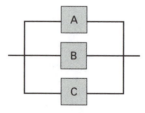

Figure 11.10 Reliability: three-component parallel network

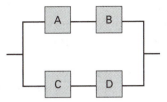

Figure 11.11 Reliability: four-component series/parallel network

Complex networks

Reliability networks can become quite complex by incorporating the basic networks described above with what are referred to as voting systems, standby systems, bridge systems and star systems. The mathematics associated with these systems, however, becomes much more complex and therefore specialist texts should be consulted (Andrews and Moss, 1993).

It is important when incorporating diversity and redundancy into systems to avoid the problems associated with common cause failures. These result in the failure of two or more different safety components as a result of the same cause, such as a power failure. Common mode failures in a system result from the same safety components failing as a result of a common weakness, such as a design fault. Because common cause events lead to more than one safety component in a system failing at the same time, the system possesses apparent diversity rather than real diversity as the components are not truly independent. In addition, overloads on one component can cause a failure in a second component, and this again negates the independence of the two components.

The use of equipment performance data is an important aspect of reliability predictions. Therefore, after a new facility or piece of equipment has been commissioned, it is important to gather performance data in order to ensure that the facility or equipment is operating to specification. This information can then be used in future designs in order to improve long-term performance. Reliability assessments require the collection of a range of data that is dependent on whether the assessment relates to availability or safety:

> In safety studies the objective will be to identify those failure modes which are potentially dangerous whereas in availability studies the proportion of failures which cause forced outage or reduction in performance will be the main focus of interest.
>
> Andrews and Moss (1993: 263)

Maintainability

Maintainability is the probability that a system will be restored to its operational condition within a specified period of time. This is related to the design features and the quality of the components incorporated within the system. Equipment designers are always striving for the most cost-effective solution to operational requirements, which include the equipment's maintenance schedules. Therefore trade-offs are invariably made in design and construction based on cost–benefit arguments associated with component costs, reliability and the costs of repair and maintenance. A key aspect of building maintainability into a system is referred to as the system's *mean time to repair* (MTTR). The importance of this can be appreciated by considering the MTTR for a fire alarm system: clearly, if a fire alarm system is broken, the longer the system takes to be repaired the more vulnerable the organisation will be to the risk of fire. Greater detail on the mathematical and theoretical aspects of the maintainability of equipment can be obtained from specialist texts (Andrews and Moss, 1993).

Assessing organisational risks

There are a number of ways in which organisational risks may be assessed: the preferred option is usually dependent on the purpose of the risk assessment. Two approaches are discussed here. The first approach defines the risk profile based on the potential consequences and likelihood of occurrence using a two-dimensional risk matrix. The second approach defines the overall risk acceptability of new projects based on a three-dimensional risk matrix using the potential technical, economic and socio-political impacts of projects.

Risk profiling

Risk profiling at a strategic level enables organisations to identify and assess the major areas of risk to their business. Organisational risk profiling does not consider the detail of each risk but rather the general level of risk within broad areas, such as finance, environment or health and safety. One reason for doing this is so that a diverse range of organisational risks can be assessed and compared in order to make semi-quantified strategic decisions on the financing of risk mitigation measures. The first stage in this process is to identify the various generic sources of risk that may affect the organisation. These may originate either from internal sources, in which case the organisation should have a significant level of direct control over them, or from external sources, which means that the organisation may have only limited direct and/or indirect control over them. Generic sources of risk include (Standards Australia, 1999):

- *commercial and legal issues*, such as contractual arrangements, changes in market demand and issues related to suppliers, customers, contractors and tenants;
- *economic issues*, such as operational costs, exchange rates and the financial rating of international markets;
- *human resource issues*, such as the loss of key employees, employee behaviour, vicarious liability, vandalism and terrorism;
- *natural events*, such as storms, floods and earthquakes;
- *political issues*, such as a change in the leadership of a country's ruling party, a change in the ruling party and the introduction or a change of legislation; and
- *technological issues*, such as changes in production methods, developments in the organisation's products/services and information technology.

The second stage of the assessment identifies those areas of the organisation's activities where these risks may have an impact (Standards Australia, 1999):

- *assets*, such as buildings, equipment, raw materials and products/services;
- *people*, such as employees, contractors, suppliers, customers and the public;
- *income*, such as sales and return on investments;
- *operational costs*, such as raw material supplies, fuel and transport;
- *operational performance*, such as production capacity, output, quality and efficiency; and
- *intangibles*, such as reputation, goodwill and quality of life.

A risk-profiling exercise is undertaken by arranging for senior managers within each of the organisation's functional groups to define those risks that, in their opinion, represent the greatest threat to the business success of the organisation. Those risks that have been identified by each business function are consolidated into a single organisational list. At this stage the consolidated list of key risks is presented to each of the senior managers, who must then independently rate the levels of risk in terms of their probability of occurrence and severity of impact on the business using a rating scale of the type presented in Table 11.1. The risk is judged by its perceived impact on the ability of the business to deliver its corporate strategy and objectives.

Table 11.1 Examples of frequency and severity rating scales for assessing organisational risks

Rating level	Frequency of occurrence (likelihood)	Severity of impact (consequence)
1	**Rare:** The loss is unlikely to occur within the next 50 years	**Insignificant:** Disruption to the business's operations will be trivial
2	**Unlikely:** The loss may occur at least once in the next 10–50 years	**Minor:** A small disruption to the business's operations may occur with a possible short-term loss of output equal to no more than 1 week's production or the loss of a minor customer
3	**Possible:** The loss may occur at least once in the next 2–10 years	**Moderate:** A limited disruption to the business's operations may occur with a possible loss of output equal to no more than 1 month's production or the loss of a medium customer
4	**Likely:** The loss may occur at least once within the next 1–2 years	**Major:** A significant disruption to the business's operations may occur with a possible loss of output equal to no more than 6 months' production or the loss of a major customer
5	**Probable:** The loss is almost certain to occur at least once within the next 12 months	**Catastrophic:** Total loss of stakeholder credibility or loss of at least 50% of production capacity or market share

The outputs from these assessments can be summarised on a simple 5 × 5 risk matrix, in order to provide a corporate overview of how vulnerable the organisation may be to the various types of risk. The average scores obtained for each area of risk can be plotted on the matrix together with an indication of the spread of values obtained: see Figure 11.12.

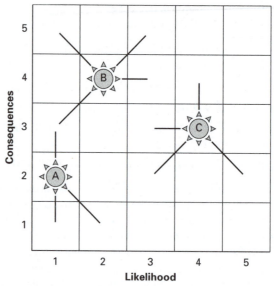

Figure 11.12 Overview of organisational risks

Figure 11.12 illustrates three organisational risks (A, B and C) with average risk values of 2 ($L=1$; $C=2$), 8 ($L=2$; $C=4$) and 12 ($L=4$; $C=3$), together with the spread of values obtained. These levels of risk may be interpreted using a risk evaluation scale, such as that shown in Table 11.2.

Table 11.2 Evaluation of organisational risks

Risk rating (score)	Evaluation
Acceptable (1–4)	No further action required
Tolerable (5–9)	Continue to manage the organisational risks through good practices and keep risks under review
High (10–19)	A detailed action plan is required in order to reduce the level of risk to the organisation to a tolerable level
Very high (20–25)	Urgent action is required in order to avoid a potentially major disaster for the organisation

At this stage of the risk assessment a management working group should be established so that those risks where there are significantly divergent views among managers or where risks fall into the high and very high categories can be reviewed. These risks should be scrutinised in order to identify reasons for the divergent views and/or high levels of risk and to address any shortcomings in the organisation's risk control measures. The principal objectives of this working group should, therefore, be to address:

■ the origins of each risk and the functions responsible for creating the risks;

■ the effectiveness of the organisation's existing control measures;

■ cost-effectiveness and cost–benefit analyses of providing improved control options; and

- the establishment of an improvement plan to ensure that high and very high risks are, at least, reduced to tolerable levels.

The advantage of the risk-profiling approach is that, although it provides only a semi-quantified summary of the risks, it enables senior management to compare their views over a wide range of issues and to reach a consensus view.

Risk acceptability in strategic decision-making

An important aspect of risk management involves decision-making over the viability of new projects. In this case managers are required to make decisions about whether the level of risk attached to a project is unacceptable in terms of costs compared with the potential benefits in terms of income. In an approach discussed by Chicken and Posner (1998), potential organisational risks are assessed under the three categories of technical, economic and socio-political risks.

Technical risks include issues such as:

- harm to people;
- harm to the environment;
- project performance operating to specification;
- lifetime of project meeting expectations; and
- requirements to upgrade project during its lifetime in order to meet improved standards.

Economic risks include issues such as:

- project completion within budget;
- project completion on time;
- interest rates varying during the period of borrowing;
- availability of sufficient financial resources to complete the project; and
- continuation of a viable market for the product or service throughout the projected lifetime of the project.

Socio-political risks include issues such as:

- public acceptability of the technology;
- public acceptability of the product or service;
- project compatibility with current social and political views; and
- changes in social and political views about the acceptability of the product, service or process during the project lifetime.

Each of these risks is assessed against the four risk acceptability criteria, shown in column 1 of Table 11.3, and then assigned the appropriate category score of 1, 2, 5 or 14. The three category scores are summed in order to arrive at an overall risk score (ranging from 3 to 42). The overall project risk score is then assessed against the same risk acceptability criteria (column 1, Table 11.3) in order to see whether the project, as defined, is acceptable to the organisation.

Table 11.3 Risk ranking scale for assessing risks associated with new projects

Risk acceptability criteria	Individual risk category score	Overall project risk score
Acceptable without reservation	1	3
Requires some action in order to make the risk acceptable	2	4–6
Requires significant action in order to make the risk acceptable	5	7–15
Unacceptable level of risk	14	16–42

Source: Chicken and Posner (1998). Reproduced by permission of Thomas Telford

Assessing operational risks

The options and techniques available for identifying and assessing operational risks are much more diverse than those available for assessing organisational risks. The techniques available are normally subdivided into the two general categories of hazard/adverse event identification and risk assessment.

Hazard and adverse event identification

The identification of hazards and adverse events is an important aspect of the risk assessment process because, if the hazards and adverse events are not identified, the risks associated with them cannot be assessed. Hazards are present in any operational activity, and some of these are generic in nature and can be identified as such through the use of checklists. Other hazards arise specifically under certain adverse operating conditions, and these are identified through the use of more sophisticated techniques, such as hazard and operability (HAZOP) studies, event tree analysis (ETA) and failure modes and effects analysis (FMEA). These techniques are referred to as *inductive* or *what if* methods of analysis because they look forward in order to determine what might happen as a result of certain initiating events. Related approaches, such as fault tree analysis (FTA), are used in accident causation analysis: in this case the approaches are referred to as *deductive* or *what could have caused thi*s analyses because these techniques look backward to see why an adverse event took place.

Scenario building is a technique of developing *risk scenarios,* and involves making assumptions about operational parameters and how these may affect operations. *Flow charts* are a graphical depiction of risk scenarios and operational activities and the ways in which these are linked together. Scenario building includes the use of the techniques referred to as *future forward*, which works out logical paths that may occur from present situations, and *simulation modelling,* which attempts to model possible actions and the reactions that may occur within an operational activity. These techniques are used in an attempt to predict and control future adverse events. *Influence diagrams* are pictorial models that are used to describe or summarise the relationships between various hazards and adverse events in a scenario. *Decision trees* summarise the options available in the decision-making process within a particular risk scenario.

Hazard checklists

Generic checklists are used by many organisations in order to identify the range of hazards present, the activities where the hazards may be encountered, and the people who may be affected by the hazards in the workplace. A typical example of a hazard checklist is shown in Table 11.4.

Table 11.4 Example of an operational hazard checklist

Work location: *Construction site*

Ref no.	Hazard group	Is the hazard present? (Yes/No)	Tasks involved	People affected	Is the work compliant with procedures? (Yes/No)
1	**Physical:** *For example:*				
	Excavation	Yes	Trench work	JCB operators	Yes
	Fencing	No			
	Pressure	No			
	Scaffold	Yes	Access platforms	Scaffolders	Yes
2	**Mechanical** *For example:*				
	Cranes	Yes	Moving steelwork	Crane operator and steel erectors	Yes
	Lifts	No			
	Machinery	No			
	Vehicles	No			
3	**Health** *For example:*				
	Chemicals	Yes	Lubricating oils	Fitters	Yes
	Legionellosis	No			
	Noise	Yes	Compressed air	Fitters	Yes
	Radiation	Yes	Weld testing	Radiographers	Yes
4	**Electrical** *For example:*				
	Discharge	No			
	Electrostatic	No			
	High voltage	No			
	Mains electricity	Yes	Mains wiring	Electricians	Yes
5	**Environment** *For example:*				
	Confined spaces	Yes	Trench entry	Contractors	Yes
	Lighting	No			
	Temperature	No			
	Wind	Yes	Steel erection	Steel erectors	Yes

Hazards assessed by: Completed checklist approved by:

Date: Date:

This approach is suitable as an *aide-mémoire* and for workplaces where complex operational activities are unlikely to be encountered; however, it should not be solely relied on in situations where complex or high-risk activities are involved. This approach is often used as a precursor to more detailed analysis techniques, such as HAZOP or FMEA.

Hazard and operability (HAZOP) studies

HAZOP studies were developed in the chemical industry in order to assess the impacts that changes in operational parameters might have on the integrity of a process. A HAZOP team should be comprised of experts in the HAZOP methodology who understand the processes being assessed and appreciate the effects that deviations from normal operational conditions may have on the safety of the process. Within the HAZOP approach certain phrases are used that have defined meanings (Andrews and Moss, 1993):

- *Intention* defines how a part or process is expected to function.
- *Deviation* is a departure from the intention that is determined by the application of the HAZOP guidewords.
- *Cause* is the reason behind the deviation; causes have a probability of occurrence associated with them, and causes that have a very low probability of occurrence are often discounted.
- *Consequence* is the outcome or harm resulting from a deviation.
- *Guideword* is a qualifying causal word that acts on the intention causing a deviation that may result in undesirable consequences.

The HAZOP approach uses a number of guidewords as a form of checklist in order to ensure that the assessor approaches possible operational changes in a methodical and logical manner. The guidewords cover physical and operational changes and also human factor changes, such as the way in which employees undertake the operations. Table 11.5 lists some common HAZOP guidewords used for assessing the impacts of physical changes to a process.

Table 11.5 Examples of HAZOP guidewords for physical changes to a process

Guideword	Interpretation examples
NONE	No power, no flow, no reagent
MORE OF	High pressure, high flow, high reagent quantity
LESS OF	Low pressure, low power, low temperature
AS WELL AS	Heat is applied in addition to an increase in pressure
PART OF	A reagent is missing from the specified list of reagents
REVERSE	The direction of a feed conveyor belt is reversed

In addition to process changes, it is also possible to incorporate potential human errors into a HAZOP study; examples of human factor guidewords (Kirwan, 1994) are shown in Table 11.6.

Table 11.6 Examples of HAZOP guidewords for human factor errors

Guideword	Interpretation examples
NOT DONE	Power not switched on or temperature not reduced
REPEATED	Reagent added twice or pressure increased twice
LATER THAN	Reagent added or temperature increased later than required
AS WELL AS	Heat or power applied in addition to an increase in pressure
READING ERROR	A meter or operating instruction is read incorrectly
SOONER THAN	Pressure or temperature increased sooner than required

Kennedy and Kirwan (1998) also suggested that the HAZOP approach could be used to predict and prevent failures in health and safety management systems. They argued that although documentation such as policies and procedures may define how organisational health and safety risks should be managed, the reality was not necessarily the same as the theory. The difference between these two states is often influenced by the organisation's safety culture. Examples of management system guidewords and the areas of potential impact (Kennedy and Kirwan, 1998) are shown in Table 11.7.

Table 11.7 Examples of HAZOP guidewords for safety management systems

Guideword	Impact on	
MISSING		
SKIPPED	People	Resources
MISTIMED	Skill	Detail
MORE	Procedure	Protection
LESS	Specification	Decision
WRONG	Training	Control
AS WELL AS	Information	Communication
OTHER		

Source: Kennedy and Kirwan (1998)

HAZOP studies should normally be implemented at the process design stage using process line drawings or flow sheets together with full details of the specified operational conditions and the number and competences of the operators involved in the process. Studies should follow a systematic and documented procedure using the appropriate physical and human factor guidewords for the process. All conclusions and recommendations from the study should be recorded so that the reasons for proposed changes are documented and these can be referred to in the future. An example of a simple HAZOP record is shown in Table 11.8.

HAZOP analysis involves a vertical logic analysis of the process, and because of this it can sometimes 'miss' potential hazards through the lack of lateral logic analysis. For example, a HAZOP analysis may consider the impact of an increase in pressure on an operational process but overlook the possibility that the containment vessel may not be able to withstand the pressure generated. However, modern computer-based guideword prompt systems can go some way towards

LLYFRGELL COLEG MENAI LIBRARY

Table 11.8 Examples of records from a HAZOP study

Intention	Deviation	Cause	Consequence	Action
1. Transfer raw material from silo to reaction vessel.	1.1 **No** power to conveyor	1.1 Failure to reset emergency stop	1.1 Process fails to start up	
	1.2 **Reverse** conveyor direction	1.2 Direction changed during cleaning process	1.2 Failure to transfer raw material to vessel	
	1.3 **Low** flow of raw material	1.3 Raw material level low in silo	1.3 Process reaction time increased	
2. Transfer hospital patient from stretcher to bed.	2.1 **No** bed available	2.1 All hospital beds occupied	2.1 Patient left on stretcher in corridor	
	2.2 Assistance **not** available to lift patient	2.2 Shortage of auxiliary nurses	2.2 Nurse receives back injury through lifting patient alone	

addressing these shortcomings. Tyler and Simmons (1995) summarised the limitations of the HAZOP technique and identified the following issues as the main causes for inadequate studies:

- *Basic assumptions*. It will usually be assumed that a facility has been designed and constructed to certain standards and codes, and therefore there will be a baseline level below which it will be assumed that there are no problems.

- *HAZOP team*. Lack of experience in the team may mean that certain deviations are excluded because they are considered to be insignificant.

- *Incomplete information*. This may lead to a failure to identify or an underestimation of the significance of a potential deviation.

- *Lack of knowledge and experience*. The guideword approach used in HAZOP studies is not a substitute for knowledge and experience; guidewords provide only a prompt list to assist the process.

- *Choice of guidewords*. The guidewords coupled with the choice of appropriate operational parameters will be adequate in the vast majority of HAZOP studies. However, it is important that the HAZOP team considers all potential sources of risk and does not limit itself to the standard parameters.

Event tree analysis (ETA)

Event trees are specific examples of the more general approach termed *probability trees*. Whereas probability trees often involve several potential outcomes from an initiating event, event trees normally deal solely with two potential outcomes, which are that the specified event either occurs or does not occur. ETA is an inductive binary logic analysis technique that is closely linked to the technique termed *fault tree analysis*, which is a deductive technique normally used in accident and incident investigation. ETA begins at a defined point in a process and then identifies, in a logical and sequential manner, potential adverse events and their possible consequences. The technique can be used as a simple qualitative approach, or as a quantitative technique if probability values are assigned to each event. Event trees, which identify potential outcomes from events, are applicable where the initiating events proceed in a time or event driven sequence of actions.

The conventions used in ETA are as follows:

- Events proceed from left to right on the page.

- The upper branch identifies that the defined action occurs and the lower branch identifies that the action does not occur.

- The branches are sometimes labelled with Yes and No to confirm the convention of upper and lower branches.

- Probability data may be included on the appropriate branches of the event tree.

Final event probability values are obtained by multiplying the individual probability values for each of the branches leading to the final event. The sum of all the final probability values must add up to 1 if the process events have been analysed correctly.

An event tree analysis should include all significant sources of risk associated with an activity and all operating regimes. An analysis therefore begins with the identification of initiating events for all internal and external sources of risk that may lead to significant consequences. One general problem associated with the use of probability trees is the complexity and size that the trees can grow to. For example, if there are x possible outcomes at each decision node on a probability tree and there are y stages in the tree, the number of end nodes is given by y^x; whereas, in the specific case of event trees, the number of end nodes is greatly reduced because each node has only two possible outcomes, and the total number of end nodes is therefore reduced to $y + 1$. Therefore it is common practice to boundary-limit the scope of individual analyses to reduce the assessments to manageable proportions.

A probabilistic safety analysis of events provides quantified information about the risks associated with each potential outcome, and this enables judgements to be made about the distribution of risks across the whole operation. Figure 11.13 illustrates a simplified ETA for the potential failure of a 400 kV electricity generator transformer's cooling water pump and the starting up of the standby cooling water system. In this example, if the generator transformer oil temperature exceeds 100°C for any significant period of time, the cellulose in the paper insulation surrounding the copper conductors will degrade, become brittle and eventually break down, resulting in a catastrophic transformer failure, caused by arcing between the copper conductors; replacement costs will be in excess of £1m. Transformer oil is therefore normally maintained at or below 50°C in order to minimise insulation degradation. If the main cooling water pump fails (*the initiating event*), a pump failure alarm should be signalled in the control room and the control room operator should then switch to the standby cooling water pump. This system, together with the estimated failure probabilities, is described within the event tree shown in Figure 11.13.

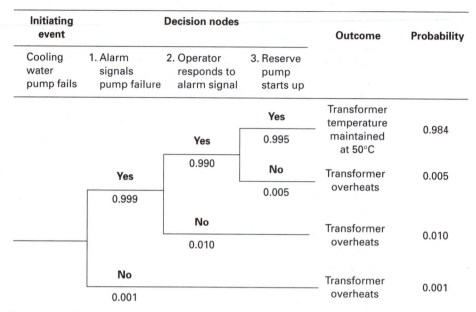

Figure 11.13 Event tree for a high-voltage transformer cooling water pump failure

The event tree shows that, if the main cooling pump fails, the pump failure indicator will operate 999 times out of every 1000 occasions. The second step in the process is that the control room operator observes and responds to the pump failure signal 99 times out of every 100 occasions. The final step in the process shows that the standby pump operates 995 times out of every 1000 demand calls. The event tree analysis identifies that the probability of the standby cooling water pump not coming on line, *if* the main cooling pump fails, is 16 times in 1000 occasions. This is the sum of the probability values displayed on the 'No' arms of the event tree (0.005 + 0.010 + 0.001) and represents a 1.6% failure rate. For such a critical and expensive piece of equipment this reliability would be deemed to be inadequate. The event tree identifies the weakest link in the process as the reliance on the operator to activate the standby system ($p = 0.990$). This stage of the process could be upgraded to an automatic switching system, which responds to the pump failure signal; this type of system would have a reliability factor of at least 0.999 and would result in the overall reliability of the standby cooling system increasing from 0.984 to 0.993 with the failure rate reduced to 0.7%.

Fault tree analysis (FTA)

Fault tree analysis is a deductive analytical technique that describes the relationships that exist between an incident and the events and conditions that led up to the incident. FTA is therefore a retrospective analysis technique that is more appropriately used for investigating the causes of accidents and incidents.

The fault tree is based on the concept that a specific incident results from a set of specific antecedents or conditions. The fault tree approach combines the contributions made to an accident by physical, management and human factor control measures. It is in this context that the technique provides a very effective and powerful accident investigation tool.

Conventions used with fault trees

The main element of the fault tree process involves the use of AND and OR logic gates. The application of these logic gates can be simply explained and understood by comparing them to the existence of physical switches in an electrical circuit and how these switches must be operated in order to pass an electric current.

Consider first the AND logic gate: see Figure 11.14. Electric power can reach point B only if the three switches p, q and r are all closed at the same time. If one switch (or gate) remains open then current cannot flow. In fault tree analysis the AND logic symbol is used to describe the situation where two or more conditions must coexist for an event to occur. If either condition does not exist then the event cannot take place.

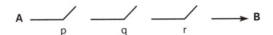

Figure 11.14 The AND logic gate

Consider now the OR logic gate: see Figure 11.15. In this case it is necessary only for switch p, q or r to be closed for electricity to pass from A to B. In fault tree analysis the OR logic symbol is used to describe the situation where only one of two or more conditions must exist for an event to occur. Provided that at least one of these conditions exists the state of the other qualifying conditions is immaterial. The AND and OR logic gates therefore describe the relationships that can exist between the input and the output conditions in one element of a fault tree scenario. Table 11.9 describes the possible output conditions that can exist for varying conditions of two inputs operating under AND and OR logic gates.

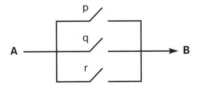

Figure 11.15 The OR logic gate

Greater detail of the mathematical issues associated with the use of fault trees can be obtained from specialist texts (Andrews and Moss, 1993).

Failure modes and effects analysis (FMEA)

Failure modes and effects analysis is an assessment technique that assesses the effect of failures in individual components within an operational system. The technique is inductive and is usually undertaken at the design stage of facilities

Table 11.9 The relationships between the input and output conditions of a device controlled by two AND or OR logic gates

Logic gate	Operational state		
	Input A	Input B	Output
AND	+	+	+
	+	−	−
	−	+	−
	−	−	−
OR	+	+	+
	+	−	+
	−	+	+
	−	−	−

and equipment. The FMEA process involves identifying each individual component within a system and assessing all the possible failure mechanisms and the effects that these may have on the system. A key aspect of this approach is to identify whether individual components will fail to safety or fail to danger. Probability values and impact levels can be ascribed to each mode of failure at each stage of the process in order to quantify the reliability and safety of individual components as well as of the overall system. The prime objective of FMEA is to identify those aspects of a system that do not achieve the desired level of safety in order that these can be rectified.

Andrews and Moss (1993) identified the following critical steps in the FMEA approach:

■ Define the system to be analysed and its required reliability performance.

■ Construct functional and reliability block diagrams (if necessary) to illustrate how the different subsystems are interconnected.

■ Note the assumptions that will be made in the analysis and the definitions of system and subsystem failure modes.

■ List the components, identify their failure modes and, where appropriate, their modal failure rates (alternatively failure rate ranges can be used).

■ Complete a set of FMEA worksheets analysing the effect of each sub-assembly or component failure model on system performance.

■ Enter severity rankings and failure rates or ranges as appropriate on to the worksheets and evaluate the criticality of each failure mode on the system reliability performance.

■ Review the worksheets to identify the reliability-critical components and make recommendations for design improvements or highlight areas requiring further analysis.

Andrews and Moss (1993: 67)

The typical elements of an FMEA report form are shown in Table 11.10.

Table 11.10 Essential components of an FMEA report proforma

Location:			Date:			
System:			Prepared by:			
Subsystem:			Approved by:			
Component identification	Component function	Failure effects	Control measures in place	Severity	Probability	Risk rank

Hazard ranking

Morgan *et al.* (2000) proposed that practical ranking techniques should group hazards into a manageable number of categories that are defined by a set of risk attributes. However:

> Although experts may be able to describe a risk objectively in terms of specified attributes, deciding which of two hazards is more risky requires value judgements.
>
> Morgan *et al.* (2000: 52)

For health and safety risks, Morgan *et al.* (2000) proposed that a suitable categorisation strategy could involve a causally linked process of work activity leading to accident initiating events, which in turn lead to consequences that are perceived and valued by stakeholders. They argued that a risk categorisation scheme should be:

- logically consistent, such that risks are not overlooked or double accounted;
- administratively compatible, such that it fits with existing risk management systems;
- equitable, so that ethical issues and the interests of all stakeholders are considered; and
- compatible with cognitive constraints and biases, such that perceptions, framing effects and mental models, for example, are considered.

Rapid hazard ranking was developed as a screening technique for use in the chemical industry in order to identify significant areas of risk and to avoid spending too much time on low-risk activities. The approach involves categorising the severity and frequency of potential incidents arising from hazards using guide values on logarithmic scales, such as those shown in Table 11.11.

The risk values presented in Table 11.11 use financial severity descriptors that can be applied across a range of hazards; however, other severity descriptors can be employed to describe specific consequences associated with different hazards. Alongside each guide level of severity there is a guide frequency value that is set

Table 11.11 Guide values for rapid risk ranking

A: Estimated severity	B: Risk category	C: Estimated frequency
Less than £1000	1	1 event per year
£1000 – £10 000	2	1 event per 10 years
£10 000 – £100 000	3	1 event per 100 years
£100 000 – £1 000 000	4	1 event per 1000 years
£1 000 000 – £10 000 000	5	1 event per 10 000 years

at a level such that the overall risk defined by the product of the severity and the frequency is approximately constant across all risk categories (in this case £100 to 1000 per event per year).

A rapid hazard ranking assessment is undertaken by addressing each section of a facility, equipment or activity in order to identify potential adverse events that could take place. For each adverse event, the likely consequences are estimated based on the impact of the event on people, environment, production, etc (column A). This enables the appropriate risk category to be identified (column B). Taking each adverse event in turn, the next stage is to determine the probable frequency of occurrence of the event. If the estimated frequency of occurrence is greater than the guide frequency associated with the risk category (column C) then the potential incident is considered to be significant and worthy of a more detailed investigation. If the estimated frequency is less or equal to the guide frequency then the risk level is regarded as acceptable, and a more detailed assessment is considered unnecessary. The more the estimated frequency exceeds the guide frequency then the greater the significance of the risk and the more thorough the subsequent detailed risk assessment should be.

Risk assessment

Risk is generally regarded as the product of two independent variables: the probability of an event occurring, and the consequences of the outcome of the event. However, probability of occurrence and consequences of an incident cannot always be regarded as independent variables. Many adverse events have a range of possible outcomes: for example, one appreciates intuitively that a fall at height will, on average, be more severe than a fall at ground level (see Figure 11.16).

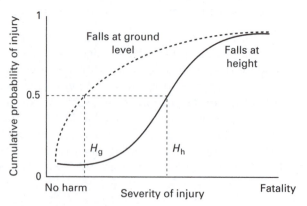

Figure 11.16 Probability–severity curves

In this example it can be seen that the 50% probability of injury value occurs at a lower level of harm for falls at ground level (H_g) than it does for falls at height (H_h). By presenting the number of days lost from work, as a result of an accident, as a probability density function, Cuny and Lejeune (1999) (electricity generating industry) and Drawer and Fuller (2002) (professional football) demonstrated that the consequences of injury follow log-normal distributions in quite different organisational settings.

One of the most important aspects of risk assessment is to ensure that an appropriate technique is employed. The technique chosen should take into account the hazards involved, the range and number of people that may be affected by the hazards, the expertise available to undertake the risk assessment, and the size of the operation. Simple hazards are generally better assessed with simple, qualitative techniques, whereas complex hazards are better assessed by thorough quantified or semi-quantified techniques.

Qualitative approaches

Qualitative approaches are usually descriptive in nature, and do not use standards for values of likelihood, harm or acceptability of risk. Qualitative approaches are also often generic in nature, and are most often used in low-risk environments, such as offices, and in small and medium-sized organisations. The generic approach is normally implemented using a standard risk assessment proforma, such as that shown in Table 11.12. The Health and Safety Executive (1994) provided guidance on a similar approach for assessments in organisations within the commercial, service and light industrial sectors, and prepared case studies to illustrate its application in office, workshop, warehouse, bricklaying and gardening settings (Health and Safety Executive, 1998b).

Table 11.12 An example of a qualitative risk assessment proforma

| Location: | *Garage* | **Assessment prepared by:** | | **Date:** |
| | | **Assessment approved by:** | | **Date:** |
A. Tasks	*B. Hazards*	*C. People affected*	*D. Control measures in place*	*E. Further action required*
Changing used car engine oil	New oil	Mechanic	Protective gloves and hygiene	None
	Used oil (carcinogenic)	Mechanic	Protective gloves and hygiene	Provide annual skin inspection by nurse
	Vehicle exhaust fumes	Mechanic; other employees in the garage	Garage doors remain open	Install local exhaust ventilation
	Hot engine	Mechanic	Protective gloves	None
	Hydraulic lift	Mechanic	Fixed retention bolts	None

In Table 11.12, column A identifies the specific task being undertaken and column B lists each of the hazards associated with this task. Column C identifies those people who may be affected by the hazards, and column D lists the existing control measures in place. If standard procedures are available, the titles of the procedures and the reference numbers for these procedures can be added here. Finally, the person completing the risk assessment makes a subjective assessment of the level of risk and identifies in column E whether any improvements are required in order to ensure that the risks are reduced to an acceptable or tolerable level. When these improvements have been made they should be verified and signed by the responsible manager in order to indicate that the actions have been completed.

Trivial risks, although not necessarily requiring a formal risk assessment, can be easily incorporated into this approach with only the minimum of effort. Inclusion of these risks identifies that they have been considered, and this avoids the situation arising whereby it may not be apparent whether certain risks have been evaluated and considered to be trivial, and therefore have not been recorded in the risk assessment, or whether they have not been considered at all.

Risk ranking

In order to compare levels of risk it is necessary to use quantified or semi-quantified measures to evaluate the risks. A problem with attempting to evaluate risks is that the data available may not be accurate and almost certainly will not be precise. One possible way around this problem is simply to rank the risks rather than to rely on absolute values. Although fatalities and major injuries are the most common currency in defining risk consequences in health and safety management, other consequences, such as product damage, lost production and environmental damage, should not be ignored. By evaluating risks in this holistic manner, severity scales can be used to compare a range of risks within a common framework.

In developing an accident severity scale, there are several factors that must be taken into account:

- the stakeholders for whom the scale is intended;
- the interests of stakeholders;
- the measures that can be used in order to assess the issues;
- the relative importance or weighting applied to each of the individual measures; and
- the format of the overall severity scale.

Addressing each of these factors will ensure that the scale enables the severity of accidents to be ranked and to be understood by the stakeholders concerned. A generic approach showing three issues (people, production, environment) is presented in Figure 11.17.

Floyd and Footitt (1999) reviewed the options available for risk ranking and concluded that although risk ranking did provide a useful technique its application in small and medium-size enterprises was difficult. A number of ranking scales have also been developed to assess the impact of major incidents.

The *Bradford disaster scale* is a ranking approach that deals with the consequences of natural and anthropocentric disasters arising from different sources. The scale generally refers to disasters where there are 10 or more fatalities, insurance losses are in excess of $1m, or 50 or more people are evacuated as a result of

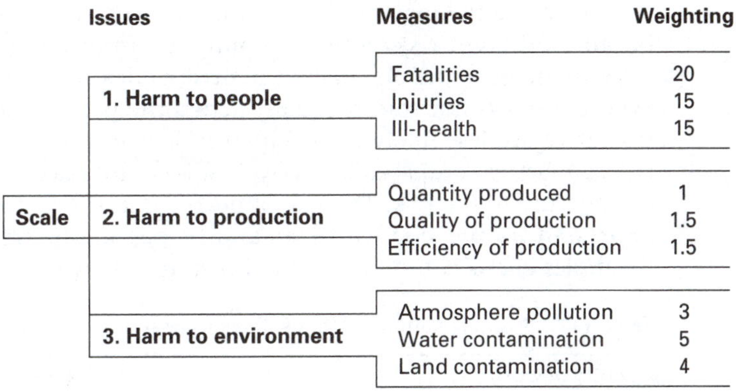

Issues		Measures	Weighting
Scale	1. Harm to people	Fatalities	20
		Injuries	15
		Ill-health	15
	2. Harm to production	Quantity produced	1
		Quality of production	1.5
		Efficiency of production	1.5
	3. Harm to environment	Atmosphere pollution	3
		Water contamination	5
		Land contamination	4

Figure 11.17 Generic approach to developing a risk ranking scale

the disaster. Measures for each of these descriptors are defined using logarithms of the numbers of casualties. The stakeholders for this scale are not defined, but they are most likely to be government departments and the emergency services.

The *Swiss scale* refers to an index introduced by the Swiss Government for defining the consequences and emergency measures required to deal with major industrial accidents. This scale is used to assess the potential impact of an industrial facility on the surrounding environment and population. For each facility nine descriptors that are related to impacts on man, animals and the environment are used, each of which is linearly scaled from 0 to 1. If the impact from one descriptor does not dominate the others, the nine values are combined to provide a single value. In this case the stakeholders targeted are government authorities.

The *major accident reporting scale (MARS)* was introduced by the European Commission in 1984 in order to establish a database of all non-nuclear, non-military, non-mining and non-transport major accidents. The Major Accident Hazards Bureau of the European Commission's Joint Research Centre in Italy manages the MARS database. The information supplied for the database is prepared by the competent authority in each country and is made up of text and numerical data that includes information on the events and circumstances leading up to the accidents, the progress of the accident events, direct and indirect consequences, emergency responses, and the results of the accident investigation.

Risk comparisons

Risk comparisons are often proposed as a way of communicating health and safety risks to the public because, it is argued, the public can more easily understand new risks if they are compared to risks associated with events, activities and technologies with which they are familiar. Risk comparisons provide a number of advantages in risk assessment:

- They do not require levels of risk, in particular those associated with ill-health and fatalities, to be translated into equivalent monetary values.

- They present information in a way that is naturally understood by most people.

- They avoid the difficult concept (for many people) of probability values.

Comparing the magnitude of risks, however, is not necessarily straightforward because different risks must be compared in different ways. Some risks affect large numbers of people, such as the risk of death in a road traffic accident; however, the risk is not spread equally across the population because people who do not drive are less likely to be killed in a road traffic accident. Therefore some risks are better compared in a way that takes into account the form and the level of exposure to the risk. The risk of death from travel, for example, may be better expressed as the chance of a fatality per kilometre or per hour travelled. Examples of risk comparisons are shown in Tables 11.13 and 11.14.

Table 11.13 Average annual risk of death as a consequence of the country of work

Country of work	Annual risk of a fatality
Portugal	1 in 12 500 employees
Austria	1 in 19 600 employees
Spain	1 in 21 300 employees
France	1 in 29 400 employees
Italy	1 in 30 300 employees
Greece	1 in 37 000 employees
Germany	1 in 47 600 employees
United Kingdom	1 in 58 800 employees
Sweden	1 in 90 900 employees

Refer to Health and Safety Commission; National Statistics (2003) for further data

Table 11.14 Average annual risk of death from accidents in various industrial sectors

Industrial sector	Annual risk of a fatality
Agriculture, hunting, forestry, fishing	1 in 13 900 employees
Construction	1 in 19 200 employees
Manufacturing – metal products	1 in 32 300 employees
Extractive and utility supply	1 in 66 700 employees
Manufacturing – chemicals	1 in 111 000 employees
Manufacturing – food products	1 in 143 000 employees
Service industries	1 in 333 000 employees

Refer to Health and Safety Commission; National Statistics (2003) for further data

Covello (1991) summarised the main limitations associated with the risk ranking approach as the failure to identify and emphasise uncertainties in the risk estimates, failure to consider all the dimensions that define and measure the risk, and failure to consider all the dimensions that define people's perceptions about the acceptability of risks and technology. However, he also claimed that well-constructed and well-documented risk comparisons were useful for communicating risk information because they provide:

- a benchmark against which new risks can be compared;
- a means for determining and communicating the relative importance of new risks; and
- a means for informing and educating people about the range and magnitude of risks to which they may be exposed.

Risk matrices

The risk matrix approach is a very common risk assessment technique used in health and safety management (Franks *et al.*, 2002). This approach is fundamentally the same as that described earlier for organisational risks but with minor changes to the severity, probability and risk acceptability scales. The most common matrices employed are the 3×3, 5×5 and 10×10 sized matrices.

The *3×3 matrix* is the simplest version of the risk matrix but the least quantified in nature. The standards used for probability, severity and acceptability in this approach are normally very subjective, such as those shown in Table 11.15.

Table 11.15 Probability, severity and acceptability standards used with a 3×3 risk matrix

Level	Probability, P	Severity, S	Risk levels, P×S	Risk acceptability
1	Low	Low	1–2	Trivial
2	Medium	Medium	3–4	Acceptable
3	High	High	5–9	Unacceptable

The 3×3 matrix provides very little differentiation between low, medium and high levels of risk, and therefore this approach is normally only used with simple hazards in low-risk environments.

The *5×5 matrix* is the most common version of the risk matrix encountered. The standards used for probability, severity and acceptability in this approach are often descriptive, but can be quantified by the use of values such as those shown in Table 11.16.

Table 11.16 Probability, severity and acceptability standards used with a 5×5 risk matrix

Level	Probability, P	Severity, S	Risk levels, P×S	Risk acceptability and actions
1	Very unlikely (10^{-6})	Insignificant (non-injury)	1–4	Trivial risk with no further action required
2	Unlikely (10^{-5})	Minor (first aid)	5–9	Acceptable risk but look for areas of improvement
3	Possible (10^{-4})	Moderate (≤3 days' absence)	10–16	Tolerable risk but improve risk control measures if possible
4	Likely (10^{-3})	Major (>3 days' absence)	17–25	Stop operations and make immediate improvements
5	Very likely (10^{-2})	Severe (fatality)		

The 5×5 matrix provides an adequate level of differentiation between a wide range of risks: therefore this approach can be applied in most work environments and with most hazards.

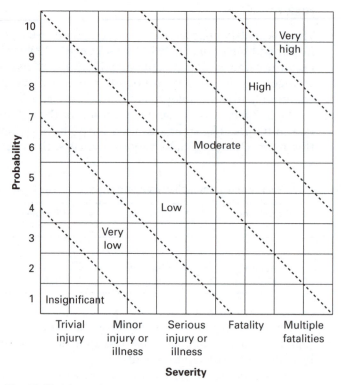

Figure 11.18 The 10×10 risk matrix

The *10×10 matrix* provides the highest level of discrimination between different types and levels of risk, but it is applicable only in those cases where this level of discrimination is essential. The matrix structure may be an expanded version of the 3×3 and 5×5 matrices, but it can also be presented in the format shown in Figure 11.18. In this example the probability and the severity scales are similar to those described previously but the acceptability scale, which is overlaid directly onto the risk matrix, covers a wider range of risk levels. Descriptive or quantified values can be applied to the probability scale in a similar way to those used with the 5×5 matrix.

Hazard rating number

The hazard rating number (HRN) approach (Steel, 1990) uses four factors, which are defined as:

- the probability of exposure (PE) or contact with the hazard;
- the frequency of exposure (FE) to the hazard;
- the number of people (NP) exposed to the risk; and
- the maximum probable loss (MPL) from the adverse event.

Weighted standard values are ascribed to each of these parameters: see Table 11.17.

Table 11.17 Standard scales employed with the HRN

PE values		FE values		NP values		MPL values	
Value	Description	Value	Description	Value	No of people	Value	Description
0	Impossible	0.1	Infrequent	1	1–2	0.1	Scratch
1	Unlikely	0.2	Annual	2	3–7	0.5	Laceration
2	Possible	1.0	Monthly	4	8–15	1	Minor break
5	Even	1.5	Weekly	8	16–50	2	Major break
8	Probable	2.5	Daily	12	> 50	4	Loss of limb
10	Likely	4	Hourly			8	Loss of limbs
15	Certain	5	Constantly			15	Fatality

Source: Steel (1990)

The HRN is derived from the product of the four values:

$$HRN = PE \times FE \times NP \times MPL$$

The HRN is then interpreted by reference to the risk acceptability values shown in Table 11.18 (Steel, 1990).

Table 11.18 Risk acceptability values for the HRN

HRN range	Risk acceptability	Action timetable
0–1	Acceptable	Accept risk
1–5	Very low	Action within 1 year
5–10	Low	Action within 3 months
10–50	Significant	Action within 1 month
50–100	High	Action within 1 week
100–500	Very high	Action within 1 day
500–1000	Extreme	Immediate action
>1000	Unacceptable	Stop activity

Source: Steel (1990)

Although a reduction in the value of any one of the contributing factors will reduce the overall risk, one major benefit of this approach is that the method highlights the particular area that will have the greatest impact on the overall risk value. Therefore risk control measures can be directed to those areas providing the greatest return. However, if the value of PE can be reduced to zero (see Table 11.17), the overall risk level, in theory, is also reduced to zero.

Risk indices

Integrating all probabilities over all consequences for all events provides a total view of the risks associated with an organisation's activities. However, this is frequently very complex and it also proves to be very difficult to communicate the results to stakeholders. There are advantages, therefore, in producing simple risk indices that effectively provide short summaries of the risks. Indices are normally presented as a single measure for a particular type of hazard or consequence. Individual risk (IR) is the probability of a defined individual suffering a fatality over a specified time period. *Fatal accident rates* (FAR) are used to summarise the number of deaths that occur for a range of hazards over a defined period of time: this is normally 10^8 hours of risk exposure, which equates approximately to 1000 employee-working lifetimes. The *individual hazard index* (IHI) is defined as the FAR for a particular type of hazard or type of accident and is calculated on the basis of actual exposure time.

Calverd (2000) proposed a simple risk index that allowed the public to understand the relative risks of different sources of hazard. He proposed that the risk index of an event is defined as

$$R = 10 + \log_{10}P$$

where P is the probability of the adverse event occurring, on a scale from 0 to 1. Therefore an event that is certain to occur will have a probability of 1 and a risk index or R-value of 10 (10 + log1). Calverd (2000) proposed that the R-value could be computed as an annual or a lifetime risk value. An adverse event with a 5% chance of occurring has a probability value of 0.05 and an R-value of 8.7 (10 + log 0.05). R-values could also be calculated on the basis of exposure. The R-values for fatalities in a range of activities are shown in Table 11.19.

Table 11.19 Risk index values as a consequence of an activity

Activity	Risk of a fatality per event	Annual Risk Index
Pregnancy	1 in 10 000	6.0
Air sports	1 in 20 000	5.7
Mountaineering	1 in 100 000	5.0
Anaesthetic	1 in 190 000	4.7
Horse riding	1 in 600 000	4.2
Football	1 in 900 000	4.0
Golf	1 in 10 000 000	3.0
Badminton	1 in 20 000 000	2.7
Air travel	1 in 100 000 000	2.0

There have been around 200 employee fatalities per year, in the UK, in the period 1993–2003, within a workforce of around 20 million people. This represents a probability of death at work of 1×10^{-5}: therefore the average R-value for work-related fatalities in the UK is 5.0. Calverd (2000) therefore suggested that any activity with a fatality R-value greater than 5 should be assessed in order to see whether legislation is appropriate, and any activity with a fatality R-value greater than 6 should have public funds allocated in order to reduce the risks.

Fuzzy logic

Decision-making has been based largely on calculations involving probability, consequence and maximum utility values. However, this approach can have limitations because the real world does not deal just in black and white evaluations. Falconer (1998) argued that the world is uncertain and vague, and that most things exist in grey areas rather than the extremes of safe and unsafe or well and unwell. Everyone may feel unwell to some extent at some time, but they may classify themselves as fit for work: therefore methods of classifying shades of 'unwellness' would be beneficial. This is the main concept underpinning fuzzy set theory, whereby levels are set between 0 (definitely no) and 1 (definitely yes). Because fuzzy theory and probability both use the scale from 0 to 1, it may be argued that fuzzy theory is simply another way of describing probability, but this is not the intention. The key difference is that probability theory defines the probability that a specified accident will or will not occur, whereas fuzzy theory defines the level of the consequences or how injured a person may be as a result of an accident. Therefore a value of 0.95 in probability theory describes the likelihood of someone having a specified injury as 95%, whereas 0.95 in fuzzy theory describes the state whereby someone is likely to be 95% towards the state of complete injury.

The fuzzy theory approach is useful in assessments of operational conditions. One can rarely state that a health and safety management system does not exist, but rather that it exists in a state that is, for example, 75% effective. In fuzzy set theory the safety management system would be ascribed a value of 0.75. For a detailed understanding of fuzzy set theory, specialist texts should be referred to (McNeill and Thro, 1994).

Summary

- Risk assessment enables employers to identify and evaluate the risks associated with their work activities. The responsibility for undertaking work-based risk assessments rests solely with the employer, although, if necessary, an employer may seek specialist external advice.

- Risk assessment provides an effective management process for drawing together operational information and summarising the justification for the implementation of control measures. Risk assessment reports should be reviewed on a regular basis and when changes in operational conditions indicate that risk levels may have changed.

- Organisational risks are dependent on, for example, commercial, legal, economic, human resource and natural events. Risk profiling an organisation's existing risks enables management to prioritise the allocation of financial resources.

- Operational risks can be assessed through a wide range of qualitative, semi-quantified and quantified risk assessment techniques.

■ Uncertainty exists in the results of all risk assessments. Where there is a high level of uncertainty associated with the consequences of an adverse event, greater emphasis should be placed on reducing the probability of the event taking place, and vice versa.

■ Probabilities can be defined through structural, frequentist or subjective approaches. Whenever possible, standards for probability, consequences and risk evaluation should be defined and used with risk assessments.

■ The probability of adverse events taking place and the reliability and maintainability of plant and equipment are important issues in quantified risk assessment. The reliability of plant and equipment can be improved by incorporating redundancy and diversity into control systems.

■ Government risk assessments are more wide-ranging than organisational risk assessments because they must consider the wider social and political implications of risk.

Issues for review and discussion

■ Consider whether the approach for risk assessment adopted within your organisation is driven by legislation or by the desire to gain operational benefits.

■ Consider the sources of information used in your organisation's risk assessments and discuss the level of uncertainty associated with the data.

■ List the ways in which the results of risk assessments are communicated to your organisation's stakeholders.

■ Describe how strategic risks are assessed within your organisation.

■ Describe how operational risks are assessed within your organisation.

■ Discuss whether the current risk assessment techniques employed within your organisation provide an adequate level of information to support management risk decisions.

References

Adams, J. (1995) *Risk*. London: University College London.

Andrews, J.D. and Moss, T.R. (1993) *Reliability and Risk Assessment*. Harlow: Longman Scientific & Technical.

Calverd, A. (2000) An index of risk. *Physics World* (February), **13**, 60.

Chicken, J.C. and Posner, T. (1998) *The Philosophy of Risk*. London: Thomas Telford.

Cooke, R.M. (1997) Uncertainty modelling: examples and issues. *Safety Science*, **26**(1/2), 49–60.

Covello, V.T. (1991) Risk comparisons and risk communication: issues and problems in comparing health and environmental risks. In: R.E. Kasperson and P.J.M. Stallen (eds), *Communicating Risks to the Public*, 79–124. London: Kluwer Academic Publishers.

Cuny, X. and Lejeune, M. (1999) Occupational risks and the value and modelling of a measurement of severity. *Safety Science*, **31**, 213–229.

Drawer, S. and Fuller, C.W. (2002) Evaluating the level of injury in English professional football using a risk based assessment approach. *British Journal of Sports Medicine*, **36**, 446–451.

Elms, D.G. (1992) Risk assessment. In: D. Blockley (ed.), *Engineering Safety*, 28–46. London: McGraw-Hill.

European Commission (1996) *Guidance on Risk Assessment at Work*. Luxembourg: Office for Official Publications of the European Communities.

Evans, A.W. (2003) *Transport Fatal Accidents and FN-curves: 1967–2001*. Sudbury: HSE Books.

Falconer, L. (1998) A review of fuzzy decision-making and its application to managing occupational risks. *Journal of the Institution of Occupational Safety and Health*, **2**(1), 29–36.

Floyd, P.J. and Footitt, A.J. (1999) *Risk Ranking for Small and Medium Enterprises*. CRR 256. Sudbury: HSE Books.

Franks, A., Whitehead, R., Crosswaite, P. and Small, L. (2002) *Application of QRA in Operational Safety Issues*. RR025. Sudbury: HSE Books.

Gadd, S., Keeley, D. and Balmforth, H. (2003) *Good Practice and Pitfalls in Risk Assessment*. RR151. Sudbury: HSE Books.

Health and Safety Commission (1999) *Management of Health and Safety at Work Regulations 1999: Approved Code of Practice*. L21. Sudbury: HSE Books.

Health and Safety Commission (2003) *Health and Safety Statistics: 2002/03*. Sudbury: HSE Books.

Health and Safety Executive (1994) *5 Steps to Risk Assessment*. IND(G)163L. Sudbury: HSE Books.

Health and Safety Executive (1998a) *Assessment Principles for Offshore Safety Cases*. Sudbury: HSE Books.

Health and Safety Executive (1998b) *5 Steps to Risk Assessment: Case Studies*. HSG183. Sudbury: HSE Books.

Health and Safety Executive (1999) *Preparing Safety Reports: Control of Major Accident Hazards Regulations 1999*. Sudbury: HSE Books.

Health and Safety Executive (2001) *Reducing Risks, Protecting People: HSE's Decision-making Process*. Sudbury: HSE Books.

Institution of Chemical Engineers (1985) *Nomenclature for Hazard and Risk Assessment in the Process Industries*. Rugby: Institution of Chemical Engineers.

Kennedy, R. and Kirwan, B. (1998) Development of a hazard and operability-based method for identifying safety management vulnerabilities in high risk systems. *Safety Science*, **30**, 249–274.

Kirwan, B. (1994) *A Guide to Practical Human Reliability Assessment*. London: Taylor & Francis.

McNeill, F.M. and Thro, E. (1994) *Fuzzy Logic: A Practical Approach*. Cambridge: Academic Press.

McQuaid, J. (1995) Improving the use of risk assessment in government. *Transactions of the Institution of Chemical Engineers*, **73B**, S39–S42.

Morgan, M.G., Florig, H.K., DeKay, M.L. and Fischbeck, P. (2000) Categorizing risks for risk ranking. *Risk Analysis*, **20**(1), 49–58.

Standards Australia (1999) *Risk Management*. AS/NZS 4360:1999. Strathfield: Standards Association of Australia.

Standards Australia (2000) *Occupational Health and Safety Management Systems: Specification with Guidance for Use*. AS4801-2000. Strathfield: Standards Australia International.

Steel, C. (1990) Risk estimation techniques. *The Safety & Health Practitioner*, **8** (June), 20–21.

Tyler, B. and Simmons, B. (1995) Hazop studies: knowing their limitations. *Loss Prevention Bulletin*, **121**, 6–8.

Risk control

Try imagining a place where it's always safe and warm.
– Bob Dylan, 'Shelter from the storm' (1974)

Chapter contents

- Introduction
- Safety culture and safety climate
- An integrated approach to risk control
- Designing safe plant and equipment
- An organisation's safe system of work
- Accounting for people in a risk control strategy
- Influencing employees' behaviours
- Health surveillance and epidemiology

Introduction

Risk control strategies are dependent on the various aspects of an organisation's activities. These activities include the control of inputs to the organisation, such as physical, human and information resources, the work environment, such as employees, premises, procedures and processes, and the outputs from the organisation, such as products, services, waste and information. It is not the aim of this chapter to attempt to discuss the individual risk control options available for every hazard in all operational settings; instead, the aim is to discuss the general principles of risk control in terms of physical, management and human factor control measures within the context of an organisation's safety culture. The discussion focuses on the underlying principles of designing and operating safe plant and equipment, the roles of the various layers of an organisation's safe system of work, and the ways in which people can influence the implementation of a health and safety control strategy.

Safety culture and safety climate

Anthropologists used the concept of culture in the nineteenth century in order to explain and understand human societies, but its use was subsequently extended in the twentieth century in an attempt to explain the way in which organisations operated. Although the concept of safety culture has been widely accepted, it has prompted much debate about its utility. The original concept of culture was used to describe and explain differences between long-standing, stable societies. However, modern organisations are constantly under review and subject to change in order to adapt to changing market forces: therefore it has been argued that culture is an inappropriate model for understanding risks in modern organisational settings (Back and Woolfson, 1999).

All organisations can be said to have a culture of some kind because culture is merely a reflection of the way in which an organisation operates (Schein, 1992). For example, the name of any well-known organisation will invariably create an image of the organisation within one's mind: this image will be dependent on a wide range of factors, such as media profile, marketing strategy and environment, health and safety performances. Organisational culture, however, is not a uniform, constant or enduring property; culture can develop or diminish depending on how people within the organisation operate and behave. It may sometimes be strong and at other times be weak; it may be strong in some parts of an organisation while weak in other parts. Strong organisational cultures are claimed to have (Northcraft and Neale, 1990):

- a corporate philosophy;
- a belief that people are an important organisational resource;
- charismatic leaders;
- rituals and ceremonies; and
- a clear view of where the organisation is heading.

Culture, however, is much more than just these five elements; it also describes how, where, who, when and why an organisation operates in a particular way. Organisational culture may be regarded as a buffer or moderating effect on the way in which an organisation, and the people within the organisation, react to new and/or existing situations and events. An organisation's culture is fashioned mainly by the leadership style of the senior management, because it is very difficult, if not impossible, for employees to create or change an organisation's culture by themselves. However, if it can be said that senior management creates an organisation's culture, it is almost as true to say that a significant change in organisational culture can be achieved only by a change in organisational leadership.

Safety culture

The idea of safety culture developed from the underpinning concept of organisational culture. However, there are still variations in the definitions of safety culture and the related issue of safety climate (Guldenmund, 2000). The phrase 'safety culture' came to prominence following a number of major accidents in the late 1980s – in particular the Chernobyl nuclear accident in Russia in 1986, the *Piper Alpha* oilrig explosion and fire in the North Sea in 1988, and the Clapham Junction train crash in London in 1988. In the UK, the Confederation of British Industry (1990) adopted a simple definition of safety culture as 'the way we do things around here'. The UK Advisory Committee on the Safety of Nuclear Installations (ACSNI), however, provided a more detailed definition of safety culture as:

> The product of individual and group values, attitudes, perceptions, competencies and patterns of behaviour that determine the commitment to, and the style and proficiency of, an organisation's health and safety management.
>
> Health and Safety Commission (1993: 23)

This definition relates safety culture very strongly to human factor issues, and removes it from the way in which physical and management issues may impact on an organisation's safety culture. The Health and Safety Executive (1991) identified the implementation of the following activities as key factors in promoting a positive health and safety culture in an organisation:

- methods of *control* within the organisation;
- the means of securing *cooperation* between individuals, safety representatives and groups;
- the methods of *communication* throughout the organisation;
- the *competence* of individuals.

> Health and Safety Executive (1991: 16)

However, the Health and Safety Executive (HSE) later adopted the ACSNI definition of safety culture, but added:

> Organisations with a positive safety culture are characterised by communications founded on mutual trust, by shared perceptions of the importance of safety and by confidence in the efficacy of preventive measures.
>
> Health and Safety Executive (2000a: 16)

The HSE therefore recognised the important influence that risk control measures can have on an organisation's safety culture in addition to the contribution from employees' attitudes, perceptions and actions. In a report prepared for the HSE about the measurement of the maturity of an organisation's safety culture, it was also acknowledged that:

> Cultural or behavioural approaches to safety improvement are at their most effective when the technical and systems aspects of safety are performing adequately and the majority of accidents appear to be due to behavioural or cultural factors. The safety culture maturity model is therefore only of relevance to organisations that fulfil a number of specific criteria. These include:
>
> - an adequate Safety Management System
> - technical failures are not causing the majority of accidents

- the company is compliant with health and safety law
- safety is not driven by the avoidance of prosecution but by the desire to prevent accidents.

Fleming (2001: 4)

It is clear, therefore, that if these precursors must be in place before a safety culture is worth measuring, then clearly these issues must also form a strong underpinning element of an organisation's safety culture. This change in approach to safety culture is embodied in the definition offered by Toft and Reynolds (1999):

> Safety culture can be defined as those sets of norms, roles, beliefs, attitudes and social and technical practices within an organisation which are concerned with minimising the exposure of individuals to conditions considered to be dangerous.

Toft and Reynolds (1999: 5)

This approach to safety culture takes into account an organisation's full range of physical, management and human factor risk control measures, and it is this holistic approach that is adopted here for discussions of best-practice health and safety management. Guldenmund (2000) proposed a framework that took account of these varied elements of risk control, and described how they influence safety culture within an organisation: see Table 12.1.

Table 12.1 Layers of safety culture that can be studied within an organisation

Layer of culture	Visibility of layer	Examples
Outer layer: comprises artefacts	Visible issues that are not always discussed in terms of safety culture	Management statements, audit reports, use of protective equipment, accidents and incidents, safety campaigns
Middle layer: comprises values and attitudes towards physical, management and human factor controls and behaviours	Explicit and conscious statements that are clearly related to organisational safety culture	Employee attitudes, health and safety policies and procedures, training, accident reports, job descriptions
Central core: comprises basic assumptions about time, space, human nature, activity and relationships	Implicit statements and actions about the way in which health and safety is managed within the organisation	Issues related to outer layer artefacts and middle layer values and attitudes

Source: Adapted from Guldenmund (2000)

Safety culture is often perceived to be a measure of organisational performance, whereas the incidence of accidents and ill-health is more often considered to be a measure of individuals' performance. However, these two measures are closely related, because accidents are dependent on individuals' actions and behaviours and the organisational standards for physical, management and human factor control measures. Accidents and incidents in many organisations are infrequent events, and so it is difficult to demonstrate an association between organisational safety culture and this measure of safety performance. Therefore, the absence of accidents, and in particular the absence of low probability/high consequence accidents, is not necessarily an indication of good safety performance or the presence of a good safety culture within an organisation.

There are concerns about the use and pervading nature of the term 'safety culture' and its adoption within organisations. It has been claimed, for example, that safety culture is little more than a manipulative management tool to control the actions and beliefs of the workforce (Back and Woolfson, 1999). Clearly, if this is the case, it must be questioned whether such an approach to health and safety management is justifiable. There is also an argument that the development of a specified safety culture could, in reality, be self-defeating in its aim of achieving improved safety performance:

> Company imposed safety cultures are likely to devalue and erode the collective understanding that the workforce has about itself and workplace dangers through its practical day-to-day experience. Culture, far from facilitating free and open communication between the top and bottom of the hierarchy, can actively impede the collective articulation of the view from below.
>
> Back and Woolfson (1999: 16)

In addition, Back and Woolfson expressed strong concerns that safety professionals, rather than empowering employees to understand and address safety concerns, disenfranchised employees through the use of technical and social languages that were incomprehensible to the workforce:

> Perhaps, before we jump on the bandwagon of 'culture-speak', it is time to remind ourselves that we live in a diverse society, with diverse interests and even a diverse language. In order to effectively improve safety in the modern workplace, we will therefore have to improve our ability to exchange, adopt and integrate diverse views, rather than smothering 'discordant' voices under a blanket which we then label 'safety culture'.
>
> Back and Woolfson (1999: 16)

Safety climate

There is much debate about the concept of organisational climate and its relationship with organisational culture (Guldenmund, 2000). Reichers and Schneider (1990: 29) concluded that 'Culture exists at a higher level of abstraction than climate, and climate is a manifestation of culture.'

In terms of health and safety management, safety culture can be viewed as an organisation's long-term experiences and practices, whereas safety climate can be viewed as the current variations or nuances of the long-term culture. Davies *et al.* (2001) described safety climate as follows:

> This term tends to be used at a more local level to describe the tangible outputs of an organisation's health and safety culture as perceived by individuals or work groups at a point in time. In general terms a company may have, or aspire to, an overall health and safety culture with specific attributes, but underlying this will be a range of health and safety climates that may differ over time, between groups of people, between sites and so on.
>
> Davies *et al.* (2001: Part 1, 1)

From this perspective it can be seen that safety climate may be reflected in the results obtained from employee questionnaires and site audits, and hence measures of safety climate may provide useful management information for assessing the changing patterns of employees' views about health and safety management.

Safety culture maturity model

Assessments of cultural maturity have been used in a number of contexts including software development, project management, human resources and quality. Fleming (2001) developed a safety culture maturity model with five levels of organisational maturity, with the aim of establishing an organisation's current level of safety cultural maturity, and identifying those actions required to improve the safety culture. Although the model was developed for the offshore oil and gas industry and was based only on human factor issues, the concept should be equally applicable in other industrial and commercial sectors, especially if the wider context of physical and management controls were to be incorporated within the model. The model utilised 10 elements to describe the safety culture of an organisation (Fleming, 2001):

- management commitment and visibility;
- communication;
- productivity versus safety;
- learning organisation;
- safety resources;
- participation;
- shared perceptions about safety;
- trust;
- industrial relations and job satisfaction; and
- training.

The five levels of maturity were defined as follows (Fleming, 2001):

- *Emerging:* where safety is defined in terms of physical and management controls and where compliance with legislation is a driving factor. Health and safety are not viewed as important issues by line management, and therefore health and safety do not appear high on the business agenda.
- *Managing:* where health and safety are considered as business risks and therefore management will spend time reducing the levels of accidents and ill-health. Health and safety is controlled within the business through physical and management controls, and accidents and incidents are perceived by management to be a consequence of employees' unsafe acts and omissions. Performance is measured through reactive measures such as accident rates.
- *Involving*: where management understands that an improved health and safety performance will come from employee involvement. Management also appreciates that accident causation is multifaceted and cannot generally be ascribed to a single causative factor. Employees are keen to work with management to improve health and safety performance.

- *Cooperating*: where employers view the control of health and safety risks as a moral as well as an economic issue. Although employers accept that accident causation is multifaceted, it is also recognised that most accidents have their roots in management decisions. Organisations are proactive in their approach to accident reduction, and performance is monitored using proactive as well as reactive measures.

- *Continuous improvement*: where the prevention of accidents and ill-health is a core activity of the business. Although the organisation is likely to have experienced an extended period of low accidents and cases of ill-health, it continually reviews performance and seeks to find ways of sustaining its high level of performance.

Although it is generally assumed that health and safety performance improves as the level of maturity of the safety culture increases, the evidence to support this hypothesis is limited. This issue is particularly important in the developing trend of partnership arrangements, which first came to prominence when organisations began to downsize and concentrate their resources on core activities (Fuller and Vassie, 2002). Cultural alignment is considered important in partnership arrangements because it generates mutual understanding and cooperation between the partners, and because significant differences between the partners' cultures could create conflicts and barriers to cooperative methods of working (Vassie and Fuller, 2003).

Measurement of safety climate and culture

Culture and climate are abstract concepts that are used to provide a holistic measure of the way in which an organisation operates. However, the variations in the definitions and the multidimensionality of the constructs create difficulties, because different researchers focus on different issues and consequently meaningful measurement and verification of an organisation's climate/culture prove to be very difficult. Dimensions that are normally incorporated into measures of safety climate and culture include the perceptions, beliefs and attitudes of the people within the sample population, but some studies include data from audits and interviews covering a broader range of issues.

Broad-based measures

Fuller (1999) described a broad-based measure of safety climate/culture that used horizontal slices through an organisation's operational activities and vertical slices through the management/employee structure. The approach assessed issues related to how well employees understood what they were expected to achieve, how well employees implemented what they were expected to do, and how well the organisation performed. This approach utilised information obtained from questions, observations, site inspections, document inspections and accident and incident reports. Results from the assessments enabled the strengths and weaknesses of the organisation's safety climate/culture to be addressed and hence appropriate health and safety improvement programmes to be identified.

Questionnaire-based measures

The largest proportion of research carried out on safety climate/culture measurement has involved employee questionnaires. Davies *et al.* (2001) reviewed a range of questionnaires that were developed for the offshore oil industry. These identified the key issues that organisations should consider when developing a safety climate/culture measure, and provided a core set of questions for use within the questionnaires. They recommended that questionnaires should be limited to 60 questions selected from a core set of 114 questions. These questions, however, could be supplemented with questions about the demographics and accident history of the sample population. At least one free response question should also be incorporated into the questionnaire to provide information about the concerns of employees. The bank of 114 core questions suggested for the surveys was categorised into 11 sections:

Section 1: Training and competence (8).
Section 2: Job security and job satisfaction (6).
Section 3: Pressures for production (7).
Section 4: Communication (12).
Section 5: Perceptions of personal involvement in health and safety (7).
Section 6: Accidents, incidents and near misses (11).
Section 7: Perceptions of organisational and management commitment to health and safety – general issues (16).
Section 8: Perceptions of organisational and management commitment to health and safety – specific issues (14).
Section 9: Merits of health and safety procedures, instructions and rules (14).
Section 10: Rule breaking (14).
Section 11: Workforce view on the state of safety and organisational culture (13).

Eight of the 114 core questions that were identified by Davies *et al.* (2001) provided information in two sections of the questionnaire and, therefore, this resulted in the total of 122 questions in the eleven sections identified above.

Responses to the questions and/or statements included in the survey instrument are gathered using five-point Likert scales graded from 1 (very dissatisfied or strongly disagree) to 5 (very satisfied or strongly agree).

An integrated approach to risk control

It is essential when addressing the issue of risk control that all options are considered in order to develop a coherent, cost-effective strategy. The results obtained from all relevant risk assessments should be reviewed during this process in order to ensure that the overall level of organisational risk is reduced rather than merely moving risks from one area of work to another, such as from the production function to the maintenance function.

Developing a risk control strategy

Risks arise from three contributory factors: the hazards, such as electricity, forklift trucks and chemicals; operations, such as office work, production and transportation; and people, such as crowds, managers, administrators and lone and shift workers. The overall level of risk is dependent on the interactions existing between these three contributory factors, and the magnitude of the resultant risk can be represented by a three-dimensional matrix such as that depicted in Figure 12.1.

Plotting the risk levels associated with each factor onto the three-dimensional matrix identifies the overall level of risk. For example, if the work involves using a harmful chemical, the hazard rating may be assigned a value of 2; if this chemical is used on a medium-sized production facility the operations rating may also be 2; and if the number of operators involved in the process is high the people rating may be 3. These ratings would therefore give an overall risk level of 12 (2×2×3). This level of risk must be mitigated by the application of physical, management and human factor control measures that achieve an overall level of control equivalent to the risk. If the matrix presented in Figure 12.1 represents the sources and levels of risk then the combinations of control measures available to mitigate them can be represented within the matrix illustrated in Figure 12.2.

If, as in the previous example, the overall level of risk is 12, the levels of physical, management and human factor controls implemented must at least be at level 2 with at least one control factor at level 3 in order to achieve an overall level of control equal to 12. This method of representation illustrates clearly an important issue: the higher the overall level of risk, the more important it becomes to have a balanced range of control measures in order to attain an acceptable overall level of risk control.

The hierarchy of controls principle

Although the approach adopted for health and safety controls should provide a balanced portfolio of physical, management and human factor measures, it is normal also to take into account what is referred to as the *hierarchy of controls principle*. This principle is embedded within the goal-setting approach of modern UK health and safety legislation, such as the Management of Health and Safety at Work Regulations 1999, and the principle of 'as low as reasonably practicable' (ALARP).

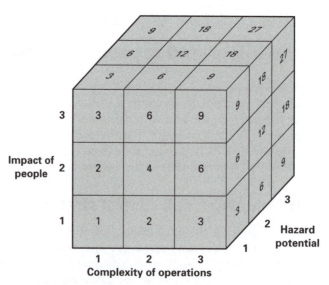

Figure 12.1 Contributory factors influencing the level of risk

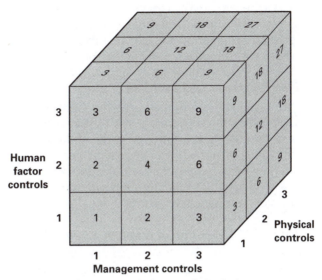

Figure 12.2 Control levels achieved through the use of physical, management and human factor measures

The six levels of control

The hierarchy of controls provides six levels or types of control measure, which should be taken into consideration when defining a risk control strategy. The higher up the list a control measure appears, the larger the number of 'at risk' people who are protected. Therefore, although the costs associated with the implementation of control measures at the top of the list may appear to be greater, because they protect a larger proportion of the workforce they are often more cost effective.

Level 1: Elimination or substitution of the hazard

Clearly, eliminating a hazard ensures that no one will be affected by the risks associated with the hazard. The option of hazard elimination is only achieved realistically at the process or equipment design stage: the elimination of hazards in an existing piece of equipment or process is more difficult, and can often be achieved only through a major change or by shutting down an operation. Substituting a hazard, which is often a more achievable option, entails avoiding the use of a product, avoiding a process or avoiding a procedure. However, although the original hazard may be substituted, it is always important to understand that one hazard is invariably replaced by another hazard, which in turn brings its own risks.

Level 2: Enclosing or modifying a process

Enclosing a hazard normally involves the application of engineered controls and attempting to physically separate people from the source of risk in order to avoid contact. The success of engineered controls is based on the assumption that, once they have been installed, they do not require day-to-day interventions through the use of, for example, safe systems of work or personal protective equipment. However, because engineered controls introduce a strong sense of security to a workforce, employees may forget to implement commonsense measures of control in their normal working environment, or the controls may even engender a feeling that greater risks can be taken with impunity. In addition, most engineered controls introduce issues related to their reliability and maintainability.

Level 3: Use of safe systems of work

Safe systems of work may take the form of verbal communication between a supervisor and an operator, or a formal written operational procedure. The success of a safe system of work is dependent on its rigorous implementation by everyone concerned. It is important to recognise that there may be more than one way of carrying out an activity safely: therefore, if different people carry out the same activity in different but safe ways the overall result may still be the creation of an unsafe environment.

Level 4: Modification of employee behaviour

Throughout the working day, employers rely on employees to carry out operations in a safe and healthy way. Human factor issues therefore form a very important part of providing a safe working environment. Ensuring that a person is competent to carry out his or her work is no different from the accepted business practice of ensuring that equipment is fit for purpose. Before purchasing a major new piece of equipment, management will spend time defining the capability and performance characteristics required and the maintenance schedules for the equipment. This process produces a detailed specification for the equipment; a similar approach is equally applicable to the selection and training of employees and contractors.

Level 5: Use of personal protective equipment

It is very unusual and certainly undesirable for personal protective equipment (PPE) to provide the only control measure for a particular operation. However, PPE does provide valuable point-of-contact protection for various vulnerable parts of the body, such as the head, eyes, hands and feet. PPE is normally used to provide a back-up or second line of defence to an engineered control measure or a safe system of work. It may appear that the provision of PPE is economically preferable to the installation of engineered controls; however, the cost of PPE for a large workforce on a regular basis may prove to be the most expensive option in the longer term while also providing a lower level of protection for the workforce. It is only in exceptional circumstances that PPE provides the only or first line of defence. This situation may occur where it is clearly impracticable to provide any other means of protection, such as during emergency situations where, for example, a rescuer uses respiratory protective equipment or heat-resistant clothing in order to enter a hazardous environment to rescue someone or to isolate a leaking vessel.

Level 6: Use of workplace monitoring and health surveillance

Workplace monitoring and employee health surveillance should be the last lines of defence in any control strategy, as they are identifying conditions of failure in control. These control measures may, however, be used to provide a retrospective back-up or second line of defence for an engineered control measure or a safe system of work. Workplace monitoring and health surveillance are used more as means of confirming that adequate control has been achieved by other means than as means of control in themselves. In a similar way that health surveillance provides a last line of control, it can be argued that accident statistics provide the ultimate indication of how effective an organisation's control strategy is.

Designing safe plant and equipment

An integrated approach to risk control involves the use of physical, management and human factor control measures. Management controls can be developed and modified over a period of time, but they still depend on employees implementing them correctly every time a task is carried out. However, provided that plant and equipment are designed with inbuilt safety features, they should operate safely over an extended period of time and be relatively tolerant of employee errors. Plant and equipment should therefore be designed with sufficient integral safety to cope with operator error and/or equipment failure. The standard approach for protecting stakeholders from operational risks is to provide several *layers of protection* through design principles, process alarms, critical alarms, automatic responses, physical barriers and emergency response procedures (Bollinger *et al.*, 1996).

Kletz (1979, 1990) provided the seminal discussions on the safe design of plant for hazardous operations, and stated:

> The best way of preventing a large leak of hazardous material is not to use the hazardous material; or not to use so much of it; or to use it at lower temperatures and pressures. We are coming to realise that we may be able to develop processes that require low inventories, or use safer materials, or use the hazardous ones at lower temperatures and pressures; that we can keep lambs instead of lions.
>
> Kletz (1979: 7–8)

Inherently safe design principles

The underlying principle of inherent safety is the elimination of hazards at the design stage rather than controlling them through the addition of layers of protection. Many of the ideas on inherent safety were developed in the chemical industry (Health and Safety Executive, 2000b), where the concept was taken to have the following meaning:

> A chemical manufacturing process is inherently safer if it reduces or eliminates the hazards associated with materials and operations used in the process, and this reduction or elimination is permanent and inseparable.
>
> Bollinger *et al.* (1996: 7)

The inherently safe design approach involves managing the three main steps involved in major accidents (Bollinger *et al.*, 1996):

- *Initiation*. Eliminate the events that can create an accident.
- *Propagation*. Eliminate the processes that may maintain or amplify an accident.
- *Termination*. Improve the processes that could stop or attenuate an accident.

Adopting the principle of inherent safety therefore concentrates on making plant and equipment safe at the drawing board stage rather than relying on the addition of physical, management and human factor controls at or after commissioning. Kletz (1990) described 11 factors that should be taken into account during the design of plant and equipment, and claimed that these factors could lead to safer operations.

Intensification or minimisation. Safe plants should use, generate and store the lowest possible quantities of hazardous substances. Ideally the quantities should be so low that, if an accident or leakage of the substance occurred, there would be no significant risk to people or the environment. Intensification can be achieved through process design, standard engineering principles and reductions in the quantities of stored materials. Intensification is normally the preferred option on the grounds of economics, because the smaller the quantities of substances used in a process, the lower the fixed costs invested in the plant and the lower the operational, maintenance and energy costs.

Substitution. Where intensification is not appropriate or possible in a plant design, replacement of the hazardous substances with a safer alternative should be considered. Substitution is normally the preferred option on purely safety grounds.

Attenuation or moderation. This provides a different approach to intensification by, for example, storing a hazardous substance such as chlorine at low temperatures in liquid form rather than in gaseous form at high pressures. A disadvantage of the attenuation process is that additional processes may be required to cope with the changed conditions: in the example presented an evaporation process may be required to return the liquid chlorine to the desired gaseous reaction state.

Limitation of effects. Plant should be designed so that if leakages of hazardous materials can occur they will occur at the minimum possible rates and/or will be contained safely. Leakages can be minimised, for example, by reducing the sizes of pipes and storage and reaction vessels. Operational procedures should also be considered at the plant design stage so that issues such as hazardous exothermic reaction conditions cannot create runaway reactions.

Simplification. The concept of simplification is based on the premise that simple plant designs create fewer opportunities for operator errors. Plant simplification is often a by-product of the intensification, substitution and/or attenuation processes. A process can be simplified, for example, by designing a reaction vessel to withstand the maximum or minimum (vacuum) conceivable process pressures, as this avoids the need for high/low pressure interlock systems and the use of bursting discs.

Domino effect. It is important to avoid a situation where a minor incident can escalate into a disaster. This is a major issue when building hazardous plants in congested areas where there is the potential for *knock-on* or *domino effects* to occur. These dangerous situations can arise, for example, when the debris from a fire and/or explosion at one facility impacts on adjacent facilities.

Construction and commissioning errors. Plant designs should minimise the potential for components to be incorrectly assembled at the construction stage and/or inadequately tested during the commissioning stage.

Plant and equipment status. A well-designed plant should aid routine operations by visually indicating the status of, for example, valves, pumps, motors and fans, and should avoid the generation of spurious or invalid status signals.

Plant design tolerance limits. Safe plant and equipment should have sufficient tolerance levels incorporated into the design to ensure that foreseeable excursions from normal operational conditions will not create unsafe situations.

Operability. Design principles should ensure that the necessary physical control systems are considered and incorporated into plants at the conceptual stage rather than relying on the addition of control systems at or after the commissioning stage. Process designs that incorporate minimal or measured responses to foreseeable changes in operational conditions are preferable to those designs that are very susceptible to minor changes in operating conditions, as these designs are more vulnerable to the possibility of catastrophic failures.

Maintenance. It is often safer and more economic to minimise the range of components installed in a plant. If there is a wide range of pumps, valves and pipes used in a plant design then sooner or later the wrong replacement type will be fitted during a maintenance outage. It is safer, therefore, to minimise the range of replacement options, even if this requires fitting a higher specification component in some situations than is strictly necessary. Although the actual unit replacement cost may be higher in these circumstances, quite often these additional costs may be recovered through the reduced levels of stores stock that are required and through a reduction in the number of plant failures caused by incorrect components being fitted.

The inherently safe design principle can be implemented by utilising the key words described above during the design of plant and equipment, and by considering the impacts that a new process or piece of equipment may have on stakeholders. Kletz (1990) estimated that the potential savings available from operating inherently safe plant and equipment amount to between 5% and 10% of the capital cost of the plant. These savings accrue from factors related to the reduced levels of add-on protective systems, such as trips, alarms, leak detectors, isolation valves and firefighting systems. However, reduced inventories of hazardous substances produce the biggest savings through the reductions made in the size of plant items such as reactors, heat exchangers, storage vessels and piping. There are also significant potential savings from the reduced levels of testing, inspections and maintenance required for add-on safety-related control systems.

Lines of defence

When the inherent hazards associated with a process have been minimised, other layers of protection can be built into operational processes in order to lower the level of residual risk even further:

- *passive systems,* such as operating a chemical process in a reaction vessel that has been built to withstand much higher pressures than those that could conceivably be generated;

- *active systems,* such as incorporating control systems that shut off feedstock to a reaction vessel in the event of high temperatures or pressures that might lead to runaway reactions; and

- *procedural systems,* such as incorporating instruments for indicating operational parameters that require an operator to take remedial action if there are excursions outside the desired operational conditions.

Passive protection systems are inherently safer than active systems, but both of these systems are inherently safer than procedural systems. A line of defence (LoD) is effectively one level or one unit of risk reduction. Risk assessment techniques should be used at the design stage in order to define the number of LoDs required to reduce the risks associated with plant or equipment to an acceptable level, or to a level that can be defined as 'as low as reasonably practicable'. If the number of LoDs implemented meets or exceeds the number defined by the risk assessment then the 'as low as reasonably practicable' requirement has been met. The number of LoDs incorporated into an installation can therefore be used as a measure of the margin of acceptability of the control system.

The margin of acceptability is defined as:

$$\text{Margin of acceptability} = \text{LoD}_{available} - \text{LoD}_{required}$$

Therefore, for each possible system fault sequence i, the resultant value for the margin of acceptability should be greater than zero for the control measures to be regarded as acceptable:

$$[\text{LoD}_{available} - \text{LoD}_{required}]_i > 0 \qquad (\text{for } i = 1 \text{ to } n)$$

A quantified system can be used for assessing the margin of acceptability that is based on the probability of failure (PoF) of a control system, where the PoF lies between 0 and 1:

$$\text{LoD} = - \log_{10} (\text{PoF})$$

Hence a protection system with an LoD rating of 1 would have a probability of failure of 10^{-1} whereas a protection system with an LoD rating of 2 would have a probability of failure of 10^{-2}, and so on. Therefore, as the probability of a failure becomes smaller, the LoD value increases. It can be seen, therefore, that in *this* case the LoD value does not indicate the number of protection systems but the quality of the systems in place.

Quantified risk assessments based on this approach require the definition of an acceptable level or standard of risk and a consequence criterion that enables numerical calculations to be undertaken (Maddison and Kirk, 1995; Stansfield, 1998). The usual criterion used in these cases is a societal risk parameter, which is normally represented by the FN-curve.

An alternative way of assessing the overall acceptability of the LoDs is to use a simple subjective approach. This may entail an examination of the number and quality of the LoDs provided as a safeguard against each potential fault sequence i. An evaluation and a level of acceptance are then adopted whereby the $\text{LoD}_{available}$ is greater than the specified criterion, such as the number and quality of safety controls. This approach requires a compromise to be reached in the assessment process between the value of a small number of high-quality protection systems compared with a large number of low-quality protection systems. This qualitative approach is considered to be particularly useful where the risks associated with a hazard are defined largely by human errors.

The safety lifecycle

New plant and equipment goes through a number of development stages before it is operational and a number of post-operational stages before it is demolished. These stages are referred to as the plant or equipment's lifecycle, and they encompass all activities in the development and use of plant and equipment:

- conception;
- specification;
- design;
- manufacture;
- installation and commissioning;
- operation and maintenance;
- modifications and retrofits; and
- decommissioning.

There are opportunities at each stage of the lifecycle to consider how to minimise risks and how the benefits afforded by the principles of inherent safety can be adopted. The International Electrotechnical Commission (1998, 2000) standard IEC 61508 presented a framework containing these stages known as the *safety lifecycle*: see Figure 12.3.

In order to ensure the success of the safety lifecycle approach, it is important to develop a documented procedure and a record for each new item of plant or equipment. The procedure should specify that a risk assessment be completed at each stage, and should assign management responsibilities for approving and recording the completion of each stage of the lifecycle.

Conception

At the research and conception stage there is a significant opportunity to influence the level of inherent safety built into a process, because this stage defines the fundamental approach of a new project. It has been claimed that if a safety problem costs $1 to be eliminated at the conception stage, it would cost $10 to eliminate it at the flow sheet stage, $100 at the final design stage, $1000 at the production stage, and $10 000 at the post-incident stage (Bollinger *et al.*, 1996). Key elements of this stage include defining:

- the scope and use of the plant or equipment;
- the boundaries of the project, such as whether the process or equipment will be a stand-alone operation or whether it will be an integral part of a more complex new or existing process; and
- the scope of the risk assessment, such as whether it should include only the specific new process, encompass the surrounding and/or connected processes and address the competence levels of the potential operators and maintenance staff.

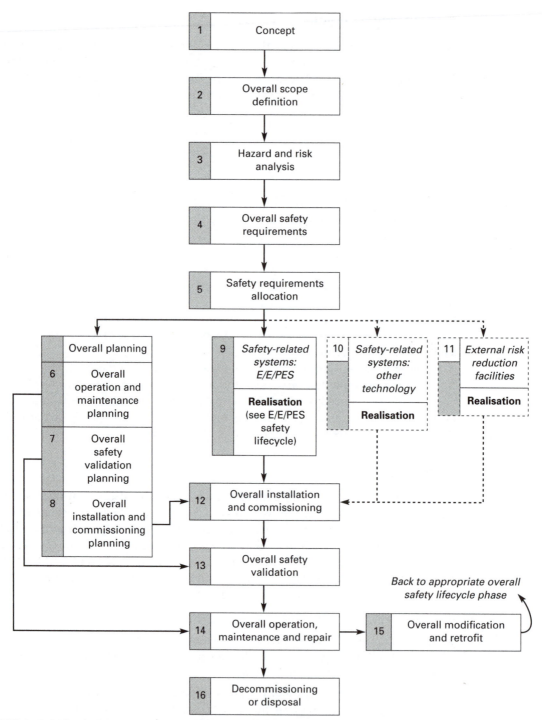

NOTE 1 – Activities relating to *verification, management of functional safety* and *functional safety assessment* are not shown for reasons of clarity but are relevant to all overall, E/E/PES and software safety lifecycle phases.
NOTE 2 – The phases represented by boxes 10 and 11 are outside the scope of this standard.
NOTE 3 – The IEC 61508-2 and IEC 61508-3 deal with box 9 (realisation) but they also deal, where relevant, with the programmable electronic (hardware and software) aspects of boxes 13, 14 and 15.

Figure 12.3 The safety lifecycle model
Source: IEC (1998, 2000); Copyright © 1998, IEC, Geneva, Switzerland. www.iec.ch

Specification

The specification stage involves ensuring that the appropriate safety control measures are identified and included within the plant or equipment. HAZOP, ETA and FMEA provide useful risk analysis techniques at this stage. It is important to consider previous accidents and incidents at similar plant and equipment at this stage because it will be inherently safer if the causes of these incidents are designed out of the process. Key elements of this stage include:

- identifying the presence of intrinsic hazards, such as electricity, pressure, temperature and flammable substances;
- identifying the presence of extrinsic hazards, such as the choice of automatic or manual operational systems; and
- completing a risk assessment for normal, abnormal and emergency conditions.

Acceptable and/or tolerable risk levels and standards for the process or equipment and the types and levels of risk control measures required to achieve these levels should also be specified at this stage.

Design

The design stage involves ensuring that the specified control procedures are incorporated into the plant or equipment design in an inherently safe way. This is achieved by defining the critical control levels (Bollinger *et al.*, 1996) required for each operational parameter: see Figure 12.4.

An important control issue contained within Figure 12.4 is that plants are designed to operate under optimum conditions, or at a specified *control point* for each parameter, but they actually operate within *quality assurance limits* around this control point. The plant should, however, be designed to function over a wider operational envelope with *upper and lower mandatory action values*, where preventive actions should be taken to correct and reset the operational conditions to the correct levels. In addition, the plant instrumentation should be designed to monitor and control the plant or equipment over an even wider range of values. The boundaries of this range provide *upper and lower critical action values*, where

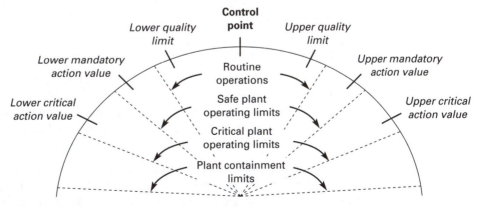

Figure 12.4 Plant operational ranges and control limits

further corrective action should be taken in order to maintain operational conditions within the process's safe operating limits. Finally, an inherently safe plant should be designed so that vessels, pipes, reactors etc operate within all conceivable values of the parameter. Key elements of this stage include:

- implementing appropriate design standards and guidance documents; and
- preparing a design document that contains a record of the specified safety systems.

Design standards that are intended for control systems should be based on issues related to the three criteria of functionality, availability and survivability:

- *Functionality* refers to the duty that a control system component is expected to perform, such as a requirement for a safety switch to operate at 10 kV for up to 30 times per day or for a reaction vessel to operate at 10 bar and 250°C in an inert atmosphere.
- *Availability* refers to a component's reliability to perform one or more desired operations, such as less than 1 failure per 10^5 operations.
- *Survivability* refers to the performance of a component under, for example, emergency conditions, where the control system may be at its most vulnerable.

Manufacture

The manufacture stage involves ensuring that the plant or equipment is produced to the design criteria specified, and ensuring that any changes that are made at this stage are subjected to a further risk assessment and approval before the changes are formally incorporated into the design. Key elements at this stage include:

- establishing a defined management approval system for accepting changes to the agreed design;
- conducting risk assessments for all aspects of the plant or equipment that may be affected by the design changes;
- obtaining approval signatures on the risk assessments for the acceptance of the design changes; and
- maintaining documented records of all the changes made during manufacture in order that these changes can be incorporated into the final operational and maintenance procedures.

Installation and commissioning

The installation and commissioning stages of new plant and equipment provide the last opportunity to check for weaknesses in the safety control systems. An important issue at this stage is ensuring that all plant items have been correctly labelled and identified so that they can be incorporated into operational and maintenance procedures. Key elements at this stage include:

- checking that procedures operate satisfactorily, and that interlock and protection systems have been tested for weaknesses during potentially hazardous situations, which should have been identified as requiring tests during the design stage risk assessment;

- assessing, approving and documenting all changes that are made to the operational and maintenance procedures before they are implemented; and

- maintaining an approved record of all the installation and commissioning checks that have been carried out as part of the final plant or equipment acceptance tests.

Operation and maintenance

Safety during operational and maintenance activities should have been thoroughly analysed and assessed at the design stage, and the suitability of the control procedures should have been confirmed during the installation and commissioning stages. Key elements at this stage include ensuring that:

- operating and maintenance procedures cover all foreseeable plant conditions;

- test procedures for plant and equipment have been identified and are available; and

- maintenance procedures address issues related to the availability of safety devices; these procedures should avoid, whenever possible, the need to override or bypass safety-critical systems.

Modifications and retrofits

Modifications to plant and equipment at some stage in their operational lifetime are not unusual occurrences. However, it is unusual for organisations to control this stage effectively, and this gives rise to conditions that are a common cause of accidents at work. Key elements at this stage include ensuring that:

- defined management approval routes exist for implementing changes to the plant design;

- risks associated with design changes are subjected to a risk assessment, which should receive formal approval and documentation before the changes are implemented; and

- documented records of all changes to plant, equipment and procedures are maintained.

Decommissioning

It is often difficult to provide procedures for decommissioning plant and equipment at some unspecified time in the future. However, it is important to avoid the situation where a plant is designed, built, commissioned, operated and maintained safely over many years but has a continuing uncertainty throughout its lifetime as to how it can be safely decommissioned. Key elements at this stage include ensuring that:

- detailed decommissioning information is available as part of the final handover documentation, particularly for those parts of the plant or equipment that contain or may contain hazardous substances; and

- information is provided on the potential for recycling components from the defunct plant or equipment.

Safety-related control systems

A control system is a system that responds to an input signal from a plant or a piece of equipment and then operates in a defined way by producing a desired output action. Control systems consist of at least one input device, a safety controller and an output device (Health and Safety Executive, 1995). If the control system is linked through a safety protection system, such as a safety interlock, it represents a *safety control system*: see Figure 12.5.

Input signals may be created by:

- binary systems that operate in just two modes, such as the operational states of 'on' and 'off', which indicate that a valve is in the open or shut position; or
- analogue systems that provide a continuous signal that corresponds to the value of the parameter measured, such as a temperature or gas concentration. Analogue signals may be converted to digital signals prior to transmission.

Output actions may result from signals received by operational devices such as:

- valves for controlling reagent flows, fans for operating fume exhaust ventilation systems, motors for operating conveyors and brakes for operating high-speed centrifuges; and
- electronic systems that run a process in an automatic cycle or that initiate a shutdown or start-up procedure.

The output actions of control systems may be implemented by electric, pneumatic or hydraulic devices, which can vary in complexity from on/off switches to computers, programmable logic controllers (PLC) or programmable electronic systems (PES). Computers are used extensively in production operations, and although these devices have many benefits in terms of their reliability, they provide an additional source of risk. It should also be remembered that computer-controlled systems are not always visible, as many modern devices have built-in microprocessor chips as part of the plant or equipment's integrated control circuits. The complexities of most computer programs mean that many systems cannot be reliably tested for all eventualities. Furthermore, changes to one aspect of a computer program may have a significant impact on an apparently unrelated part of the process control system. Computers that form part of the safety function of a process or equipment should be subjected to a thorough risk assessment during all stages of the lifecycle process.

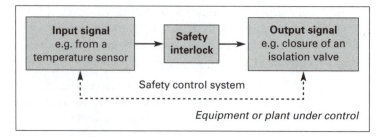

Figure 12.5 Schematic example of an automatic safety control system

Two major examples of safety-related control systems that are used with plant and equipment are interlocking and protection systems (Health and Safety Executive, 1995).

Interlocking systems provide a means for preventing operations or access taking place during a hazardous situation. Interlocks may be provided by a mechanical device, such as a bolt or limit switch, or through the immobilisation of plant or equipment, such as the removal of power.

Protection systems normally provide process control by monitoring the operational state of a plant or equipment. Protection systems are normally *operate-on-demand* devices, which alter the operational conditions of the process in order to return a plant or equipment to a safe condition.

When carrying out risk assessments for safety-related control systems, it is important to differentiate between the two key applications of computers, namely those related to *process control* and *process protection*. These two applications should ideally be maintained as independent control systems because of their sometimes conflicting requirements and in order to minimise the possibility of common cause failures: see Figure 12.6.

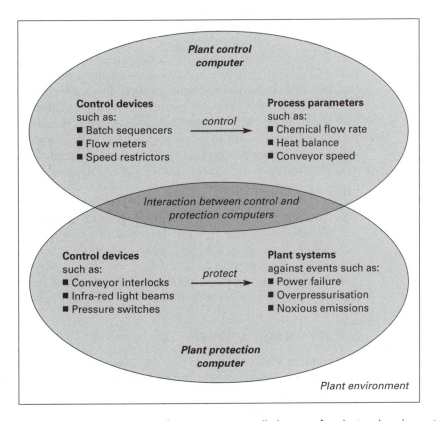

Figure 12.6 Schematic description of a computer-controlled system for plant and equipment operation and protection

Important questions that should be considered with computer-controlled safety protection systems are the following (Health and Safety Executive, 1997a):

- To what extent does the process or equipment rely on the computer for safety?
- What other physical, management and human factor control systems are available to support the computer-controlled system?
- Has the reliability of the computer control system been thoroughly assessed?
- Was the system subjected to a full risk assessment?
- Has the system been tested during start-up and shutdown and for routine, abnormal and emergency operational conditions?
- Does the system operate in a fail-safe mode?

Functional safety of safety-related systems

As electromechanical and solid-state electronic safety systems were more and more replaced by computerisation, the level of concern over whether computerised systems would perform effectively increased. It was also increasingly clear that testing procedures that were used on conventional safety-related systems were less and less applicable to computer-controlled systems. The International Electrotechnical Commission (IEC, 1998, 2000) developed a standard consisting of a series of substandards for safety-related control systems, referred to as IEC 61508. This standard focused on instrumented and computer-based safety control systems, and introduced the concept of *safety integrity levels* (SILs). The principle of SILs, however, was subsequently adopted as a generic control approach, and is now used in a much broader context. The IEC standard on functional safety in industrial automation was published in seven separate documents (IEC, 1998, 2000), and was developed as an overarching performance-based standard for use with any industrial process using electronic safety-related systems (IEC, 2002).

Implementation of IEC 61508

The standard is constructed so that all relevant stages of the safety lifecycle are considered when assessing safety-instrumented systems. The standard provides a framework for defining the safety specification required to achieve an acceptable level of risk: see Figure 12.7.

This framework model explains how the levels of risk reduction required to reach tolerable and acceptable (operational) levels of risk can be achieved.

Safety integrity levels

A key concept introduced in the IEC Standard 61508 was the safety integrity level and the linkage of SILs to the probability of failure on demand of a safety-related protection system. The standard defines SILs for systems on a scale from 1 (the lowest level) to 4 (the highest level). Therefore, where a plant failure has a high consequential risk associated with it, a high SIL should be associated with the control system; where a plant failure has a low consequential risk associated with it, there is only a necessity for a low SIL for the control system.

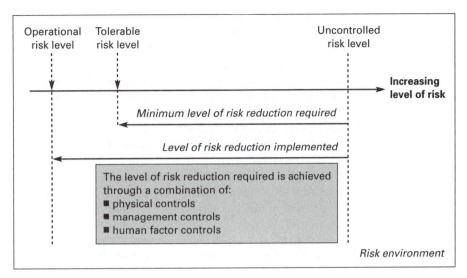

Figure 12.7 Framework model for specifying control measures to achieve an acceptable level of risk

Defining safety integrity levels

The probability values associated with SILs are dependent on the context of the working environment of the control system. Where a system is operated continuously, such as machinery, there is clearly a constant requirement for the safety system to be available: in this context SIL values are linked to the probability of failure to danger per hour. However, where the demand is only periodic, such as in an emergency shutdown system, the value of the SIL is linked to the probability of failure to danger per demand: see Table 12.2.

Table 12.2 Safety integrity levels

Safety integrity level	Low demand mode	High demand/continuous mode
	Probability of a dangerous failure to perform a design function on demand	*Probability of a dangerous failure to perform a design function per hour*
4	$\geq 10^{-5}$ to $<10^{-4}$	$\geq 10^{-9}$ to $<10^{-8}$
3	$\geq 10^{-4}$ to $<10^{-3}$	$\geq 10^{-8}$ to $<10^{-7}$
2	$\geq 10^{-3}$ to $<10^{-2}$	$\geq 10^{-7}$ to $<10^{-6}$
1	$\geq 10^{-2}$ to $<10^{-1}$	$\geq 10^{-6}$ to $<10^{-5}$

Source: IEC (1998, 2000); Copyright © 1998 IEC, Geneva, Switzerland. www.iec.ch

The probability values quoted in Table 12.2 therefore refer to the confidence or reliability that the control system will operate when required.

Implementing the concept of safety integrity levels

The performance requirements of a protection system associated with part of a plant or piece of equipment are assessed and defined using, for example, event tree analysis. This performance requirement then provides the basis for the specification and design of that particular part of the plant or piece of equipment. The IEC standard defines SILs on the basis of the level of risk reduction required to achieve an acceptable level of residual risk rather than on the consequences of failure. The derivation and application of the SIL required for the ith potential event in a process or piece of equipment is illustrated in the event tree shown in Figure 12.8.

If a plant in a high-demand mode, for example, is assessed as high risk and requires a safety device capable of operating at a SIL value of 3, the device specified must be capable of performing efficiently with a failure rate no worse than once in 10^7 operations (see Table 12.2). An operation in a low-demand situation, however, that is assessed as low risk and requiring a safety device capable of operating at a SIL value of 1 will only be required to perform with a failure rate no worse than once in 10 operations.

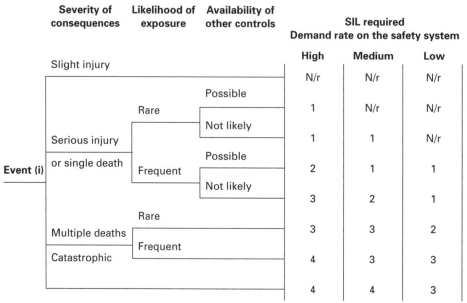

N/r: Not required

Figure 12.8 Defining the SIL required for a safety-related control system using event tree analysis
Source: IEC (1998, 2000); Copyright © 1998, IEC, Geneva, Switzerland. www.iec.ch.

A comparison of lines of defence and safety integrity levels

The two concepts of LoDs and SILs are very closely linked. The LoD approach requires an estimation of the risk associated with a plant or piece of equipment and identifies the level of risk reduction required. The procedure then allocates an LoD rating to the specified protection systems and compares this value with the level of protection actually implemented. If the difference between the specified and the actual levels is greater than or equal to zero then the protection systems implemented are adequate. The SIL approach uses event tree analysis in order to identify the level of safety required for a control system and then relates this to the probability of failure of the protection system under low-, medium- and high-demand operational conditions.

The LoD value has been defined previously as:

$$LoD = -\log_{10}(PoF)$$

where PoF is the probability ($0 \leq PoF \leq 1$) of the protection system failing on demand and

$$SIL\ (n) = LoD\ (n\ to\ n+1)$$

Therefore, if the defined LoD value is compared with the SIL value (n) shown in Table 12.2, it is possible to obtain a comparison of the two procedures under equivalent operational conditions: see Table 12.3.

Table 12.3 A comparison of LoD and SIL ratings

Probability of failure on demand	Level of risk reduction achieved	LoD value	SIL value
10^{-4}–10^{-5}	10^4–10^5	4–5	4
10^{-3}–10^{-4}	10^3–10^4	3–4	3
10^{-2}–10^{-3}	10^2–10^3	2–3	2
10^{-1}–10^{-2}	10^1–10^2	1–2	1

An organisation's safe system of work

An effective health and safety management system is essential for an organisation to control its operations, and a major part of this management system is the organisation's safe system of work. The term 'safe system of work' is often used just to describe procedures for routine operations; however, the effective and efficient management of workplace health and safety risks requires the implementation of a much wider range of procedures. An organisation should establish an overall *generic* safe system of work consisting of several interconnecting layers of management control that covers both corporate and operational issues. All aspects of this generic safe system of work will be informed and influenced by factors such as legislation, standards, business ethics and corporate philosophy. A safe system of work forms an integral part of risk management, and it is a key input to the process of risk control. A framework describing a generic organisational safe system of work is presented in Figure 12.9.

This generic safe system of work outlines the mechanisms by which an organisation's standards and performance targets can be implemented and monitored. The system should form an integral part of the organisation's quality and risk management systems. The number of elements from this generic safe system of work that should be adopted by an organisation will depend on:

■ the complexity and range of risks associated with the operations;

■ the skills and competences of the people involved with the operations;

■ the products and services provided;

■ the number and locations of the operational sites; and

■ the level of development of the countries within which the organisation operates.

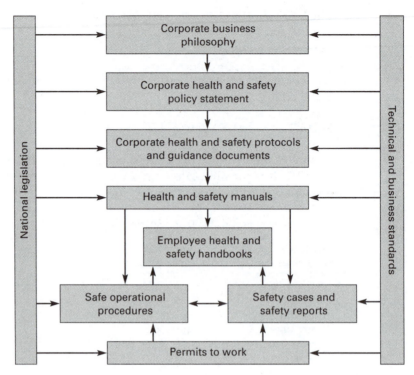

Figure 12.9 Framework for a generic organisational safe system of work and those factors influencing the system

The following sections discuss components of this generic safe system of work.

Corporate policy statement

The corporate policy, which represents the top tier of the documented safe system of work, should define the overarching organisational approach to the management of health and safety risks. The way in which health and safety is managed within an organisation reflects the perceptions and motivations of the senior management and the chief executive officer in particular. The health and safety policy provides a statement of the organisation's philosophy of what it desires to achieve and how it intends to achieve it.

The Health and Safety Executive (2000a) provided guidance on the minimum requirements of an organisation's health and safety policy statement:

Written statements of health and safety policy should at the very least:

Set the *direction* for the organisation by:

- demonstrating senior management commitment;
- setting health and safety in context with other business objectives;
- making a commitment to continuous improvement in health and safety performance.

Outline the *details* of the policy framework, showing how implementation will take place by:

- identifying the Director or key Senior Manager with overall responsibility for formulating and implementing the policy;
- having the document signed and dated by the Director or Chief Executive;
- explaining the responsibilities of managers and staff;
- recognising and encouraging the involvement of employees and safety representatives;
- outlining the basis for effective communications;
- showing how adequate resources will be allocated;
- committing the leaders to planning and regularly reviewing and developing the policy;
- securing the competence of all employees and the provision of any necessary specialist advice.

Health and Safety Executive (2000a: 25)

There is a recommendation in this guidance that corporate policy statements should contain *details* of how an organisation intends to achieve its health and safety standards. However, because many larger organisations operate in a world market, it is impossible to create a single corporate policy statement that includes the specific details of how health and safety issues should be managed within each sector, each subsidiary and each country in which the organisation operates. A health and safety policy statement by its nature should be a relatively short document and cannot, and should not, contain the details of how health and safety issues will be managed. The document should, however, provide an unequivocal statement to all parts of the organisation of the direction and general philosophy of the way in which the organisation wants and expects health and safety risks to be managed. A copy of the health and safety policy statement should therefore be available to every employee.

Corporate protocols and guidance documents

In large organisations, which may incorporate subsidiaries and/or autonomous national and international companies, there are very good management reasons why the policy statement cannot contain specific details of how health and safety issues should be managed. Apart from the difficulties associated with interpretation and understanding translations into local languages, there are variations in culture, legislation, perceived risk, levels of risk, competences and human and financial resources. The approach adopted by many large multinational organisations is therefore to produce a series of health and safety protocols, which are often supported by additional guidance documents that describe how the corporate health and safety policy statement should be implemented locally. Each protocol will provide brief details of the purpose and scope of a process or activity, the actions required, and the responsibilities for undertaking the actions in order to achieve compliance with the organisation's health and safety policy statement. Protocols should also describe the roles and responsibilities of groups and interested parties in arrangements such as joint ventures and alliances. Protocols and supporting guidance documents should always be presented in a goal-setting format rather than as prescriptive requirements. This approach allows the senior management of each subsidiary company to identify the most appropriate approach for them to adopt in order to achieve the corporate goals.

Corporate protocols

Different organisations will clearly need to address different business risks but, typically, protocols may cover issues such as:

- management roles, responsibilities and accountabilities;
- employees' training and behaviours;
- health and safety plans and reports;
- risk assessments;
- dissemination of information and documentation;
- reporting of accidents and ill-health and incident investigations;
- management of organisational change;
- acquisitions and divestitures;
- project design and construction;
- purchasing of goods and services;
- crisis and disaster management;
- external and community relations; and
- auditing and review.

Corporate guidelines

In addition to protocol documents, an organisation may provide guidance documents to outline how senior management will be assessed for their compliance with the protocols. Because implementation procedures will vary from country to country and from company to company, the guidance should only indicate which aspects of the protocol document will be audited in order to demonstrate compliance. The following two examples illustrate the way in which this information can be presented.

Example: Management guidelines for training

The existence of the following elements will serve to confirm that the training requirements for health and safety, which are outlined in the company's training protocol, have been adequately implemented. Each company should expect audits of their company to investigate the existence of:

- induction training programmes for all new staff that raise awareness of the policy and organisational structures for dealing with health and safety issues;
- training programmes that achieve defined levels of competence in health and safety issues for directors, managers, supervisors and all other employees and contractors;
- refresher training programmes for all staff;
- records of training and levels of competence achieved by all employees; and
- risk assessments that identify the minimum level of competence required by employees to undertake their work activities.

Example: Management guidelines for external relations

The existence of the following elements will serve to confirm that the external relations requirements for health and safety, which are outlined in the company's external relations protocol, have been adequately implemented, and each company should expect audits of their company to investigate their existence:

■ procedures for liaising with enforcement authorities with respect to compliance with legislative requirements;

■ procedures for implementing and recording actions arising from enforcement authorities; and

■ procedures for preparing, authorising and issuing statements or responses to the public and the media.

The management of organisational change

One important aspect of a corporate safe system of work relates to the way in which major organisational changes can impact on health and safety management:

> There has been immense media attention on the issues of delayering, outsourcing, flexible labour and the purported effects of these aspects of working life on stress and industrial health and safety. However, there has been little research on these issues to either confirm the existence of such trends or to evaluate the effect of business re-engineering on health and safety. At the same time, much health and safety guidance is based, if implicitly, on the presumption that organisations retain a hierarchical management structure with a 'command and control' style of management. These presumptions may no longer hold true for latter day 'delayered' forms of flatter management structures advocated by strategies such as Business Process Re-Engineering.
>
> Wright (1996: iii)

It is important, therefore, that strategic changes to organisational management incorporate an assessment stage whereby the potential impact of the management changes may be considered. This part of the safe system of work should incorporate issues related to:

■ identifying management changes that may have a detrimental impact on the organisation's ability to manage health and safety risks effectively;

■ developing systems for monitoring and controlling management changes;

■ the levels of risk associated with the management changes; and

■ formally assessing the impact of management changes after implementation of the changes.

Typical issues that should be included within the change management review are adequacy of revised operational manning levels, retention of organisational competence, identification of health and safety responsibilities, and outsourcing of activities to contractors.

Health and safety manuals

Health and safety manuals contain generic statements on specific hazards encountered in the working environment. These statements make a significant contribution to the organisation's generic safe system of work by:

- providing a common generic assessment of the risks associated with an organisation's workplace hazards;
- ensuring that managers and supervisors have a common basis around which to design and implement local safe systems of work; and
- ensuring that health and safety advice is available in a consistent and reliable format throughout the organisation.

Taking work with display screen equipment in the UK as an example, one would expect information on the following issues to be provided as the minimum level of guidance in a health and safety manual.

Example: Work with display screen equipment

Legislation

Work with display screen equipment (DSE) is covered by:

- the general requirements of the Health and Safety at Work etc Act 1974 to provide a safe system of work;
- the general requirement of the Management of Health and Safety at Work Regulations 1999 to carry out a risk assessment; and
- the specific requirements of the Health and Safety (Display Screen Equipment) Regulations 1992.

Areas of risk

Potential areas of harm to users of DSE are:

- shoulders, arms and hands through work-related upper limb disorders;
- eye fatigue through extended periods of use;
- headaches caused by screen glare and image quality and/or user's poor eyesight; and
- body aches caused by poor ergonomic design of the display screen equipment work station.

Risk assessment

The Health and Safety (Display Screen Equipment) Regulations 1992 define a user as someone who habitually uses DSE as a significant part of their normal work; however, all employees using DSE for more than one hour per day should be regarded as at-risk users. Risks associated with DSE work should be assessed under the following headings:

User's assessment

- Is there any evidence of pain or restricted use in the upper limbs?
- Is there any evidence of impaired vision, eyestrain or headaches?

- Is the display screen easy to read?
- Has an eyesight test been undertaken?
- Are regular rest breaks from working with DSE provided?

Manager's assessment
- Is the user's posture correct?
- Can the user's chair be fully adjusted?
- Is a document holder available?
- Is the local lighting adequate?
- Are there any electrical hazards created by the DSE?

Inspections/review of risk assessment
- Has the risk assessment been recorded?
- Has the work environment changed since the last inspection/risk assessment?

Training
- Has the user been trained in the correct use of DSE?
- Has the user received an information leaflet on the correct use of DSE?

Employee handbooks

Employee handbooks are normally issued as pocket-sized booklets that are intended to provide a simplified version of the information provided in an organisation's health and safety manual. These booklets should contain general health and safety information for the range of hazards encountered within the work environment rather than specific detailed operational procedures. Good-quality employee handbooks normally include diagrams and pictures in order to illustrate the risks and the control measures associated with each of the hazards. Handbooks are sometimes used as a convenient way of summarising health and safety issues related to specific operational activities, such as procedures for working with contractors, providing the schedules and activities associated with major plant outages and, in some high-risk environments, providing an outline of the permit to work.

Safe operational procedures

There is a legal requirement, in the UK, to provide and maintain systems of work that are, so far as is reasonably practicable, safe and without risks to health. However, there is no legal definition of what a safe system of work is and whether it is any different from a system of work or an operational procedure. The Health and Safety Executive (1989) defined a safe system of work as:

> A safe system of work is a formal procedure which results from systematic examinations of a task in order to identify all the hazards. It defines safe methods to ensure that hazards are eliminated or risks minimised.

Health and Safety Executive (1989: 3)

In reality, organisations aim to implement systems of work that are safe: therefore most routine operational procedures are *de facto* 'safe systems of work' because they incorporate a wide range of safety-related issues. The Health and Safety Executive (1989) described when it was appropriate to have a safe system of work in place as follows:

> Many hazards are clearly recognisable and can be overcome by physically separating people from them, e.g. by using guarding on machinery. A safe system of work is needed when hazards cannot be physically eliminated and some element of risk remains.
>
> Health and Safety Executive (1989: 3)

Most operational procedures represent a compromise between the aims and objectives of various organisational functions. For example:

■ the finance manager will seek to maximise profits;

■ the quality control manager will seek to achieve the highest or most consistent quality of products and/or services;

■ the production manager will seek to produce the highest level of saleable products and services;

■ the environment manager will seek to minimise the impact of the organisation on the environment; and

■ the health and safety manager will seek to maintain a safe and healthy work environment.

A safe system of work may be a verbal instruction or a written or computer-based procedure. Only designated managers and supervisors should prescribe operating procedures verbally, and individual operators should not be allowed to develop and implement their own procedures without prior formal approval from their supervisor or manager. Systems of work are sometimes referred to as *method statements* when they provide only a broad outline of how a particular task should be carried out. Contractors often use method statements as generic procedures to indicate to clients how particular jobs will be completed.

Task analysis

The development of operational systems of work is normally implemented through the process of task analysis, which is a systematic procedure involving:

■ identifying the task to be carried out;

■ defining the aims and objectives of the task;

■ identifying the actions that are needed to achieve the task objectives;

■ describing the ways in which the actions should be carried out in order to complete the task objectives;

■ identifying the hazards associated with the actions carried out; and

■ specifying the control measures required to minimise the risks associated with the hazards identified.

It should be apparent from this list that the processes of defining safe operational procedures and carrying out risk assessments are closely linked. Task analysis, in effect, provides the detailed description of the steps identified in an event tree analysis. One way in which a task analysis can be carried out is to start with an overview of the task, work through the high-level operations required for the task, and then gradually break these down into lower-level actions or subtasks. Each subtask may have a set of safe operating procedures associated with it in order to explain how to carry out the actions safely. An important aspect of task analysis is that the process may identify a range of important actions that do not have to be carried out every time the main task is completed. For example, plant/equipment may have to be serviced annually, and employees may have to be trained and approved initially and then follow an annual retraining and reassessment.

Safe systems for working with contractors

A contractor can be defined as anyone who is brought into an organisation to carry out work and who is not a direct employee of that organisation. Contractors are employed by many organisations to carry out, for example, routine operations, maintenance, design, installation and demolition activities. Employers should take the same level of care over the management of contractors as they do over their own employees, but they should be aware that contractors are often at greater risk of injury because they may be less familiar with the work environment, hazards and activities than employees. There are four important stages in developing a safe system for working with contractors: plan the contract, select the contractor, monitor and review the contractor's performance. In order to achieve an effective system of work with contractors it is essential to discuss and agree the health and safety arrangements for the activities before a contract is placed.

Permits to work

The Health and Safety Executive (1997b) defined a permit to work system as:

> A formal written system used to control certain types of work that are potentially hazardous. A permit-to-work is a document which specifies the work to be done and the precautions to be taken. Permits-to-work form an essential part of safe systems of work for many maintenance activities. They allow work to start only after safe procedures have been defined and they provide a clear record that all foreseeable hazards have been considered.
>
> Health and Safety Executive (1997b: 2)

Although this definition refers to a written system, some large organisations successfully employ computer-based permit to work documentation because this has a number of advantages over a written system (Iliffe *et al.*, 1999), such as legibility and the potential for retrieval of information on performance. The aims of a permit to work system are to ensure that:

- people are aware of the hazards and the nature, extent and timescales of a hazardous work activity;
- formal checks, such as plant isolations and gas tests, are completed before the work commences;

- activities are coordinated if more than one group of people are involved in activities; and
- authorisation to work is obtained before the work commences.

The specific objectives of a permit to work are to:

- identify the scope of the work and the associated hazards;
- establish the standards of protection required;
- identify the responsibilities for requesting work and being involved in the work;
- provide a formal written transfer of information from those requesting work to those people executing the work; and
- provide a mechanism for returning plant and equipment to an operational state after the work has been completed.

The permit to work certificate

A permit to work should not normally be used for carrying out routine operational activities. Examples of situations and hazards where a permit to work may be appropriate include repairs to electrical systems, entry into confined spaces, hot work such as welding, and work at heights and in excavations. The outline of a typical permit to work and the information required in such a document are shown in Figure 12.10.

During the lifetime of a permit to work, there may be changes in the type of hazards encountered, the level of risk, the timescale of the work or the scope of the work. Whenever a significant change occurs, the existing permit to work should be withdrawn and a new permit issued that takes account of the changes in circumstances.

Two key personnel are involved in the administration of a permit to work certificate, namely the *permit issuer* and the *permit acceptor*. The responsibilities taken on by issuers and acceptors of permits to work cannot be overstated. Therefore it is important that these key personnel receive full and appropriate training, which has been assessed and validated, and that their competence has been authorised in writing by a senior manager.

The permit to work issuer

The permit to work issuer should be a competent person who has been trained, assessed and approved to issue permits to work. The issuer will normally be:

- a manager, supervisor, senior operator or technician;
- someone who has knowledge of the plant, equipment, hazards and procedures involved; and
- someone who has the means or authority to eliminate hazards and implement control procedures.

1. **Document reference No.:**	
2. **Work activity:** Scope of the work should be defined, such as: ■ replace pump/fan; ■ repair tank lining; ■ install control module.	
3. **Job location:** Information should be provided on: ■ plant location; ■ plant identification, including reference numbers if available; ■ diagrams and/or plans of location and/or equipment, if necessary.	
4. **Withdrawal of plant/equipment from service:** Provide confirmation of when the named plant has been removed from service and how long the permit is valid for. Available from: (*Date and time*) Available until: (*Date and time*) Signature: (*ISSUER*) Date: Time:	
5. **Hazard identification:** List the hazards associated with the work activity and those introduced as a consequence of the work being undertaken. Authorised signature: (*ISSUER*) Date: Time:	6. **Control measures:** List all control measures, including personal protective equipment, required for the hazards identified in Section 5. Authorised signature: (*ISSUER*) Date: Time:
7. **Isolations and other permits associated with the work:** Include information on issues such as electrical isolations and testing of confined spaces: ■ Electrical: Reference no: Signature: (*ISSUER*) Date: ■ Confined space: Reference no: Signature: (*ISSUER*) Date:	
8. **Permit issue:** Authorisation that the job has been inspected, all the precautions identified have been implemented, and the people undertaking the work have been briefed. Authorised signature: (*ISSUER*) Date: Time:	9. **Permit acceptance:** Acceptance by those people undertaking the work that they have been shown the job and are satisfied that all the precautions indicated have been implemented. Authorised signature: (*ACCEPTOR*) Date: Time:
10. **Completion/extension of work:** Statement of whether the job has been: ■ completed; ■ not completed; or ■ a time extension is required to complete the work. Authorised signature: (*ACCEPTOR*) Date: Time:	11. **Cancellation of job/return to service:** Confirmation that the work has been completed satisfactorily and the plant/equipment have been recommissioned. Authorised signature: (*ISSUER*) Date: Time:

Figure 12.10 Example layout and information required in a permit to work

The issuer may not, however, be aware of the hazards and risks introduced by the work being undertaken, so cooperation between the issuer and the acceptor of a permit to work is essential. Key responsibilities involved in the preparation of a permit to work are:

- identification of equipment, location and boundary of the work activities;
- definition of the work to be undertaken;
- identification of the hazards present or created;
- isolations required to contain/control hazards such as electricity, chemicals and mechanical power;
- assessment of the residual risks;
- timescales for the validity of the permit to work; and
- identification of who will undertake the work and accept the permit.

The issuer of a permit to work must issue a permit to the person carrying out the work only when *all* aspects of the preparation have been completed satisfactorily. The issuer is responsible and accountable, because he or she has signed and issued the permit to work (Section 8), thereby taking responsibility for the completion of the preparations (Sections 5 and 6) and isolations required (Section 7) and for ensuring that they are valid for the lifetime of the work activity, as defined on the permit (Section 4). The issuer is also responsible for ensuring that the acceptor understands the details of the work activity (Section 2) and location (Section 3).

The permit to work acceptor

The permit to work acceptor should be a competent person who has been trained, assessed and approved to accept permits to work (Section 9). The acceptor must:

- ensure that the requirements of the permit are fully understood;
- examine the workplace or be familiar with the work area where the activity is to be undertaken;
- ensure that all team members understand the requirements of the permit;
- ensure their own and the team members' safety throughout the lifetime of the permit; and
- accept ownership of the plant or equipment until the job has been completed or suspended.

When the work has been completed the acceptor must demonstrate to the issuer that the work has been completed, suspended or requires additional work from that identified on the permit (Section 10). The acceptor must ensure that the issuer, in accepting the plant back, understands the limitations, if any, of the plant or equipment being received.

Safety cases and safety reports

The main purpose of safety cases and safety reports is for organisations that operate in certain high-risk work environments to formally demonstrate that they have systems of work in place in order to prevent major accidents and to limit the consequences of a major accident, if one were to occur. The requirements of safety cases and safety reports are very similar; they differ only in their contextual setting and because of the specific requirements of health and safety legislation. Generally, the requirements of a safety case are more far reaching than those of a safety report, because a safety case usually refers to an entire operational activity, such as an offshore oilrig. An offshore oilrig includes, for example, power-generating plant, a heliport, boat-docking facilities, oil storage tanks, deep-water diving facilities, pipeline distribution system and an accommodation facility; any one of these activities could give rise to an accident that could create multiple fatalities. A safety report, however, may refer only to specific parts of an operation, such as the use of certain hazardous chemicals within a chemical processing plant.

The Health and Safety Executive provided information and guidance on what should be incorporated within a safety report for the chemical industry (Health and Safety Executive, 1999a) and within a safety case for the offshore oil industry (Health and Safety Executive, 1998a). These examples can be used as general guidance for the preparation of safety reports and safety cases in other industrial sectors. Other aspects of safety cases and safety reports are discussed in Chapter 11.

Accounting for people in a risk control strategy

Cox and Edwards (2000), who discussed the importance of matching individuals to jobs, proposed a range of tests for assessing an employee's physical and mental fitness for work. These tests included assessments of the employee's mobility, locomotion, posture, strength, dexterity, coordination, sensory functions, communication, cerebral function, mental state and motivation. The contribution that people have on the level of risk and the ways in which employees behave raise a number of interesting generic issues in relation to the risk control strategy. Some important aspects of how people impinge on the working environment are discussed in other chapters, such as culture and human error (Chapter 3), risk perception (Chapter 4), risk communication (Chapter 5), and competence and training (Chapter 13). A number of other issues are discussed here.

The influence of human factors on work procedures

Safe systems of work play an important part in the day-to-day operations of all industrial and commercial organisations: therefore it is essential that the perceptual and mental abilities of the people who will be expected to implement them are taken into account. For example, procedures that contain unnecessary and/or overly complex details are less likely to be followed correctly and, if insufficient detail is provided, inexperienced operators may be unable to perform the task. The Gestalt theory of perceptual organisation, which was discussed in Chapter 4, provides a useful insight into how information can be presented in order to enhance employees' perceptions. Gestalt principles suggest that information should be presented in a way that enables the user to perceive the material in a holistic way rather than as a series of individual steps. Highlighting important parts of textual information through the use of typographical techniques, such as italicising or underlining, and through the use of colour, may also have beneficial effects for reading and comprehension; however, overuse of these techniques should be avoided (Osborne, 1998).

Consideration should be given to the structure of written procedures through, for example, sentence length, sentence activity, use of positives and negatives and the temporal order of wording. Sentences should always be constructed concisely in plain language and should avoid overly complex structures. Evidence suggests that people respond more quickly to active instructions, such as 'press the red button' than to passive instructions, such as 'the red button is pressed'. Presenting instructions and operational steps in the order in which they should be carried out also aids comprehension. For example, 'press the red button, wait two minutes and then press the green button' is preferable to 'before pressing the green button press the red button' (Osborne, 1998).

There is often a tendency to automatically produce information in the printed word format; however, studies have indicated that some non-prose formats can enhance a reader's ability to absorb and apply the information. For example, information that simply informs an operator about the location of controls on a piece of equipment may be better presented pictorially, whereas information that informs the operator about how to use the equipment is better presented using a combination of pictures and prose (Booher, 1975). Illustrations and symbols are used widely in the communication of safety information through, for example, safety signs. Features that improve a picture's perceptibility are again based on the Gestalt principle, such as:

- A solid boundary provides a good contrast between the symbol and its background.
- A simple shape is perceived more easily.
- Closure of the figure within a frame helps the user to perceive the 'whole' image.
- Stability in a figure avoids one's perceptual system from imposing different and often ambiguous interpretations on the sensory information.
- Symmetry in the figure makes recognition easier.

In multinational organisations it is important to consider cultural differences when designing and presenting pictorial information because, if a user does not understand the picture, the symbol's meaning will be lost. For example, in some countries a penguin symbol is used to imply frozen goods:

> This involves an inferential relationship between the picture (penguin) and what it is intended to signify (frozen goods). As long as the inference is made, then the connection should also be made. However, people who have never seen a penguin or do not know where it comes from may not understand the picture's meaning.
>
> Osborne (1998: 115)

A particular and important type of safety information is provided by hazard warnings, which may form part of a procedure or be stand-alone features. The human response to warnings is important in all work situations, but it is particularly important where risks have not been completely eliminated at the design stage, as human intervention may be necessary to respond, for example, to protection alarms. Warnings fulfil three main functions:

- alerting someone that a product or situation is hazardous;
- specifying the potential seriousness of the hazard and the consequences of the wrong action; and
- specifying the preventative actions to be taken.

Health and Safety Executive (1999b: 29–30)

Most people notice written warnings; however, only half the people actually read them and only a third of those who notice the warning will comply with it (Health and Safety Executive, 1999b). The perceived importance of audible warnings can be influenced by changes in pitch, repetition and volume, because loud, high-pitched, increasing tones and frequent repetitive sounds are synonymous with situations requiring urgent action. In some situations a number of audible warning systems may be in operation at the same time, so it is important that employees are able to discriminate between their relative importances. Audible warning systems, which are normally associated with urgent action, should therefore not be used for low-priority warning signals.

The influence of human factors on work design

Technological advances have contributed to safer and more efficient ways of working, but they also often reduce the skill requirements of employees and reduce the time available for them to perform tasks. Consequently, some jobs become monotonous, which in turn may impact on employees' attitudes to work and their mental well-being (Parker *et al.*, 1998). To prevent this situation arising, four job characteristics should be considered:

- variety of tasks or skills (increased use of capabilities);
- autonomy (higher control over when and how tasks are done);
- completeness (whether the job produces an identifiable end result which makes the task more significant and meaningful for the worker); and
- feedback from the job (improved knowledge of the results of the work activities).

Health and Safety Executive (1999b: 25)

These job characteristics can be incorporated into procedures through job rotation, job enlargement, job enrichment, or autonomous working.

Job rotation allows employees to move frequently through a cycle of different but similar jobs. Although this may increase the variety of tasks, other job characteristics may be unchanged, and therefore this approach may have little impact on employees' job satisfaction.

Job enlargement increases the number of tasks carried out by employees so that they gain a variety of skills. Although horizontal enlargement adds tasks to an employee's job description, these tasks may have a limited effect on job satisfaction if they simply result in an accumulation of equally mundane tasks. Vertical enlargement, on the other hand, can provide additional interests, which increases variety and autonomy within a job.

Job enrichment is similar to vertical job enlargement, but this process also adds other aspects to the job, such as scope for personal achievement, recognition and opportunities for progression.

Autonomous working gives groups a collective responsibility for planning, implementing and reviewing their work. This type of working has been associated with improvements in quality, and it provides improvements in all four of the job characteristics described above. However, it is important that employee teams are equipped with the appropriate skills and competences in order to deal with their new roles and responsibilities.

The influence of employee work patterns

Lone workers, shift workers and crowds present unique problems in health and safety management and therefore require quite different control scenarios.

Lone working

Employers are responsible for the health and safety of employees, and these responsibilities cannot be avoided even when employees work alone. Lone workers are defined as people who work by themselves without close supervision.

Lone workers at fixed locations include employees who are:

- the only person on the premises, such as in small shops, petrol stations and at home;
- working independently from other groups of workers, such as in stores, research establishments and parking areas of large organisations; and
- working outside normal daytime hours, such as cleaners and security staff.

Lone peripatetic workers include employees who are:

- on other people's premises, such as subcontractors carrying out field repairs;
- in remote locations, such as farm and forestry employees; and
- at constantly changing locations, such as sales representatives, estate agents and home care workers.

Although there are some situations where lone working is unacceptable, such as entry into confined spaces, lone working is generally acceptable, and for many people it represents their normal mode of working. Training, instruction and supervision are important control measures for lone workers, and it is important that employers audit lone workers' operations. Whenever lone workers are operating at a third-party site, the third party should provide information about the site risks and the control measures in place. Defining systems of work for lone workers is, in principle, no different from defining a safe system of work for other groups of workers; however, there are particular issues that must be considered (Health and Safety Executive, 1998b):

- The risks associated with the work should be capable of being adequately controlled by the lone worker.
- The lone worker should be medically capable of working alone.
- The lone worker should have been trained and deemed to be competent to complete the work alone.

- The lone worker should receive adequate supervision.
- Appropriate arrangements should be in place to deal with cases of accident, ill-health and emergencies.

Violence to staff is a problem in many areas of work (Health and Safety Executive, 1997c), but it is particularly important for lone workers.

Shift working

Manufacturing and service sectors have traditionally been associated with shift work; however, consumers now demand a wider range of services to be available on a 24-hour basis, and this has further increased the need for shift working. The root of many shift-based health and safety problems is the fact that shift work requires employees to operate against the body's biological clock or circadian rhythm, which controls bodily functions such as temperature and hormone production. Employees on a night or evening shift are working at times when the circadian rhythm is calling for the generation of melatonin, the sleep-inducing hormone, and they are trying to sleep when the circadian rhythm is calling for the generation of cortisol, the waking-up hormone. As a result of the endogenous nature of the circadian rhythm, changing from a day working routine to a night working routine cannot be accomplished biologically in a short period of time (Froberg, 1977; European Foundation, 2000). The nature of the circadian rhythm means that shift systems that have a forward rotation, for example from morning to evening to night shift, correspond better to the natural circadian rhythm than backward rotations. The effects of this rotation are comparable to long-distance flights going westwards, where there is prolongation of the day, and the jet-lag effect experienced by travellers on long-distance flights eastwards, where the day is effectively shortened. Folkard and Monk (1979) proposed a conceptual model in which shift performance was regarded as a function of different factors that interact directly with performance or affect the adjustment process: see Figure 12.11. The three major inputs to the model were the:

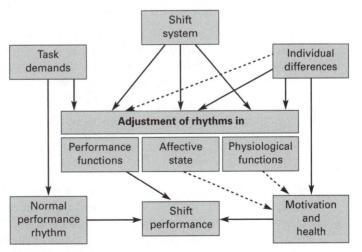

Figure 12.11 A conceptual model of factors affecting shift performance
Source: Folkard and Monk (1979)

- task demands, such as the levels of vigilance and the physical and cognitive work required;
- type of shift system used, for example fixed or rotating system; and
- personal factors, such as age, health, sleep needs and behavioural patterns.

These inputs may affect the performance functions, affective state and physiological functions of employees, and the interaction of these may influence shift performance either directly or indirectly through the shift worker's health and well-being.

Managing the risks associated with shift working requires an input from both the employer and the employee on issues such as:

- work organisation;
- shift scheduling;
- workplace design; and
- worker education and instruction.

Work organisation

Shift work should be limited to essential jobs, and employees' workloads should be organised so that, if possible, the most hazardous and strenuous tasks are completed early in the shift and less demanding tasks are planned for later in the shift. Work activities during a shift should be adjusted to prevent boredom, and effective supervision should be provided for high-risk activities.

Shift scheduling

There is no single optimum shift system for all sectors, workplaces and activities. Knauth (1993), however, made a number of general recommendations:

Nightwork should be reduced as much as possible. If this is not possible, quickly rotating shift systems are preferable to slowly rotating ones. Permanent nightwork does not seem advisable for the majority of shift workers.

Extended workdays (9–12h) should only be contemplated if the nature of the work and the workload are suitable. An early start for the morning shift should be avoided.

Quick changeovers (e.g. from night to afternoon shift at the same day or from afternoon to morning shift) must be avoided. The number of consecutive working days should be limited to 5–7 days. Every shift system should include some free weekends with at least two successive full days off.

The forward rotation of shifts (phase delay, clockwise rotation) would seem to be recommendable at least in a continuous shift system.

Knauth (1993: 15)

Workplace design

The main factor for shift working is the promotion of workplace alertness by, for example, maintaining good levels of lighting and ventilation. Where shift workers also work alone, a supervisor or manager should maintain regular communication with the shift worker in order to avoid feelings of isolation.

Worker education and instruction

Employers should provide sufficient information regarding organisational systems in order to:

- control and reduce the risks associated with shift work;
- minimise the effects of shift work on health, safety and well-being by, for example, protecting sleep periods and meal routines; and
- recognise symptoms of poor health that may be associated with shift work, especially during the first year when the effects are often more prominent.

Crowds

Many activities involve crowds, particularly in the leisure industry at events such as sports meetings, pop concerts, fun fairs and carnivals; they also occur at other locations, such as shopping centres, rail and underground stations and trade exhibitions (Au *et al.*, 1993). There is always the possibility of minor accidents occurring through slips, trips and falls, but the major safety problem arises when these minor incidents develop into major disasters. For example, in football, 66 spectators were fatally crushed and 145 spectators were injured as a result of crowd movement near the end of a match at the Glasgow Rangers' Stadium in 1971, and 95 spectators were fatally crushed and over 400 were injured as a result of crowd pressure at the start of the match at Sheffield Wednesday's Hillsborough Stadium in 1989 (Frosdick and Walley, 1997).

The main issues (Health and Safety Executive, 2000c) that should be addressed in order to control crowd risks are related to:

- transport to and from the event, such as use of buses, trains and cars;
- parking, such as signposts, capacity and pickup and drop-off points;
- access routes, such as separating pedestrians from vehicles, access for emergency services and lighting;
- entrances and exits, such as queues, barriers, stewards and security;
- start and finish times, such as coinciding with transport; and
- provision of toilet facilities and catering.

Influencing employees' behaviours

Employees' behaviours at work make a key contribution to their own and their colleagues' health and safety (Keil Centre, 2000). However, a risk control strategy addressing employees' behaviours cannot be effective unless it is implemented within a framework of physical and management controls. Employees' behaviours at work can be influenced by education and training, ergonomic design and behavioural safety programmes. The behaviour-based safety approach focuses on promoting employees' safe behaviours, exploring motives that underpin behaviour, and understanding what issues support safe and unsafe behaviours

(Sulzer-Azaroff, 1987). This approach is largely based on the behaviourist or stimulus response theory of behaviour. A key advocate of the behaviourist approach was Skinner (1938), who identified two types of behaviour:

- *respondent behaviour*, which refers to the behaviour produced when a stimulus triggers a natural response (classical conditioning), such as that observed during excitement or fear; and
- *operant behaviour*, which refers to the response to environmental features, such as that observed while driving a car.

Operant behaviour is learned and reinforced by a process of conditioning, which is used to shape future behaviours in a way that produces behaviours that would not normally appear spontaneously (Keil Centre, 2000). For example, a schoolteacher may use praise and/or prizes as a means of encouragement and reinforcement for pupils who have demonstrated that they have learned a particular skill. There are three elements in operant conditioning, which are referred to as ABC: the stimulus or *antecedent* (A), the response or *behaviour* (B) and the reinforcement/punishment or *consequences* (C) that the behaviour produces. Reinforcement is any consequence that increases the probability that a desirable behaviour will be repeated, such as the use of complimentary comments. Analysing the antecedents and consequences of unsafe and safe workplace behaviours therefore provides valuable information for reinforcing safe and eliminating unsafe behaviours (Fleming and Lardner, 2002). For example, an operator may lift heavy boxes incorrectly (the behaviour). The reason for this may be that he or she has not been trained correctly (the antecedent). The reinforcement (the consequence) of this behaviour is that the operator may have practised this behaviour for an extended period without injury. The safe behaviour of lifting correctly could be reinforced through appropriate training and through praising operators who use correct procedures.

Behavioural safety approaches were developed in the United States in the 1970s. Komaki *et al.* (1978), for example, applied the behavioural approach within the food processing industry. Krause and Hidley (1989) combined the work of Komaki *et al.* (1978) with lessons from quality management, and prescribed the use of training, performance indicators, feedback and employee participation as key factors for providing a sustainable continuous improvement process. Krause *et al.* (1990) found that immediate peer-to-peer verbal feedback was the most effective way of achieving behavioural change in an industrial setting. From the 1980s onwards, safety initiatives based on the observation of safe and unsafe acts have been implemented in a number of sectors, such as construction (Duff *et al.*, 1993; Robertson *et al.*, 1999), manufacturing (Cooper *et al.*, 1994), nuclear (Finlayson *et al.*, 1996) and chemical/research (Vassie, 1998).

The key attributes (Behavioural-Safety.com, 2003) of a behavioural safety programme are as follows.

Significant workforce participation. Full engagement of the workforce is an essential element, and without this engagement it is difficult to bring about improvements.

Specified unsafe behaviours. The programme should focus on a small number of unsafe behaviours that cause the largest percentage of accidents and incidents.

Observational data collection. Trained observers monitor their colleagues' work behaviours on a regular basis. The greater the number of observations, the more reliable the data become. Additionally, increasingly frequent observations increase the probability that safety behaviour will improve, as every act of observing and measuring behaviours alters the behaviour of those people being observed.

Data-driven decision-making processes. Data, such as the percentage of behaviours performed safely, provide a measurement of safety performance, and an examination of the trends in these data enables the identification of operational areas where improvements are desirable. Positive reinforcement is provided to employees working safely, and corrective actions are taken where employees exhibit unsafe behaviours.

Organised improvement intervention. Planned interventions begin with briefing sessions within the work areas and departments that will be involved, and these are followed by the formation of volunteer groups, such as a steering committee and observers.

Regular focused feedback about ongoing performance. Feedback is the key ingredient of any improvement initiative. Within behavioural safety programmes, feedback usually takes three forms: verbal feedback to people at the time of observation, visual feedback using charts placed at strategic work locations, and weekly/monthly briefings where detailed observational data are provided and discussed. This feedback provides the basis for focused improvements to be targeted.

Visible ongoing support from managers. Visible and demonstrable commitment, leadership and behaviours from management to the process is vital (Marsh *et al.*, 1998). This commitment can be demonstrated by:

- allowing observers sufficient time to conduct their observations;
- giving praise and recognition to those people working safely;
- providing the necessary resources and assistance for remedial actions to take place; and
- promoting the initiative whenever and wherever the opportunity arises.

Fleming and Lardner (2002) considered that behavioural safety programmes had addressed only a limited number of unsafe behaviours and, in particular, that reported programmes had not addressed senior management behaviours. Although behavioural safety programmes have made a substantial contribution to improving health and safety performance in several industrial sectors, there are a number of potential difficulties that may arise when implementing these programmes (Keil Centre, 2000). Success is dependent on employee involvement, and therefore employees must be involved in the process from a very early stage: it is particularly important that targets and goals are set participatively rather than being imposed by managers (Locke and Latham, 1990; Cooper *et al.*, 1994). An employee's desire to 'buy in' to a behavioural safety programme and the effect of operant conditioning within the programme will be affected by employees' personalities, and where they fall within the typology of human nature (Thompson *et al.*, 1990):

It is obvious that what motivates one person turns off another. Many motivational models acknowledge this and the issue of individual differences is not one that should be overlooked.

Gilby (1996: 13–14)

Several interventions have reported short-term improvements (McAfee and Winn, 1989); however, there is limited evidence of long-term improvements (Vassie, 2000). Krause *et al.* (1999) reported a longitudinal evaluation of behaviour-based safety interventions based on injury data from 73 companies in the USA over a five-year period, and found that on average companies improved their safety performance by 26% in the first year, increasing to 69% in the fifth year. Post-intervention mainte-nance of behavioural safety programmes is an important issue (Cooper *et al.*, 1994; Vassie, 2000): therefore embedding the process within the organisation's safety cul-ture can help to support the sustainability of the programme (Vassie, 1998).

Health surveillance and epidemiology

Work-related ill-health should be prevented by the implementation of an appro-priate combination of physical, management and human factor control measures. In some cases, however, the potential ill-health consequences from work are such that it may be beneficial to monitor those people who may be at the greatest risk. In these cases, information on ill-health and its causes is col-lected through health surveillance and/or epidemiological studies.

Health surveillance

The purpose of health surveillance is solely to protect the health of employees, and therefore it should be implemented only in cases where there is a clear bene-fit to be gained. Health surveillance programmes are used to ensure that an employee's health is appropriate for the job and continues to be appropriate.

Pre-employment and pre-placement health checks

Health surveillance may be used by organisations during staff recruitment in order to:

- assess the general fitness of potential employees for work;
- identify people, such as asthmatics, who may be vulnerable to certain work conditions;
- identify any health conditions that may present a hazard to other people affected by the person's job, such as airline pilots and train drivers; and
- exclude those people who have a history of medical absence.

Pre-employment health surveillance is useful for identifying the existing health status of employees, and this process may provide valuable information for employers if they have to defend themselves against compensation claims for ill-health. During pre-employment medical assessments the primary responsibility of an occupational physician must be to the employer rather than to the job applicant, because no duty of care exists between the physician and the applicant. It is important, however, that employers do not use pre-employment screening in place of an adequate risk control strategy in the workplace.

Workplace health surveillance

The first level of occupational health surveillance is achieved through regular assessments of employees' sickness records and patterns of absence. The second level of surveillance involves employees carrying out self-assessment inspections for the presence of ill-health, such as skin blemishes. The third level may involve a medical assessment of an employee's physical and mental health by an occupational nurse or physician. Specific periodic health assessments may be required for occupations such as airline pilots, train drivers, offshore divers, radiographers and users of compressed air.

Health surveillance programmes should always be accompanied by the preparation and maintenance of a health record, which should summarise issues such as the individual's exposure to potentially hazardous conditions and a conclusion as to the suitability of the employee to continue working in a particular environment. The physician or occupational nurse dealing with the health assessment should retain the confidential medical information. In carrying out health surveillance, employers will clearly have access to sensitive personal information, and therefore all record systems must conform to the very highest ethical standards (Royal College of Physicians, 2001).

It may be necessary to produce a workforce state-of-health review in support of an organisation's health management policy; this is an acceptable practice provided that the information is presented in an anonymous fashion and it is not possible to identify individuals from the information published. Although health information should not be routinely disclosed to line managers, there are instances where it is important for managers and supervisors to be aware of an employee's limitations in order to ensure that they and/or others are not exposed to unacceptable levels of risk.

Epidemiology

The causes and effects of workplace injuries are relatively easy to determine, but this is not usually the case for diseases and ill-health. Epidemiology, which is the study of how and why ill-health and disease occur among different groups of people, provides information that can be used to plan, implement and evaluate health control strategies. Epidemiological studies measure adverse health effects in relation to specific populations and specific risk factors. In this context, *occupational epidemiology* relates to employees who are exposed to workplace hazards, such as chemicals, noise and radiation, and *environmental epidemiology* refers to the study of non-workplace populations who may be exposed to the consequences of work activities, such as the effects of air pollution. *Medical surveillance* covers the collection, analysis and evaluation of health data for specific hazards, particular types of workplaces or particular groups of workers, whereas *disease surveillance* covers the collection, analysis and evaluation of health data, among the general population, for the detection and control of specific diseases and ill-health.

There is a close relationship between clinical assessments and epidemiological studies. *Clinical assessments* deal with individuals and involve recording their medical history and exposures to occupational health hazards, carrying out physical and medical examinations and making clinical judgements that produce medical diagnoses, prognoses and treatments for patients' illnesses. *Epidemiological studies* deal with groups of people and involve collecting and analysing data on adverse health effects and exposures obtained through, for example, questionnaires and health surveillance programmes; these results are used to produce summaries of the causes of adverse health effects, to make predictions about risk levels, and to identify potential intervention strategies.

A key feature of epidemiological studies is that measurements are made and data are collected in relation to a specified population. A specified *population at risk* refers to that group of people who would be counted as cases if they suffered the type of adverse health effect being studied. Measuring the frequencies of ill-health and disease in a working population requires standardising diagnostic criteria. In clinical practice people are divided into those people affected and those people who are not affected. However, diseases rarely exist as clear cases of 'yes' or 'no'; they are more likely to occur over a continuous range of severities. For example, in the case of work-related noise-induced hearing loss, employees affected can suffer from only minor loss of hearing to complete deafness. Therefore, in most cases of occupational disease and ill-health, it is a matter of how severe the adverse health effect is. There are four approaches that can be used to define when a non-case becomes a case:

- *Statistical values.* Normal or average values can be defined as those states or conditions that fall within two standard deviations of, for example, the mean value for the target population.
- *Clinical values.* These describe the level of a condition above which clinical symptoms and/or complications become more frequent.
- *Prognostic values.* Some patients with clinical observations such as high blood pressure may exhibit no adverse symptoms, but they may still have an adverse prognosis.
- *Operational values.* A case might be based on the threshold point for receiving treatment; this threshold point will take into account both the observed symptoms and the prognosis, but neither will solely determine it.

The *incidence* of a disease is the rate at which new cases occur in a target population during a specified period of time. The *prevalence* of a disease is the proportion of a population that are cases at a given point in time. Prevalence is an appropriate measure only in relatively stable conditions, and it should not be used for acute disorders. In cases of chronic disease the outcomes are often intermittent, and therefore point prevalence, based on a single examination at a single point in time, may underestimate the total frequency. *Mortality* is defined as the incidence of death from a disease, whereas *morbidity* is defined as the incidence of any departure (using subjective or objective criteria) from a state of physiological or psychological well-being.

Epidemiological data, *per se*, do not provide useful information apart possibly from setting benchmark levels for future comparisons. Data are normally used to compare the incidence rates and/or prevalence of ill-health and disease among different populations or among the same population at different points in time. This type of information can be used to address workplace issues such as the following:

- Has the occurrence of an adverse health effect changed over a period of time?
- Is the rate of occurrence of an adverse health effect in one workforce higher than rates found in other comparable workforces?
- Can an observed adverse health effect be associated with particular workplace conditions?
- Have changes in risk control measures changed the incidence of an adverse health effect?

In each of these cases it is necessary to compare and evaluate two sets of epidemiological data in order to produce meaningful conclusions from the information. The collection of occupational epidemiological data is also of paramount importance in establishing acceptable occupational exposure standards for a wide range of health hazards, such as chemicals, noise and radiation.

Occupational exposure standards

Occupational exposure to a health risk factor is measured in terms of the intensity and extent to which employees are subjected to the hazard and, normally, the higher the exposure the greater the risk that an employee will suffer an adverse health effect. This causative effect is normally referred to as an exposure–response or dose–response relationship. Occupational exposure standards are set using the principle that there is an exposure level at or below which the majority of the working population will experience no or only a very low risk to their health. There are no definitive definitions of an occupational exposure standard, as the definition will depend on the nature of the hazard; however, the key parameters are the time of exposure and the intensity of exposure to the hazard. Exposure standards are not determined solely by the properties of a hazard or the results from epidemiological studies, as social and economic factors are also taken into account: see Figure 12.12.

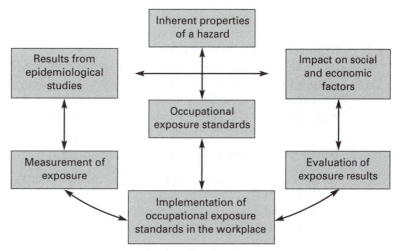

Figure 12.12 Factors affecting values ascribed to occupational exposure standards

Causation criteria for occupational exposure standards

When creating and defining occupational exposure standards, it is important to confirm that an exposure to a hazard actually causes the adverse health effect. In this context there are a number of factors that must be considered and taken into account.

Temporality. The presumed cause or presence of the hazard must precede the adverse health effect. However, it does not automatically follow that, if an exposure to a cause or the hazard precedes the adverse health effect, the latter is a direct consequence of the former.

Reversibility. The removal of a presumed cause or hazard should lead to a reduction in the risk of the adverse health effect. If a reduction in exposure is followed by a reduced risk of the adverse health effect then the presumption of a cause and effect relationship is strengthened. However, as with temporality, reversibility is not a confirmation of a cause and effect relationship.

Strength of association. Exposure should be associated with a high relative risk of acquiring the adverse health effect.

Exposure–response or dose–response. An increased exposure to the possible cause or hazard should be associated with an increased likelihood of the adverse health effect. Exposure is normally measured as intensity, and dose is measured as a quantity of exposure over a specified time period. The existence of an exposure–response relationship has three implications:

- It provides evidence of a true causal relationship between the exposure and the adverse health effect.

- It may provide a measure of the level of risk of an adverse health effect resulting from an exposure.

- It may define the level of exposure to a causal agent below which the adverse health effect is unlikely to occur or even impossible.

Consistency. The results obtained should agree with other published information, because it follows that if several studies (especially if they use different research methodologies) reach the same conclusion, then a cause and effect relationship is more likely to exist.

Biological plausibility. The postulated cause and effect relationship should be consistent with a reasonable biological mechanism.

Analogy. It should be possible to make analogies with examples from other established cause and effect relationships.

Specificity. Many adverse health effects can be the result of several causes, and many causes of ill-health have different effects on the body.

Setting occupational exposure standards

Occupational exposure standards are normally set after considering the following issues.

Nature and magnitude of the health effect. These factors will establish the level of priority that should be allocated to creating a standard for the hazard, because it is more important to allocate resources to establish exposure standards for major health effects than it is for minor health effects.

Critical adverse health effect. Where more than one health effect can occur from exposure to a hazard, the critical adverse health effect is the one that occurs at the lowest exposure level.

Exposure–response relationships. The sample population from which the exposure–response data were obtained must relate to the target population for which the occupational exposure standard is intended. The level of the standard will then be determined by factors such as the acceptability and tolerability of the residual risk and the uncertainty associated with the exposure–response data.

Effectiveness of the exposure standard. The implementation and value of occupational exposure standards should be reviewed on a regular basis using the results obtained from workplace monitoring exercises and epidemiological studies.

Summary

- Safety culture is a long-term measure of the attitudes, perceptions and behaviours of employees and reflects the way in which risks are controlled within an organisation. Safety climate provides a measure of the current safety culture in an organisation.

- Risk control should be achieved through a balanced mixture of physical, management and human factor controls. The hierarchy of controls provides a framework for determining the preferred risk control strategy.

- Plant designed using inherently safe principles provides better long-term safety than plant using add-on safety features. Passive control systems are inherently safer than active control systems, and these are in turn safer than procedural control systems.

- The IEC standard 61508 discusses the role of the safety lifecycle in the design of safe plant and equipment. The safety lifecycle principle provides a framework around which to implement inherently safe design principles. The concepts of lines of defence and safety integrity levels are used to define the performance of safety-related protection systems.

- An organisation's generic safe system of work should be composed of several layers of management control, the top layer of which is the organisation's health and safety policy statement. Other layers of the system include a health and safety manual, employee handbook, safe operating procedures and permits to work.

- The behavioural approach to safety, which is based on the principle of operant conditioning, explores the motives behind employees' behaviours and determines the issues supporting safe and unsafe behaviours.

- Epidemiological studies provide information on the causes of workplace ill-health and allow comparisons to be made of the incidence of ill-health between different workforces and different workplaces.

Issues for review and discussion

■ Consider how employees can contribute to improvements in an organisation's safety culture.

■ Review the layers of management control required in a generic safe system of work.

■ Evaluate the approaches available for managing risks within a major hazard work environment.

■ Assess the management difficulties associated with implementing a permit to work system.

■ Consider the personal, organisational and social costs and benefits of implementing an epidemiological study.

References

Au, S.Y.Z., Ryan, M.C., Carey, M.S. and Whalley, S.P. (1993) *Managing Crowd Safety in Public Venues: A Study to Generate Guidance for Venue Owners and Enforcing Inspectors*. CRR 53/1993. Sudbury: HSE Books.

Back, M. and Woolfson, C. (1999) Safety culture: a concept too many? *The Safety and Health Practitioner*, (January), **17**,14-16.

Behavioural-Safety.com (2003) http://www.behavioural-safety.com

Bollinger, R.E., Clark, D.G., Dowell, A.M., Ewbank, R.M., Hendershot, D.C., Lutz, W.K., Meszaros, S.I., Park, D.E. and Wixom, E.D. (1996) In: D.A. Crowl. (ed.), *Inherently Safer Chemical Processes: A Life Cycle Approach*. New York: Center for Chemical Process Safety of the American Institute of Chemical Engineers.

Booher, H.R. (1975) Relative comprehensibility of pictorial information and printed words in proceduralized instructions. *Human Factors*, **17**, 266–277.

Confederation of British Industry (1990) *Developing a Safety Culture: Business for Safety*. London: Confederation of British Industry.

Cooper, M.D., Phillips, R.A., Sutherland, V.J. and Makin, P.J. (1994) Reducing accidents using goal setting and feedback: a field study. *Journal of Occupational and Organizational Psychology*, **67**, 219–240.

Cox, R.A.F. and Edwards, F.C. (2000) Introduction. In: R.A.F. Cox, F.C. Edwards and K. Palmer (eds), *Fitness for Work: The Medical Aspects*, 1–25. Oxford: Oxford University Press.

Davies, F., Spencer, R. and Dooley, K. (2001) *Summary Guide to Safety Climate Tools*. Sudbury: HSE Books.

Duff, A.R., Robertson, I.T., Cooper, M.D. and Phillips, R.A. (1993) *Improving Safety on Construction Sites by Changing Personnel Behaviour*. HMSO Report Series CRR51/93. London: HMSO.

European Foundation (2000) *Shiftwork and Health: BEST European Studies on Time*. Dublin: European Foundation for Living and Working Conditions.

Finlayson, L., Fishwick, T. and Morton, A. (1996) Reducing accident rates: the behavioural approach. *Loss Prevention Bulletin*, **130** (August), 3–6.

Fleming, M. (2001) *Safety Culture Maturity Model*. Sudbury: HSE Books.

Fleming, M. and Lardner, R. (2002) *Strategies to Promote Safe Behaviour as Part of a Health and Safety Management System,* CRR 430/2002. Sudbury: HSE Books.

Folkard, S. and Monk, T.H. (1979) Shiftwork and performance. *Human Factors,* **21**, 483–492.

Froberg, J.E. (1977) Twenty-four hour patterns in human performance, subjective and physiological variables and differences between morning and evening active subjects. *Biological Psychology,* **5**, 119–134.

Frosdick, S. and Walley, L. (1997) *Sport and Safety Management.* Oxford: Butterworth-Heinemann.

Fuller, C.W. (1999) Benchmarking health and safety performance through company safety competitions. *Benchmarking: An International Journal,* **6**(4), 325–337.

Fuller, C.W. and Vassie, L.H. (2002) Assessing the maturity and alignment of organisational cultures in partnership arrangements. *Employee Relations,* **24**(5), 540–555.

Gilby, R. (1996) Bogus behaviour. *The Safety and Health Practitioner,* **14**(8), 13–15.

Guldenmund, F.W. (2000) The nature of safety culture: a review of theory and research. *Safety Science,* **34**, 215–257.

Health and Safety at Work etc. Act 1974. London: HMSO.

Health and Safety Commission (1993) *ACSNI Study Group on Human Factors, Third Report.* Sudbury: HSE Books.

Health and Safety (Display Screen Equipment) Regulations 1992. London: HMSO.

Health and Safety Executive (1989) *Safe Systems of Work.* IND(G)76L. Sudbury: HSE Books.

Health and Safety Executive (1991) *Successful Health & Safety Management.* HS(G)65. Sudbury: HSE Books.

Health and Safety Executive (1995) *Out of Control: Why Control Systems Go Wrong and How to Prevent Failure.* Sudbury: HSE Books.

Health and Safety Executive (1997a) *Computer Control: A Question of Safety.* IND(G)243L. Sudbury: HSE Books.

Health and Safety Executive (1997b) *Permit-to-work Systems.* INDG98. Sudbury: HSE Books.

Health and Safety Executive (1997c) *Violence at Work.* IND(G)69L. Sudbury: HSE Books.

Health and Safety Executive (1998a) *Assessment Principles for Offshore Safety Cases.* HSG181. Sudbury: HSE Books.

Health and Safety Executive (1998b) *Working Alone in Safety: Controlling the Risks of Solitary Work.* INDG73. Sudbury: HSE Books.

Health and Safety Executive (1999a) *Preparing Safety Reports: Control of Major Accident Hazards Regulations 1999.* HSG190. Sudbury: HSE Books.

Health and Safety Executive (1999b) *Reducing Error and Influencing Behaviour.* HSG48. Sudbury: HSE Books.

Health and Safety Executive (2000a) *Successful Health and Safety Management.* HSG65. Sudbury: HSE Books.

Health and Safety Executive (2000b) *Designing and Operating Safe Chemical Reaction Processes.* HSG143. Sudbury: HSE Books.

Health and Safety Executive (2000c) *Managing Crowds Safely: A Guide for Organisers at Events and Venues.* HSG154. Sudbury: HSE Books.

Iliffe, R.E., Chung, P.W.H. and Kletz, T.A. (1999) More effective permit-to-work systems. *Transactions of the Institution of Chemical Engineers,* **77**(**B**), 69–76.

International Electrotechnical Commission (1998, 2000) *Standard IEC 61508: Functional Safety of Electrical / Electronic / Programmable Electronic Safety-related Systems; Parts 1 to 7*. London: British Standards Institution.

International Electrotechnical Commission (2002) *Functional Safety and IEC 61508: A Basic Guide*. Geneva: IEC.

Keil Centre (2000) *Behaviour Modification to Improve Safety: Literature Review*. OTR 2000/003. Sudbury: HSE Books.

Kletz, T.A. (1979) *Industrial Safety: The Shaking of the Foundations*. Loughborough: Loughborough University of Technology.

Kletz, T.A. (1990) *Plant Design for Safety: A User-friendly Approach*. New York: Hemisphere.

Knauth, P. (1993) The design of shift systems. *Ergonomics*, **36**(1), 15–28.

Komaki, J., Barwick, K.D. and Scott, L.R. (1978) A behavioral approach to occupational safety: pinpointing and reinforcing safe performance in a food manufacturing plant. *Journal of Applied Psychology*, **63**(4), 434–445.

Krause, T.R. and Hidley, J.H. (1989) Behaviorally based safety management: parallels with the quality improvement process. *Professional Safety*, **34**(10), 20–25.

Krause, T.R., Hidley, J.H. and Hodson, S.J. (1990) *The Behavior-based Safety Process: Managing Involvement for an Injury-Free Culture*. New York: Van Nostrand Reinhold.

Krause, T.R., Seymour, K.J. and Sloat, K.C.M. (1999) Long-term evaluation of a behavior-based method for improving safety performance: a meta analysis of 73 interrupted time-series replications. *Safety Science*, **32**, 1–18.

Locke, E.A. and Latham, G.P. (1990) *A Theory of Goal-setting and Task Performance*. Englewood Cliffs, NJ: Prentice Hall.

Maddison, T. and Kirk, P.G. (1995) Application of pilot risk study methods to the safety inspection of industrial plant. *Loss Prevention Bulletin*, **125**, 11–16.

Management of Health and Safety at Work Regulations 1999. London: HMSO.

Marsh, T., Davies, R., Phillips, R., Duff, R., Robertson, I., Weyman, A. and Cooper, D. (1998) The role of management commitment in determining the success of behavioural safety intervention. *Journal of the Institution of Occupational Safety and Health*, **2** (2), 45–55.

McAfee, R.B. and Winn, A.R. (1989) The use of incentives/feedback to enhance workplace safety: a critique of the literature. *Journal of Safety Research*, **20**, 7–19.

Northcraft, G.B. and Neale, M.A. (1990) *Organizational Behaviour*. Chicago: Dryden Press.

Osborne, D.J. (1998) *Ergonomics at Work: Human Factors in Design and Development*. Chichester: John Wiley & Sons.

Parker, S.K., Jackson, P.R., Sprigg, C.A. and Whybrow, A.C. (1998) *Organisational Interventions to Reduce the Impact of Poor Work Design*. CRR 196/1998. Sudbury: HSE Books.

Reichers, A. and Schneider, B. (1990) Climate and culture: an evolution of constructs. In: B. Schneider (ed.), *Organisational Climate and Culture*. San Francisco: Jossey Bass.

Robertson, I.T., Duff, A.R., Marsh, T.W., Phillips, R.A., Weyman, A.K. and Cooper, M.D. (1999) *Improving Safety on Construction Sites by Changing Personnel Behaviour: Phase Two*. Sudbury: HSE Books.

Royal College of Physicians (2001) *Guidance on Ethics for Occupational Physicians.* London: Royal College of Physicians.

Schein, E.H. (1992) *Organisational Culture and Leadership.* San Francisco: Jossey-Bass.

Skinner, B.F. (1938) *The Behaviour of Organisms.* New York: Appleton Century Crofts.

Stansfield, R. (1998) *Report on the Development of the Technical Risk Audit Method (TRAM).* Oxford: AEA Technology.

Sulzer-Azaroff, B. (1987) The modification of occupational safety behavior. *Journal of Occupational Accidents,* **9**, 177–197.

Thompson, M., Ellis, R. and Wildavsky, A. (1990) *Cultural Theory.* Boulder, CO: Westview Press.

Toft, B. and Reynolds, S. (1999) *Learning from Disasters: A Management Approach.* Leicester: Perpetuity Press.

Vassie, L.H. (1998) A proactive team-based approach to continuous improvement in health and safety management. *Employee Relations,* **20**(6), 577–593.

Vassie, L.H. (2000) Effectiveness of safety improvement processes: behaviour-based approaches to safety. *The Safety and Health Practitioner,* **18**(5), 28–33.

Vassie, L.H. and Fuller, C.W. (2003) Assessing the inputs and outputs of partnership arrangements for health and safety management. *Employee Relations,* **25**(5), 490–501.

Wright, M.S. (1996) *Business Re-engineering and Health and Safety Management: Literature Survey.* Sudbury: HSE Books.

Training and competence

A company must, for its very existence, make use of the store of knowledge that exists within the company, and learn how to make use of help from outside when it can be effective.

– Deming (1982: 466)

Chapter contents

- Introduction
- Workforce competence, training and education
- The learning process
- Designing a training programme
- Health and safety training

Introduction

As organisations strive to meet competitive demands, they will seek to achieve higher standards and greater employee flexibility; this in turn brings demands for increased skills levels throughout the workforce. Establishing the necessary competences within an organisation and providing the appropriate training therefore becomes an important objective. Health and safety training and instruction is a requirement of most national regulatory systems, but from a risk management perspective it is also essential to ensure that employees are competent to deal effectively and safely with workplace situations and activities. Health and safety training should therefore be seen as a fundamental part of a business management system. Failure to continuously review the competence and training needs of employees, particularly in the light of organisational change, can have serious consequences. For example, the Health and Safety Executive identified a lack of team leader competence as an underlying causation factor in the fire and explosion at the Hickson and Welch chemical plant in 1992 that killed four employees (Health and Safety Executive, 1994). Prior to this incident, the company had undergone a reorganisation, in which layers of management were removed and team leaders were given greater responsibilities; however, the competences of these employees were not reviewed in the context of their new responsibilities.

The main aim of this chapter is to discuss the principles of effective training using theories and practices that are applied to adult learning. Emphasis is placed on training needs analysis, designing training programmes, and evaluating training. These general principles are then discussed in terms of health and safety training.

Workforce competence, training and education

The terms 'competence', 'training' and 'education' are often used interchangeably; however, they each have specific meanings:

- *Competence* is a combination of knowledge, skills and practical experience that a person acquires in order to perform a particular task correctly.
- *Training* is a planned activity with narrow goals and with a specific application that is undertaken by a person; it is largely, but not exclusively, concerned with learning and being able to apply new skills.
- *Education* is the acquisition of knowledge that has general applicability across a range of activities; it enables people to identify different ways of thinking and behaving, and encourages the development of choice.

In order to meet the demands of a competitive marketplace, many organisations had to reconsider the way in which they operated. From the 1970s onwards, organisations continuously reorganised in order to reduce costs and improve productivity. Having realised that it was not possible to continuously downsize, organisations then focused on achieving greater flexibility in their operating procedures as a means of maintaining a competitive edge. This was achieved largely by removing tiers of management, empowering the workforce, and focusing on teamwork. Consequently, decision-making moved from being solely a management activity to a management–workforce activity, which created a need for organisations to ensure that employees were competent to deal with their new and changing roles.

> The effect of empowerment means constant education and training of the whole workforce, not just in tools, techniques and methods but also in the wider aspects of business, management and international competition.
>
> Longworth and Davies (1996: 59)

Whereas employee competence in general is linked to improving an organisation's operational performance, management competence is linked with achieving competitive advantage and business performance (Winterton and Winterton, 1996). Organisational performance in a changing environment is dependent on the participation and cooperation of groups and individuals within the organisation. Therefore, with the increased emphasis on team working, empowerment and flexibility, there was a need to develop ways of managing these new working arrangements. Management training and education and the development of competences became critical objectives (Fonda, 1989).

Wright *et al.* (2003), in discussing competence in hazardous industries, highlighted the fact that training should not be equated with competence. European health and safety legislation places requirements on employers to appoint competent persons to assist them in meeting their safety obligations; however, there are significant variations across the European Union in how the issue of competence is treated (Engineering Employers Federation (South), 2003). Rasmussen (1997) identified that to achieve effective risk management, organisations required a workforce that was capable. In the UK, the Management of Health and Safety at Work Regulations 1999 also recognised the importance of and the need for employee capabilities in order to carry out their work activities. Capability is related to but differs from competence, training and education. Stephenson (1994) suggested that capability was concerned with the effective and appropriate application of a combination of knowledge, skills and personal qualities in a range of situations. From this it can be seen that competence does not necessarily mean that someone is capable in all situations, as personal and situational factors also affect the way one works. As training programmes cannot cover all potential personal and situational factors that may be encountered in work situations, training can realistically pursue competence but not capability. Levels of competence and capability directly affect the level of supervision required by employees. Low levels of employee competence, particularly when working in high-risk situations, dictate that a high degree of supervision is required, whereas high levels of employee competence, particularly when working with low-risk activities, allow a high degree of self-supervision (Health and Safety Executive, 2000).

The learning process

The development of effective training and education programmes requires an understanding of the way in which adults learn. Learning is essentially a change process that is achieved through the acquisition of new knowledge, skills and abilities that influence and alter the way people behave in certain situations. There are usually two aspects of the learning process: the first is the reception of and engagement with new ideas, and the second is the response to these new ideas. Learning takes place in a number of ways, including:

- acquisition of new or the development of existing physical and mental *skills*;
- acquisition of *knowledge* from information that is largely memorised;
- development of *understanding* through experiences and drawing upon and applying knowledge and skills; and
- acquisition of new *attitudes*.

Theories of learning

Educational theorists differentiate between the various aspects of the learning process, such as the acquisition of a new skill or insight and the process by which this learning takes place, and have offered several theories to describe the process (Rogers, 1986). These typically fall into three groups: behaviourist, cognitive and humanist.

Behaviourist theories regard the learning process as a stimulus–response mechanism, which takes place when a stimulus from the environment provokes a response. Skinner (1969) argued that the learning process was accelerated by the use of reinforcement, which was referred to as operant conditioning. The teacher manages this process by implementing stimuli and reinforcing desired responses and discouraging undesirable responses through the use of rewards and penalties respectively. The association between the response and the reinforcement brings about learning. This process is frequently used in a variety of circumstances to shape behaviour. As an educational tool, however, it fails to take account of other aspects of human behaviour, such as motivation, and it is possible that employees develop resistance to the conditioning process. In practice, this theory relies on the positive role of the teacher, with the learner taking a more passive role in the process. The teacher controls the stimuli, chooses the correct response, and rewards it accordingly. Opportunities for feedback from the learner to the teacher are somewhat limited, and where it does occur it takes place after rather than during the learning process.

Cognitive theories are considered by some to be a subgroup of behaviourist theories. These theories place emphasis on the processes involved in creating learner responses, organisation of perceptions that take place in the mind, and the development of insights. In this approach, understanding is considered to be a fundamental stage in the learning process, and therefore subject matter must be assembled systematically before it can be understood. Goal-setting, in relation to the material and feedback throughout each stage of the learning process, is seen as important. The subject matter is seen as the dominant factor in the learning process, with the teacher structuring the material and the learner seeking to master it.

Humanist theories of learning, which are associated with the work of Rogers (1967), have dominated recent approaches to learning. These theories emphasise that the learner is at the heart of the process, with personality and social setting providing the drivers for learning. The approach emphasises that significant and effective learning takes place only when the learner can see that the material is relevant to his or her personal needs and when the learner is able to participate responsibly in the learning process. The role of the teacher is to facilitate the process by helping to create the learning conditions and providing the resources needed. In contrast to the two previous theories, significantly less control is exerted over the learner, with the increased level of learner autonomy providing conditions that are considered to be conducive to learning. The self-directed learning approach, emphasised in humanist theories, is one of the main bases of competence-based education and training, and it emphasises individualised learning programmes and a greater focus on the needs and aspirations of the learner.

Experiential learning

Learning takes place in different ways: from formal structured activities such as lectures, case studies and books, and also from experiences, which often occur in an unconscious way. Kolb (1984) proposed a model of experiential learning that drew upon the different ways in which people learn. He considered that it was not sufficient to just have an experience in order to learn, because without reflecting upon the experience the learning potential could easily be lost. The feelings and thoughts that emerged from the process of reflection enabled generalisations or concepts to be produced by the learner that could then be applied to tackle new situations. Furthermore, if learning is about change, then new ideas should be tested in new situations. The learner must therefore make the link between theory and action, plan for action, carry out the action, reflect upon the outcomes of the actions, and then relate what happened back to theory.

Kolb (1984) postulated a four-stage cycle of experiential learning to improve competence:

- involvement in real experiences;
- reflection on experiences;
- development of abstract conceptualisations or generalisations about the experiences; and
- active testing of the concepts in new situations.

Learning therefore combines the processes of experience, perception, cognition and behaviour, and is not simply the imparting and assimilation of knowledge. The learning cycle is illustrated in Figure 13.1 in the context of health and safety.

Honey and Mumford (1986) proposed that individuals had their own preferred learning styles, and that these preferences could be related to the stages in Kolb's learning cycle. For example, some people preferred learning through active experience, whereas others preferred to reflect upon their experiences. However, the best learners benefited from all components of the learning cycle. Honey and Mumford (1986) identified four learning styles, which were referred to as the reflector, theorist, pragmatist and activist. These learning styles demonstrate close links with the dimensions of human nature discussed in Chapter 3.

The *reflector* is keen on considering experiences from a variety of perspectives before arriving at cautious decisions. The thorough collection and analysis of data about experiences and events are important issues for reflectors, so they tend to postpone reaching a decision for as long as possible. Typically, reflectors will hold back their views in meetings and discussions as they will listen to other people's discussion before making their own points.

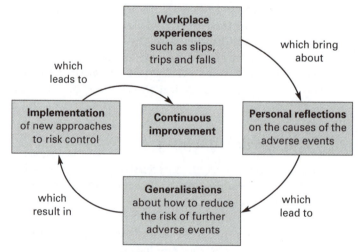

Figure 13.1 The experiential learning cycle
Source: Adapted from Kolb (1984)

The *theorist* prefers to assimilate information and analyse it rationally. Theorists think problems through in a step-by-step, logical way and adapt and integrate observations into complex but logically sound theories. They tend to be perfectionists, who will not feel comfortable unless they can explain all the facts in a logical and rational way. They will also be extremely uncomfortable with subjective judgements, lateral thinking and flippant remarks.

The *pragmatist* is most comfortable testing out an idea and seeing it work in practice; pragmatists are experimental and impatient to make things work well. They positively search out new ideas, grasp opportunities to experiment with applications, and like the challenge of making practical decisions and solving problems. They have a low tolerance of rumination and open-ended discussions.

The *activist* seeks immediate experiences and welcomes the challenge of any new learning opportunity. Activists are very open minded, flexible, and enjoy the excitement of change and novelty. However, they quickly become bored with routine, long-term detailed matters. Activists involve themselves fully and without bias in new experiences; they have a tendency to act first and consider the consequences later. As soon as the excitement from one activity has faded they are busy looking for the next activity. They often tackle problems by brainstorming.

By appreciating the different learning styles, trainers can match learning opportunities with the preferred learning styles of individuals. In this context, Honey and Mumford (1986) designed a questionnaire that enabled learners to assess their preferred learning styles. Ideally, training situations should take account of the different learning styles in order to maximise training effectiveness. Although preferred learning styles should influence training methods, there are a number of other issues, such as learner motivation, that will influence learning, irrespective of an individual's preferences.

Dale and Nyland (1985) proposed a *cone of learning*, which related the degree of involvement of the learner in the learning process to the extent to which the information presented was retained. This suggested that the more active the learner was in the training activity the higher the proportion of information presented that would be retained (Table 13.1).

Table 13.1 The cone of learning

Involvement level	Proportion of information likely to be remembered
Active (doing): performing a job or task, simulating a real experience	90%
Active (receiving and participating): taking part in a discussion or giving a presentation	70%
Passive (visual and receiving): seeing something being done, watching a demonstration or a video	50%
Passive (verbal):	
■ looking at pictures	30%
■ hearing words	20%
■ reading	10%

Source: Dale and Nyland (1985)

Designing a training programme

Although training can make a significant contribution to performance, a training programme may not necessarily be the most beneficial and cost-effective course of action for an organisation to follow. In some cases it may be more appropriate to select staff who already have the knowledge and skills required, or to contract out specific types of work to specialists rather than train existing employees in new skills. However, once a need for training has been established, the training should follow a logical sequence involving six stages (Patrick, 1992): determine job content, identify training needs, set objectives, implement training programme, evaluate training programme, and assess effectiveness of the training. The job analysis defines the type of activities and actions involved. Rasmussen (1986) broke activities into three categories, which he referred to as:

- *skill-based activities*, which involve routine and repetitive tasks that may be performed automatically, such as driving a car or making a cup of tea;
- *rule-based activities*, which involve following a defined sequence of steps that require thought to put them into action, such as determining airborne asbestos fibre levels; and
- *knowledge-based activities*, which involve dealing with new situations from first principles, such as preparing an action plan for reducing the accident rate in a factory.

In order to undertake each of these types of activity effectively, an employee will require a specific mix of abilities in the psychomotor, cognitive (intellectual) and affective (attitudinal) learning domains. If the employee designated to carry out a task does not possess the required mix of abilities then there is a 'gap' in their abilities, which may be filled by appropriate training. This 'gap' defines the training needs, which in turn define the training objectives.

Having established the training objectives, the next step in the sequence is the implementation of a training programme, which first requires identification of the most appropriate techniques and methods to meet the specified objectives. The most effective training techniques will depend on the learning domain (Daines *et al.*, 1993):

- *psychomotor domain*: demonstration, individual practice and coaching;
- *cognitive domain*: lectures, syndicate work and problem-solving tasks; and
- *affective domain*: discussion, case studies, role play and simulation.

Training for skill-based activities should ensure that there is sufficient repetition of the task provided in order to reinforce the skill. Where a skill is rarely required but needs to be implemented automatically when it is required, such as in emergency situations, the training programme should involve an element of 'overlearning' because this increases the likelihood that the skill will be retained and be available when needed. Training for rule-based activities should ensure that the complete operational sequence is taught each time, to reduce the likelihood that steps may be omitted, and to emphasise that the sequence of steps must be retained. Training for knowledge-based activities should concentrate on the basic principles and deal at length with problem-solving scenarios that involve assessing a wide range of options developed through activities such as brainstorming. It is important that employees are able to recognise a situation requiring a knowledge-based activity and do not try to treat it through rule-based activities by applying familiar routines. Training for knowledge-based activities presents a considerable challenge for health and safety training, as it involves training for situations that may not be foreseeable and which therefore cannot be simulated or modelled. Case studies provide a useful way for participants to consider scenarios that offer similar circumstances and to develop ways of dealing with them. For example, consider the learning outcome for trainee managers 'to prioritise their problems and tasks so that they can decide when and how to tackle them'. This requires the development of abilities in the cognitive and affective domains, which can be addressed through methods such as lectures, case studies, simulation and discussion. In contrast, the learning outcome for an electrician 'to fit a plug' requires development of abilities in the psychomotor and cognitive domains, which can best be addressed through methods such as demonstration and practice.

The evaluation of *training effectiveness* is an important stage in the training programme, but one that is often neglected. The evaluation process should explore issues such as how far learners have progressed from their starting points, the effectiveness and suitability of the training methods, activities and resources used, and what the learners felt about the programme. Additionally, a long-term evaluation of training should be undertaken by monitoring the effectiveness with which employees carry out jobs for which they were trained. In particular, training output should be measured by setting appropriate criteria against which performance can be measured, in advance of the training programme.

Measuring the effectiveness of a training programme requires a measurement of ability before and after the training programme is implemented (Hale, 1984). In the absence of a benchmark starting position on which to base the measurement of change, training is usually 'evaluated' using an end-of-course questionnaire, which is often simply a measure of the trainees' enjoyment of the course rather than a measure of their increased competence.

> The safety literature and anecdotal evidence suggest that many interventions in occupational safety and health are implemented with the sincere hope that they work, but with a lack of solid evidence of their effectiveness, especially in the area of safety training and education...'
>
> Shannon *et al.* (1999: 161)

Training evaluation should always be linked to training objectives. Kirkpatrick (1994) identified three key questions for the evaluation of training:

- Have trainees learned the new knowledge and skills?
- Are trainees applying the new behaviours in the workplace?
- Is there a demonstrable change in the organisation's performance?

The method of evaluation employed, however, will depend on the abilities being taught, i.e. psychomotor, cognitive or affective. Abilities that are learned for knowledge and skill-based activities are usually assessed through methods such as written examinations, practical tests, coursework and simulations. These assessments will indicate whether any learners need additional support or require further opportunities to test their new abilities. However, such evaluative methods cannot provide data on how well learners will retain their newly acquired abilities, or how well they will be applied within the workplace.

In cases where a training programme is aimed at providing new abilities in order to undertake a specific task, the assessment should ideally take place shortly after the completion of the training programme. Where the purpose of the training programme is targeted at improving employee performance in their current role, and further practice and experience may be part of the learning process, the assessment should take place at an appropriate interval of time after completion of the training programme. The most appropriate evaluation methods, in this case, are direct observations of workplace practice, which may be undertaken by a supervisor, manager, trainer or external assessor. Self-completion questionnaires and interviews have also been used, largely because they are easy to implement and offer a lower cost option; however, they offer poor reliability for measuring changes in behaviour resulting from training. Changes in behaviour can provide essential information on whether the new abilities are actually applied in the workplace, and this can aid identification of problems with the design and delivery of training programmes. There are, however, some behaviours that cannot easily be observed, such as emergency preparedness, because they will be implemented only in specific and rare situations. Evaluating training effectiveness through one-to-one observations is clearly a time-consuming and expensive task: therefore equipping employees with the abilities to undertake workplace observations can provide a cost-effective option. This approach is used in many behavioural safety intervention programmes, which are discussed in Chapter 12.

Changes in organisational performance can be assessed over a period of time by reviewing the levels of prosecutions, accidents, incidents etc. Although this type of evaluation may indicate a link between training and a particular business objective, it can sometimes be difficult to prove a true causal link, as other confounding factors may have contributed to the change in performance. Other difficulties that may occur with this type of evaluation are that certain reactive performance measures, such as accident rate, may be insensitive to the impact of individual training programmes if the values are already low. It is also difficult to carry out cost–benefit analyses of training programmes because of the problems associated with assigning monetary values to many health and safety issues. The selection of appropriate performance measures for assessing health and safety management performance is considered in detail in Chapter 14.

Health and safety training

Health and safety training, like any other business training, should have a rational basis. However, health and safety training is often used as a response to a serious incident or a visit from an enforcing authority. This unstructured approach to training usually results in money being wasted. The effective management of health and safety requires competences throughout the organisation and, in particular, among those people who occupy senior positions in the organisation. The Health and Safety Commission (1990) recognised that the acts or omissions of senior management were capable of influencing the actions at operator level, and therefore the training needs of everyone within an organisation should be addressed. Although their recommendations were based on the nuclear industry, the proposals are applicable generally across all industries. Usually, there are three main types of health and safety training needs in an organisation: organisational, managerial and operational.

Organisational needs cover issues relating to the organisation as a whole. For example, the organisation must provide advice on health and safety matters and undertake health surveillance for specific hazards.

Managerial needs relate to the knowledge, skills and attitudes required by all managers. These include: knowledge of relevant legislation, risk assessment and control methods and the organisation's health and safety management system; an understanding of risks within their area of responsibility; and the skills of leadership, communication, coaching, training and problem solving in relation to health and safety.

Operational needs relate to the knowledge, skills and attitudes that people need in order to perform in a safe and healthy manner in a given environment. These include detailed knowledge and understanding of the hazards and risks associated with an individual's job as well as more personal needs that arise in specific circumstances and at certain stages in an employee's development. Personal needs that can be identified through performance appraisal may also arise from observations of safe and unsafe acts, workplace inspections and incident investigations. Vidal-Gomel and Samurçay (2002) presented a framework for the systematic analysis of accidents and incidents in order to identify competence requirements for operators in the context of electrical maintenance. Circumstances such as staff changes caused by promotion or absence, the introduction of new equipment or technology and the performance review of established staff provided appropriate opportunities for the assessment of operational/personal training needs.

A structured approach to health and safety training should be achieved by considering how the training and education of employees can contribute to the achievement of health and safety goals. Glendon and McKenna (1995) suggested that the basis for health and safety training could be identified from two perspectives: corporate strategy and risk management. First, corporate objectives create implications for functions such as production and maintenance and, as a result, the human resources department should develop policies on issues such as employee recruitment, selection and appraisal. This in turn requires the training department to develop training programmes to support corporate objectives, including induction, job-specific and refresher health and safety training. A second rationale for health and safety training lies in considering it as part of an overall risk management process. For example, employees require specific abilities in order to develop and implement policies, plans and risk assessments. The case for the provision of health and safety training can be argued from a strategic perspective, but there is also a legal requirement for appropriate training in most national health and safety regulatory systems.

Training needs analysis is an opportunity to ensure that training provides the right solution to a problem. Although there has been significant growth in the provision of training and education programmes for health and safety practitioners

(Hale, 2002), few health and safety professionals in the UK adopt a strategic approach to training needs analysis (Training Solutions, 1998). The issue of health and safety training has also been overlooked in management education. Many undergraduate and postgraduate qualifications in general management, which are intended to equip students with an understanding of all the major functions of business, do not cover health and safety management as a component within their syllabi. For example, Hawkins and Booth (1998) showed that the occupational health and safety content of MBA programmes in British university management schools was non-existent or very limited, and that management academics did not consider it to be relevant for contemporary business managers. Middle managers, in particular, were identified as a target group for education in health and safety management (Van Dijk, 1995). Inadequate management education in the area of health and safety has been highlighted in a number of sectors, such as construction (Carpenter *et al.*, 2001) and engineering (Lee, 1999). However, enquiries into many major accidents in the UK have highlighted serious failings in senior managers' awareness of health and safety issues (Health and Safety Executive, 1996). This suggests that there is a need for health and safety management to be given the same level of importance as other management issues within the academic study of business management.

In other areas of education, and in particular in primary and secondary schools, there is a range of initiatives in place aimed at the integration of occupational health and safety into the education system. For example, in the UK health and safety forms part of the National Curriculum, in Australia and New Zealand resource packages were developed for schoolchildren and teachers, and in Ireland on-line resources were made available for students and teachers (European Agency for Safety and Health at Work, 2003).

Summary

- Workforce, and in particular, management competence and capability are essential pre-requisites for sustainable business performance.

- There are three major theories of learning, namely behaviourist, cognitive and humanist. Humanist theories, which emphasise that the learner should be at the heart of the learning process, have dominated recent approaches to learning. In order to achieve this type of learning, the learner needs to engage in a cycle of experience, perception, cognition and behaviour.

- Where the need for training has been identified, a six-stage approach is advocated that commences with a job analysis in order to define training needs. The setting of training objectives, implementation of a training programme and an evaluation of the training follows this and the final stage considers the effectiveness of the training.

- In order to enable training to influence human performance in the desired way, post-training levels of performance should be matched to the learning objectives. Training effectiveness can be assessed at various levels but assessing whether trainees apply what they have learned in the workplace and the impact that this has on health and safety performance provide the most useful indicators of training effectiveness.

■ A structured approach to health and safety training should be developed. Usually there are three types of training needs: organisational, job and individual. Training needs analysis and the health and safety competences of managers are important issues.

Issues for review and discussion

■ Consider whether training or selection is the most appropriate option for an organisation to follow.

■ Consider the contribution of health and safety training to organisational performance.

■ Review the key aspects of evaluating the effectiveness of health and safety training.

■ Assess the impact of senior management health and safety competence on an organisation's health and safety performance.

■ Review the organisational, managerial and operational health and safety training needs within an organisation.

References

Carpenter, J., Williams, P. and Smith, N.C. (2001) *Identification and Management of Risk in Undergraduate Construction Courses*. CRR392/2001. Sudbury: HSE Books.

Daines, J., Daines, C. and Graham, B. (1993) *Adult Learning Adult Teaching*. Nottingham: Nottingham University.

Dale, E. and Nyland, B. (1985) *Cone of Learning*. University of Wisconsin: Eau Claire.

Deming, W.E. (1982) *Out of the Crisis*. Cambridge, MA: MIT Press.

Engineering Employers Federation (South) (2003) *Benchmarking the Competent Person in Manufacturing and Engineering Sectors*. RR121/2003. Sudbury: HSE Books.

European Agency for Safety and Health at Work (2003) http://europe.osha.int

Fonda, N. (1989) Management development: the missing link in sustained performance. *Personnel Management*, December, **21**, 50–53.

Glendon, I.A. and McKenna, E.F. (1995) *Human Safety and Risk Management*. London: Chapman & Hall.

Hale, A.R. (1984) Is safety training worthwhile? *Journal of Occupational Accidents*, **6**, 17–33.

Hale, A.R. (2002) New qualification profiles for health and safety at work specialists. *Proceedings of the XVth World Congress on Safety and Health at Work, Vienna, 26–31 May 2002, Session B2*.

Hawkins, J. and Booth, R.T. (1998) Safety and health management system guidance: a view founded on BS 8800:1996. *Journal of the Institution of Occupational Safety and Health*, **2**(1), 7–24.

Health and Safety Commission (1990) *Advisory Committee on Safety in Nuclear Installations: Study Group on Human Factors First Report on Training and Related Matters*. Sudbury: HSE Books.

Health and Safety Executive (1994) *The Fire at Hickson and Welch Ltd: A Report of the Investigation by the Health and Safety Executive into the Fatal Fire at Hickson and Welch Ltd, Castleford on 21 September 1992.* Sudbury: HSE Books.

Health and Safety Executive (1996) *Reducing Error and Influencing Behaviour.* HSG48. Sudbury: HSE Books.

Health and Safety Executive (2000) *Successful Health and Safety Management.* HSG65. Sudbury: HSE Books.

Honey, P. and Mumford, A. (1986) *The Manual of Learning Styles.* Maidenhead: Peter Honey.

Kirkpatrick, D. (1994) *Evaluating Training Programmes: The Four Levels.* San Francisco: Berret-Koehler.

Kolb, D.S. (1984) *Experiential Learning.* Englewood Cliffs, NJ: Prentice Hall.

Lee, J.F. (1999) *Education of Undergraduate Engineers in Risk Concepts.* London: Health and Safety Executive.

Longworth, N. and Davies, W.K. (1996) *Lifelong Learning.* London: Kogan Page.

Management of Health and Safety at Work Regulations 1999. London: HMSO.

Patrick, J. (1992) *Training: Research and Practice.* London: Academic Press.

Rasmussen, J. (1986) *Information Processing and Human–Machine Interaction: An Approach to Cognitive Engineering.* Amsterdam: Elsevier.

Rasmussen, J. (1997) Risk management in a dynamic society: a modelling problem. *Safety Science,* **27,** 183–213.

Rogers, A. (1986) *Teaching Adults.* Milton Keynes: Open University Press.

Rogers, C. (1967) The Facilitation of Significant Learning. In: L. Siegel (ed.) *Instruction: Some Contemporary Viewpoints.* Scranton: Chandler Publishing.

Shannon, H.S., Robson, L.S. and Guastello, S.J. (1999) Methodological criteria for evaluating occupational safety intervention research. *Safety Science,* **31,** 161–179.

Skinner, B.F. (1969) *Contingencies of Reinforcement: A Theoretical Analysis.* Englewood Cliffs, NJ: Prentice Hall.

Stephenson, J. (1994) Capability and competence: are they the same and does it matter? *Capability: Education and Training for Life and Work,* **1**(1). http://www.lle.mdx.ac.uk/hec/journal/1-1/0-2.htm

Training Solutions (1998) Health and safety training standards. *Training Solutions for Health and Safety,* **1** (March), 8–12.

Van Dijk, F.J.H. (1995) From input to outcome: changes in OHS-education and training. *Safety Science,* **20,** 165–171.

Vidal-Gomel, C. and Samurçay, R. (2002) Quality analyses of accidents and incidents to identify competencies. The electrical systems maintenance case. *Safety Science,* **40,** 479–500.

Winterton, J. and Winterton, R. (1996) *The Business Benefits of Competence-Based Management Development.* DfEE Research Studies 16. London: HMSO.

Wright, M., Turner, D. and Horbury, C. (2003) *Competence Assessment for the Hazardous Industries.* Sudbury: HSE Books.

Performance measurement

> *'No data yet', he answered. 'It is a capital mistake to theorize before you have all the evidence. It biases the judgement.'*
>
> – Conan Doyle (1974: 36)

Chapter contents

- Introduction
- The principles of performance measurement
- Developing performance indicators
- Measuring health and safety performance
- Reporting health and safety performance

Introduction

Increasingly, organisations in the private and public sectors have recognised that performance measurement is an important element of continuous improvement, organisational growth and prosperity. The role of performance measurement is captured by the frequently cited phrases *you can't manage what you can't measure* and *what gets measured gets done*. Moreover, as stakeholders take a greater interest in the activities of organisations, performance data enable stakeholders to assess whether organisations have discharged their responsibilities. Health and safety performance can be measured reactively, in terms of, for example, the harm to people and property, and proactively, in terms of, for example, the level of training and the number of audits carried out. The main aim of this chapter is to discuss the principles of performance measurement and, in particular, the approaches adopted for health and safety. The relative merits and difficulties associated with reactive and proactive monitoring techniques are also discussed.

The principles of performance measurement

According to Drucker (1999), the specific purpose of a business enterprise is to achieve a certain level of economic performance, which is in contrast to public services, whose main purpose is to provide acceptable levels of service. On this basis, economic performance should be a key performance indicator in business. Although economic performance is considered the *raison d'être* for most businesses, this overall objective should be translated into subobjectives that reflect the various activities within the business, such as environment, health and safety, quality, production, marketing, supply chain and human resources. Within the public sector, on the other hand, the fundamental objective of performance measurement is to secure continuous improvement in the provision of public services and accountability (Audit Commission, 2000a).

Financial measures have been at the heart of organisational performance measurement systems for many years. However, as organisations changed, they became driven by a desire to achieve customer satisfaction, and therefore financial performance measures became only one of a much wider set of business performance measures.

> In today's worldwide competitive environment companies are competing in terms of product quality, delivery, reliability, after-sales service and customer satisfaction. By focusing mainly on financial variables there is a danger that the performance reporting system will motivate managers to focus exclusively on cost-reduction and short-term profitability and ignore many of the critical factors that determine long-term business success.
>
> Zairi (1994: xi)

Although the terms 'performance indicator' and 'performance measure' are often used interchangeably, a distinction can usefully be made between them (Jackson and Palmer, 1989).

Performance measures usually refer to those criteria and parameters that can be used to determine, precisely and explicitly, an organisation's economy, efficiency and effectiveness. For example, the number of units produced per hour on a production line is a measure of efficiency.

Performance indicators usually refer to those data and criteria that cannot provide precise measures of an organisation's economy, efficiency or effectiveness but which can provide indicative data that are useful for highlighting particular issues. For example, inspection data that show poor levels of housekeeping in a work area may be indicative of an increased risk of a slip, trip or fall injury, and this in turn is indicative of poor safety management.

Performance data have a wide range of users and uses, and therefore the specific requirements of the data should be considered when defining performance indicators and measures so that these requirements can be addressed. Typical users and uses of performance data include:

- chief executives and senior managers, to assess the level of achievement of corporate objectives, such as return on investment;

- employees, to assess the level of achievement of operational objectives, such as production rates;
- external bodies, to assess the level of compliance with legislation, such as emissions to land, water and air;
- the public and interest groups, to assess the level of achievement of social objectives, such as waiting times for hospital treatment; and
- politicians, in order to assess the level of achievement of political objectives, such as education standards.

Performance measurement may be linked to the process of benchmarking, in which comparisons are made between business units within an organisation or between different organisations in order to identify best practice and opportunities for improvement (see Chapter 15). Additionally, because it can be considered to be a part of an organisation's continuous improvement cycle (Figure 14.1), performance measurement should not be viewed as an end in itself. Well-designed performance measures and indicators will raise questions and identify problems in a management system, but they should also indicate where the answers to these problems can be found.

The Audit Commission (2000a) defined six principles or attributes of an effective performance measurement system.

Clarity of purpose requires that a performance measurement system be defined in terms of, for example, the target audience, how the data will be used, and for what purpose the data are required.

Focus on organisational objectives requires that performance measures be determined by the objectives of a particular operational activity or strategic objective of an organisation.

Alignment of operational and corporate performances requires that there is a link between the performance measurement system and the objective-setting and review processes of an organisation. For example, managers' personal targets should be described in terms of operational performance measures or indicators, which in turn should be linked to corporate objectives and performance.

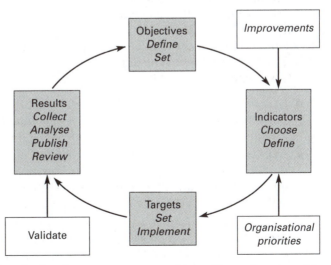

Figure 14.1 The role of performance measurement in continuous improvement

Balanced view of organisational performance requires that the performance measurement system reflects a balanced view of the organisation's activities.

Regular refinement requires that the performance measurement system, like other parts of a management system, incorporates a periodic evaluation and review process in order to ensure that the system continues to achieve its desired aims.

Robust performance indicators are those that display a number of characteristics, including:

■ relevant to the overall mission and activities of the organisation;
■ accurate and statistically valid;
■ understandable and usable by stakeholders;
■ comparable across departments, sites, organisations and over time;
■ verifiable by third party auditors and inspectors;
■ cost-effective;
■ responsive to changes in performance;
■ providing accountability for performance;
■ enabling innovation and continuous improvement; and
■ timely for operational and strategic purposes.

Developing performance indicators

The selection and application of performance indicators may have a major impact on the operation and overall direction of an organisation. In developing a set of performance indicators, an organisation should consider which activities are important and which reflect the organisation's objectives. Poor definition of objectives leads to misunderstandings, and this is often at the root of problems with performance measurement (Zairi, 1994). In order to obtain a full and balanced picture of performance, the indicators should focus on activities at each operational level within an organisation and measure what needs to be measured rather than what can be easily measured. There are a number of ways in which balanced indicator sets can be developed, but one of the most common ways is to base the selection on the dimensions of economy, efficiency and effectiveness (Jackson and Palmer, 1989).

■ *Economy* is concerned with the acquisition of the necessary human and material resources of a specified quality and quantity at the lowest cost. An example of an economy-based measure is the cost of raw materials.
■ *Efficiency* is concerned with producing the maximum output from a given resource input or using the minimum inputs for the production of a defined quantity and/or quality of output. An example of an efficiency-based measure is the amount of electricity consumed per unit of production.
■ *Effectiveness* is concerned with delivering the requirements of the customer and having a service or product that satisfies its aims or intended use. An example of an effectiveness-based measure is the proportion of satisfied customers.

The dimensions of cost, quality and time can also be used to obtain a balanced set of performance measures. The cost dimension reflects production economics; the quality dimension reflects the performance of a product or service and/or its suitability for the user; and the time dimension reflects the responsiveness and speed with which products and services are produced and/or delivered. For example, a balanced set of performance indicators might include the average cost per unit delivered (cost); the percentage of deliveries made to the correct location (quality); and the average time from receipt of order to despatch of order (timeliness).

The *balanced scorecard* approach (Kaplan and Norton, 1992) links short-term operational control with long-term business strategy, and focuses management's attention onto a limited number of critical performance measures in the four key areas of stakeholders, economics, operations and development: see Figure 14.2. In order to accommodate both short- and long-term performance measures, the balanced scorecard approach uses three time bases to cover yesterday's, today's and tomorrow's activities.

Outcome measures

An important but sometimes problematic part of performance measurement is determining outcome measures that reflect an organisation's objectives. Often the outcomes from initiatives may take some time to emerge, and they may be influenced by several confounding factors over time. Outcome measures of effectiveness require a clear understanding of what the organisation is trying to achieve; in contrast, economy and efficiency indicators can be constructed more easily by assessing costs and the use of resources.

The *ripple effect* approach (Audit Commission, 2000b) is a useful means of identifying and providing links between an organisation's objectives and outcome measures. An analogy can be drawn with a pebble tossed into a pond, which causes concentric ripples of effect to reach the furthest extremes of the pond. The ripples or outcomes furthest from the centre point reflect the overarching objectives or philosophy of the organisation, and are achieved as a result of the immediate ripples created at the centre: this analogy reflects the indirect measurable operational aspects of an activity. Figure 14.3 illustrates the ripple effect by linking the immediate objective of a company's sales function to a range of outcomes related to this objective.

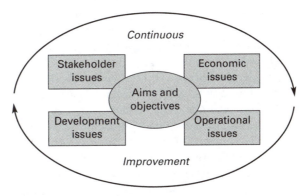

Figure 14.2 The balanced scorecard approach to performance measurement

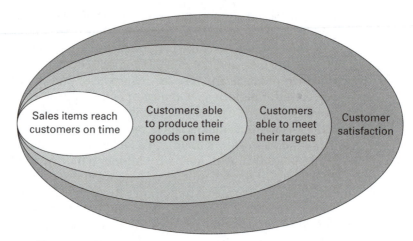

Figure 14.3 The ripple effect of performance measurement
Source: Adapted from Audit Commission (2000b)

The principle of the ripple effect can be used effectively to develop a range of performance indicators that are linked to an organisation's objectives and it is particularly useful in situations where an immediate outcome measure does not exist. In some cases the outcomes from a particular activity may take time to appear, such as the impact of carcinogenic chemicals on employees' health. In these cases performance measures of intermediate activities or effects, which reflect the final outcome, can be used. However, a causal relationship must be established between these intermediate process measurements and the final outcome.

Measuring health and safety performance

Despite the proliferation of guidance in the management and public sector literature on the measurement of performance and the development of non-financial indicators, there is little information on the measurement of health and safety performance (OECD, 2003). The work of Bird and Germain (1986) and the Health and Safety Executive (1999) highlights the impact that poor accident or loss control can have on the financial and operational well-being of an organisation. Whereas organisations have developed a strong recognition of the benefits of matching performance measures to organisational objectives, specific measures for health and safety are not well developed. However, developments in corporate governance have created a renewed focus on the control of health and safety risks and the identification of health and safety performance measures (Health and Safety Executive, 2001).

Clearly 'health and safety' can be defined as the absence of harm, which suggests that health and safety performance can be measured in terms of the presence or absence of harm. Recording instances of harm, such as injury, ill-health and damage to equipment, provides a bottom-line measurement of health and safety performance. These types of measure are referred to as *reactive* or *lagging* measures. However, this output-focused approach to health and safety management has several limitations. For example, when injury and loss rates are low, measurements cannot provide useful information about changes in performance. Reason (1997) considered that, in these circumstances, lagging measures provided more 'noise' than 'signal', and where the likelihood of severe accidents is low, the absence of injuries is not a suitable indicator of health and safety management performance. Measures of harm are subject to random fluctuations, and values can lag influential inputs, such as training and auditing. Lagging indicators also do not provide information about why a level of performance is achieved, and as a result they can mask underlying or latent issues (Royal Society for the Prevention of Accidents, 2001).

An alternative and complementary approach to the use of reactive measures is the linkage of output performance, such as accidents and ill-health, with inputs to the health and safety management system, such as inspections and training. This type of measurement is referred to as *proactive performance measurement* and the measures as *proactive* or *leading* measures. Measures of this type provide an opportunity to monitor the effectiveness of risk control systems and to gain advance warning of weaknesses or deficiencies before actual failures occur. In order for proactive/leading performance measures to be effective in improving health and safety performance there must be a causal relationship between the proactive/leading inputs and the reactive/lagging outputs. Figure 14.4 illustrates the relationships between reactive/lagging and proactive/leading indicators. Where leading and lagging indicators fall in Region I, both input and output performances are poor. In Region II the good input performance achieved is not matched by the output performance. This may be the result of a time delay between an improvement in inputs and a corresponding improvement in output performance, or it may simply be that there is no causal link between the inputs and outputs. In Region III the good output performance may be a result of luck and the insensitivity of lagging measures to changes. In Region IV the good input performance is matched by a good output performance.

Reactive performance measurement

Reactive measurement is concerned with the collection of information on the outputs of a health and safety management system, such as accidents and ill-health. Output measures have the advantage of being easily understood, easily

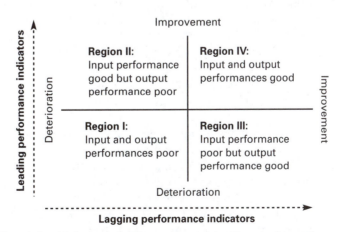

Figure 14.4 The relationship between leading and lagging health and safety performance indicators

communicated and easily calculated. However, the Audit Commission (2000b) highlighted the importance of organisations measuring activities because they are relevant and not just because they are easy to measure. In most industrial nations certain specified accidents and ill-health occurrences are recorded as a requirement of the national regulatory system. The accuracy of national data on injuries at work is clearly dependent on employers complying with these regulatory reporting requirements; unfortunately, under-reporting is a serious problem in some industrial sectors. Therefore organisations with good reporting procedures that operate in sectors with high levels of under-reporting may find that their performances appear to be poor compared with the published rates for their sector. Despite this cautionary note, accident rates do provide an absolute measure of performance over time and an effective way of comparing performances between similar business units within an organisation.

Gathering information on minor injuries and other non-injury incidents is usually more challenging; however, it is important to collect information on all injuries and potential losses in order to take steps to prevent more serious injuries associated with the same risks from occurring. Many organisations committed to improving health and safety performance operate near-miss or learning-event reporting systems in order to gather this type of information.

In order to facilitate comparisons of health and safety performance between organisations, over time and with statistics published by external sources, such as regulatory bodies, accident data are usually normalised and expressed as an incidence of injuries or ill-health. Incidence can be calculated as the number of injuries or cases of ill-health in a defined period of time (normally a year) per 100 000 employees:

$$\frac{\text{Number of reportable incidents in the period}}{\text{Average number of employees during the period}} \times 100\,000$$

However, this formula takes no account of variations in working arrangements, such as part-time working or overtime, and may therefore give rise to discrepancies in the incidence rate between different organisations if the working patterns are not the same. Therefore incidence can also be calculated as the number of injuries or cases of ill-health per hours worked. By counting the number of hours worked, rather than the number of employees, discrepancies that may be caused in the incidence rate calculation by part-time workers and overtime are avoided. The calculation applies to any chosen period of time.

$$\frac{\text{Number of reportable incidents in the period}}{\text{Total number of hours worked during the period}} \times 100\,000$$

Where employee numbers are small, the incidence may not be the best way to illustrate or monitor health and safety performance, as the measure will be extremely sensitive to small changes in the total number of accidents. For example, a company with 10 employees working 40 hours per week will have an incidence of injury of 0 for zero accidents and 5 for one reportable accident in a year. For an organisation with 500 employees working the same number of hours, the incidence only changes from 0 to 0.1 for one reportable accident. In small and medium-size enterprises the use of a rolling or cumulative incidence, which measures the value over a period of several years, may be a more representative measure of performance.

Proactive performance measurement

Proactive performance measurement provides an organisation with an indication of its health and safety performance before an accident, incident or ill-health occurs. In order to develop performance measures for proactive monitoring it is necessary to consider those inputs that lead to effective health and safety management, such as:

- plant and equipment which is 'fit for the purpose' of reducing the risks from identified hazards as far as is reasonably practicable;

- systems and procedures to operate and maintain that equipment in a satisfactory manner and to manage all associated activities;

- people who are competent, through knowledge, skills, and attitudes, to operate the plant and equipment and to implement the systems and procedures.

European Process Safety Centre (1996: 3–4)

The premise is therefore that the provision of positive inputs to a health and safety management system should prevent or reduce negative outputs (or failures). Proactive or leading performance measurements that reflect the three positive input areas of health and safety management should complement the reactive or lagging output performance measures and compensate for their limitations. The input performance measures must be linked via a causal relationship to the outputs of the health and safety management system: for example, measuring employees' compliance with a particular safety procedure could be linked to the level of accidents and incidents in this activity. The ripple effect (Audit Commission, 2000b) can also be used to develop input performance measures that are linked to outputs. However, a lack of understanding of the linkage between input and output measures can lead to the targeting of inappropriate measures. For example, if eye injuries occur it would be appropriate to measure the use of eye protection in the work area, but in the absence of such injuries this measure would be of little value. Similarly, if the value of an input measure is already high this measure will not provide useful data for monitoring improvements in performance. There is clearly no single universal proactive measure of health and safety performance but a range of measures that fall within the three categories of inferential, semi-quantitative and quantitative.

Inferential indicators are based on the number of non-conformances found and the number, nature and type of recommendations made following audits and inspections. For example, in a workplace inspection it may have been noted that particular work areas were cluttered and had poor housekeeping; although this non-conformance is not a direct measure of safety performance, it can be inferred that poor housekeeping is indicative of poor hazard management, which may in turn lead to slips, trips and falls. Similarly, evidence of repeated audit recommendations to address the same problem indicates poor procedural and people control and inadequate management actions to rectify workplace deficiencies.

Semi-quantitative measures of health and safety performance include descriptive scale measures, such as poor, satisfactory or good. In the case of workplace inspections, cluttered work areas may be rated on a scale with qualitative descriptions, such as 'poor' (floor and surface areas cluttered), 'satisfactory' (generally clear but some clutter on floors and surfaces) and 'good' (no or very little clutter on floors and surfaces).

Quantitative measures include percentage compliance figures for activities and ratings of the quality or effectiveness of these activities. For example, employers have a duty to provide training for employees. Therefore an efficiency performance measure for this activity would be the percentage of the workforce requiring manual handling training who have actually completed the training. An effectiveness performance measure will relate, in this case, to the quality of the training, such as how well the trainees perform in respect of manual handling in the workplace. A high level of efficiency and a high level of effectiveness predict a high level of performance: see Figure 14.5.

Understanding the contribution that different inputs make to outputs will increase the value of leading performance indicators, and therefore a periodic analysis of the relationship between leading and lagging indicators is good practice. It is appropriate to use statistical tests in order to identify and verify cause–effect relationships between inputs and outcomes. Although several indicators may be available for monitoring the range of inputs, it can often be difficult to measure and convey an overall level of performance. Individual performance indicators can be combined to produce a compound performance indicator. The reporting of leading and lagging performance indicators, however, can create confusing messages when the leading and lagging indicators appear to be out of line with each other. It can therefore be useful to plot the values of leading performance indicators against the values of lagging performance indicators to assess overall performance (Step Change in Safety, 2003). This method of presentation enables a visual check to be made on the relationship between

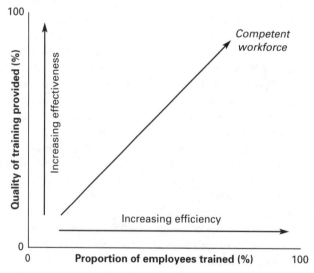

Figure 14.5 Quantitative measures of health and safety performance

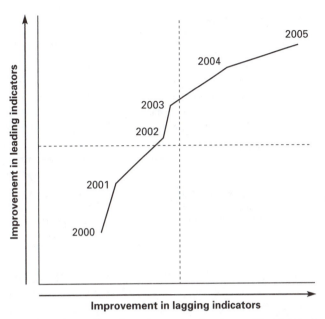

Figure 14.6 Presentation of overall performance using leading and lagging indicators
Source: Adapted from Step Change in Safety (2003)

input and output performance measures. Figure 14.6, which shows the perform-ance of a company over a period of several years, illustrates how improvements in the leading performance indicators are not immediately reflected in the lag-ging indicators. However, the lagging performance indicators eventually reflect the continuous improvement achieved in the performance of leading indicators.

Robust proactive performance measures should provide data over timescales that reflect the nature of the indicators (Audit Commission, 2000a) and should reflect operational, strategic and thematic issues.

- *Operational* performance measures reflect the day-to-day management of health and safety risks, and should be collected by local line management at monthly, weekly or daily frequencies.

- *Strategic* or corporate performance measures reflect senior management views on the management of health and safety risks, and should be undertaken by independent third parties, typically at one- to three-year intervals.

- *Thematic* performance measures address generic aspects of the health and safety management system, and may be undertaken internally or externally by specialists.

Table 14.1 provides examples of the measurement activities that can be under-taken within each section of the performance matrix; in practice some measurement activities will provide data for more than one section of the matrix.

The categories of proactive measures and their linkage to outputs have been discussed, but a number of organisational factors influence their development, such as size of organisation, available resources, existing level of health and safety performance and the nature and risks associated with the work. For example, small and medium-sized businesses typically have limited health and safety resources compared with large multinational organisations. Whereas the main

Table 14.1 Health and safety performance measurement matrix

Input	Performance measures		
	Operational	Strategic	Thematic
Physical systems	Inspections of equipment and facilities, such as conveyor guards	Review specified safety integrity levels on high-risk equipment	Mechanical integrity assessments, such as lifting equipment
Management systems	Compliance audits, such as permits to work	Senior management review of company policies and protocols	Systems integrity audits
Human factors	Employees' safe and unsafe acts, such as manual handling	Senior management involvement, such as health and safety committees	Attitude and perception surveys

concern of small and medium-sized enterprises may be achieving legal compliance, large organisations may strive for standards that achieve performance levels in excess of the minimum legal compliance. Scotney (2000), for example, reported a performance measurement tool for UK Health and Safety Executive inspectors based around legal compliance specifically for use in small and medium-sized companies. Step Change in Safety (2003), on the other hand, proposed three levels of proactive/leading performance indicators for measuring an organisation's safety culture maturity. At level 1, organisations are concerned with compliance, and leading indicators should focus on legislation and the health and safety management system. At level 2, performance indicators should focus on monitoring the effectiveness of the health and safety management system, such as the number of health and safety audits planned and completed, and the frequency and effectiveness of safety talks. It is also appropriate to retain some compliance-based indicators at level 2 in order to assess whether legal compliance is still maintained. At level 3, an organisation has developed a culture of continuous improvement and learning, and therefore performance indicators should reflect local issues. First- and second-level indicators, however, should continue to be used in order to warn of developing weaknesses in the management system. The three levels of performance indicator provide the foundation for a continuous improvement process that seeks to increase the positive input measures while decreasing negative outputs.

Reporting health and safety performance

The publication of performance data enables stakeholders to assess whether an organisation's commitments and obligations to the management of risk have been fulfilled. For example, a company that has environmental obligations to prevent defined emissions to the atmosphere may publish environmental performance data on carbon dioxide, sulphur dioxide and toxic metal emissions in its annual report. Performance measures should therefore be used as a means to promote the accountability of organisations to their stakeholders. Guidance on reporting health and safety performance (Institution of Occupational Safety and Health, 2002) suggested that there were three levels of health and safety reporting: minimal, comprehensive internal and external reports.

Minimal reporting covers workplace injuries/ill-health, significant adverse events, comparisons with long-term organisational or national targets, and priorities and targets for the forthcoming year.

Comprehensive internal reports are usually produced as organisations develop a risk management approach to health and safety rather than a compliance-led approach. In addition to statistics that are largely based around lagging indicators, these reports include information on leading performance indicators and a commentary on a range of health and safety activities, such as employee involvement in health and safety.

External reports on health and safety performance are produced by organisations that recognise the importance of discourse with their external stakeholders as part of their long-term sustainability. Such reports should be considered within the overall context of corporate social responsibility reporting, for which the Global Reporting Initiative (2002) produced guidelines that were consistent with good practice health and safety reporting.

Peebles *et al.* (2002) described the level and quality of health and safety reporting in the annual reports of the UK top companies. Less than half of the company reports contained information on health and safety issues, and there was considerable variation in the quality of the reporting. For example, some organisations devoted complete sections of their annual report to health and safety matters, whereas others included only brief statements on compliance with national legislation. The number of companies including health and safety information in their annual reports increased from 1995 to 2000, but there were still some top UK companies that did not report health and safety information. A later study (Peebles *et al.*, 2003) indicated that the level of health and safety reporting had increased further by 2002. However, the nature and quality of the reporting remained variable. For example, virtually all companies reported on the company health and safety policy, but under half reported on their health and safety performance, and lagging indicators were the most common source of data. The overall quality of reporting of health and safety performance raises questions about companies' recognition of the importance of public reporting to stakeholders.

In most industrial nations the recording of certain accidents and ill-health is a requirement of the national health and safety regulatory system. It is therefore possible to gain a national perspective of health and safety performance based on the collection of reactive data. These statistics enable injury data to be analysed by, for example, industrial sector and nature of accident: this enables stakeholders to pinpoint key issues and trends within sectors. Companies may also use this type of data in order to compare their performance with sector average figures as part of a benchmarking exercise. International comparisons of health and safety performance may also offer some potential for identifying routes to improvement, particularly within similar industrial sectors, similar hazards or within groups of countries operating under similar regulatory frameworks, such as within the European Union. However, cross-country comparisons must be treated with some caution, as many countries have different reporting requirements and different definitions of reportable injuries.

Summary

- Performance measurement is an essential part of business management at all levels of an organisation. There are six key characteristics or attributes of an effective performance measurement system, namely: clarity of purpose, focus, alignment, balance, regular refinement and robustness.

- The development of effective performance indicators requires the linkage of indicators to the objectives of an organisation. The ripple effect provides a means of linking operational performance indicators and measures to organisational objectives.

- Reactive/lagging health and safety performance measures focus on outputs such as organisational failures and non-conformances. Although reactive/lagging measures are often easily gathered they have limitations, such as not providing feedback on influential activities and underlying or latent issues.

- Proactive/leading performance health and safety measures focus on the inputs to health and safety management systems and provide a means of overcoming many of the limitations of reactive/lagging performance measurement. However, it is important to establish a cause–effect relationship between inputs and outputs when using leading indicators.

- The level of monitoring and reporting of health and safety performance is influenced by an organisation's size, available resources, current standards of health and safety and nature of the risks associated with the organisation's activities.

Issues for review and discussion

- Evaluate the importance of the six principles of an effective performance measurement system as defined by the Audit Commission (2000a).

- Review the use of reactive measures of health and safety management performance.

- Review the use of proactive measures of health and safety management performance.

- Consider the advantages and disadvantages of compound health and safety performance indicators based on reactive and proactive measures.

- Consider the advantages and disadvantages of organisations using the minimal, comprehensive internal and external reporting approaches for communicating health and safety performance.

References

Audit Commission (2000a) *Aiming to Improve: The Principles of Performance Measurement.* London: Audit Commission.

Audit Commission (2000b) *On Target: The Practice of Performance Indicators.* London: Audit Commission.

Bird, F.E. and Germain, G.L. (1986) *Practical Loss Control Leadership*. Loganville: International Loss Control Institute.

Conan Doyle, Sir A. (1974) *A Study in Scarlet*. London: J. Murray and J. Cape.

Drucker, P.F. (1999) *Management: Tasks, Responsibilities, Practices*. Oxford: Butterworth-Heinemann.

European Process Safety Centre (1996) *Safety Performance Measurement*. Rugby: Institution of Chemical Engineers.

Global Reporting Initiative (2002) *Sustainability: Reporting Guidelines*. Boston: GRI.

Health and Safety Executive (1999) *The Costs to Britain of Workplace Accidents and Work-Related Ill-Health in 1995/96*. Sudbury: HSE Books.

Health and Safety Executive (2001) *A Guide to Measuring Performance*. www.hse.gov.uk/opsunit/perfmeas.htm

Institution of Occupational Safety and Health (2002) *Guidance on Including Health and Safety Performance in Annual Reports*. Wigston: Institution of Occupational Safety and Health.

Jackson, P. and Palmer, R. (1989) *First Steps in Performance Measurement in the Public Sector: A Management Guide*. London: Public Finance Foundation.

Kaplan, R.S. and Norton, D.P. (1992) The balanced scorecard: measures that drive performance. *Harvard Business Review*, Jan–Feb, **70**, 71–79.

OECD (2003) *Guidance on Safety Performance Indicators*. Paris: OECD.

Peebles, L., Kupper, A. and Heasman, T. (2002) *A Study of the Provision of Health and Safety Information in the Annual Reports of the Top UK Companies*. CRR 446/2002. Sudbury: HSE Books.

Peebles, L., Kupper, A., Robertson, V. and Heasman, T. (2003) *The Provision of Health and Safety Information in the Annual Reports, Websites and Other Publicly Available Documents Produced by the UK's Top Companies and a Sample of Government Departments, Agencies, Local Authorities and NHS Trusts*. RR134. Sudbury: HSE Books.

Reason, J. (1997) *Managing the Risks of Organisational Accidents*. Aldershot: Ashgate.

Royal Society for the Prevention of Accidents (2001) *Measuring and Reporting on Corporate Health and Safety Performance: Towards Best Practice*. Birmingham: Royal Society for the Prevention of Accidents.

Scotney, V. (2000) *Development of a Health and Safety Performance Measurement Tool*. CRR309/2000. Sudbury: HSE Books.

Step Change in Safety (2003) *Leading Performance Indicators: Guidance for Effective Use*. http://www.stepchangeinsafety.net

Zairi, M. (1994) *Measuring Performance for Business Results*. London: Chapman & Hall.

CHAPTER 15

Auditing, benchmarking and continuous improvement

She knows there's no success like failure
And that failure's no success at all.

– Bob Dylan, 'Love minus zero/No limit' (1965)

Chapter contents

- Introduction
- The role of auditing
- The audit process
- Format of an audit report
- Health and safety auditing
- Quality management
- Continuous improvement
- Development of benchmarking
- The benchmarking process

Introduction

Auditors were originally employed to assess an organisation's financial accounts and provide a statement of authenticity (or not as the case may be); a statement to this effect is still required in annual reports. The word 'audit' originates from the Latin verb audire, which means 'to hear', because, when audits were first introduced, an audit involved an oral presentation. Now the term is used in a much broader sense, and covers a wider range of activities, such as management audits, equipment inspections, accident investigations and performance checks. The use of the word 'audit' in this context is linked to the management belief that 'if it gets measured it gets done', even though in many audits nothing is actually measured. The terms 'audit' and 'inspection' are often used interchangeably in health and safety management; however, the terms may be viewed as the two extremes of a continuum process, with high-level strategic management audits at one end and specific operational inspection programmes at the other end. In the discussion within this chapter the term 'audit' is used throughout, unless otherwise specified, to cover both terms.

In the search for improved performance, some organisations have compared performances across operational units for many years. These internal comparisons were generally undertaken when particular operations were going through bad times, and comparisons were made to bring the poorer operations up to what were perceived to be the better standards of the successful parts of the organisation. Comparisons of this type were rarely, if ever, undertaken when an organisation was prospering, because there appeared to be no incentive to question current management practices. This approach, however, led to complacency, as there was an absence of a continuous improvement philosophy. Although Japan and the USA have employed intra- and inter-company comparisons or benchmarking for many years, other countries have only recognised the benefits more recently.

The aims of this chapter are to discuss the principles of effective auditing, to relate these principles to health and safety management, and to present the main elements of a health and safety audit programme. The principles and practices of benchmarking are also discussed, together with the roles of auditing and benchmarking in the process of continuous improvement.

The role of auditing

Auditing is defined as:

> A systematic process of objectively obtaining and evaluating evidence regarding assertions about economic actions and events to ascertain the degree of correspondence between those assertions and established criteria and communicating the results to interested users.
>
> Committee on Basic Auditing Concepts (1973: 2)

Assertions refer to the claims and/or representations made by management about an issue, and the job of the auditor is to determine whether these claims are fair. In order to determine whether the claims are fair, an auditor must gather qualitative and/or quantified data to support or refute the claims. In most organisations there are systems that are designed to produce performance data, and the auditor should first test the veracity of these systems: this is referred to as *system testing*. When the systems have been validated, it is then possible to test the data derived from the system: this is referred to as *substantive testing*.

Auditing fulfils many roles within an organisation, and it is important to be clear about the purpose of a proposed audit before undertaking the audit itself. Figure 15.1 summarises the main activities controlled by an organisation's audit function.

Internal and external auditing

Internal auditing provides support for an organisation's management in order to assist them in achieving organisational aims and objectives. The Institute of Internal Auditors (2003) defines internal auditing in the following terms:

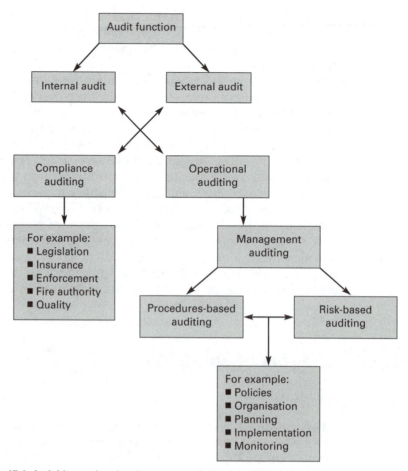

Figure 15.1 Activities undertaken by an organisation's audit function

> Internal auditing is an independent, objective assurance and consulting activity designed to add value and improve an organization's operations. It helps an organization accomplish its objectives by bringing a systematic, disciplined approach to evaluate and improve the effectiveness of risk management, control and governance processes.
>
> The Institute of Internal Auditors (2003)

External auditing provides an independent view of the assertions made by an organisation's management. External auditors normally represent the interests of stakeholders other than the organisation's management team. However, the senior management group, and directors in particular, can also employ external auditors in order to provide an independent view of the assertions made by their own middle and lower management team. Both internal and external auditing may address issues of compliance and operational performance.

Operational auditing

Operational auditing assesses an organisation's activities against criteria for efficiency and effectiveness, and concentrates on procedural issues such as health and safety management. Operational auditing should provide line management with support by identifying strengths and weaknesses in the management system and by assisting managers in identifying solutions in areas of weakness. Operational auditing traditionally involved a series of efficiency and effectiveness audits within functions and across the organisation as a routine activity. This process, however, is quite time consuming and expensive, so the modern approach is to concentrate on specific organisational activities, and to focus on those areas of risk where the cost–benefit return will be the greatest.

Management auditing forms that part of operational auditing that measures the effectiveness of an organisation's management system. The terms 'efficiency' and 'effectiveness', in the context of auditing, are used to describe different aspects of management performance. *Efficiency*, which is considered to be an input parameter, refers to minimising the costs of operation. *Effectiveness*, which is considered to be an output parameter, refers to the utilisation of an organisation's resources, and is particularly relevant for assessing an organisation's long-term profitability. The more senior the management level at which audits are implemented, the more important it is to assess effectiveness rather than efficiency.

Procedure-based auditing is normally based on standard auditing packages that address organisational issues irrespective of whether they are perceived to be of high or low risk. This approach clearly has two major disadvantages:

- low-risk activities are over-audited and high-risk activities are under-audited; and
- the risk of not detecting significant errors and omissions is greatly enhanced.

Risk-based auditing is based on the premise that auditing operations with the highest levels of risk provides the highest return on investment. Areas that are considered to be of higher importance in a risk-based audit may include issues where:

- there is a significantly higher than average level of accidents and incidents;
- there are conflicts between the levels of production output and the health and safety of employees and other stakeholders;
- employees continually raise concerns over health and safety; or
- enforcement agencies target their resources.

Compliance auditing

Internal auditing traditionally concentrated on ensuring that an organisation's assets were safe and secure, in particular those related to financial issues. However, as legislation and standards developed, directors needed to be assured that the organisation was meeting these new requirements: hence compliance auditing of operational activities developed as an assessment tool. These developments were particularly important in the case of health and safety, where compliance auditing may be undertaken voluntarily, as a specific requirement of legislation or in conjunction with enforcement agencies. Compliance auditing may also be undertaken for non-legislative reasons, such as part of a quality management system or insurance control measure.

The audit process

Successful audits require a significant amount of preparation in order to ensure that the strategy adopted addresses the relevant issues and provides the necessary information.

Planning

First the audit objectives and second the audit evaluation criteria should be defined.

Audit objectives should be realistic and achievable, and should address the risks associated with the activities being audited. Objectives can vary from a company-wide strategic view of health and safety management to very specific audits, such as the condition of ladders and personal protective equipment.

Audit evaluation criteria are essential in order to determine whether non-conformances exist. The evaluation criteria should be specific to the audit undertaken and can range, for example, from the existence of a health and safety policy statement to the presence or absence of a signature on a permit to work. Audit evaluation criteria provide the basis for the development of the audit programme.

The planning process should consider:

- background information, such as health and safety plans, employee job descriptions and responsibilities, health and safety manuals, operational procedures, budgets and the conclusions from previous audit reports;

- resource requirements, such as the number of auditors and their competence, as these may lead to the need to recruit external auditors with specific skills; and

- communication requirements, such as meetings with management groups, ongoing communication, and the methods and timescales for reporting.

Implementing

Audits are implemented in three stages.

The *preliminary survey* provides an auditor with the opportunity to acquaint him or herself with the operations, locations and personnel involved in the audit, and to confirm potential sources of data and documentation that may be required for the audit. The preliminary survey should include gathering general information about the activities, identifying areas of concern, obtaining general information, and confirming the scale of the audit. The survey may include the use of interviews, discussions and focus groups with employees, on-site observation of activities, a brief assessment of procedures, and a brief review of documentation.

The *audit programme* forms the heart of the audit, and its content, therefore, must be carefully prepared in order to ensure that all aspects of the issues under assessment are included. The audit programme should state the objectives of the audit programme, define the activities that should be assessed, and describe the procedures for collecting the audit data and information. Documentation to be inspected and validated within the programme may include, for example, management correspondence, working procedures, maintenance schedules and accident and incident data. The audit may also include interviews, discussions, questionnaires and site inspections.

Conducting the audit requires preparation of visit timetables and site contacts and allocation of times for interviews and inspections. Audits may require interaction with a wide range of personnel from directors to operators: therefore it is important that everyone involved is aware of the purpose of the audit. The auditors should preferably have an *aide-mémoire* or checklist available during interviews in order to guide them through the programme in a structured manner. An important aspect of operational auditing is to confirm that management answers to questions are matched by observations and employees' actions during site visits.

Evaluating and reporting

Evaluation and reporting should always be based on *factual* and/or *inferential* evidence.

Factual evidence is obtained from direct information that an auditor can confirm, such as accident and incident statistics and management records. Factual evidence provides stronger evidence than inferential evidence in support of audit conclusions and recommendations.

Inferential evidence is obtained, for example, from general observations and assumptions about the current or past state of affairs, the ways in which activities are carried out by employees, and responses to questions. Inferential evidence alone cannot normally lead to direct audit conclusions or recommendations.

Sources of audit evidence can be classified as physical, confirmatory, documentary, mathematical, analytical and hearsay. Any or several of these sources of evidence are acceptable for health and safety audits, but the validity of some evidence will clearly be greater than other evidence:

- *Physical evidence* includes direct data and/or information that have been gathered by counting, examination or observation, such as the proportion of employees using hard hats on a construction site.

- *Confirmatory evidence* includes information that has been obtained from third parties, such as whether health and safety induction training programmes are implemented for contractors working on site.

- *Documentary evidence* includes information obtained from company sources, such as shift log sheets, instrument calibration records, computer files.

- *Mathematical evidence* includes calculations carried out by the auditor as a means of confirming evidence presented by management, such as accident statistics.

- *Analytical evidence* includes comparisons between current performance and previous performance, results about an issue from different sources of information, results from similar operational units, and results from other organisations within the same sector.

- *Hearsay evidence* includes answers from employees to questions about health and safety activities, such as: How often do managers take an interest in health and safety issues? This type of evidence should wherever possible be supported by other sources of information. Hearsay evidence is sometimes very useful for identifying areas that may require further investigation.

The evaluation process should identify strengths and weaknesses in the ways in which an organisation's activities are performed, and how the performance of these activities could be improved. The audit conclusions and recommendations should be discussed with the management within the function audited in order to identify a strategy for progressing the recommendations and actions; it is always preferable if an agreement on the way forward from the audit can be agreed before the final audit report is produced. However, if an agreement cannot be reached, this should not deter an auditor from reporting the audit findings, conclusions, recommendations and proposed actions in full.

Audit risk

Audit risk should not be confused with risk-based auditing. Audit risk is the risk that an auditor will fail to identify errors that exist in an organisation's health and safety management system. These errors may be errors of commission or errors of omission.

Errors of commission arise where management report that a state of affairs exists or certain activities or actions have been completed when this is not actually confirmed by the audit. This may occur either through a weakness in the design of the audit programme, a lack of time for the auditor to complete that aspect of the audit programme, or a deliberate failure by the auditor to address the issue.

Errors of omission arise where an auditor fails to report that certain adverse events, such as accidents and incidents, have occurred and have not been reported by the organisation's management. It is much harder for an auditor to achieve the completeness (or omission) objective of an audit than to achieve the existence (or commission) objective of an audit, because the auditor is always trying to identify the existence of a non-specified unknown event rather than attempting to confirm whether specified known events took place.

Format of an audit report

The audit report provides the vehicle for auditors to report their opinions, summary and conclusions based on the evidence gathered from the audit. In general, a substantive audit report should follow a general format consisting of the following sections: title, addressee, introduction, scope, findings, conclusions and the auditor's disclaimer notice.

An audit report should always have a clear title, which includes the key features of the audit. The audit title should also indicate whether the audit is independent and carried out by an external auditor, an internal audit carried out by the organisation's audit function, or an internal audit carried out by line management. The audit report should state who commissioned the audit and for whom the audit report was prepared. The introduction should describe the auditor's position and their independence or otherwise from the functions and activities being audited. The scope of the audit report should provide the boundaries of the audit, when and where the audit was undertaken, and any qualifying statements about the content and extent of the audit.

The main part of the audit report should describe the auditor's findings, and should include any qualifications on the validity of the findings that the auditor thinks are appropriate to make. These opinions and comments may include statements to the effect that the results allow an *unqualified opinion*, a *qualified opinion* or an *adverse opinion* to be expressed. An unqualified opinion implies that the auditors were confident that they had gathered enough evidence to be certain that there were no errors of omission or commission in the audit report. In addition, the findings must have confirmed the assertions made by management about the state of management within the organisation. Where a qualified opinion is presented, the auditors are implying that the information gathered indicated that there were some discrepancies between the claimed performance and the actual performance, but these differences were not major. If the auditors express an adverse opinion, it implies that the information gathered indicated that there were major discrepancies between the claimed performance and the actual performance. If the auditors express a *disclaimed opinion*, it implies that restrictions were imposed on the audit, such as time limitations and accessibility and availability of data. Konrath (1993) described a decision-making framework that enabled auditors to determine whether they should report an unqualified, qualified, adverse or disclaimed opinion: see Figure 15.2.

Audit follow-up refers to the adequacy and effectiveness of actions taken by management in order to address and rectify issues that were raised in the audit report. Line management should prepare an action plan after considering the following factors:

- significance of the audit findings;
- levels of risk associated with the deficiencies identified;
- costs involved in addressing the actions compared with the benefits that may be gained from correcting the deficiencies;
- difficulties associated with implementing the corrective actions; and
- timescales required to complete the actions.

Some issues identified may be so important that immediate action is required, whereas other issues may be insignificant and present only limited risks to the organisation. The auditors should preferably identify high-, medium- and low-risk issues in their report.

Health and safety auditing

The Health and Safety Executive (2000) defined auditing as:

> The structured process of collecting independent information on the efficiency, effectiveness and reliability of the total health and safety management system and drawing up plans for corrective action.
>
> Health and Safety Executive (2000: 68)

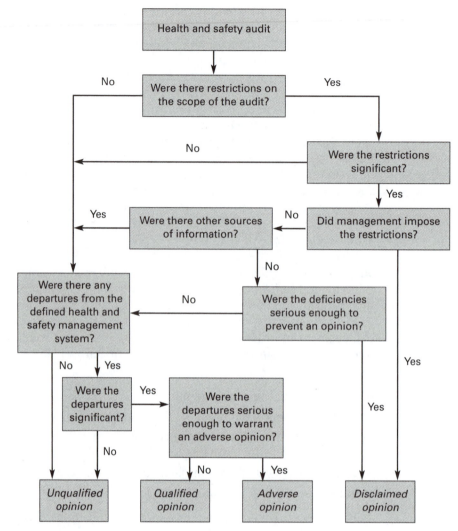

Figure 15.2 A decision-making framework for determining an audit report's opinion statement
Source: Adapted from Konrath (1993)

Auditing is included as an important element of most health and safety management systems (see Chapter 10) but few systems provide clear guidance and
contents for audit programmes. The Health and Safety Executive (2000), however, described issues that should be incorporated and assessed within an audit of
health and safety management systems: see Table 15.1.

Table 15.1 Issues incorporated within a health and safety management system audit

Element of the management system	Examples of activities included
Policy	Philosophy Scope Board level commitment
Organisation	Management responsibilities Employee consultation Employee competence
Implementation	Risk assessment procedures Risk control systems Resource allocation Continuous improvement philosophy
Measurement	Proactive performance measures Reactive performance measures
Review	Corporate governance Performance compared to sector average Developments in management system

Health and safety audit programmes

A range of formal and informal and proprietary and non-proprietary audit programmes has been developed for use in health and safety. Many of these programmes are generally similar in their aims and objectives, but there are some differences in the detail in terms of the scope, content and assessment methodology. These audit programmes are generally procedure-based rather than risk-based, because they have normally been developed for general use within a wide range of organisations: they cannot therefore address specific risk issues found within individual organisations. Proprietary audit programmes do not, in general, give guidance on how to interpret audit results or introduce improvement strategies in order to address deficiencies in performance. Three approaches are outlined here as examples of the content of typical commercial audit programmes.

Responsible Care programme

The Chemical Industries Association's (CIA) Responsible Care programme (Chemical Industries Association, 1991) was developed specifically for the chemical industry, but the framework and content of the programme are equally valid for many other sectors. The CIA programme provides a range of audit checklists for safety and occupational health topics and guidance for four levels of performance within each issue. It is not essential that every issue or even every element of the Responsible Care programme be included in every audit, rather that the auditor selects the elements and issues that are appropriate for individual audits. The safety audit consists of 11 sections (Chemical Industries Association, 1991): see Table 15.2.

Table 15.2 Issues covered within the CIA Responsible Care safety audit programme

Element of the audit programme	Examples of safety issues covered
Management controls	Safety policy Operational procedures Emergency plans Performance measurement
Hazard control	Chemical data sheets Safety lifecycle approach Maintenance procedures
Training and motivation	Induction training Ongoing training Refresher training
Accident investigation	Legal requirements Internal reporting Root cause analysis
Communication	Internal communications External communications with local community, media and interest groups
Emergencies	Availability of emergency equipment Emergency training exercises
Personal control measures	Provision of personal protective equipment Use of personal protective equipment on site
Physical controls	Bursting discs Electrical isolations Lifting equipment Guarding
Workplace	Access and egress Lighting Ventilation Stairs and walkways
Distribution	Warehousing facilities Internal traffic External traffic
Employee welfare	Amenity facilities Storage and drying facilities Rest rooms and food areas

Source: Adapted from Chemical Industries Association (1991)

The occupational health audit also consists of 11 sections (Chemical Industries Association, 1991): see Table 15.3.

The safety and occupational health audit programmes both follow an assessment system whereby ranking improves from level 1 through to level 4, as the performance reaches defined higher standards.

International Safety Rating System

The International Safety Rating System (ISRS) (International Loss Control Institute, 1990) is a comprehensive health and safety audit package consisting of

Table 15.3 Issues covered within the CIA Responsible Care occupational health audit programme

Element of the audit programme	Examples of health issues covered
Management controls	Resource allocations Communication procedures Employee competence
Hazard control	Inventories of hazardous agents Safety data sheets Risk assessment Analysis of occupational health statistics
Control of exposure	Compliance with occupational exposure limits Local exhaust ventilation Maintenance procedures
Exposure monitoring	Monitoring programmes Quality assurance schemes
Health surveillance	Compliance with legal requirements Confidentiality of personal data
First aid	Legal requirements Medical treatment facilities Rehabilitation
Health promotion	Employee health education Overseas travel procedures
Emergency response	Liaison with emergency services Exercises with emergency services
Information and training	Training procedures Operational procedures
Health records	Legal requirements Confidentiality of personal data
Audits	Legal compliance Action plans

Source: Adapted from Chemical Industries Association (1991)

20 sections with detailed assessment criteria contained within each section. The full ISRS audit programme is extremely comprehensive but also extremely time consuming and expensive to implement. However, ISRS also provides a Basic Program Audit, which is an abbreviated version of the full audit that may be more appropriate for all but the most complex and highest hazard operations. The composition of the full audit package is summarised in Table 15.4.

The ISRS audit programme uses one of three possible scoring systems, with the scoring system dependent on the issue being assessed:

- A simple no/yes answer is provided, corresponding to the absence or presence of the particular audit item. Zero or the specified score is awarded as appropriate.
- Scores are awarded in a range from zero up to the specified score based on the auditor's judgement of the level of compliance.
- Scores are awarded in a range from zero up to the specified score, based on a measured level of compliance with the issue.

Table 15.4 Outline content of the ISRS audit programme

Element	Examples of issues covered
Leadership and administration	Policy; safety coordinator; management participation and performance standards; management meetings; reference manual; management audits; individual responsibility; joint committees; safe working policy
Management training	Induction; formal; refresher
Planned inspections	General; follow-up procedures; reports; preventive maintenance; equipment inspections; hazardous conditions; general inspections; programme monitoring
Task analysis and procedures	Task inventory; task analysis; hazard analysis; programme monitoring
Accident/incident investigations	Procedures; scope of investigations; follow-up actions; major accidents; near misses; management participation
Task observation	Defined programme of observation; programme monitoring
Emergency preparedness	Leadership and administration; emergency plan; training; emergency lighting and power; protective and rescue equipment; emergency team; planning; communication
Organisational rules	General rules; specialised rules; work permits; education and review; compliance; monitoring
Accident/incident analysis	Statistics; analysis; property and equipment damage; problem-solving teams; near-miss analysis
Employee training	Training needs analysis; training programmes; evaluation
Protective equipment	Standards; records; enforcement; monitoring
Health control	Hazard identification; control; information; training; hygiene; health maintenance; assistance; communication; records
Programme evaluation	Management compliance; physical conditions; fire prevention; health; records
Engineering controls	Design; process; monitoring
Personal communications	Training; job induction; task instruction; personal interviews; monitoring
Group meetings	Group meetings; management involvement; records; monitoring
General promotion	Notice boards; statistics; awards; publications; performance; housekeeping; records
Hiring and placement	Physical capabilities; induction training; pre-employment assessment
Purchasing controls	Procurement; selection and control of contractors
Off-the-job safety	Identification; education

Source: Adapted from International Loss Control Institute (1990)

The scores obtained for each item within a section are summed to provide a total section score, and the individual section scores are then summed to provide an overall audit score. Increasing levels of performance in the audit programme enable operational sites using the audit programme to achieve awards at five levels under the Standard Programme and a further five levels under the Advanced Programme.

DuPont STOP audit system

The DuPont organisation regards auditing as a fundamental part of an effective health and safety management system, and the ability to audit as a core management skill. DuPont, however, treats health and safety auditing in a less structured and less formal manner than that used in many other approaches. Auditing is regarded as a means of preventing losses, improving safe behaviours, raising safety awareness, enforcing operational standards, and identifying weaknesses in the health and safety management system. The Safety Training Observation Programme (STOP) (DuPont, 1986) teaches line managers how to identify unsafe acts in order to minimise or eliminate injuries and ill-health from the working environment. STOP adopts a five-stage approach:

1 *Decide*. Managers consciously make time for safety audits to the exclusion of other activities.
2 *Stop*. Managers consciously observe employees' working behaviours.
3 *Observe*. Managers observe employees' behaviours using STOP checklists in order to structure and categorise the observed unsafe acts: see, for example, Table 15.5.
4 *Act*. Managers discuss their observations with the employees concerned.
5 *Report*. Managers make a summary of their observations and discussions with employees in order that unsafe act statistics can be established.

Table 15.5 Examples of observable elements in a STOP safe and unsafe acts audit

Section	Examples of observable elements
Actions of people	Adjusting personal protective equipment; changing position; stopping job; performing lockouts
Use of protective equipment	Head, eyes, ears and face; respiratory system; arms and hands; legs and feet
Positions of people	Striking or being struck by objects; falling; contacting temperature extremes; contacting electric current; awkward positions and postures
Tools and equipment	Wrong tool or equipment for job; used incorrectly; in unsafe condition
Procedures	Procedures or standards inadequate; procedures or standards not known or understood; procedures or standards not followed

Source: Adapted from DuPont (1986)

Strengths and weaknesses of auditing systems

Proprietary audit systems are procedure-based rather than risk-based, whereas in-house audit systems can be developed specifically to address important risk issues within the organisation. The effectiveness of a proprietary audit system should therefore be determined by the adequacy of the issues incorporated within the programme to meet the needs and address the risks of an organisation. Most proprietary audit systems provide a balanced view of an organisation by using question sets that:

■ address vertical and horizontal slices through an organisation's operational structure;
■ involve a mixture of formal and informal interviews and questions; and
■ assess site conditions.

The main advantages of proprietary audit systems are that they are well planned and well structured, and are prepared from a non-biased viewpoint. From this perspective, therefore, they provide an independent assessment of an organisation's performance. The main disadvantages of proprietary audit programmes are that they are often too general and too bureaucratic, do not necessarily address the issues that are important to an organisation, and some organisations may even develop management systems that will score highly on the audit programme rather than address the main risk issues.

Quality management

The main purpose of adopting a quality management system is to increase the probability of achieving the organisation's aims and objectives. Quality is an interesting concept because it has different meanings for different people. For this reason, it is possible for different organisations to provide different levels of quality within the same product range: this is referred to as a *quality niche*. Quality management systems have developed around important issues such as finance, budget, operations and information technology.

Total quality management

Total quality management (TQM) is a management system aimed at achieving continuous improvements in the quality of products and services provided by an organisation. Total quality management originated in the USA with Deming, who took his ideas to the more receptive economies in Japan in the late 1940s. His ideas were later supported and developed by others, such as Juran and Ishikawa in the 1950s. These three 'quality gurus' identified the key issues behind the TQM philosophy as follows (Bartol and Martin, 1998):

- Quality is cheaper than poor workmanship.
- Employees will improve quality if they are provided with the appropriate management support.
- Real improvements in quality are achieved through cross-functional cooperation.
- Improvements in quality can be achieved only with senior management support.

Quality has been defined by the American Society for Quality (2003) as the totality of features and characteristics of a product or service that bear on its ability to satisfy stated or implied needs. Quality is an issue that should be implemented strategically within an organisation for it to be effective: this depends on senior management understanding the underpinning elements of quality, which Bartol and Martin (1998) described as:

- *performance* of the primary operating characteristics of the product or service;
- *additional features* provided over and above the primary operating characteristics;
- *reliability* of the product or service;
- *conformance* of the product or service with defined standards;

- *durability* or length of service provided by the product;
- *serviceability and support* provided for the continued operation of the product;
- *aesthetics* of the product or service; and
- *perceived quality* of the product or service by the person using it.

An important aspect of quality management is achieving a balance between these eight issues, because improvements in some elements may be achieved only at the expense of performance in other elements.

Lau and Anderson (1998) reviewed attempts to introduce TQM into organisations and identified three important dimensions: philosophical, strategic, and measurement.

Philosophical dimension

Deming described 14 important management points that need to be addressed when attempting to improve quality, and these have had a major impact on the philosophy and development of TQM (Bartol and Martin, 1998):

- Create a constancy of purpose in the drive towards improvements in products and services.
- Take on the challenge, leadership and responsibilities for change.
- Eliminate the need for quality inspections by building quality into the product or service.
- Move towards cooperation with suppliers on a basis of total cost rather than component price.
- Aim for constantly decreasing costs through a continuous improvement philosophy.
- Employ job training.
- Encourage leadership and supervision.
- Eliminate employee fear in order to encourage effective working.
- Reduce inter-departmental barriers.
- Eliminate work slogans, as these do not improve quality.
- Use effective leadership rather than target numbers to achieve output.
- Use product quality rather than target numbers to achieve output.
- Introduce employee education and self-improvement programmes.
- Work towards a quality philosophy by utilising the talents and abilities of the whole workforce.

Lau and Anderson (1998) summarised the important facets of each element of the philosophical dimension of TQM as:

- *Total:* Ensure employee participation and teamwork, develop a sense of ownership by everyone, involve all levels and functions within the company and apply systems management.
- *Quality:* Focus on customers (internal and external), emphasise the continuous improvement ideal (*kaizen*), train employees to achieve competence and capability and encourage innovation.

■ *Management:* Develop commitment and leadership by senior management, establish aims, objectives and standards for the company and improve the organisational culture.

Strategic dimension

This relates to the implementation of the quality targets and actions needed to satisfy stakeholder aspirations. However, because there is no single way to ensure quality, there is no single way to establish TQM within an organisation. Therefore the design and implementation of TQM initiatives vary from company to company and country to country, because what may be effective in one organisational setting will almost certainly not be appropriate or as effective in another setting. An important aspect of TQM is the necessity to plan effectively in order to ensure that implementation programmes make the transition from the philosophical to the strategic dimension. The key outcomes from the strategic dimension are aligning TQM with the organisation's operational strategy, encouraging employee commitment to the issue of quality, and achieving organisational targets.

Measurement dimension

Organisations may expend significant effort on establishing performance measures and collecting performance data; however, if managers do not receive this information in a usable format it is very difficult for them to act on the results. Therefore collection, analysis and communication of performance data are of fundamental importance.

The link between TQM and organisational performance

Terziovski and Samson (1999) claimed that there were limited data available that established a link between TQM and organisational performance:

> The common rationale for many TQM initiatives is that they will pay off 'five to six years down the line' and the CEOs can only hope that shareholders are willing to wait that long.
>
> Terziovski and Samson (1999: 226)

In fact it was claimed that it was not TQM *per se* that improved organisational performance but the management factors implemented alongside the programmes that really achieved the improvements.

> The findings suggest that most features generally associated with TQM, such as quality training, process improvement, and benchmarking, do not generally produce advantage, but that certain tacit, behavioural, imperfectly imitable features can produce advantage. The author concludes that these tacit resources, and not TQM tools and techniques, drive TQM success, and that organisations that acquire them can outperform competitors with or without TQM.
>
> Terziovski and Samson (1999: 228)

With or without demonstrable evidence, senior managers still desire and strive to convert strategic quality initiatives into practical management systems, and a number of national and international schemes for recognising this performance have been established, such as the ISO 9000 quality management system, European Quality Awards, the Malcolm Baldridge National Quality Award, and the Deming Prize.

Continuous improvement

The application of quality criteria has developed, since the early 1900s, through the approaches of inspection, quality control, quality assurance and quality management. Although each approach developed and improved on the previous one, the emphasis was always on solving the problem of quality. It was only with developments in the era of quality management that emphasis shifted to a philosophy of prevention rather than cure. Now the emphasis has shifted even further to one of continuous improvement, which entails an organisation adopting a flexible and responsive approach to the whole issue of quality management. Adopting a continuous improvement philosophy requires questioning operating procedures with the intention of identifying ways for improving performance and eliminating organisational weaknesses. Here the focus is on measuring an organisation's current performance against a defined model that is claimed to represent business excellence, such as the European Foundation for Quality Management (EFQM, 2003) *Business Excellence Model*: see Figure 15.3.

The Business Excellence Model provides a non-prescriptive framework against which continuous improvements can be monitored. The model defines five organisational inputs – leadership, people, policy and strategy, resources and

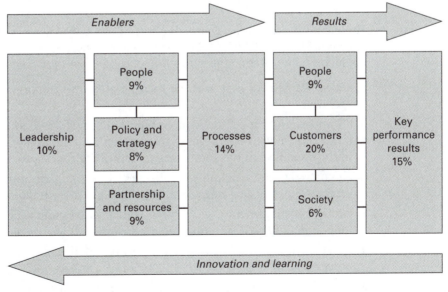

Figure 15.3 The EFQM Business Excellence Model
Source: EFQM (2003)

processes – which act as quality enablers, and four organisational outputs – people, customers, society and business performance – which provide quality results. Each of the nine components is assigned a fixed maximum proportion of the total score available for the performance assessment: see Figure 15.3. If an organisation improves the enabling components with the model, it is claimed that this should improve results for stakeholders. Although excellence is dependent on balancing the needs of all stakeholders, the customer provides the ultimate assessor of organisational quality.

Kaye and Anderson (1999) defined 10 criteria that must be in place for organisations to achieve and maintain continuous improvement:

(1) Senior management commitment and involvement.

(2) Leadership and active commitment to continuous improvement demonstrated by managers at all levels.

(3) Focusing on the needs of the customer.

(4) Integrating continuous improvement activities into the strategic goals across the whole organisation, across boundaries and at all levels.

(5) Establishing a culture for continuous improvement and encouraging high involvement innovation.

(6) Focusing on people.

(7) Focusing on critical processes.

(8) Standardizing achievements in a documented quality management system.

(9) Establishing measurement and feedback systems.

(10) Learning from continuous improvement results, the automatic capturing and sharing of learning.

Kaye and Anderson (1999: 489)

These criteria are clearly identifiable within the EFQM Business Excellence Model (Figure 15.3). Bessant *et al.* (1994) also argued that there were six principles for achieving successful long-term implementation of continuous improvement programmes:

■ a clear framework that must be incorporated into the organisation's strategic agenda;

■ an underlying supportive culture with widespread recognition of the importance and value of continuous improvement, and an acceptance that everyone in the organisation has something to contribute to the process;

■ an enabling infrastructure with the adoption of organisational structures that promote efficient two-way communication and decentralised decision-making;

■ strategic management that includes regular targets and milestones (short- and long-term) and well-communicated measurement and display routines;

■ process management with the adoption of learning or problem-solving processes; and

■ a range of supporting techniques that includes problem-solving tools and training in their application.

Development of benchmarking

Historically, the aim of most organisations has been to operate their businesses in a way that allows them to compete effectively in local, national and international markets. It is accepted that, where an organisation has a competitive edge over the competition, it is more likely to be successful; however, business performance in a world economy has changed to become more an issue of how effectively resources are used.

> Once, competitive advantage lay with those who had access to and control over physical resources. Later, possession of technology became the deciding factor. But the increasing internationalisation of markets in physical resources and technology has reduced the influence of these factors in themselves, and an increasingly sophisticated and discriminating customer base means low prices alone are no longer a guarantee of business success.
>
> The competitive edge now is with those who manage their resources most effectively in offering a timely response to the demands of the market.
>
> Department of Industry (1992: 2)

Although most organisations understand the need for strong financial controls, many do not appreciate the importance of meeting stakeholders' interests. The problem for many organisations is understanding that today's business solutions may not be tomorrow's solutions, because technology, employees, customers, standards and legislation constantly change. Therefore procedures and technology should be constantly under review, and a philosophy of continuous improvement should be adopted in order to maintain a competitive position within world markets. There are many management approaches for achieving continuous improvement, but the application of benchmarking provides the best long-term solution to the problem (Yasin, 2002; Dattakumar and Jagadeesh, 2003). It is important, however, not to confuse benchmarking with the management technique of reverse engineering. The key activities in benchmarking are the identification and analysis of operational processes in organisations that achieve industry best practices, whereas reverse engineering is the comparison and analysis of similar but superior competitor products and services.

Defining benchmarking

The term 'benchmarking' is used in different ways. For some organisations the technique is used simply as a process of comparison between organisations and/or activities. For other organisations it includes the process of identifying the ways in which improved performances may be achieved. Camp (1989) reported three definitions of benchmarking.

A *formal definition* is:

> Benchmarking is the continuous process of measuring products, services, and practices against the toughest competitors or those companies recognized as industry leaders.
>
> Camp (1989: 10)

This definition, which was developed by the chief executive officer of the Xerox Corporation, emphasised the importance of benchmarking as a continuous process, the need for performance measurement, the application of the technique to products, services and practices, and the need to compare performances with industry best practices.

A *dictionary definition* is:

> A surveyor's mark ... of previously determined position ... and used as a reference point ... standard by which something can be measured or judged.
>
> Camp (1989: 12)

Historically, the term 'benchmark' referred to a well-defined land surveyor's mark on a permanently fixed object, which is used as a reference point for altitude measurements. This interpretation of a permanently fixed mark or reference point from which to take measurements was adopted within the business community, but it was adapted later in order to allow the reference mark to be continuously changed or raised as standards of business performance improved.

A *working definition* is:

> Benchmarking is the search for industry best practices that lead to superior performance.
>
> Camp (1989: 12)

This last definition, which was adopted by Camp (1989) after many years of developing the technique, provides a simple compromise between the two earlier definitions, and incorporates the image of *dantotsu* or the philosophy of 'the best of the best'. Camp (1989) preferred this last definition because it concentrated on practices, which he felt were the key to benchmarking, and because he felt that this definition was easier for organisations to understand, and therefore it was easier for them to embrace and implement the principles of benchmarking.

The benchmarking process

Benchmarking is most effective when it forms part of everyday business practice. Whereas TQM achieves a slow but continuous improvement in performance, the aim of benchmarking is to provide a quantum jump in performance: see Figure 15.4. This approach requires a leap of imagination for some managers, as it requires them to accept that they may not currently be carrying out their activities in the most effective way. They must also accept that other people may be more effective at certain parts of their job than they are.

There are various types of benchmarking, such as internal, external, competitive, functional, generic, process, cost, performance, customer, strategic and operational benchmarking. However, these can be grouped into four basic categories:

- *Internal benchmarking* compares an organisation's performance in activities or functions with those achieved at other locations within the same organisation.

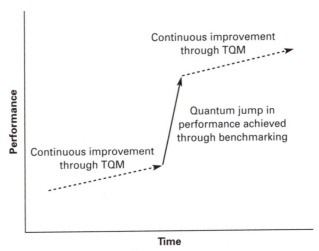

Figure 15.4 The roles of TQM and benchmarking in continuous improvement

- *External benchmarking* compares an organisation's performance in activities or functions with those achieved within similar organisations.
- *Functional benchmarking* compares an organisation's performance in products, services and/or processes with those achieved by the top companies regardless of their business sector.
- *Generic benchmarking* compares an organisation's performance in an activity or function with the performance achieved in any other relevant activities or functions by the best performing companies regardless of their business sector.

Camp (1989) summarised the underpinning philosophy behind the process of benchmarking as follows:

Know your operation. You need to assess the strengths and weaknesses of the internal operation. That assessment must be based on the understanding that competitors will analyze your operation also to capitalize on the weaknesses they uncover. If you do not know the operation's strengths and weaknesses you will not be able to defend yourself. You will not know which operations to stress in the marketplace and which will require strengthening.

Know the industry leaders or competitors. In a similar fashion you will only be prepared to differentiate your capabilities in the marketplace if you know the strengths and weaknesses of the competition. More importantly, it will become clear that only the comparison to and understanding of the best practices of industry or functional leaders will ensure superiority.

Incorporate the best. Learn from industry leaders and competition. If they are strong in given areas, uncover why they are and how they got that way. Find those best practices wherever they exist and do not hesitate to copy or modify and incorporate them in your own operation. Emulate their strengths.

Gain superiority. If careful investigations of best practices have been performed, and if the best of those best practices have been installed, then you will have capitalized on existing strengths, brought weaknesses to match the marketplace, and gone beyond to incorporate the best of the best. This position is clearly a position of superiority.

Camp (1989: 4)

Camp (1989) emphasised the importance of separating the benchmarking process into its two fundamental parts of *practices* and *metrics*. In this context, practices were regarded as the organisational methods used, and the metrics were the quantifiable effects observed from the practices. Whereas the key to performance measurement and auditing is identifying activities that can be monitored to provide quantified data on organisational performance, the key to benchmarking is identifying industry best practices. It is fundamental to the process of benchmarking that metrics will not define why weaknesses in organisational performance exist, as it is the differences in the practices on which the metrics are based that provide this level of information. The underpinning framework of the benchmarking process is presented in Figure 15.5.

Implementing the benchmarking process

Benchmarking should not be regarded simply as finding out what other organisations have done and adopting their processes within one's own organisation. The objective of benchmarking is to develop the ideas and processes of other organisations on a continuous basis. The two main elements of benchmarking are the processes of *metric benchmarking* and *process benchmarking*, both of which are normally included within a benchmarking exercise. Metric benchmarking involves comparisons of quantified performance data across the benchmarking organisations, whereas process benchmarking involves an examination and comparison of the processes that produce the levels of performance identified by metric benchmarking. Using the benchmarking framework described in Figure 15.5, the important implementation stages are:

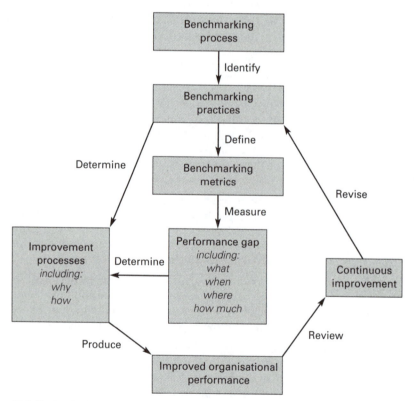

Figure 15.5 Underpinning framework for the benchmarking process

- defining the organisation's and the benchmark partners' performance standards;
- measuring the organisation's and the benchmark partners' performance;
- identifying the differences between the organisation's and the benchmark partners' performances;
- establishing, where appropriate, new performance standards for the organisation;
- defining targets and timescales for achieving these improved performance levels; and
- reassessing the organisation's performance standards on a continuous basis.

These stages, which are summarised in Figure 15.6, emphasise the close link between benchmarking and a continuous improvement philosophy.

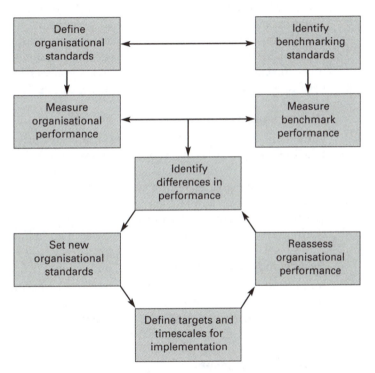

Figure 15.6 Key stages in the benchmarking process

Identify organisational activities

It is true to say that almost any *strategic* and *operational* issue can be benchmarked. For strategic issues one would generally be assessing standards of performance within an organisation, whereas for operational issues one would be considering systems of work. However, as benchmarking is neither an easy nor a cheap management exercise, it is important to limit benchmarking activities, at least to begin with, to those business activities that are critical to an organisation's success. Answering the following two questions is helpful in identifying important issues:

- Will improvements in the issue have a significant impact on stakeholder satisfaction?
- Will improvements in the issue have a significant impact on financial performance?

Identify benchmarking partners

Broadly speaking there are five categories of benchmarking partner, together with the possibility of making comparisons on an international basis as well as a national basis.

Internal partners

The first option is to use internal benchmarking partners, whereby comparisons are made between an organisation's own operational sites or management performances. The benefit of this category of benchmarking is that comparisons are made between very similar operations, and therefore it is relatively easy to analyse the results and identify improved practices. This approach is very useful for organisations setting out on the benchmarking process because it allows them to gain experience before involving external partners. This approach is limited because it does not enable new ideas to be identified and brought into an organisation at a strategic level.

Direct competitor partners

For larger organisations this is an important and often the most useful category to adopt. For smaller organisations, however, it can present difficulties if comparisons are not made with similar-sized organisations. Larger organisations invariably have greater resources available and if small or medium-sized organisations attempt to emulate them, they may be trying to reach an unachievable target. This category is the most difficult option to implement for all organisations, as few competitors will knowingly cooperate in benchmarking exercises.

Parallel industry partners

A major source of innovative ideas comes from working with partners from other industries. The reasoning behind this is that organisations within the same industry often resolve problems in similar ways, whereas organisations in other industries may address them in quite different ways.

Cross-sector partners

In this case comparisons are made of similar activities between completely different industries. This approach offers the same advantages as working with parallel industry partners.

Cross-function partners

The final option for identifying benchmarking partners is to consider benchmarking one activity against a different kind of activity. Although at first sight this may appear to be inappropriate, there are in fact many good comparisons that can be made. In the case of health and safety management systems, for example, comparisons could be made with environment and quality management.

Develop the benchmarking programme

Development of the benchmarking programme depends very much on the issues that are being assessed. In many cases the information required may already be available in the public domain: for example, financial data are included in company annual reports, environmental emissions are often accessible from public records, and health and safety statistics are available from enforcement authorities. In other cases detailed audit programmes may be required in order to extract the relevant information from customers, suppliers or employees. Other common approaches adopted for gathering data in benchmarking programmes include the use of questionnaires, interviews, focus groups and audits.

Whereas some organisations are quite happy to exchange information in some operational areas, other organisations may prefer to exchange information through a third party in order that the information provided is non-attributable. In these cases benchmarking partners receive from the third party facilitator their own performance data together with the average performance and the non-attributable best and worst performances within the benchmarking group. The disadvantage of this approach is that, although best performance is identified, it is not always possible to identify how the best organisation achieved its performance.

Analyse the benchmarking data

Only information that is relevant to the benchmark issue(s) should be collected, otherwise useful data will be masked by other irrelevant information. When a company has been identified as a superior performer in one or more aspects, the data should be analysed in order to:

- quantify the differences in performances;
- ensure that similar issues are being compared; and
- identify those management practices that are transferable.

Implement the benchmarking findings

The final stage of the benchmarking programme is the most important. However, some organisations take part in a benchmarking exercise because they have assumed that they are already the best at their business, and if this illusion is destroyed by the results they may find it difficult to accept new practices from other organisations. The outputs from a benchmarking exercise should include:

- new operational standards for performance;
- communicating the new standards and the reasons for the changes to employees and other people affected by the changes;
- targets, timescales and responsibilities for implementing the changes in standards;
- allocation of resources for implementing the changes in standards; and
- monitoring of progress against the targets for achieving the changes.

Benchmarking health and safety management systems

Most businesses operate in an environment of risk, and the key to success is to reduce the levels of risk to acceptable or tolerable levels. Health and safety represents one of the many risks to which organisations are exposed, and therefore benchmarking health and safety performance should potentially be as important as benchmarking any other business risk. One major advantage with benchmarking health and safety management is that many organisations are more than willing to share their experiences in order to raise performances throughout industry and commerce. The Health and Safety Executive (1999) addressed health and safety benchmarking, and identified three areas where benchmarking could generate improvements in performance:

reduce accidents and ill-health;

improve compliance with health and safety law; and/or

cut compliance costs

Health and Safety Executive (1999: 1)

Health and safety should be a strategic issue for senior management in most organisations, as good performance brings rewards beyond a reduction in the levels of accidents and ill-health. Health and safety management systems provide the basis for efficient and effective performance, but a move towards excellence is accelerated by the adoption of a continuous improvement philosophy supported by the process of benchmarking. Fuller (2000) developed a theoretical model using safety benefit curves in order to explain the management benefits that effective benchmarking and continuous improvement processes could provide. Issues that should be addressed when benchmarking health and safety include:

- how health and safety is managed within the organisation;
- how stakeholder satisfaction with health and safety performance is achieved;
- how health and safety is perceived by stakeholders within the organisation;
- how much health and safety management costs the organisation in terms of prevention and failures;
- how health and safety issues are communicated to stakeholders; and
- how employees and others are trained in health and safety issues.

Good practice management systems are well documented in publications such as the Health and Safety Executive's (2000) *Successful Health and Safety Management*, the British Standards Institution's (1996) *Guide to Occupational Health and Safety Management Systems* and the International Labour Organization's (2001) *Guidelines on Occupational Safety and Health Management Systems*. Although benchmarking can be applied to any aspect of a health and safety management system, it is preferable to prioritise issues and assess performances in those operational areas where risks are high. Accident statistics provide a useful guide to indicate where an organisation's main risks exist; however, it should always be remembered that the absence of accidents in some operational areas, especially those involving low-probability and high-consequence events, does not necessarily indicate that these areas are managed effectively. Prior to the benchmarking process it is often helpful to assess an organisation's current position in order that any improvements achieved through the benchmarking process can be quantified. Baseline assessments of this type can be made using proprietary or in-house audit packages coupled with questionnaires to ascertain employees' views on current management practices and performances (Fuller, 1997, 1999; Fuller and Vassie, 2001).

Summary

- Auditing is a process of obtaining and evaluating evidence about management's assertions of current performance. Effective auditing is an essential element of an effective health and safety management system.

- Operational auditing may be procedure- or risk-based. Proprietary audit programmes tend to be procedure-based rather than risk-based.

- Internal auditing should provide added value to an organisation's management system by evaluating and improving the effectiveness of the risk management process. External auditing provides an independent view of the assertions made by an organisation's management.

- Quality relates to the characteristics of a product or service that affect its ability to satisfy stated or implied needs. Total quality management is a management system aimed at achieving continuous improvement in organisational performance. The continuous improvement philosophy requires organisations to continuously question their operating procedures.

- Benchmarking is a management technique aimed at achieving significant improvements in organisational performance by identifying industry best practices. The key stages in the benchmarking process are defining the activities to be assessed, identifying partners, developing the programme, analysing the data, and implementing the results.

- The two main elements of benchmarking are metric benchmarking, which compares the performances of benchmarking partners, and process benchmarking, which compares how organisational performances are achieved.

Issues for review and discussion

- Consider the costs and benefits of using external auditors for auditing the performance of senior managers.

- Evaluate the advantages and disadvantages of procedure- and risk-based approaches in health and safety auditing.

- Review the advantages and disadvantages of using commercial health and safety audit programmes.

- Review the internal barriers that exist to carrying out a benchmarking exercise.

- Review the complementary roles of auditing and benchmarking in an organisation operating with a continuous improvement philosophy.

References

American Society for Quality (2003) http://www.asq.org.

Bartol, K.M. and Martin, D.C. (1998) *Management*. Boston: Irwin McGraw-Hill.

Bessant, J., Caffyn, S., Gilbert, J., Harding, R. and Webb, S. (1994) Rediscovering continuous improvement. *Technovation*, **14**(1), 17–29.

British Standards Institution (1996) *Guide to Occupational Health and Safety Management Systems*. London: British Standards Institution.

Camp, R.C. (1989) *Benchmarking: The Search for Industry Best Practices that Lead to Superior Performance*. Milwaukee: ASQC Quality Press.

Chemical Industries Association (1991) *Guidance on Safety, Occupational Health and Environmental Protection Auditing*. London: Chemical Industries Association.

Committee on Basic Auditing Concepts (1973) *A Statement of Basic Auditing Concepts*. Sarasota: American Accounting Association.

Dattakumar, R. and Jagadeesh, R. (2003) A review of literature on benchmarking. *Benchmarking: An International Journal*, **10**(3), 176–209.

Department of Industry (1992) *Management Best Practice: Managing into the '90s*. London: Department of Industry.

DuPont, E.I. (1986) *Safety Training Observation Program*. Wilmington: E.I. DuPont de Nemours & Co. (Inc).

European Foundation for Quality Management (2003) *Introducing Excellence*. Brussels: European Foundation for Quality Management.

Fuller, C.W. (1997) Key performance indicators for benchmarking health and safety management in intra- and inter-company comparisons. *Benchmarking for Quality Management & Technology*, **4**(3), 165-174.

Fuller, C.W. (1999) Benchmarking health and safety performance through company safety competitions. *Benchmarking: An International Journal*, **6**(4), 325–337.

Fuller, C.W. (2000) Modelling continuous improvement and benchmarking processes through the use of benefit curves. *Benchmarking: An International Journal*, **7**(1), 35–51.

Fuller, C.W. and Vassie, L.H. (2001) Benchmarking the safety climates of employees and contractors working within a partnership arrangement: a case study in the offshore oil industry. *Benchmarking: An International Journal*, **8**(5), 413–430.

Health and Safety Executive (1999) *Health and Safety Benchmarking: Improving Together*. C250. Sudbury: HSE Books.

Health and Safety Executive (2000) *Successful Health and Safety Management*. HSG65. Sudbury: HSE Books.

Institute of Internal Auditors (2003) *Definition of Internal Auditing*. http://www.theiia.org

International Labour Organization (2001) *Guidelines on Occupational Safety and Health Management Systems*. ILO-OSH 2001. Geneva: ILO.

International Loss Control Institute (1990) *International Safety Rating System*®. Loganville: Institute Publishing.

Kaye, M. and Anderson, R. (1999) Continuous improvement: the ten essential criteria. *International Journal of Quality and Reliability Management*, **16**(5), 485–506.

Konrath, L.F. (1993) *Auditing Concepts and Applications: A Risk Analysis Approach*. Minneapolis: West Publishing Company.

Lau, R.S.M. and Anderson, C.A. (1998) A three-dimensional perspective of total quality management. *International Journal of Quality and Reliability Management*, **15**(1), 85–98.

Terziovski, M. and Samson, D. (1999) The link between total quality management practice and organisational performance. *International Journal of Quality and Reliability Management*, **16**(3), 226–237.

Yasin, M.M. (2002) The theory and practice of benchmarking: then and now. *Benchmarking: An International Journal*, **9**(3), 217–243.

CHAPTER 16

Responsibility and accountability for health and safety

It's too bad for his wife and kids he's dead,
But if he was sick, he should have said.
It wasn't me that made him fall.
No, you can't blame me at all.

– Bob Dylan, (1964) 'Who killed Davey Moore?'

Chapter contents

- Introduction
- Individual responsibility and accountability
- Corporate responsibility for health and safety risks
- Corporate social responsibility
- Corporate commitment to health and safety management

Introduction

It is important for organisations and individuals that create risks to acknowledge their responsibilities and accountabilities for managing these risks. A survey of the UK FTSE 100 companies (Disaster Action, 1997) showed that fewer than 50% of companies reported on health and safety issues in their annual reports, although later surveys showed that the level of reporting had increased to over 90% by 2002 (Peebles *et al.*, 2003). These levels of company disclosure compare very favourably with results reported across the rest of the world (Roberts, 1990): see Table 16.1.

The aim of this final chapter is to briefly discuss the responsibilities and accountabilities of individuals and organisations for the management of health and safety risks, and their wider duty to help to improve health and safety performances at the organisational, national and international levels.

Table 16.1 Level of disclosure of health and safety information across the world (1987)

World region	No. of companies	Proportion of companies reporting health and safety information (%)
Europe	99	21
Australia/New Zealand	15	20
Southern Africa	11	19
Asia	15	13
North America	40	10
Japan	19	0

Source: Adapted from Roberts (1990)

Individual responsibility and accountability

The issues of responsibility, accountability and blame are of some importance in health and safety management because the way in which they are regarded within an organisation will contribute to the development of the organisation's safety culture. Some people regard an employee who has an accident and reports it to senior management as a fool on two counts: a fool for having the accident, and a bigger fool for reporting it. This attitude is a major problem for organisations because, if employees fail to report an accident or incident, the organisation loses an opportunity to learn from the mistakes that have been made. For this reason, many organisations operate what is referred to as a 'no-blame' safety culture in order to encourage employees to report all accidents, incidents and near misses without the threat of disciplinary action or recrimination. A disadvantage associated with this management approach is that employees may feel, because of the absence of the disciplinary threat, that they have no necessity to take ownership of the causes and consequences of an accident or incident. This may lead to a general lack of will and desire among employees to work to the highest standards, and this will ultimately lead to lower health and safety standards within the organisation.

In business environments, where organisations are competing in national and international markets, employees are assigned responsibilities and accountabilities and set performance targets within most business functions. In this context, line managers and employees will already have indirect responsibilities and accountabilities for health and safety performance because these have close links with, for example, an organisation's output, quality, finance and environment performance. It is also unreasonable to expect the public to accept that an organisation's senior management, who may be responsible for multiple deaths arising from a major accident, should not be blamed and held accountable for the fatalities. In fact, the legislation in most countries already provides the means for the prosecution of individuals working within organisations for causing accidents. Organisations are therefore realising that a 'no-blame' safety culture is not aligned and not compatible with the responsibility and accountability cultures adopted within most business functions.

An increasing number of organisations are adopting what is referred to as a 'just' or 'accountable' safety culture. This approach establishes the concept within health and safety management that employees have an obligation to account for their actions. It must be recognised, however, that one can only be held accountable for those issues for which one is responsible. Whereas the chief executive officer of an organisation has responsibility for all business activities, and therefore should be accountable for all business successes and failures, other line managers have delegated responsibilities and accountabilities for specific defined work activities. Therefore the difference between 'blame' and 'just/accountable' safety cultures relates to the level of delegated responsibility that an individual has for the activities involved. A 'just' culture is more difficult to implement within an organisation than the extremes offered by the 'blame' and 'no-blame' cultures because it requires an understanding of the basis of human error. This in turn makes it essential to implement accident investigation procedures that will identify the real causes of accidents rather than superficial causes that may be sufficient to satisfy the requirements of a non-committed senior management group.

The relationships between the organisational approach adopted for accident investigation and the organisation's safety culture have given rise to many non-attributable but revealing quotes, such as the following:

Safety culture:

Our organisation operates a no-blame culture and looks for the underlying reasons for accidents rather than scapegoats.

Our organisation may operate a no-blame culture but that doesn't stop them wanting to find out whom they are not blaming.

Accident investigation:

Our organisation learns from its mistakes by treating accidents and incidents as opportunities for continuous improvement.

The workforce would follow him anywhere out of a morbid curiosity to find out what he could possibly do wrong next.

Our managers normally use 'blame-storming' sessions as the method of accident and incident investigation.

Corporate responsibility for health and safety risks

The major reasons why organisations manage health and safety risks have been identified as a fear of prosecution and/or legal liability (Ashby and Diacon, 1996; Wright, 1998; Wright *et al.*, 2003) and concerns about corporate responsibility (Wright, 1998; Wright *et al.*, 2003). Neither stakeholder pressures nor the formal requirements of corporate governance appeared to influence the reporting of health and safety performance. As a consequence of the generally low levels of corporate disclosure of health and safety performance observed in the early 1990s, Disaster Action (1997) prepared guidelines for the provision of health and safety information in company reports. It was suggested that companies should provide the following information annually:

Policy statement

- Describe the company's overall approach to health and safety.

Organisation and responsibility

- Identify the board member responsible for health and safety.
- Describe the way in which health and safety is organised.

Performance

- State the level of performance compared with the company's industry sector.
- Note improvements or decline in the company's level of accidents occurring during the immediate preceding years.

Fatalities and serious accidents

- Report the number of fatal accidents and number of serious accidents.
- State the measures taken to prevent recurrence.

Non-compliance with health and safety legislation

- State the number of prosecutions and provide a brief description.

Review procedures

- State method of health and safety review adopted.
- Report whether internal or external resources are used.

Awards

- Indicate awards received from recognised safety organisations for specific achievements.

Special items

- Describe any major health and safety factor, such as impending litigation, which affects the company's business position.

Disaster Action (1997: 7)

Disaster Action (1997) described the main advantages of reporting as a corporate demonstration that a strategic approach was adopted for health and safety management and that changes in performance provided an important business performance indicator. These recommendations have in some part also been adopted within national and international corporate governance and internal control reporting systems. For example, the Organisation for Economic Co-operation and Development (1999) *Principles of Corporate Governance – Section IV: Disclosure and transparency* recommended:

The corporate governance framework should ensure that timely and accurate disclosure is made on all material matters regarding the corporation, including the financial situation, performance, ownership, and governance of the company.

Organisation for Economic Co-operation and Development (1999: 8)

Corporate social responsibility

One view of business is that the directors of a company are merely agents acting on behalf of the owners (the shareholders) and, as such, their sole responsibility is to maximise the return on the investments of these owners: this is referred to as the *principal agent theory*. Corporate social responsibility, on the other hand, is a concept derived from a wider perspective that businesses have responsibilities to a range of people in addition to shareholders: this is referred to as the *stakeholder theory*. These two opposing views can provide a dilemma for senior management because, although it may be deemed socially acceptable and altruistic to provide benefits to employees, the local community and even society in general, shareholders may view this as a misappropriation of their investment. The middle ground is that management should be aware of the needs of all stakeholders, and balance their varied interests on an equitable basis. Closely linked to the concept of corporate social responsibility is the issue of ethical and unethical management practices. Unethical management takes the perspective that 'profit at any price' is acceptable, whereas ethical management involves the desire to make profits within the principles of fairness and justice for all parties affected by the business activities. Between the extremes of ethical and unethical business behaviour is the approach of indifference that is adopted by many organisations. Indifference to the views of non-shareholders can result from either a conscious or an unconscious management decision to ignore the rights and needs of others.

Definitions of corporate social responsibility (CSR) generally refer to the voluntary integration of social and environmental concerns into business operations beyond the levels required by legislation and corporate governance. The Organisation for Economic Co-operation and Development (2003) have expanded on this simplistic explanation by describing CSR as:

> The search for an effective 'fit' between businesses and the societies in which they operate. The notion of 'fit' recognises the mutual dependence of business and society – a business sector cannot prosper if the society in which it operates is failing and a failing business sector inevitably detracts from general well-being. Corporate responsibility refers to the actions taken by businesses to nurture and enhance this symbiotic relationship. Of course, societies can also act to nurture this relationship by providing such services as law enforcement, investment in the many public goods used by business and appropriate regulation and by financing these activities via a well designed, disciplined system of public finance. If the actions of both business sectors and societies are successful, then the 'fit' between the two helps to foster an atmosphere of mutual trust and predictability that facilitates the conduct of business and enhances economic, social and environmental welfare.
>
> Organisation for Economic Co-operation and Development (2003)

The European Commission (2001) published a discussion document entitled *Promoting a European Framework for Corporate Social Responsibility* in order to bring the debate on the subject to the forefront of the European and international business agenda. The European Commission posed the idea that CSR should be regarded as a long-term investment by organisations in the same way as quality management. The document also proposed that European companies should foster the ideals of CSR internationally as well as nationally. This approach supported the OECD views presented in their document *Guidelines for Multinational Enterprises*:

> Multinational enterprises, like their domestic counterparts, have evolved to encompass a broader range of business arrangements and organisational forms. Strategic alliances and closer relations with suppliers and contractors tend to blur the boundaries of enterprises.
>
> Organisation for Economic Co-operation and Development (2000: 15)

The health and safety of employees and others have traditionally been safeguarded through legislation, but changes in working practices have offered wider opportunities for proactive organisations to raise standards nationally and internationally. Modern businesses develop rapidly, and this necessitates organisational changes in order to meet and benefit from the opportunities and challenges created nationally and internationally. Rapid developments and changes in an organisation, however, lead to new risks and the breakdown of poor quality management systems: if this happens, low-risk activities may be transformed into high-risk activities. However, an effective and efficient health and safety management system can deal with the rapidly changing demands of a modern work environment and still remain equitable for all stakeholders; these systems can be achieved through the use of proactive management based on best practice principles and a corporate philosophy of social responsibility.

One problem with advocating the benefits of CSR has been the difficulty of establishing clear empirical relationships between socially responsible management policies and profitability. This has occurred mainly because of the attendant problem of defining a performance measure for CSR. Burke and Logsdon (1996), however, suggested that a more appropriate way of looking at CSR was to determine under what conditions an organisation could serve its own interests and the interests of its stakeholders. It was suggested, therefore, that because CSR was a strategic business issue, it should be linked not just to profitability but to a range of criteria that reflected the wider opportunities for business advantage. Burke and Logsdon (1996) proposed six broad criteria as components of the performance measure:

- *Centrality* measures how closely the CSR programme fits with the organisation's aims and objectives.
- *Specificity* describes the ability of the CSR programme to provide benefits for the organisation.
- *Proactivity* defines the degree to which the CSR programme anticipates new social trends.
- *Voluntarism* indicates the scope for discretionary decision-making within the CSR programme.
- *Visibility* describes the credit received from internal and external stakeholders for the CSR programme.
- *Value creation* measures economic benefits resulting from the CSR programme.

Corporate commitment to health and safety management

Management's attention is often distracted from health and safety by other issues competing for their time, such as production, costs, efficiency, quality and the environment. The workforce's awareness and understanding of health and safety issues, however, is more focused as they deal with and suffer from the consequences of operational risks on a daily basis (Fuller, 1999). The case for an improvement in health and safety performance can, for most organisations, be argued on financial, legal and social grounds. The important issue, however, is not the argument for an improvement but the process by which corporate aims are translated into a programme that will achieve the desired performance. With any management function, performance depends not just on policies and procedures but on the development of effective operational practices, which are appropriate to the working environment and which are also perceived to be appropriate by the workforce implementing them. In this respect it is essential that organisations present their health and safety philosophy carefully and constructively to all stakeholders.

Organisations cannot always rely on supporting health and safety initiatives through cost–benefit analysis and demonstrations of financial return. Directors should be presenting the view among stakeholders that resources allocated to health and safety management are provided not just to achieve a direct financial return but also to generate a number of additional intangible benefits, such as corporate image, brand recognition, customer and supplier satisfaction and employee approval and motivation.

In the UK, the Health and Safety Commission (2002) recommended that a competent board director be appointed with responsibility for ensuring that health and safety issues are properly managed within an organisation. This appointment should not, however, be seen to detract from the health and safety responsibilities of the other directors within their specific areas of accountability. In some organisations, health and safety receives corporate interest only in response to major adverse events. Following events of this type, the board agrees to a significant inflow of resources to investigate the incident, and initiates preventive interventions in order to divert attention away from the underlying deficiencies of the management system that led to the incident. This reactive influx of resources attempts to create the impression among employees, the regulators, the media and the public that health and safety is treated seriously within the organisation. However, support that is created in this environment is usually short lived, and commitment fades as media, public and governmental interest wanes. For health and safety interventions to be successful and enduring, initiatives must be supported by a genuine long-term commitment from senior management.

Changes in the world of work have created new risks arising from the use of new technologies and new patterns of work (Roy, 2003). These changes demand that organisations adopt best practice principles and new strategies for the effective management of health and safety risks. Of particular importance in this context is the trend for organisations to move undesirable risks to temporary workers, contractors and developing countries. Saari (2001) identified three strategies that proactive organisations can adopt in order to provide the impetus for the creation of healthy and safe work environments worldwide:

- *Zero-accident vision*. The direct goal is not the actual elimination of all accidents and cases of ill-health, but the replacement of the fatalistic view that accidents and ill-health will always occur with the belief that with effective management they are preventable.

- *Integrating safety measures across time segments and communities*. People normally categorise life into time zones and locations related to work, leisure, travel and home life. Consequently people relate health and safety issues and standards to the environment in which they are present rather than take the holistic view that health and safety standards relate equally to all aspects of life. This is particularly important as work patterns change and people, for example, spend more time travelling to and from work, working at home and working part-time.

- *Globalisation as a platform for accident prevention*. The health and safety performances of multinational organisations are often significantly better than those of smaller organisations and organisations in developing countries. These larger organisations therefore provide a valuable resource for exporting good practice in health and safety management nationally and internationally. In addition, these organisations are strong enough to use health and safety criteria for the selection of contractors and suppliers (European Agency for Safety and Health at Work, 2000; Winkler and Irwin, 2003).

Multinational organisations should therefore seize the opportunity to use their powers in order to raise health and safety standards throughout the world.

Summary

- Individuals working within organisations have direct and indirect responsibilities for managing health and safety, and they should be accountable for the way in which these responsibilities are carried out.

- Organisations should demonstrate their responsibility and accountability for health and safety risks by publishing performance details in company annual reports.

- The major reasons why organisations manage health and safety risks are a fear of prosecution and legal liability and concerns about corporate responsibility.

- A management approach incorporating the concept of corporate social responsibility ensures that the rights and needs of all stakeholders are included within an organisation's management practices.

- Measurement of the contribution that a policy of corporate social responsibility makes to an organisation should not just include financial issues.

- Health and safety interventions will be successful and enduring only if they are supported by a genuine long-term commitment from senior management.

References

Ashby, S.G. and Diacon, S.R. (1996) Motives for occupational risk management in large UK companies. *Safety Science, 22*, 229–243.

Burke, L. and Logsdon, J.M. (1996) How corporate social responsibility pays off. *Long Range Planning,* **29**(4), 495–502.

Disaster Action (1997) *Corporate Responsibility: Health and Safety in Company Annual Reports.* London: Disaster Action.

European Agency for Safety and Health at Work (2000) *Occupational Safety and Health in Marketing and Procurement.* Factsheet 28. Bilbao: European Agency for Safety and Health at Work.

European Commission (2001) *Promoting a European Framework for Corporate Social Responsibility: Green Paper.* Luxembourg: European Commission.

Fuller, C.W. (1999) An employee–management consensus approach to continuous improvement in safety management. *Employee Relations,* **21**(4), 405–417.

Health and Safety Commission (2002) *Directors' Responsibilities for Health and Safety.* Sudbury: HSE Books.

Organisation for Economic Co-operation and Development (1999) *Principles of Corporate Governance.* SG/CG(99)5. Paris: Organisation for Economic Co-operation and Development.

Organisation for Economic Co-operation and Development (2000) *The OECD Guidelines for Multinational Enterprises.* Paris: Organisation for Economic Co-operation and Development.

Organisation for Economic Co-operation and Development (2003) *Corporate Responsibility.* http://www.oecd.org

Peebles, L., Kupper, A., Robertson, V. and Heasman, T. (2003) *The Provision of Health and Safety Information in the Annual Reports, Websites and Other Publicly Available Documents Produced by the UK's Top Companies and a Sample of Government Departments, Agencies, Local Authorities and NHS Trusts.* RR134. Sudbury: HSE Books.

Roberts, C.B. (1990) *International Trends in Social and Employee Reporting.* London: Chartered Association of Certified Accountants.

Roy, M. (2003) Self-directed workteams and safety: a winning combination? *Safety Science,* **41**, 359–376.

Saari, J. (2001) Accident prevention today: one accident is too many. *Magazine of the European Agency for Safety and Health at Work,* **4**, 2–5.

Winkler, C. and Irwin, J.N. (2003) *Contractorisation: Aspects of Health and Safety in the Supply Chain.* RR 112. Sudbury: HSE Books.

Wright, M.S. (1998) *Factors Motivating Proactive Health and Safety Management.* CRR 179. Sudbury: HSE Books.

Wright, M., Marsden, S. and Holmes, J. (2003) *Health and Safety Responsibilities of Company Directors and Management Board Members.* RR135. Sudbury: HSE Books.

ST NO	— £39.99
ACC NO	058790
CLASS	344.047
DATE	22/7/04
STAFF	

Index

LLYFRGELL COLEG MENAI LIBRARY
SAFLE FFRIDDOEDD SITE
BANGOR GWYNEDD LL57 2TP